This book is an introductory account of the kingdom of Sicily established in 1130 by Roger II, a 'Norman' king, and ruled by Roger, his son and grandsons until 1194 when the kingdom was conquered by his son-in-law, Henry VI of Hohenstaufen. The period covered does, however, extend from 1130 to 1266, when the kingdom passed from the Hohenstaufen heirs to Charles of Anjou, a period roughly as long and as coherent as the 'Norman' monarchy of England between 1066 and 1204.

Roger II's difficulties in creating an enduring kingdom needed continuous military effort. Even when these efforts were no longer required, the monarchy had still to learn how to function in lands where traditions of local government were strong. Yet when the monarchy itself faltered, the kingdom did not fall apart. Frederick II, the grandson of Roger II, showed that it could be revived and that his sons could maintain it. The ways in which the monarchy made itself indispensable cannot be traced in detail, but pointers to its success can be seen. The kingdom did not spring full-armed at birth – it took time and experience to hammer it into shape. When at last it looked capable of assuming the leadership of all Italy, its enemies combined to prevent it from doing so with the most profound consequences for Italy, the papacy and the west.

Cambridge Medieval Textbooks

THE NORMAN KINGDOM OF SICILY

Cambridge Medieval Textbooks

This is a series of specially commissioned textbooks for teachers and students, designed to complement the monograph series Cambridge Studies in Medieval Life and Thought by providing introductions to a range of topics in medieval history. This series combines both chronological and thematic approaches, and will deal with British and European topics. All volumes in the series will be published in hard covers and in paperback.

For a list of titles in the series, see end of book.

THE NORMAN
KINGDOM OF SICILY

DONALD MATTHEW

Professor of History,
University of Reading

PUBLISHED BY THE PRESS SYNDICATE OF THE UNIVERSITY OF CAMBRIDGE
The Pitt Building, Trumpington Street, Cambridge CB2 1RP, United Kingdom

CAMBRIDGE UNIVERSITY PRESS
The Edinburgh Building, Cambridge CB2 2RU, UK http://www.cup.cam.ac.uk
40 West 20th Street, New York, NY 10011–4211, USA http://www.cup.org
10 Stamford Road, Oakleigh, Melbourne 3166, Australia

First published 1992
Reprinted 1993, 1995, 1998

Printed in the United Kingdom at the University Press, Cambridge

A cataloguing in publication record for this book is available from the British Library

Library of Congress cataloguing in publication data
Matthew, Donald, 1930 –
The Norman kingdom of Sicily/Donald Matthew.
p.   cm. – (Cambridge medieval textbooks)
ISBN 0 521 26284 4 – ISBN 0 521 26911 3 (pbk).
1. Sicily (Italy) – History 1016–1194. 2. Sicily (Italy) –
History – 1194 – 1282. 3. Normans – Italy – Sicily – History.
I. Title. II. Series
DG867.2.M38 1992
945'.804 – dc20   91-18961 CIP

ISBN 0 521 26284 4 hardback
ISBN 0 521 26911 3 paperback

UP

CONTENTS

Contents

ABBREVIATIONS

AB	*Art Bulletin*
AHR	*American Historical Review*
ANS	*Anglo-Norman Studies*
ASI	*Archivio Storico Italiano*
ASP	*Archivio Storico Pugliese*
ASPN	*Archivio Storico per le Provincie Napoletane*
ASS	*Archivio Storico Siciliano*
ASSO	*Archivio Storico per la Sicilia Orientale*
BAR	*British Archaeological Reports*
BCSFLS	*Bullettino: Centro di Studi Filologici e Linguistici Siciliani*
BISIME	*Bullettino: Istituto Storico Italiano per il medio evo*
BJRL	*Bulletin of the John Rylands Library*
BSR	*Papers of the British School in Rome*
CCM	*Cahiers de civilisation médiévale*
DA	*Deutsches Archiv*
DOP	*Dumbarton Oaks Papers*
EHR	*English Historical Review*
FSI	*Fonti per la Storia d'Italia*
JEH	*Journal of Ecclesiastical History*
Mélanges	*Mélanges d'archéologie et d'histoire, Ecole française de Rome*; from 1983 (vol. 71), *Mélanges de l'Ecole française de Rome, moyen âge–temps modernes*
MGH	*Monumenta Germaniae Historica*
PBA	*Proceedings of the British Academy*

NOTE ON COINAGE

A considerable number of different coins were struck and used in various parts of the Norman kingdom, and valuations were assessed in several monies of account. In the twelfth century, the kings struck gold coins called *tari*, which had international circulation and therefore standard equivalents, such that there were four *tari* to the Arabic *dinar*, and six *tari* to the gold *solidus* of Constantinople. The *tari*, which weighed about one gram, was considered to comprise twenty *grana*, and there were thirty *tari* to the *uncia*. Under Frederick II, a new coin, the *augustalis*, was struck such that there were four *augustales* to the *uncia*. *Schifati* were actual gold coins struck at Constantinople and said to be worth eight *tari*. Silver coins in the twelfth-century kingdom included the *provenesini*, struck outside the kingdom and valued at four *provenesini* to the *ducalis*, where ten *ducales* were worth one *solidus*. There were twelve *miliarenses* to the *solidus* as used in those parts of Italy formerly subject to Constantinople. The copper coin *romesina* was not struck after 1140, but replaced by a smaller coin, *follaris*, such that twenty-four *follari* were worth one *miliarensis*. The values of these coins fluctuated over time and local variations also occurred. This note is designed to help the reader understand the scale of values, not to calculate actual sums.

Map of Sic[ily]

d Southern Italy

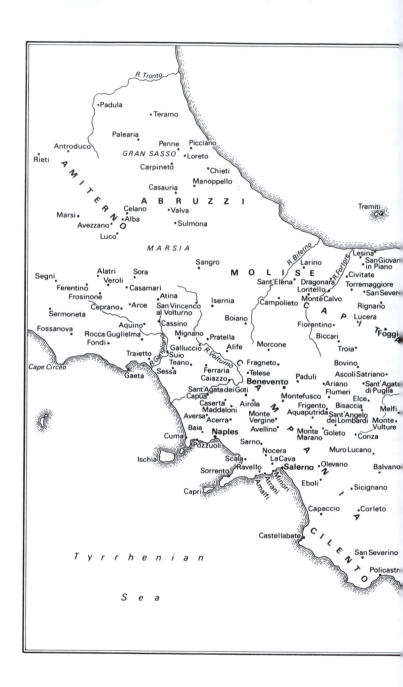

R. Tronto

•Padula

• Teramo

Palearia

Antroduco•   Penne   Picciano
                        •Loreto
Rieti•   GRAN SASSO

AMITERNO   Carpineto   •Chieti
                    Manoppello
         Casauria•

A   B   R   U   Z   Z   I

Celano• •Valva
Marsi•   •Alba
  Avezzano•   •Sulmona
    Luco•

MARSIA

Sangro•   Larino•   Lesina•
                              SanGiovan
           M O L I S E   in Piano
Segni•   Alatri   Sora   •Civitate
         •Veroli•   Sant'Elena• Dragonara• Torremaggiore
   Ferentino•   Loritello•   •SanSever
   Frosinone• •Casamari   MonteCalvo•
         •Atina   Rignano•
   Ceprano• •Arce SanVincenco Isernia   C A P Lucera•
Sermoneta•   al Volturno   Fiorentino•
Fossanova• Cassino• Boiano•   •Foggi
   Rocca Guglielma• Mignano•   Biccari•
      Fondi•   •Pratella Alife•   Morcone•   Troia•
                Galluccio•   Bovino•
   Traietto•   Suio• Alife
Cape Circeo   •Teano   Fragneto• Paduli   Ascoli Satriano•
      Gaeta• Sessa• Ferraria• •Telese   •Ariano •Sant'Agata
                Caiazzo• Benevento   Flumeri   di Puglia
          Sant'Agata dei Goti•   Montefusco•   Elce•
            Capua• Caserta• Airola• Frigento• Bisaccia• Melfi•
              Maddaloni•   Aquaputrida•Sant'Angelo Monte•
          Aversa• Acerra• Monte   dei Lombardi Vulture
            Baia•   Vergine• Avellino• Goleto• Conza•
          Cuma• Naples   Monte
              Pozzuoli•   Sarno•   Marano•
Ischia•   Nocera•   Muro Lucano•
                  Scala• LaCava•
              Sorrento• Ravello• •Salerno Olevano•   Balvano•
                Capri• Atrani   Eboli• •Sicignano
                  Amalfi   Capaccio• •Corleto

              Castellabate•   CILENTO

T y r r h e n i a n   SanSeverino•
                                      Policastr
S e a

R. Biferno
R. Fortore
R. Garigliano
R. Volturno

Tremiti

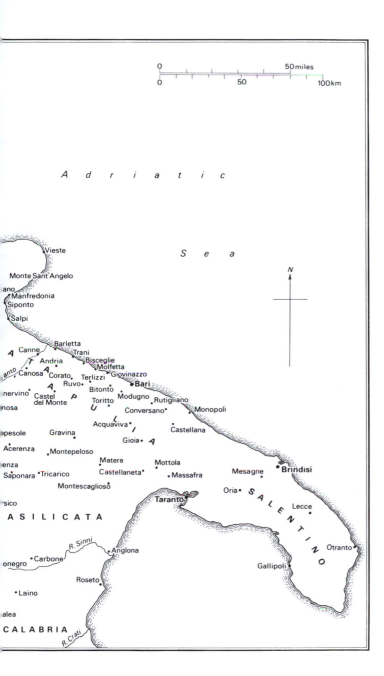

Adriatic

Sea

N

Vieste

Monte Sant'Angelo

ano
Manfredonia
Siponto

Salpi

Barletta
Canne
Trani
Andria
Bisceglie
Molfetta
Canosa
Corato
Terlizzi
Giovinazzo
Ruvo
Bari
Bitonto
nervino
Castel
del Monte
Modugno
Rutigliano
Toritto
nosa
Conversano
Monopoli
Acquaviva
pesole
Gravina
Castellana
Acerenza
Montepeloso
Gioia
enza
Matera
Mottola
Saponara
Tricarico
Castellaneta
Massafra
Mesagne
Brindisi
Montescaglioso
Oria
SALENTINO
Taranto
Lecce
sico

BASILICATA

R. Sinni

onegro
Carbone
Anglona
Otranto

Roseto
Gallipoli

Laino

alea

CALABRIA
R. Crati

T A P U L I A

0   50 miles
0   50   100 km

xv

--- • ---

ACKNOWLEDGEMENTS

--- • ---

I should like to thank formally those who have helped me with the writing of this book. In particular I am most deeply obliged to Professor Gherardo Ortalli for inviting me to Italy so that I could work extensively on this subject, and to Professor Giosuè Musca for his help and counsel over many years. Professor C. M. Kauffmann gave me invaluable advice on some special aspects of this study, and I owe a very useful reference to the kindness of Professor Hugo Buchtal. The late R. H. C. Davis kindly read and commented on a draft of this book, for which I was never able to thank him adequately before his death. Sir Richard Southern continued to give me the benefit of his wisdom, advice, criticism, support and encouragement, even when I was most at my wits' end. Mrs Elizabeth Berry took charge at all stages of turning my muddled manuscripts into readable copy. For all the help I have received in trying to get it right, I give thanks for myself and on behalf of the readers of the book. For the errrors and blemishes that remain I am responsible.

INTRODUCTION

The Norman kingdom of Sicily has an assured place in the teaching of medieval European history in this country. All teachers of it are, nevertheless, unhappy about the limited amount of reading they can recommend to students who cannot understand books in foreign languages. This has very unfortunate consequences. Since few of the original sources in Latin, let alone Greek or Arabic, have been translated, the student cannot form an impression of them at first hand. Moreover, the main preoccupations of the ample scholarly literature in Italian, French and German, as well as some other languages, cannot be grasped from what writing is available only in English. The problems of modern British students are compounded in other ways too. They inevitably approach the subject with established convictions about the Norman monarchy in England. These shape their expectations of what to expect and how to interpret what they find in southern Italy. The Norman monarchy in England may now be made to acknowledge what it owes to its Anglo-Saxon predecessor, but no one doubts that under the Normans the monarchy was powerful, authoritative and exceptionally centralised for its date. In addition, the development of political authority in the modern English state is assumed to have been continuous since at least the Norman Conquest. The southern Italian monarchy is quite another matter. No Italian looks back on it as playing an important part in the development of the modern Italian state. On the contrary, the continuing existence of its descendant, the Bourbon kingdom, deferred the realisation of unification in the nineteenth century, and far from being in the forefront of 'progress', the 'South'

I

(*mezzogiorno*) as a whole has been identified with forces of stagnation and backwardness. In the context of Italian history, the Norman creation of the monarchy is not therefore respected as a valuable stage in the development of the whole modern nation. If the Norman monarchy is viewed as an arbitrary creation, it also becomes clearer what a great difference there is between it and the Norman conquest of England. In the latter, a united kingdom changed hands as a result of one major battle. In southern Italy, it took over a century for Norman power to infiltrate to the point where a monarchy could be devised to integrate all the Norman elements into one entity. British students have to adjust their expectations in ways that obviously have no parallels for students on the continent. It is especially important for them not to be led astray by superficial similarities between monarchies more often compared than contrasted.

There are other snags lying in wait for students who live some considerable distance from southern Italy. I am not thinking so much of simple ignorance of place-names or geography, for this may be fairly quickly corrected by careful study of maps. More difficult to overcome is a common feeling, even amongst English Italophiles, that Italy south of Rome is 'different', a region more backward and alien, a world of its own. North Italians are themselves not immune to the prejudice that the 'Mezzogiorno' has its own personality. In the South itself, however, the differences between the various peoples and regions loom larger than any perception of their common features. Sicily, Calabria, Apulia, Campania, Abruzzi, to name only the most obvious, have their own distinctiveness. Even today they view the kingdom, of which they were once all part, from different angles. In Britain, the local loyalties which must have formerly prevailed over 'national' ones withered away so long ago that their importance can only be recovered by historical imagination: even in the Norman kingdom, they are assumed to have been already vestigial. In southern Italy this was not so. When the Normans came, the South was deeply divided, not just by political authority, but by speech, culture and religion. If the monarchy had any success in diminishing the force of local loyalty, it certainly never stifled it altogether. Instead of thinking about 'the South' as though it were a natural unit, students need rather to perceive how different its constituent parts were, and remained, even after the kingdom was set up.

The character of historical writing in English about the southern Italian monarchy suggests that this subject presents particular difficulties for English historians to get to grips with; but there are other, quite different problems that beset historians writing in any language. In particular, it would currently be very exceptional for any one scholar (more so now perhaps than in the twelfth century) to be sufficient master of Latin, Greek and Arabic to be able to read the sources in all three of the major languages in which they were written. Very obviously in the case of Arabic, this means that historians are likely to depend upon the research of scholars whose primary interests are linguistic or literary rather than historical. To an extent greater than with other topics of twelfth-century European history, the kingdom of Sicily has therefore to be studied, not only through a greater number of languages, but with the help of several different scholarly disciplines. Although medieval archaeology has until now made rather a modest contribution to modern understanding, the pre-eminent role of art history serves to illustrate this point. And because the kingdom has to be studied from many angles, the difficulty of defining its central focus is accentuated. The monarchy, here as elsewhere, is usually placed centre-stage, but mainly to solve what is basically an aesthetic problem of presentation. Actually, when the light is turned too brightly on the kings themselves, they cannot withstand the glare. The contrast with Norman England is obvious, even when allowance is made for modern myth-making. In England, we have Domesday Book and Magna Carta as evidence of royal authority at the heart of the system. Westminster Abbey and Windsor Castle still symbolise important aspects of royal power. In the southern Italian kingdom, there are no comparable surviving monuments of either kind. It can only be taken on faith that the monarchy is central to study of the kingdom, and political historians have not been as successful as in England in presenting their preoccupations as fundamental to modern understanding. The history of the kingdom cannot be written in terms of the monarchy alone.

The lack of any strong political 'message' in the kingdom's history probably helps to explain another striking feature of historical scholarship on Sicily: its international character. This is found even in English writing, though there is nothing like the quantity or variety of work in English that there is in German or French. German scholarship has been fostered in various ways, but is probably explained basically in terms of German involvement in the history of the medieval empire, which was linked to the kingdom most strikingly under Frederick II. Similarly, French interest originally grew from a desire to follow up the successes of the eleventh-century colonists who left Normandy to make themselves masters in southern Italy. Since the French have not, however, been so notably concerned with the history of the Normans in England, the main stimulus for modern scholarship there cannot in fact be attributed to chauvinistic sentiments. Although the history of the kingdom of Sicily has, of course, been closely studied in the South itself, it has been characteristically seen in excessively local terms and has not been generally accepted in Italy as part of the national history, unlike the history of the city republics, for example. The fact that there has been no Italian concern to monopolise study of the subject for Italian nationals, coupled with the fact that cultural history has been of equal importance as political history for the kingdom as a whole, has probably helped to swell the numbers of scholars from all over Europe who have been able to make outstanding contributions to its modern scholarly study. As a result of such divergent tendencies, the most important advances in our appreciation of the kingdom have recently tended to be published either as the proceedings of great conferences addressed by scholars from all over Europe, or in the publications of the many local historical societies. These facts also help explain how difficult it is to keep the subject clearly in focus.

I have called attention to the difficulties facing any writer when dealing with the kingdom, not only to plead extenuating circumstances for this book's defects, but also to indicate what sort of decisions have to be taken by the author at the outset. A book of this size, written in English, for the benefit of beginners in the study rather than for scholars, does not set out to resolve knotty problems of the kingdom's history. Its main purpose is to help students grasp the basic elements of interest, and it will be successful if it encourages its readers to pursue the matter further. To do this, they will need adequate linguistic competence to tackle the many substantial works in other languages. Only then can they penetrate deeper into the subject. Scholars already familiar with these books will not find this one very helpful.

When deciding how to write the book, I drew on my experience that one of the principal attractions of medieval history for students is the possibility it gives them to make direct contact with original documents of the past. I have therefore tried to make the most of the contemporary evidence. It is in my view highly desirable for students to realise not only the character of the evidence, but also its quantity, if they are to assess the strength of the base on which all conclusions must be founded. Because of the nature of the evidence, and its often limited quantity, there is bound to be controversy about how to interpret almost every piece of it. I am aware that by not pegging down every sentence with footnotes, I must appear to be presumptuously offering my own somewhat inexpert opinions. I have, all the same, done my best to make full use of all the scholarship known to me, so that the contemporary evidence should have maximum effect. Each of the topics discussed here deserves a big book to itself, in which the issues could be set out and the arguments assessed in detail. This book has been written to meet a different kind of need. I have worked on the assumption that many students are in fact much more interested in making contact with the twelfth-century kingdom than with the scholarly arguments about it, however engrossing they may be. In my view, English readers also have special problems of their own, which are not those of the Italians, Germans or French, where the southern kingdom is concerned. This book inevitably reflects not only what I have read, but also what I have learned about teaching the topic for many years.

In preparing this study, I have gathered many references and visited many libraries at home and abroad and have still not been able to find all the books and articles I have looked for. I am sorry that my reading has been incomplete, but I recognise that this must always be the case. Even as I have been writing, more work has been published, in abundance and of high quality. It seems impossible to work quickly enough to master this new material, and delays in publication mean that being up to date with the literature must be an unattainable goal. From my own efforts to locate books and periodicals in England, I have also come to see how difficult it will necessarily be for students to follow up references both to primary sources and to secondary works, even if they understand the languages in which they are written. There are a few privileged libraries in England, but even these do not always have all the books of fundamental importance. In some cases I have not found evidence that the book I needed could be read in any library in this country. I have had this in mind when preparing a guide to further reading. I had intended to list all the useful work written in English, but realised that I could not leave out certain basic books in other languages. Even if they cannot read them, students need to know what they are. To make anything like a comprehensive bibliography would itself require another book. I have therefore made a selection, giving references both to particularly useful works, or to recent ones on important topics, as well as to other publications likely to be obtainable which are worth reading – not necessarily because I regard these references as definitive, but so that interested students can get from them further guidance on bibliography. My purpose has been to show the southern kingdom of Italy as the sources I have read seem to present it.

PART I

THE NORMANS AND THE MONARCHY

I

SOUTHERN ITALY AND THE NORMANS BEFORE THE CREATION OF THE MONARCHY

·

The Norman kingdom of Italy created in 1130 for Roger II comprised the lands he had inherited in Calabria and Sicily from his father, Count Roger I, the mainland territories ruled by his cousin, Duke William of Apulia, until his death in 1127, and the lands of those great men of southern Italy who were or became Roger's vassals. These lands had never previously been united under a political authority of their own, and had not shared a common history since Justinian's reconquest of Italy six hundred years before. The establishment of the kingdom was made possible by the diffusion of Norman lordships throughout most of these lands in the hundred years before 1130, though it is misleading to regard Norman successes in those years as stages in a long-term plan to unite them eventually into a single Norman state. Norman military commanders had taken over the governments of the regions they controlled at various times, and not all these political authorities actually still survived in 1130. The units of the kingdom were as disparate as can be imagined. Apart from the leaders and their vassals, often also of Norman descent, the units had very little in common. The larger they were, the more complex their structures. Roger II's own lands combined Calabria, conquered from the Greeks, and Sicily, taken from the Muslims. Duke William, last in a line of Normans who had nominally led those Norman counts settled in Apulia since its conquest from the Greeks after 1042, was also, more effectively, heir to the Lombard princes of Salerno, for this had become the chief city of William's family on its capture by his grandfather, Robert Guiscard, in 1076. It was obviously not easy to rule territories which had only been brought together by the facts of conquest. Putting all the units into one kingdom might have seemed more likely to compound the difficulties than to simplify them. As long as Roger pressed for no more than formal deference, his new vassals were prepared to acknowledge him as king, but they did not expect to lose powers in their own lands. Nor, as Normans, had they prepared the way for this monarchy by shaping their states to Norman specifications.

To a limited extent, the imposition of Norman lordships throughout southern Italy and Sicily in the eleventh century had involved some agreement and co-operation amongst the Normans in order to further common interests. However, Norman governments had not thereby simplified the political situation of the region. Instead they had complicated it by disrupting the earlier major political authorities. They utterly destroyed the Greek imperial administration, and mercilessly exploited the weaknesses of the Lombard principalities – Benevento, Salerno and Capua. Of these, only Capua fell more or less complete to a Norman prince; the others were broken up. The one Norman in the eleventh century who managed to make himself really master over Normans and Lombards alike was Robert Guiscard, duke of Apulia (1057–85), but only by struggling constantly to keep his Norman vassals in subjection. His 'state' did not survive his death: his sons fought over the inheritance and divided it. There was nothing exceptional about family squabbling. After 1042, three of Guiscard's half-brothers, William, Drogo and Humphrey, became in succession counts of the Normans in Apulia yet, when the young Guiscard himself first came south (c. 1046–7), his brothers gave him no welcome. He was left to make his own fortune, initially more or less as a brigand and horse-thief, with a few followers in Calabria. When Count Humphrey died in 1057, Guiscard insisted on taking over his role as Norman leader in Apulia, which naturally provoked the resentment of Humphrey's own sons. In addition to the rivalries within Guiscard's family, there were other tensions, such as those between the Normans settled in Apulia and those established at Aversa in 1030, the Normans' first base in southern Italy. When Richard, count of Aversa, seized the Lombard principality of Capua in 1058, he re-launched Aversa's claim to be considered the most dynamic of the Norman centres. With the principality, however, Richard also acquired the ancient rivalry between Capua and Salerno. The Normans of Apulia had, at an early stage in their settlement, enjoyed the protection of the prince of Salerno, and they continued to take an interest in its affairs. Far from assisting their fellow Norman in Capua to defeat Lombard Salerno, the Normans of Apulia took Salerno under their own protection, until Guiscard decided to take over the city himself. To the original spirit of emulation between Normans of different bands was therefore added in due course the centuries-old rivalry of the Lombards. The Normans cannot be understood as operating in the South as a coherent force. Each Norman lord had interests of his own to look after.

THE NORMAN SETTLEMENT IN SOUTHERN ITALY BEFORE 1085

The Normans seized their opportunities with both hands, but they had not originally created the confusing situation in the South that had positively encouraged their intevention. The contemporary records insist that the Normans first came south while engaged on pilgrimage. When their military talents were revealed quite by chance, they were invited to stay on to give aid to political leaders with inadequate military forces of their own. Pious Normans are said to have been persuaded to help Salerno defend itself against Muslim raiders at the beginning of the eleventh century. Piety also appears to have played some part in persuading the Normans to fight on behalf of Lombard insurgents against the Greek government in 1016, for it was allegedly while visiting the shrine of St Michael on Monte Gargano that they first met the insurgent leader, Melo. But when the Normans entered Sicily in 1060 as allies of one Muslim emir against another, piety seems an improbable motive, even if some Normans were cunning enough to calculate that by playing off the Muslims in this way, the island might ultimately be recovered for Christendom. Everywhere, however, the Normans were drawn into conflicts they had not started. If their first interventions belong to *c.* 1000, as is now believed, it took them thirty years to obtain a real base of their own at Aversa. This they received in reward for helping the ruler of Naples to recover his duchy which the prince of Capua had seized. During those thirty years they had time to size up the situation and develop their own strength by encouraging a steady flow of recruits from Normandy to come south and join their fellows. Local princes did not perceive any danger to themselves in this development. They happily continued with their own feuds, and paid for these splendid mercenaries. The Normans cannot be blamed for this political blindness. Initially they were neither ambitious nor eager to assume political responsibilities themselves.

The extreme political confusion in the South can be most easily explained by reference to its past. In the eleventh century, it was a region where three very different major political traditions still interacted and overlapped. The Muslims arrived in Sicily in 827 and, well before completing their conquest of the island from the Greeks, they invaded and occupied parts of the mainland. Throughout the ninth century they presented a real threat of durable conquests, and stupendous efforts were called for, particularly by the Carolingian Emperor Louis II, the papacy and the Greeks themselves, to rescue southern Italy from this menace of Muslim domination. Not until a great Christian coalition managed to defeat the Muslims at Garigliano in 916 was there promise of lasting success. Even so, in no way daunted, the Muslims kept up coastal raids from their bases in Sicily and North Africa. Conditions in the South remained insecure, and it is understandable why any military help offered from Christians to the North, like the Normans, was appreciated.

The Lombards had been established in southern Italy since the late sixth century, but they had not succeeded in consolidating their political hold on the toe and heel, or over the maritime cities of Campania in the duchy of Naples; nor had they crossed over into Sicily. All these territories had remained nominally subject to the Greek empire. As the empire itself grew weaker in the seventh century, its hold on all its Italian provinces became unpopular and precarious. When the Lombard king of Italy in the North finally took imperial Ravenna in 751, the Lombard ruler of the South, the duke of Benevento, might have expected to be able to complete his conquests in the South as well. In fact, fear of the Lombard king's success incited the pope to obtain Frankish intervention in Italy. After Charlemagne's defeat of King Desiderius in 774, the rulers of Benevento, the last representatives in Italy of Lombard authority, found themselves also threatened with Frankish lordship, and keeping their own independence became more important to them than pushing the Greeks into the sea. On occasion they even found Greek support helpful. Though the dukes grandly began to call themselves princes, their territory was weakened by being split into three, and when fear of the Franks diminished in the ninth century these princely rivalries mattered more than all else. Any expectation of ousting the Greeks altogether was forgotten.

For their part the Greeks, under the new Macedonian dynasty (867–1025), discovered that they were able not only to recover on the mainland what they had lost to the Muslims, but also to resume government of regions once settled by Lombards. In the early eleventh century, the Greek empire in Italy and elsewhere was highly confident of the future. The collapse of a Lombard insurrection in Apulia in 1016 encouraged the government to try and enlarge its sphere of action in the South. It had no doubts about its ability to provide adequate government for German barbarians or Latin Christians. It was confident of the support provided by the native Greeks and the religious establishment of southern Italy. It still nursed the dream of fulfilling its moral duty to recover Sicily from the Muslims, and did actually launch an expedition for this purpose in 1038. Greek interest in the region went back to the original colonies of the eighth century BC. From this point of view, the Greeks considered the Lombards every bit as much in need of being subjected to imperial authority as the Muslims or Normans. They had no qualms about their presence in Italy. Greeks had unassailable rights in the territory.

At the time of the Normans' arrival in the South, there was no resolution in sight of the tensions set up by the interaction of these three basic groups. The Normans changed this, and rather quickly. Though they did not turn against the Greeks until 1040, by 1071 they had already captured Bari, the last stronghold of the imperial government. The Norman conquest of Sicily, begun in 1060, was completed in 1093. In a comparatively short time, therefore, the Normans, without previously consolidating their own lordships into a single political authority, were able to effect decisive change in the history of Europe. The subordination of the Greek element to the Latin had never before been made definitive in the South. Mere Norman adventurers brought the limits of western Europe to the straits of Otranto.

This astonishing achievement was of great consequence, not only to the peoples of the region, but also to the two chief leaders of the western world. Since Charlemagne, the German emperors of the west had aspired to extend their authority throughout Italy and over the last outposts of the Greeks. The Macedonian revival had made this more difficult, but with the appearance of Otto I in Italy, as emperor after 962, a new sense of purpose was apparent in the western empire too. Six successive emperors in turn pressed as far south as circumstances allowed, making at least one visit there during their reigns. When the Normans set themselves up in Apulia in 1042, Emperor Henry III lost little time in coming south to secure Norman allegiance and so take advantage for his empire of their successes. Had the German emperors been able to maintain this watchful eye on the South, the Norman kingdom would never have emerged. But after Henry III's visit in 1047, it was not until 1137 that another German emperor showed himself in the South. In the meantime, the Normans had learnt how to manage their own affairs and to take advantage of German embarrassments elsewhere, in particular, of their quarrel with the papacy.

The other western leader alert to the implications of the Normans' initial successes was the pope. Whereas the German emperors looked forward to realising the dream of making their empire effective in the South, the papacy was basically concerned to recover the authority and properties which it had once enjoyed without question. It was only as a result of the deterioration in relations between the papacy and the iconoclastic eastern emperors that the emperor Leo III deprived the Roman bishop of all jurisdiction over the churches, and of all the see's numerous and valuable properties, which were subject to his own imperial authority (732–3). Papal losses in Calabria and Sicily were considerable and painful. The papacy had anticipated that the interventions of Charlemagne and his successors, the Frankish emperors, would restore what the Greeks had confiscated. Emperors did in fact use these injuries to the papacy as part-justification of their own advances into the South, but the papacy recovered nothing. In the late ninth century, the Greek government had provided for the administration of Greek churches in the South by creating metropolitan bishops subject to the patriarch of Constantinople. The papacy had been powerless to prevent it, and saw that papal influence in the region would never count for anything again unless the Greek imperial administration in Italy collapsed. Instead, it flourished throughout the tenth century. During this time the papacy itself was mostly in the hands of great Roman families, the counts of Tusculum or the Crescentii, who for political reasons valued good relations with the powerful Greek government too much to risk souring them by reminders of their ecclesiastical grievances. The revival of German imperial power in Italy after 962 began to change the situation. However, there were complications. Imperial support for papal revindications did not reconcile all Roman parties to German control in Rome and, to advance their interests against the Greeks, the Germans had to make friends with the Lombard princes. These princes had ambitions of their own, as shown by their success in obtaining concessions of metropolitan authority for the bishops of their chief cities, Capua (966), Benevento (969) and Salerno (983). The intention with these last two was to bring the Latin churches within the Greek empire's lands under the authority of those archbishops. In effect, the Lombards planned to exclude the direct authority of the bishop of Rome in the region much as the Greeks had already done. Given these circumstances, it is hardly surprising if popes, independent enough of German influence, preferred to pursue their own policies whenever possible. Benedict VIII (1012–24), for example, was interested in taking advantage of whatever opportunities were opened up for the papacy in the South.

Imperial direction of the Roman church reached its peak in 1046 when Henry III appointed the first of a series of four German bishops to the holy see. Though naturally inclined to support imperial policies in Italy without compromising a programme for ecclesiastical reform, Pope Leo IX (1049–54), the most remarkable of the four, soon realised from his visits to southern Italy that the emperor's new Norman vassals were neither docile instruments of imperial policy nor popular with the local population. When the Lombard city of Benevento embraced papal lordship to escape Norman occupation, Leo found himself obliged to take on political responsibilities in the South. He actually organised a southern coalition to check the Normans. Battle was joined at Civitate in 1053, but the Normans were victorious. For a few more years the implications did not sink in: the Normans had come to stay and could not be easily removed. Only after the death of Henry III in 1056 and that of his last papal appointee, Victor II, in 1057 did the reforming party at Rome realise that, deprived of its necessary political support, it would need other allies. Within two years, Pope Nicholas II (1059–61) accepted that it was impossible to avoid coming to terms with the Normans any longer.

His predecessor, Stephen IX, had been abbot of Monte Cassino at the time of his election as pope (August 1057), and could also count on the support in Italy of his brother, Godfrey, duke of Lorraine. Stephen died in Tuscany in March 1058, and as soon as his death was known in Rome, a member of the Tusculum family, the bishop of Velletri, was elected Pope Benedict X, without Stephen's absent cardinals being consulted. For some months these latter hesitated over how to proceed, but in December they chose Gerard, bishop of Florence, as Pope Nicholas II, and made the decision to challenge Benedict X in Rome with the help of Duke Godfrey. In this they were successful, but Godfrey could not remain in Rome indefinitely to protect Nicholas. The pope's reforming party saw that some institutional safeguard against 'improper' papal elections was required. The papal election decree, published at Nicholas' Easter synod in 1059, was designed to prevent a recurrence of such a state of affairs. But in the meantime, there were more immediate problems for the reformers. Benedict X escaped from custody, and his supporters continued to defy Nicholas. At Monte Cassino, where Desiderius had been elected to replace Stephen IX, the abbot had that same year recognised Richard of Aversa as prince of Capua and welcomed him to the abbey. There can be little doubt that this gesture of friendship towards the Normans by a leading figure of the southern Italian church opened the way for papal negotiations with the Norman leaders. Richard of Capua provided Nicholas II with forces against Benedict X and, after Nicholas' death, assisted the cardinals, as agreed, in establishing the new pope, Alexander II, at Rome. Nicholas' reconciliation with the Normans is most famous, however, for the link it created, not so much with the Normans based so close to Rome as Capua, but with the Normans in distant Apulia. Significantly, it was Nicholas who went to

Melfi to recognise Guiscard as duke, and to approve plans for the conquest of Sicily. He received an oath of fidelity from Guiscard, couched in similar terms to those sworn by Richard of Capua. Nicholas was able to hold a church council at Melfi where he deposed two bishops. The recovery of the effective papal oversight of the southern church was shown too by the pope's decision to recognise a new ecclesiastical province for Acerenza, although his predecessor Stephen IX had only the previous year confirmed it as a suffragan bishopric of the province of Salerno. Though other evidence is wanting, the only plausible explanation for Nicholas' decision regarding Acerenza is that the Normans of the region wanted to have those churches under their authority removed from the jurisdiction of the Lombard archbishopric. Nicholas also imposed on Guiscard a personal penance of founding monasteries to atone for his sins. The Normans' willingness to co-operate with the papacy proves that they recognised the advantages of papal approval. This was in fact nothing new; it was the change in papal policy that brought about the new relationship. The rewards were immediate. The pope found that by accepting these Norman vassals, the whole area of southern Italy under Norman control was opened up for papal intervention. Leading Normans allowed the bishoprics of their chief cities, like Melfi and Aversa, to come directly under Roman authority; they offered in addition pensions from their lands in direct proportion to their extent.

The mutual acceptance of 1059 was the beginning of a long and troubled relationship between the papacy and the Norman leadership. The oaths of fealty became the basis of papal claims to overlordship, and ultimately of sovereignty when the papacy attempted to turn the Norman gift of lordship into a right to dispose of the fief as popes thought fit. In 1059, neither side could foresee what lay ahead. The practical advantages for both in the short term were real, and it is probable that neither side considered how long their alliance of expediency might endure. In the old days, papal influence in the South had been possible because there was no authority to challenge it. The recovery of papal authority was achieved thanks to the Normans, and remained dependent on their goodwill. The papacy was naturally reluctant to admit this, preferring to think the Normans only conceded papal rights out of duty. However it could only be a matter of time before the question of who was really in charge arose. The Normans had proved they could hold their own; to them it seemed that the papacy was facing the real facts. It is inconceivable that the Normans, as real masters, thought the papacy had gained the upper hand.

The papacy was in fact too dependent on Norman support over the next forty years to venture anything more than ineffective protests about intolerable Norman behaviour, as Gregory VII did, for example, when Guiscard finally annexed the principality of Salerno against explicit papal orders to the contrary. Apart from the papacy's difficulties with the German emperor Henry IV, the main reason for papal weakness in dealing with the Normans was that Guiscard, the principal Norman leader, was too headstrong and successful to be challenged. During the 1060s, he set about the conquest of Sicily and the elimination of the Greeks from Apulia. Eventually leaving his youngest brother, Roger, with the task of completing the Norman conquest of the island, he concentrated on the affairs of the Adriatic. After the capture of Bari in 1071, he committed himself to challenging the Greek empire across the sea. There was no end to his military projects, and he certainly regarded his obligations as papal vassal as much less important than his own political goals. Guiscard was, for this reason, quite prepared to ignore papal excommunication. Even when reconciliation with Gregory VII was negotiated in 1080, Guiscard remained truculent rather than abashed.

The papacy did not altogether regret the alliance. The Normans were after all interested in reviving the ecclesiastical life of the South according to the norms of the Latin church. Guiscard and his family were responsible for the foundation of several new monasteries, for setting up new Latin bishoprics for their followers in the heart of Greek Calabria, and for bringing the Greek bishops under the jurisdiction of Latin metropolitans. The slow recovery of Sicily from the Muslims created the opportunity for the re-establishment of organised Christianity by the setting up of new Latin bishoprics there. When Palermo was captured in 1072, the Normans found it had a resident Greek archbishop, Nicodemus, and Gregory VII duly confirmed his powers over (unnamed) suffragans. In practice, Nicodemus was given no say in the organisation of the church in the island, and the few bishops had to seek consecration from the pope. The papacy did not, however, recover its own former properties there.

Progress in re-making ecclesiastical life in Sicily clearly rested entirely with Count Roger. When Mazara del Vallo in the west was captured in 1072, a bishop was appointed there and not at Marsala on the site of the ancient see of Lilybaeum, though the bishop sometimes used the classical name to give distinction to his see. Another bishopric was revived at Agrigento, the major centre of authority in the south, after its capture in 1086. There was, however, no plan to restore the bishoprics of the pre-Muslim period. Roger actually set up a bishopric for his own men in his castle at Troina (1080), and this was only later transferred to Messina on the insistence of Urban II. Secular decisions on such matters could have been justified on the grounds that, until the conquest of the island was complete in 1093, it would have seemed premature to expect more, but on the mainland too the Normans showed from the beginning that they had ideas of their own about ecclesiastical organisation. For example, they desired to have metropolitan bishops for their own provinces, not only at Acerenza, but also at Conza and Cosenza, in total disregard of earlier papal privileges granted to the archbishop of Salerno. Although the popes protested, they finally confirmed what they had no power to alter. If, from some points of view, papal interests had been advanced by the Normans, overall the papacy had certainly gained less by 1085 than it may have hoped in 1059 when the Norman alliance was negotiated. Guiscard had been too domineering to serve papal interests. The papacy could only hope for more amenable leaders in the future.

Guiscard's ambitions had not obviously led him to make of his dominions a unified state capable of consolidating the Norman conquests. Although his occupation of Salerno in 1076 pushed his rival Richard, prince of Capua, into second place amongst the Normans, it did not itself lead to the loss of Capua's effective independence. Even if Guiscard had thought a united Norman dominion a practical possibility, there was no chance whatever of securing papal approval for such a Norman 'state'. It is unlikely that the Normans would ever have contemplated asking Henry IV for imperial sanction. If Guiscard had long-term ambitions for his authority, what they were must remain in doubt. When he seized the Norman leadership in Apulia, he had, like his half-brothers before him, married into the family of the Lombard princes of Salerno, certainly for political reasons. To do this meant repudiating his previous Norman wife, Alberada, by whom he had one son, Mark 'Bohemond', a great warrior, who campaigned with his father from an early age. Guiscard's Lombard wife, Sichelgaita, clearly aimed to secure Guiscard's succession for her oldest son, Roger, whose Lombard connections gave him certain advantages, particularly after Guiscard's capture of Salerno itself in 1076. Yet Guiscard himself must have anticipated opposition to Roger's succession from Bohemond and other Normans resentful of Lombard intrigue. As it happened, when Guiscard died in Corfu in July 1085, Bohemond was away sick in Italy, so Roger, backed by his mother, was able, immediately after his father's death, to get himself recognised as heir in Bohemond's absence. Back in Italy, however, a confrontation with Bohemond proved unavoidable. As a result, Bohemond eventually obtained extensive lands and authority, notably the cities of Bari and Taranto, though Roger kept the title of duke of Apulia. It is not clear whether Roger even retained feudal suzerainty over Bohemond, whose ambitions were, however, shortly diverted to the east by enthusiasm for the first crusade. Guiscard had not, in fact, created out of his conquests a state capable of surviving his death, and the Norman situation in the South remained very unsettled. After 1085, there was no single leader with any clear idea of what to do with the Normans' strength, and it is therefore not surprising that so many were caught up in the excitement of the crusade. They had eliminated the Greek, Lombard and Muslim governments of the region, but their own prospects there did not look any more durable.

NORMAN RULERS IN THE SOUTH 1085–1127

Guiscard's military and political career is mainly known from three chronicle records of the late eleventh century: by Amatus of Monte Cassino; Geoffrey of Malaterra, a Norman monk of Guiscard's foundation at Sant'Eufemia in Calabria; and in Latin verse by William of Apulia. Geoffrey is the only one of the three to provide a historical record of the years after Guiscard's death in 1085, and his narrative concludes in 1098. This means that for the forty years or so between 1085 and the death of Duke William in 1127, modern historians have no coherent narrative from which to reconstruct the changes in Norman society for the period immediately before the monarchy was devised. Only the barest outline of events is provided by Falco writing in papal Benevento after 1112.

By the time of Guiscard's death, there was no doubt that the Normans were in command of the region, even if there was no glimmer of the monarchy to come. Guiscard's duchy was divided after 1085. Count Roger in Sicily showed no desire to take Guiscard's place or forestall his son, Roger II, in claiming a dominant role for Sicily amongst the Norman lordships. Guiscard had retained certain rights in Calabria and Sicily which were claimed by his heirs. Roger I made no attempt to challenge these after 1085. To understand what Roger II was up against in 1127, it is necessary to understand what was happening in the years immediately before. Roger could not simply pick up what his uncle Guiscard had laid down in 1085. There were eventful years between. The laconic notices of the local Italian annals still concentrate mainly on military affairs, even for rulers not normally credited with reputations as soldiers. For example, Guiscard's successor, Duke Roger of Apulia (1085–1111), who was more deferential than his father to the clergy, is described as a valiant warrior able to beat even the heroic Bohemond in battle. He is presented as repeatedly successful in taking cities by siege-warfare during a long reign: Capua (for its prince); Canosa; Benevento (for the pope); Monte Sant'Angelo; and Lucera. His son William (1111–27), who died at the age of thirty, is admittedly not recorded in battle until 1121, but he is then said to have embarked on several memorable campaigns to restore peace to his dominions. Falco reports that by this once-and-for-all display of energy, William enjoyed tranquillity until his death. He is described as of medium height and graceful body, but again the emphasis is on soldiering: *miles audax et strenuus, in militare arte peritus.* When he died he was buried like a military hero. Apparently popular with his barons and vassals, William is not highly regarded by historians, mainly because of the contrast between him and his cousin, Roger II of Sicily. At the time, they were sufficiently well-matched to require Pope Calixtus II to travel all the way to Nicastro in order to try and make peace between them in December 1121. Roger would not give way to the pope's pleas, but after Calixtus' departure, they themselves came to terms in February 1122. In return for concessions, William obtained a force of knights from Roger, nominally his vassal, to help him deal with another vassal, the rebellious count of Ariano. Falco, a contemporary, reports that William at this point abandoned to Roger the rights in Calabria claimed by Guiscard and his father as dukes of Apulia; considering the protracted negotiations, William's later tranquillity, and Roger's own renewed activities in Calabria at this time, this seems very plausible. Possibly at the same time, William sold off to Roger the half-share in Palermo he had similarly inherited from his grandfather. At some stage, William may also have designated his cousin, Roger, as his heir. To modern writers, William seems insignificant when compared with Roger II, but within the limits of what was expected in the twelfth century, William was generally respected as duke, and held his own in turbulent company.

These annals give little attention to the affairs of Sicily, though its count is often assumed to have displayed more considerable authority in his lands than did the dukes of Apulia in theirs. Guiscard's brother, Roger I, had enjoyed in his dominions of Calabria and Sicily a prestige and authority derived from his leadership in the re-conquest of Sicily. After his death, however, there was some disorder, and it is not certain whether his widow and the two boys, Simon and Roger, who in turn succeeded to the title, commanded comparable respect, not, at least, before Roger II came of age (1112). The grants made by Count Tancred of Syracuse to the church there in 1104 do not acknowledge the authority of Count Simon; they are dated without reference to any kind of formal overlordship. As late as 1120, the count of Ragusa, in grants to the church of Catania, likewise made no reference to Roger II as count of Sicily, dating his document by the years of Pope Calixtus II, the direct lord of the diocese. It seems unwarranted to interpret comparable behaviour on the mainland as indicative of any inherently weaker authority of the duke of Apulia when compared with that of the count of Sicily.

Roger II of Sicily, however, soon showed signs of wanting to strengthen his authority in his lands. The hard bargaining in 1121–2 with William was presumably conducted mainly for the purpose of gaining sole responsibility in Calabria. Particularly unsatisfactory from Roger's point of view was the situation on his northern border with the principality of Taranto, where Constance of France, widow of Bohemond I, and her young son, Bohemond II, could not subdue the vassals of their dominions. They had been totally evicted from Bari. Roger II seems to have conducted military campaigns with huge forces against various enemies on the mainland every year from 1121. The departure of Bohemond II to take up his father's *regnum* of Antioch in 1126 strengthened Roger's resolve to impose himself at Taranto. His ambitions were therefore well appreciated, and had been consistently resisted by the barons of this region long before the death of Duke William in July 1127 opened up further opportunities for Roger on the mainland. Roger's attempts to extend his dominions can be paralleled by those of his cousins, the counts of Loritello, who were expanding their authority into the still-Lombard lands north of Benevento. Roger's own activities would not have impressed his contemporaries as signs that he was already planning a monarchy.

All the Normans expected to use their military resources to enlarge their lordships and overcome whatever challenges they met. The greater princes of Apulia and Sicily wielded power alongside, or over, a very much greater number of other rulers, the counts, who effectively exercised the 'sovereign' powers in their own localities. When Amatus of Cassino wrote his history of the Normans c.1080, he recorded the tradition that Norman dominion in Apulia had begun about forty years earlier, with twelve Norman chiefs each planted in his chief city. Although there are difficulties about fitting this theory *in toto* to events either for 1042 or for 1080, it undoubtedly represents an important aspect of the early settlement, and was still operative in Guiscard's last years: Norman lordships were numerous, autonomous and not beholden to the duke of Apulia, who was only their chief, not their master. At the very beginning of their settlement, at Aversa, in 1030, the Normans had obtained formal authority for their powers from the established ruler, the *magister militum* of Naples; the Lombard prince of Salerno and the German emperor had similarly authorised the Norman recuperation of Apulia. Once Norman 'counts' were established, however, the hereditary claims of their own kin prevailed in successive generations. Moreover, the steady elimination of the older authorities made endorsements by them both impossible and superfluous. The limits of these counts' powers may originally have been determined by the geographical bounds of the diocese of their chief city, but military success and political astuteness helped some counts to extend them. The greatest scope for them was opened up in the northern regions beyond Benevento. Here the survival of older Lombard counties themselves probably provided a useful model of 'states' with mainly military purposes and secular objectives.

The military strength of the Norman counts was provided by combining the existing forces of city knights (*milites*) with those of their own feudal barons and tenants. The effectiveness of their lordships is demonstrated by their charters. These credit them with responsibility for the administration of justice and the collection of financial rewards for exercising public powers. The more extensive a lord's personal dominion, the more valuable any general concession made by him within his territory became. Counts invariably disposed of their 'rights' without deference to any nominal overlord, such as the duke of Apulia. Likewise, the duke himself could only grant what was his by proprietary right. Although there were a large number of these Norman counts, information about them is slight since few of their documents have been preserved and even these have not been much studied.

At this point the records of the southern churches have to be pressed into historical service. They become the principal sources of information about the Normans and the society they governed. The bishoprics of the South were small and numerous (nearly 150 of them), and their documents have been preserved in a very casual manner. But taken together, along with equally miscellaneous monastic records, they help us to perceive how the Normans settled into southern Italy and shaped the character of their government. The range of local comital power can be demonstrated from the charter granted by Count Geoffrey of Canne in 1105 to the cathedral church of his ancient city. Son and heir of the Norman Count Amico, Geoffrey nevertheless called himself a senator of the Roman empire, and claimed to act by order of the emperor Alexius. This was probably a device intended to protect Geoffrey from any claims to lordship advanced by Guiscard's sons, Duke Roger of Apulia or Bohemond of Antioch. The Greek emperor was invoked to suit Geoffrey's convenience. In fact, Geoffrey disposed of his gifts as though he were sovereign. He confirmed the church's rights in five or six estates (*casalia*) with all their appurtenances in the sea, saltings, vineyards, fields and livestock. He protected the cathedral's clergy and laymen from demands for labour services (*angaria*) and inquests (*inquisitiones*), and allowed the cathedral to accept any man who agreed to its lordship and jurisdiction (the *potestas affidandi*). He gave permission to build ovens and mills in the city, construct jetties in the river, place fishing nets in the river down to the sea, and build shops. He exempted the church's tenants from dues for the use of the lands, grass, waters, wood and stone in their holdings, and exempted the church itself, as well as its men, from tax (*jus tributarium*). None of its men were to be forced to be a bailiff (*bailivus*), or to perform other services for the count. The property of their men who died intestate and without lawful descendants should pass to the church. The count even allowed his own men to offer themselves to the church. He renounced his rights to license the ordination of clergy, and to tolls on the cathedral's buying and selling in and out of Canne. He allowed the church to accept ploughmen as *affidati*, with special provision for those who also ploughed the count's own land; in their case the count and the cathedral would share the pension due (*affidatura*). Those who wished to live on the cathedral's estates (*casalia*) were to become the cathedral's men unless they were from the count's own domain. The cathedral was given seigneurial jurisdiction (*bandum*) over its *casalia*, but if any of the count's men had disputes with any of the cathedral's men, such disputes would be settled in the count's court, though his judges would confer with the cathedral's own magistrate, the catapan. The cathedral was granted the daily renders (*redditus*) of its harvesters and the men working its lands, and the count renounced all his public rights to exact service, tribute, *collecta*, tithe, *adjutorium*, rent or other burden. He undertook never to question the church's immunity, or to remove its men to his own lordship on account of any plea, problem, crime or dispute, reserving only open homicide or treachery (*proditores*). The cathedral was allowed to take rents, tributes and services from its own men. The count ended with a pompous endorsement of all the good old customs, and a promise to help the church enjoy its lordship or pay a penalty. The range of comital powers, claimed and bestowed, is notable and comprehensive in its petty exactitude. The charter indicates both the nature of the authority and the variety of the revenues enjoyed by this Norman count of Apulia. The powers of other counts were presumably comparable to Geoffrey's. To all intents and purposes, counts were sovereign lords in their own lands.

The rarity of surviving records makes it impossible to draw a map of comital responsibilities in southern Italy at the beginning of the twelfth century. The situation itself was not static, since in some regions, particularly in the north, counts, such as Loritello, were still extending their jurisdiction. Elsewhere, some counties had reached their limits and already taken root by *c.*1100; from later evidence, it is clear that, after one generation, such counties could survive the failure or forfeiture of their ruling families. The county of Monte Sant'Angelo, at its peak in the 1090s, survived the expropriation of its last count, William (in 1104), to become, still apparently intact as a feudal honour, the dower of Joanna of England when she married King William II in 1177. Understandably, in such circumstances, families that lost their counties as a result of political disturbances under the monarchy continued to nurse expectations of a comeback, and were sometimes surprisingly successful. Thus the old comital family of Civitate, deprived by the emperor Lothar in 1137, eventually recovered the county; the county of Alife was also recovered after more than thirty years by the nephew of Roger II's great enemy, Rainulf. These counties had become established family properties well before the monarchy was created. This was certainly not by virtue of any prevailing public law, but was influenced by Norman notions of hereditary right. The most likely explanation for this is that the counts had organised a local honour of barons and knights capable of acting together with or without the count, and not easily or usefully broken up at will. How all these counties had come to be what they were by *c.*1100 may be baffling, but the fact of their importance must not be overlooked.

Glimpses of the inner workings of a Norman county are very rare. One of the best is the confirmation of the customs of Eboli made by Count Nicholas of the Principate in 1128. He acknowledged the claims to respect of the men of Eboli at a time when he was fearful of how his new lord, Duke Roger II, might interpret the traditional relationship. Nicholas' father had already given Eboli a *cartula* and ordinances: these he confirmed. His own charter dealt specifically only with the more recent issues of contention. He began, surprisingly, by defining the area involved geographically, and proceeded immediately to the most worrying matter: what would happen if Duke Roger induced the men of Eboli to agree to a truce or pact with him, whilst the count himself remained committed to war? The count then undertook to guarantee the protection of their rights and the doing of justice, no doubt seeking to retain their loyalty by generous terms designed to diminish any appeal Roger II's lordship might otherwise have for them. The knights of Eboli got their victuals, pay and replacements for equipment lost in war. The clergy were to get their rights; new settlers were to remain secure, provided they were not the count's own men or his barons' men, and not servile (*servi* or *ancillae*); the officials of the district were all to be from Eboli and not outsiders. Finally, the count swore on oath to keep the terms. If he failed to do so, and refused to make amends within a fortnight, the men of Eboli were released from their obligations to him. The remarkable ability of the men of the region to treat their own count as an equal power may, however, indicate not so much the particular weakness of Nicholas' comital authority, as the real nature of local power in southern Italy: the counts themselves had to reckon with a strong local sense of rights and customs within a very narrow compass. Here the Norman lords came to terms with traditional societies.

The nature of the powers exercised and conceded by Norman lords proves that the content of their 'sovereign' rights could not have owed much to Norman ideas, except to the degree that Normans once installed in 'office' might have become determined to profit from their position. The specific rights claimed and granted by the counts were not derived from feudal relations but from their authority over local populations. Taxes on personal status, or on pasture, for example, did not come from Norman experience. The rarity of grants of this type surviving from before the Norman occupation makes it difficult to trace the history of all these claims, but a grant made by the Lombard count of Lesina to the monastery on Tremiti, which includes such typically 'sovereign' claims as rights of wreck, certainly suggests that later Norman assertions of rulers' rights had ancient local precedents. On the other hand, the frequency with which Normans, as distinct from earlier Lombard rulers, apparently granted away 'sovereign' privileges to others, such as churches, has raised the suspicion that the Normans encouraged the 'feudalisation' of the 'sovereign' authority. Against this, however, it needs to be recognised that insistence on formal concession of such grants proves the importance they attached to getting prior written authority for the exercise of such rights. Charters of concessions to churches, which made it possible to define exactly what was granted, also permitted great variations in what was conceded. When Duke Roger of Apulia conceded to the bishop of Troia some rights of grazing, it was not long before the bishop was back again asking for a ducal grant of the *herbaticum* as well, the dues normally rendered for pasture. The duke's officials appear to have read the ducal grants punctiliously, and were not prepared to give beneficiaries the benefit of the doubt. In this context, the Normans cannot have been casual or profligate in making concessions of potentially valuable dues.

Although there is no way of measuring seigneurial revenues, the Normans certainly amassed considerable sums from the many miscellaneous customs to which they made claim. In a society where cash transactions were commonplace, it is not surprising that even feudal relationships were given a cash value. When Guiscard in 1059 undertook to pay the pope twelve pence of Pavia for every yoke of oxen on his domain lands, he acknowledged a concept of vassal duty unknown in the North. Concern for money rents is reflected also in other ways. Concessions to churches of rights to pasture and water in certain lands were conditional on respect for the traditional rights of others, lest, as the charters state, they should suffer and the lord's exactions from them correspondingly be diminished. The use of money had implications for the feudal relationship. On the one hand, it could reduce seigneurial dependence on the performance of regular vassal-service; on the other, it provided occasional windfalls of money payments for aids and services.

When considering the more strictly military obligations of lordship, a number of local factors have to be taken into account. The persistent Norman engagement in warfare in this period continued to offer possibilities for casual enrichment from booty and conquests, which could itself have deferred the drawing-up of definitive grants of estates in return for agreed services. In Sicily, Count Roger had at his disposal contingents of Lombard, Greek and Muslim troops, both cavalry and infantry, probably paid in cash. On the mainland, there was a tradition of local militias, some paid, rather than of enfeoffed knights. Warfare itself was concerned with the problem of reducing and retaining towns, with correspondingly limited interest in the deployment of cavalry forces in open country, as conditions in northern France required. The importance of building powerful fortresses over these cities represents a long-standing local interest in fortification. Gisulf II, the Lombard prince of Salerno, held out against Guiscard in the *rocca* of Salerno for many months (1076); the Capuans defied Richard of Aversa from the *rocca* there for four years (1058–62). The Normans faced enemies with little to learn from them about the arts of self-defence: they simply built better fortresses than their predecessors. The Normans' strength lay in knowing better than their enemies how to make political capital out of their military commands.

The Normans who seized possession of the localities without bothering to obtain formal permission duly established *de facto* lordships with either more or less prospect of making them permanent. They did not acknowledge that the members of the Altavilla family who were recognised as counts of Apulia (and from 1059 as dukes), had special powers over them, entitled to their homage for lands they had acquired by their own efforts. There is no evidence that the dukes ever enjoyed powers other than by military success, or attempted to deprive vassals of their counties; nor did all counts become vassals of the duke. One of the most unexpected features of some lordships in the South at this time was their continuing use for dating purposes of the regnal years of the Greek emperor, as though he was still thought of as ultimate sovereign. In some cases, Norman counts may have deliberately sought such imperial titles to deflect any Altavilla pressure on them, but Alexius Comnenus cannot himself have taken much advantage of this deference to his authority. His main preoccupation as eastern emperor at this time was naturally the restoration of his authority nearer to Constantinople. In effect, the Normans were their own masters.

This was also the period in which the German king was least able to intervene in the South as western emperor. Not only was he preoccupied with domestic problems; in Italy, the effects of the investiture dispute prevented his appearance in the South. The only authority with any traditional pretensions to act in southern Italy after Guiscard's death was therefore the papacy. The papacy actually began to present a much more imposing and prestigious front in the South from the beginning of Urban II's pontificate. The importance of the South was further enhanced after 1095 by the crusade, for this region was naturally the main springboard from Rome to the east. Urban's predecessor, Victor III, as Desiderius abbot of Monte Cassino, had been amongst the very first to appreciate the potential value of friendship with the Normans. Gregory VII, despite his disapproval of Guiscard, recognised his need of the Normans to rescue him from Henry IV in Rome. Their conflict with the empire forced all subsequent popes to acknowledge that the Normans' help was indispensable, however distasteful this dependence became. After Gregory's death, his successors as pope had to learn how to be more flexible.

The initiative was certainly taken by Urban II, himself a Frenchman. This probably helped him make contacts in southern Italy, perhaps through the several clergy established as bishops and abbots in the conquered areas, or through the Cluniac links with the monastery of La Cava. As a Frenchman, who showed how to win support for the crusade, he clearly had a better idea than Gregory VII of how to set about making friends with the Norman rulers. At first he had no alternative, since the papacy had sunk to such a torpid level in the 1080s that Urban had to work hard to put fresh spirit into the institution and revive its faltering morale.

The southern Italian bishops were summoned to participate in Urban's own election, and no sooner was he elected (12 March 1088) than Urban went to Sicily itself to meet the last of the Altavilla brothers, Roger I, with whom he established a good relationship. Urban is one of the few popes who ever ventured to the island, and his need of Roger's support is more apparent than Roger's need of him. The pope gave advice, even warnings, about the reorganisation of Christianity in the conquered island, which had to this point not been high on Roger's agenda. The see of Troina was transferred to Messina, and a bishop appointed at Syracuse in 1092, but there was no question of giving him the archiepiscopal dignity enjoyed by his ninth-century predecessors. Catania, already a more important city along the coast, had been provided with a great Benedictine monastery, Sant'Agata, with monks sent from Sant'Eufemia. This too became a bishopric. It is notable that all later bishoprics founded in the island were provided either with monastic chapters, or with a regular community of canons. Urban's reasons for visiting the South were only incidentally ecclesiastical. He needed Roger's help in making peace between Guiscard's sons, Roger and Bohemond, in Apulia, and he wanted to warn Roger against having anything to do with the anti-pope or the German king. In return for Roger's support, Urban II was prepared to let him organise the church of his dominions without interfering. Urban made only one foolish move. In 1098, he made Roger's bishop of Messina a papal legate. Roger reacted to this with such uncharacteristic violence that Urban immediately recognised his mistake. Again in a personal meeting, he made peace by authorising Roger himself to do what a legate would otherwise have done. A little later he put the terms of his concessions into writing, and the document conferred what has somewhat misleadingly been called Roger's legatine commission. Roger would not accept that any papal nominee could acquire effective powers over the church in Sicily. In effect, Urban II was not so concerned about Sicily as he was about re-establishing the authority of the papacy in the western church. For this he needed to be sure of southern Italy as a firm base for his operations.

Just before he died, Victor III held a church council at Benevento, his home town. Urban II, in a pontificate of eleven years, held seven councils in the South. Here he could assemble an impressive company of local bishops and even distinguished visitors, such as Archbishop Anselm of Canterbury, who was present at councils in both Capua and Bari in 1098. At Bari, 185 bishops assembled for his council. Urban dealt with the main local problems involved in reorganising the church in those parts, and shared in the moments of great enthusiasm by dedicating new churches on his travels. Urban did not set out to impose papal authority so much as to build up a goodwill in the South that might eventually pay dividends.

After Urban's death, his successor, Paschal II, kept up the momentum. No pope since the early ninth century reigned longer than Paschal, but he remains both obscure and controversial. Yet despite other problems, he certainly made a strong impression in the South, often making visits of several months in all but seven of his eighteen years as pope. He held several influential councils in the South, beginning in his very first year at both Salerno and Melfi. He actually needed and obtained Norman help for the recovery of the rebellious city of Benevento which, as a papal enclave in Norman territory, could not avoid becoming the base for Paschal's southern Italian operations. The papacy counted a high number of bishoprics and abbeys under its direct protection in these parts, greater in fact than in any other part of Italy outside the patrimony. A list made for Pope Innocent II in 1136–8 gives thirty-nine bishops (including the eighteen metropolitans) and forty-nine monasteries. The prelates of these churches took their problems as naturally as their modest financial pensions to Rome, and the popes were certainly kept well informed about what went on all over the South. Authentic papal documents known to relate to southern Italy for the period of five pontificates between 1088 and 1130, number well over five hundred.

The papacy even began to assume a kind of proprietary interest in the region, for the dominant secular authorities had no objection to a papal lordship that cost so little. If the minor kings of Christendom, such as Aragon and Denmark, accepted papal lordship, why should the later dukes of Apulia or the princes of Capua balk at a commitment entered into by their heroic ancestors? Urban II took oaths from prominent Normans at Melfi in 1089 to keep the Truce of God, and such oaths were renewed at Paschal II's council at Troia in 1115. According to the Salerno chronicler, Urban went further, actually investing Guiscard's son, Roger, with the duchy of Apulia at Melfi in 1089; and Paschal did likewise at Salerno in 1100. Rather better authority records that Paschal invested Roger's son, William, as duke on the border of the papal patrimony at Ceprano in 1114. This bond between Duke William and Paschal's successors was punctiliously renewed in 1118, 1120 and 1125. Comparable ceremonies were probably enacted for the prince of Capua, and in 1120 for several counts as well: Airola, Ariano and Loritello. Nor was it all ceremony. Paschal expected to get Norman help against Henry V in 1110. It is said (though on poor authority) that William entrusted his lands to the pope's safekeeping while he went to Constantinople in 1121. The pope certainly tried to use his good offices to reconcile William and Roger of Sicily (who was formally William's, not the pope's, vassal) in the same year, though Roger's intransigence indicates that the papacy had no more power than the duke to coerce him. Throughout the period 1088–1130, popes had real impact on the political, as well as religious, life in southern Italy. In Sicily it was different. Here Roger II continued to exercise the 'legatine' powers granted to his father by Urban II, taking no notice in 1117 when Paschal II felt obliged to reprimand him for doing so. For various reasons the papacy avoided an open breach with Roger II, who was obviously not as much in papal favour as Duke William was.

Roger's aloofness from the papacy had no parallel on the mainland. Paschal II found even the generally truculent Bohemond of Antioch deferential on account of his crusading interests. In southern Italy, it was convenient for the pope to meet envoys from the Greek emperor or the crusading states, and the pope actually lived there in greater security than in other parts of Italy, even Rome itself. The deposed anti-popes of the time, when they eventually made their submissions, were not surprisingly relegated to the safe religious establishments of the South, La Cava or Aversa. Another Frenchman elected pope in France, Calixtus II, no sooner arrived in Rome in June 1120, than he too took the road to Cassino, Benevento, Troia and Bari, spending five months restoring the good relations which had been disrupted after the death of Paschal, even obtaining the performance of homage as well as taking oaths of fidelity from papal vassals there. In July 1121 he returned to the South, travelling right down into Calabria on such an extended trip that he did not return to Rome until March 1122. The papal presence in southern Italy was thus opportunely asserted in the early twelfth century when no challenge could be offered. It rested on what popes considered the legitimate rights of the Roman church over churches and princes; it also regularly brought popes for extended visits to their city of Benevento, if no further. How the laity reflected on the implications cannot even be guessed at; but the clergy at least were forcibly reminded in frequent papal synods of the reform programme, whether they were directly subjected to Roman protection or not.

The leading role of the papacy in southern Italy by the early twelfth century, however unobtrusively acquired, had a decisive impact on the whole history of the later monarchy. Hard-pressed though Paschal II and his successors had been elsewhere, they enjoyed quite a favourable reception on their frequent southern visits. This did not depend only on particularly faithful vassals, like the princes of Capua or the dukes of Apulia, because popes had discovered they could deal directly with a great many Normans of purely local importance. In addition, the links with some well-established religious corporations in the South show that the clergy there turned naturally to Rome. They did not hanker after a Carolingian-type protection of monarchy such as their brethren had found so useful in England and Normandy. Some of the greater Norman leaders in the South had themselves played a notable part in helping to draw Rome into the affairs of their churches, if only for their own purposes. After Guiscard's death, few Normans thought it necessary to keep the papacy at arm's length. Roger II was exceptional.

From their first negotiations with the two Norman princes of Capua and Apulia in 1059, the popes realised that their own freedom of action depended on not being obliged to deal with a single, over-mighty Norman in the South. Gregory VII undoubtedly recognised the dangers presented by Guiscard's success in concentrating so much authority in his own hands, though he was powerless to prevent it. In the light of this experience, it is hardly surprising that Honorius II should consider trying to block Roger II's claim to the succession of Duke William in July 1127, for if this were not prevented, Roger II would bring the papacy face to face with a ruler of unprecedented authority in the South. Moreover, his personal intractability had already given earlier popes motive to pause. Honorius therefore had good reason to try and make use of his authority as overlord to oppose Roger, but what real strength could the pope muster? He could count on his direct lordship of nearly a hundred dependent churches; he had great hopes of finding secular leaders to support him, and he certainly regarded himself as equal to meeting Roger's challenge. Roger recognised the need to get Honorius' approval, and accepted that the strength of his rights as William's next of kin was not sufficient on its own, though he did not consider that the pope had any justification for refusing him his due. Honorius chose to put this particular point to the test: if he was really lord, he could not be legally obliged to submit to Roger's pressure. He was certainly correct in believing that the South as a whole was far from eager to welcome Roger as duke of Apulia. Until battle was joined, who was to say that the pope would not prevail against the count of Sicily?

The effectiveness of Duke William's own government was proved by the disorder that erupted immediately after his death. On the day of his funeral, Count Jordan of Ariano, whom he had disinherited, set about recovering his old county by attacking Montefusco. Shortly after, Jordan went to the assistance of another disaffected Norman, Robert, son of Count Richard, who was trying to take possession of Fiorentino, where Jordan was killed. It was in such unsettled times that Roger II sailed into Salerno harbour and began to bargain with the citizens for recognition as their lord, cautiously not leaving his ships during the negotiations. Roger promised to respect their persons and their rights; he also allowed them to retain possession of the *rocca*. Their agreement was confirmed with oaths. Accepted in Salerno, Roger similarly obtained the submission of Benevento, Troia, Melfi and almost all parts of Apulia. Before returning to Sicily, he sent envoys with presents to the pope, asking for investiture as duke and attempting to buy Honorius' approval by offering him Troia and Montefusco. Honorius refused to deal with Roger, even though he had already won acceptance in most parts of the duchy.

Honorius' attitude encouraged many to repudiate the fidelity so recently sworn. In fact, the pope could himself do little to help even his own city of Benevento where, according to the local chronicler, some of the city's inveterate enemies, alleging Roger's orders, inflicted many miseries on the inhabitants. However, Honorius did excommunicate Roger, and offered remission of sins for all those who died in battle against him. In November, the pope went on to Troia to rally the opposition in Apulia, returning in December, when Jordan II, prince of Capua, died, to preside at a great ceremony in which Jordan's son, Robert, was solemnly inaugurated and anointed in the traditional Lombard manner as his successor. The pope now had a captain to command the forces opposed to Roger. Robert's first campaign was a sign of what was to come. Though supported by a great force from Benevento, the prince and his chief vassal, Rainulf, count of Alife, would not persist in their attack on a castle belonging to Roger's ally, Hugh, count of Boiano, pleading a fall of snow as their excuse. However, the assault on the castle was successfully renewed in the spring when the pope brought a contingent of soldiers from Rome. The victorious allies then advanced into Apulia, where they were joined by Grimoald, prince of Bari, and Tancred, count of Brindisi, whose cities were being attacked by Roger's forces. Roger chose to avoid giving battle and withdrew into the mountains, leaving Honorius to swelter for over a month in the heat of summer until the prince of Capua slunk away again. He could no more support the rigours of summer than of winter. Honorius at last accepted that he would have to deal with Roger after all, though Roger had still not crushed the opposition by force. He had nevertheless got his own way, despite the fact that there was no general enthusiasm for his lordship.

Honorius kept up his opposition to Roger for just over a year. Even after he recognised that it would be impossible to prevent Roger succeeding William, negotiations between the parties were protracted. When Roger at last met the pope at Benevento on 22 August 1128, it was only after sundown that Honorius agreed to come down on to the bridge outside the city for the ceremony because Roger feared to enter the city itself. Roger swore fidelity to the pope, and promised to respect papal rights in Benevento and the independence of the principality of Capua. The pope had become his lord, but was in fact at Roger's mercy. Within a year, Honorius was asking Roger to help him recover his hold on the rebellious city of Benevento. Roger had shown himself to be the strong man of southern Italy, and the forces of opposition, however considerable, had not been able to thwart his ambitions.

2

THE ESTABLISHMENT OF THE KINGDOM

THE CREATION OF THE MONARCHY

The Norman monarchy was established in the novel situation created by the general acceptance of Roger II's succession to the duchy of Apulia, but the idea of making Roger king did not emerge until 1130. It did not command universal approval, and Roger's enemies contested his pretensions for nearly thirty years. No other medieval kingdom had such strange birth pangs. Whatever hostility this plan provoked in different quarters, King Roger II (1130–54) and his son, William I (1154–66), showed unshakable faith in the possibility of holding their conglomeration of lands together as a kingdom. Although it is not surprising that the story of the monarchy's foundation is told in terms of the heroic pertinacity of these two kings in the face of persistent petty-minded opposition, there has to be more to the explanation of its ultimate success than the personal qualities of Roger and his son.

One of the critical factors throughout the monarchy's history was the attitude of the papacy. The ultimate weakness of papal resistance to it in the twelfth century was as important to its formation as the strength of the papacy in the thirteenth century proved to be for the annihilation of the Norman dynasty in 1266. Because the papacy was the most determined of the monarchy's opponents from first to last, it is paradoxical that it actually owed its inception to the altogether exceptional circumstances of Anacletus II, the Roman pope, who himself was forced to seek Roger's support in 1130. Roger seized his chance to make the monarchy possible, and never surrendered the advantage it gave him.

To understand what happened, it is therefore necessary to keep constantly in mind both the impact of events, and the clearheadedness of the Norman rulers, even in their direst extremities.

The Norman kingdom in Italy was apparently first conceived at a meeting between Pope Anacletus II and Duke Roger in September 1130. The idea of creating a monarchy is often assumed to have come from Roger, and he certainly showed consistent determination throughout his life to manœuvre the papacy into a formal position of superiority. Anacletus' written concession to Roger of a royal crown can therefore be interpreted as a mere endorsement of Roger's detailed proposals, rather than a spontaneous gesture of his own. However, since Roger would never proceed on his own initiative without papal 'authority' to legitimise his actions, it is necessary to understand why papal consent was forthcoming. Roger did not himself coerce Anacletus by military action as he did Honorius II and, later, Innocent II.

The general situation in which both Roger and Anacletus found themselves in the late summer of 1130 certainly makes their willingness to collaborate understandable. It is easy to assume now that Roger believed calling himself king might help solve some of the political problems created when he added his cousin's duchy of Apulia to his own inherited counties of Sicily and Calabria after 1127. But it was not so obvious in 1130 that this would help Roger much. Roger's claim to the succession of Duke William of Apulia in July 1127 had provoked considerable opposition. This collapsed after Honorius II was reluctantly induced to recognise Roger as duke in August 1128, and Roger was enough of a realist to appreciate that changing his title would not have dramatically reduced his remaining difficulties. Thus, whatever Roger's long-term plans for his government, the decision to found a kingdom in 1130 is better understood by reference to the anxieties of the pope than to those of the ruler.

Elected on the 14th, and consecrated on 23 February 1130 in bizarre circumstances, Anacletus II had been faced from the beginning by a rival candidate for the papacy assuming the title Innocent II, whose weakness was, however, evident when he rather quickly decided to leave Anacletus in possession of Rome and drum up support elsewhere. Anacletus, secure in Rome, may not at first have appreciated the importance of allies in northern Europe. Only in May did his uneasiness appear in his letters to France and Germany. By late August there was no room left for doubt. Archbishop Norbert of Magdeburg, one of the principal prelates of the empire and an old friend, had dared to send messages to Rome denouncing Anacletus for using force and bloodshed to secure his election as pope. Anacletus was furious, and pronounced anathemas on his enemies. The very next month, the pope left Rome for the papal city of Benevento. No ruler's benevolence and support mattered more to him as a matter of urgency than Roger's. Anacletus was certainly in greater need of a supporter with the prestigious title of king to lend credibility to his pretensions than Roger was of complicating his situation with further novelties. Anacletus was not necessarily expecting Roger to confront any northern European army attempting to impose Innocent II at Rome; though, as part of his feudal obligation to the pope, Roger would have provided military protection. Roger also had the important advantage of being ruler of the Greek Christians in Italy and Sicily. Anacletus hastened to muster church synods in southern Italy, including representatives of the eastern churches, which enabled him to boast of his ecumenical recognition, as against his rival who enjoyed merely northern European support. The practical consequences of eastern recognition may have been negligible and the basis for Anacletus' boasts insubstantial. This did not make them entirely spurious. In Bari, it was not difficult for the pope to meet representative churchmen from the patriarchates of Constantinople and Antioch, as he claimed, for the rulers of Taranto were princes of Antioch and the southern Italians maintained regular contact with both the Greek empire and the Holy Land. In southern Italy, if not elsewhere in the peninsula, a pope with such Christian contacts would anyway have commanded more respect than a cardinal backed by northern kings. For such a cardinal to impose himself in Rome must have seemed not only unlikely but unacceptable. Roger II cannot have expected such a pope to be set up in Rome. A pope backed by the empire would surely prove as much a failure as any of Henry V's puppets years before. There is therefore no reason to think that Roger secretly doubted Anacletus' own legitimacy as pope, or that he cynically exploited his anxieties. It was sufficient that Roger, like most men in southern Italy, recognised Anacletus as true pope, and was given no possible motive for changing allegiance. On his side, Anacletus must have considered that his party would look more weighty if it included at least one Latin king to match the quality of Innocent II's backers. Roger, as a 'Norman', could have been expected to command some attention in England and France. Anyway, as king in southern Italy, he would have every motive to combat the German king Lothar, should this latter venture to assert traditional imperial claims in Italy. That Anacletus was more desperate to secure Roger's loyalty than Roger was to call himself king is most surely indicated by the number of concessions Anacletus made to get Roger's agreement to the plan. If Roger was pleased to be promoted, he was certainly not prepared to have greatness thrust upon him without important guarantees.

According to Falco, a prominent figure in papal Benevento, the pope and Roger discussed these proposals at Avellino, half-way between Benevento and Salerno, Roger's ducal capital, and a likely meeting place. It was a town belonging to Roger's brother-in-law, Rainulf, count of Alife, a former ally of Pope Honorius II. The outcome was Anacletus' publication on 27 September, in his own city of Benevento, of the decision to offer Roger a crown, with royal unction to be performed by the archbishop of his lands. Sicily was declared the head of the kingdom, and the only archbishop on the island, at Palermo, was at the same time given metropolitan authority over four of the Sicilian bishops. Within three months the ceremony of coronation was duly performed in Palermo, which Roger treated as the capital city of his kingdom, in this way making explicit what Anacletus' bull had merely suggested. Granting Roger a 'crown' for the kingdom of Sicily, Calabria and Apulia indicates that there was to be a single kingdom made of three parts, formerly only of comital or ducal standing; it was not an island kingdom with a continental adjunct, as, for example, in northern Europe where Henry I was king of England and ruler in the Norman duchy. Most elements of Roger's kingdom were already ruled directly by him, but Anacletus also formally granted him suzerainty of the principality of Capua. This formerly vassal state of the papacy had been vigorously protected from Roger's ambitions by Honorius II two years earlier, but in the meantime, it had effectively become Roger's when its prince, Robert II, an unimpressive ruler, had paid homage to Roger as lord. Anacletus therefore accepted what he could no longer challenge. But when Anacletus also granted Roger the 'honour' of Naples, he went further. Naples, hitherto independent, was not the pope's to give. By declining to endorse its independence, the pope made the submission of its ruler, Sergius, to Roger inevitable. The pope also offered his king the *auxilium* (that is, the military services) of his own men in papal Benevento, retaining the sovereignty maybe, but not the substance of his military resources there. In return for these specific concessions, the pope was to receive Roger's homage and fealty and an annual pension of 600 *schifati*, a rather modest *quid pro quo*.

From Benevento, the pope moved south-east to hold a church council at Bari, where he also issued for the local archbishop a privilege authorising him to consecrate the princes of Bari, Grimoald and his heirs. Given that Roger himself attended the council, this privilege would imply that in Anacletus' eyes, Bari still formed a semi-autonomous part of Roger's kingdom. Six weeks later Roger, himself back in Palermo, celebrated his coronation in impressive style on Christmas day, receiving his crown from the prince of Capua and unction from his archbishop, while Anacletus' cardinal Comes stood by approving. The kingdom had now achieved public acclaim.

How widespread was enthusiasm in the kingdom for Roger's exaltation? Who apart from pope and king gained by it? For many great men in Roger's lands, kingship made no difference to their obligations as vassals, and they reacted to him as king much as they had reacted to him as count or duke, accepting or resisting his authority according to their variable political calculations. Yet it is obvious that the kingship could not have been proclaimed without the participation of great men, like the crown-bearer prince of Capua, and the approval of the hundreds more who made the ceremonies impressive, accompanying the processions and feasting from gold and silver dishes served by domestics dressed in silk. The king's splendour inspired awe but also fear: there were those who reckoned to lose rather than gain from the innovation.

The part that some great men played, and were invited to play, in this change of state is specially emphasised in the record of Roger's deeds written for his sister by Abbot Alexander of Telese, a few years later. In this, Anacletus is completely ignored. Instead, the abbot stresses the initiative taken by those in Roger's entourage for the proposal to make him king. He attributes the idea to the leading clergy, princes, counts, barons and others of the mainland who put it to Roger at Salerno. Telese regarded their enthusiastic approval for it as formally necessary and, according to him, it was only after receiving their encouragement that Roger returned to Sicily and convoked another meeting, where with overwhelming support he was elected king before being anointed in the cathedral. This emphasis on the enthusiasm of the leading men, both on the mainland and in Sicily, for Roger's kingship may reflect what Roger preferred to insist on by 1135, rather than the position in 1130 itself, but it cannot be altogether wrong: for the monarchy to work at all, it had to have some general approval. There is another important strand in the abbot's account that deals with the problem of why Roger's kingdom had as its capital city Palermo, on the island; he states that the great men on the mainland had freely acquiesced in this at Salerno. This is our first glimpse of the view that Palermo became the capital of Sicily because it had once been the seat of kings who ruled Sicily, a convenient historical fiction. At Salerno it was also accepted that, though these earlier kings at Palermo had ruled only in Sicily, the kingdom to be revived for Roger should comprise all those regions (Calabria, Apulia and others) which he already ruled.

The link between the kingdom and the metropolitan status of Palermo, here punctiliously explained, oddly echoes the juxtaposition of the two found in Anacletus' bull, which the abbot so deliberately ignores. Sicily itself, which was made to serve the argument, was, however, not really the problem. The positive contribution which the kingship could make, if at all, was on the mainland where there was no tradition of united government. Could the monarchy, with its *principium* and *caput* in Palermo, make itself respected by the Normans of the mainland?

Here was the problem that the abbot recognised to be fundamental, and in a way it was understandable that he should pass over Anacletus' initiative and concentrate on the internal and domestic justification for Roger's promotion. Abbot Alexander names the king's uncle, Count Henry of Paternò, as the spokesman of those who argued for the royal style, once Roger had united under his authority the lands of Prince Bohemond, of the former duke of Apulia, of the prince of Capua, of the ruler of Naples, and all the territory almost as far north as Ancona, so that all warlike disputes were stilled by his authority. The kingship conferred on him enabled him to punish the wicked and preserve justice: this was the hallowed justification for monarchy. For him, the temporary embarrassments of the papacy in the hands of Anacletus II could not be considered as the true cause of the monarchy's creation.

The discordant elements in Roger's lands were so far from submitting promptly to his jurisdiction, that the creation of the monarchy brought them into open conflict. In 1131, within a few months of the coronation, Roger required the authorities of Amalfi to surrender all their fortifications to him, and when they refused, sent forces to impose his own terms. He was so successful that Sergius of Naples thought it wiser to submit to Roger without waiting to be forced. However, the following year, when similar pressure was put on the Adriatic ports, resistance proved to be less easy to crush decisively. The enemies of the king took heart and thought of alliances against him. Out of common antipathy to Roger and Anacletus, they also began to look beyond his territories to see how the rival pope and his northern supporters could be made to serve their interests. These external complications, which Roger cannot originally have anticipated, prevented him from immediately getting the better of his domestic enemies. They were not illusory dangers: his most ignominious moments came when the aged German king Lothar invaded his kingdom in April 1137 and carried all before him as far south as Bari. Yet as soon as Lothar returned north in September, Roger was able to recover his own, for unlike Lothar, who was essentially a figure in transit, Roger had the long-term advantage of total commitment to southern Italy. Year after year he was able to return to the mainland from tranquil winter months in Sicily to renew the conflict with his opponents, showing no signs of being discouraged or deterred even by spectacular defeats, determined to prevail in the end and have his revenge on his enemies. Roger had a further important advantage. He had a clear and coherent aim: to make his kingship a reality. By contrast, his enemies thought only of defending their own positions, and therefore only made alliances of expediency. The willingness of many Norman lords to accept Roger's monarchy and find new scope within it for their own ambitions compromised the hopes of men like the prince of Capua, who only hankered after the old kind of autonomy. The German king and Innocent II had even more diverse ambitions.

From Sicily, where Roger was most secure, there are no contemporary records apart from legal documents: likewise for Calabria and the Adriatic provinces. Two or three accounts of these years, on the other hand, were significantly written in the region south of Rome, the most satisfactory coming from the papal city of Benevento. Its author, Falco, a layman who obtained the office of *judex* (a civil magistrate rather than a judge) under Pope Innocent II, had no sympathy for Roger and his monarchy, but his partisan spirit makes him as eloquent a spokesman for the opposition as could be desired. His personal experience of the period and the troubles that befell Benevento, together with his awareness of how the fortunes of war swept aside feeble local resistance, makes his breathless narrative of events enthralling. His rhetorical appeals to the reader's sense of wonder and the set speeches of the leading characters display his sense of art as well as his malice. Because of his fundamental concern for Benevento, rather than for Roger, Falco is of course no guide to Roger's frame of mind. For the historian, however, as Falco himself makes plain, this must be one of the most important elements for making sense of what happened.

Abbot Alexander's *Gesta Rogeri* could in other hands have been just such a revelation of the king's character. Its major shortcoming appears to be the abrupt way it breaks off in the middle of the account of 1135, for reasons unknown, but most likely because of the abbot's own death. Written at the behest of Roger's sister, Mathilda, estranged wife of Count Rainulf of Alife, and offered incomplete to the king by the author, the *Gesta* certainly records Roger's strenuous activities on the mainland from the time of his succession to Duke William of Apulia, but without giving the impression of being informed at first hand, either about Roger or about the events. The most vivid passages seem to express the abbot's misgivings or anxieties about Roger's rule, which may explain his initial reluctance to accede to Mathilda's request. Telese was not in the front-line of campaigning. It is only mentioned in the text because Roger himself made two brief visits there. He commended himself to the community, particularly by restoring the ownership of the mountain behind the abbey, and by offering enough silver for a chalice and two censers to replace those appropriated by the count of Alife to finance his campaign against Roger. The rather unworldly abbot probably wrote his *Gesta* as a thank-offering. He went as far as writing a eulogy, but took the opportunity to remind Roger of the need to show mercy and humility. For the mainland, he reports what he had heard, not what he had seen. Like Falco's, his account makes it quite clear that, for many contemporaries, what mattered was not the fate of Roger's monarchy, but rather that of their own community. In this sense, both of them provide an unexpected context in which to set Roger's activities. It is probably not fortuitous that Roger's activities provoked more written comment in this part of southern Italy, and that his arduous struggles with enemies on the Adriatic side failed to inspire similar accounts. There, the opposition to his rule could draw little comfort from an older order of things, and nursed no hopes of help from beyond Roger's frontiers to aid the cause: opposition was no less instinctive, but it nourished fewer illusions. In the west, however, hopes of thwarting Roger in the end protracted the agony and explain why it was there that Roger had to prove his mettle. The main question at issue was the principality of Capua.

Anacletus' bull indicates that to create his kingdom, Roger had demanded more than his own lands; he had insisted on additional papal concessions over Capua, Naples and Benevento. Events in the next five years proved why. For several years, Roger struggled to retain, and then recover, the allegiance of Robert of Capua. When this proved impossible, he conquered Capua and made one of his own sons prince there. There was still no question of quietly absorbing it into the kingdom: its separate identity could not be forgotten. This must have been Roger's major concern from the beginning. With the prince of Capua, his crown bearer, loyal to the monarchy, Naples and Benevento of themselves could do no harm; without Capua, the whole kingdom threatened to revert again to its constituent parts.

Until Anacletus' change of policy, Capua had normally been able to count on papal support in its earlier efforts to resist domination by the Altavilla family, because the papacy, recognising the dangers of becoming dependent on one great ruler in southern Italy, had striven since 1076 to keep up the friction between the rulers of Capua and Salerno. Even when Honorius recognised Roger as duke in August 1128, he still insisted that Roger swear to respect Capua's autonomy. Nevertheless, since then, Roger had known how to take advantage of Honorius' recognition. In his campaigns of 1129 he had subdued Adriatic Apulia, and taken fealty from the great men. He had so clearly become master of southern Italy that the pope himself personally visited Roger to obtain his help in punishing the rebellious city of Benevento. Since Honorius was himself so dependent on Roger's assistance, he had no further power to save Capua, and sometime that summer Robert, over-awed (*timore commotus*), did homage to Roger. Without papal support, Robert of Capua could not maintain his independence.

Anacletus' disputed election initially gave Robert no chance of breaking free, for at least in southern Italy Anacletus' cause seemed likely to prevail. From the first, therefore, news of Innocent II's success in northern Europe must have encouraged Robert to hope for better days. In the early summer of 1132, Roger sent forces to reinforce Anacletus' position in Rome. According to Falco, both Robert of Capua and Rainulf of Alife took two hundred knights with them. While they were away, Roger took advantage of Alife's absence, not only to occupy his town of Avellino but to seize his son and his wife, Roger's sister, as hostages. Falco and Telese marvel at the king's apparently callous behaviour, presumably reflecting contemporary indignation; yet Roger's move is much less likely to have been an unwarranted provocation than a calculated move, and reveals how little trust Roger by then placed in these important vassals. Falco reports Robert's indignant protests of injured innocence, but in fact the breach between king and Robert was probably accepted as inevitable on both sides. Robert certainly lost no time in exploiting tensions in Benevento to help drive out Anacletus' supporters there. On his own, however, he could not prevail; the success of his cause was definitely tied to the outcome of the schism, while Roger found that his kingship was threatened not merely by Robert and Innocent II, but by the hostility of northern Christendom.

For another twenty years Roger had to cope with the consequences. However tiresome this was, Roger may not have become unduly pessimistic about the eventual outcome. Whatever motive the northern princes and clergy had for supporting Innocent and seeking to oust his rival from Rome, none of them were expected to have any interest in, or intention of, making more than the most perfunctory visit to southern Italy, in the manner of so many previous German emperors with territorial pretensions. Roger's main problems in the years 1132–7 were not, therefore, of papal making. It was in the South itself that his monarchy really had to be defended. Likewise, it was in the South that any challenges had to be sustained. Robert of Capua's attempt to save his cause by calling on external aid, rather than by organising the local opposition to Roger, showed how little real confidence he had in the future of his cause. Roger's strength lay both in his sense of Robert's fatuity and in his belief in eventual triumph.

Fortunately, Falco's partisan feelings in this struggle made him a forceful advocate of the parties hostile to Roger, as may be judged from the long speech he put into the mouth of Robert of Capua, addressing his forces after rejecting the king's offers to negotiate. Robert had asked Roger to restore Alife's estates and family before there could be any question of discussions, but in the speech to his three thousand knights and forty thousand infantry (!) the prince insisted not on the personal wrongs done to Alife, but on the willingness of all the combatants to leave their homes, wives and children to defend their freedom. He reminded them how the king had by then treated Bari, and sent its prince, Grimoald, chained into Sicilian exile; likewise Count Geoffrey and Tancred of Conversano, whose city and towns had been taken by guile. The king had an insatiable thirst for the riches of all the great men (*omnes ... potentes viros*), whose reputations were to be trampled mercilessly in the dust. Whilst they still had time to do so, they had to act to escape from this man's clutches. Some of their goods had already been lost to him; now with faith in God and their weapons, they would shed their blood to defend their freedom and avoid falling into the hands of another (*in alienas manus*). They had to put aside fear of death and die together defending justice, and the whole world would speak of their valour. Robert's speech here takes an elegiac tone, more appropriate for the historian who knew the outcome than for the ostensible occasion, but the note of desperation could actually be authentic. The prince urged that death with honour was preferable to death in misery or even exile. A reference to Maccabees brings out the sacred parallels to the cause, but the speech ends with a very contemporary demand for the mutual exchange of hostages to forestall defection from the united ranks. The speech betrays only too clearly the anxieties of the *potentes*, and why they feared Roger so much.

In Falco's account, these brave words were followed by further fruitless parleys with the king. Roger then suddenly began negotiating with the papal city of Benevento, whose aid had been offered by Anacletus in 1130, and which Roger now secured, with a promise to free the property (*haereditates*) of the citizens from Norman 'servitude' and tribute-payments. However, the willingness of the papal rector, Cardinal Crescentius, and the leading citizens to confirm these terms on oath prompted rumours in the city that it was about to be handed over to the king. In the ensuing tumult the cardinal fled to the king, and the insurgent Beneventans repudiated the terms negotiated. Here Falco provides another summary of their position: 'We do not want to be bound by oaths in this way to the king, and obliged to weary ourselves in his service; fatigued and sweating in the burning sun with his Sicilians, Calabresi and Apulians. We are placed here in a delectable position, and have never been accustomed to military dangers, so let us have no truck with such a king as this.' Whereupon Robert, Alife and others immediately entered into a compact with the Beneventans, renouncing for their part all their customary financial dues (*fidantias et tributa*) from Benevento, and claims to military aid, in return for promises of security. The Beneventans concluded that this pact was preferable to Roger's. Falco describes its triumphant publication and Roger's own dejection that his schemes had come to nothing. After a show of preparing to fight, Roger instead ordered a strategic withdrawal at dead of night and took refuge in Salerno.

Robert's army, cheated of battle, nevertheless made a show of pursuing the king, and managed to take prisoner some of the king's Saracen soldiers. One of them was summarily executed and Robert of Capua, for the sake of glory (*nomine gloriae*), sent the head to his city to boost his reputation (*ut fama laudis ejus attolleretur*). This injury to his Saracens spurred Roger on to seek revenge by laying siege to Robert's *castellum* of Nocera. Here, on the fifth day of the siege, the princely allies arrived to succour the place. A difficult battle was fought at Scafati, in which Roger was driven ignominiously from the field and his great army scattered; prisoners were taken, and immense booty seized from the king's baggage train. This tremendous victory was greeted at Benevento as though it had been achieved by the citizens' own efforts, and Falco appropriately gloated at great length over Roger's downfall.

Yet within a month Roger was back at Melfi, rallying his forces against Tancred of Conversano, still apparently at large, and then back in Salerno with others of his nobles (*proceres*), planning his revenge on Robert of Capua and Alife. He also set upon the Beneventans, taking many captives, men, women and beasts. He ravaged their vineyards just at harvest time, and would not relax his pressure, despite pleas made by the cardinal–rector himself. Early in December, Roger sailed back to Sicily after gaining possession of the *castellum* of Balba, a *castellum* belonging to a vassal of Rao of Fragneto, one of Robert's allies, which they failed to recover. Their great victory in July had therefore yielded little fruit, and at the end of the year Falco shows that the effort of keeping up the struggle against the king had devolved upon the supporters of Innocent II in Benevento itself, under Cardinal Gerard and the new constable he had appointed. This development clearly owed much to the dissensions in the city since the summer, and to the hopes placed by some in the eventual triumph of Innocent. The arrival of the German king Lothar in Italy made the descent of the Innocentians on Rome appear imminent. However, the king and pope did not actually reach Rome till late April 1133, and since they stayed barely two months, Anacletus' party was certainly more securely ensconced there than they wanted to believe. Both Robert and Alife hastened to Rome to beseech Lothar to intervene in the South, for neither had confidence in their own unaided efforts to defeat Roger, despite their successes of the previous year. Whereas it cannot have taken Roger long to realise how little help Lothar could give, Robert characteristically appears to have continued hoping that Lothar would pluck his chestnuts out of the fire.

While the situation in and south of Rome remained uncertain, Roger wisely concentrated his efforts on restoring Apulia to obedience. Roger became very angry that the firmness he had shown in Apulia since 1127 had not been sufficient to bring barons and cities to their senses. Since the death of Duke William, Apulia had proved very unreliable in its loyalty to the new duke. It is understandable that with Capua and Benevento, where Roger's claims as king were recent and novel, he had had to proceed circumspectly. But in Apulia, Roger claimed as duke, and consistently from 1127 demonstrated, that he would not tolerate any subversion of his ducal rights. For the details of his merciless conduct in Apulia we are dependent on the abbot of Telese, who recorded only what he thought the most important, very soon after they occurred. Some of these details could have been derived from Roger himself, who made his two visits to the abbey at moments of triumph and security. But Falco also has some of the same stories, and though neither chronicler was particularly knowledgeable about Apulia, the news of Roger's campaigns must have spread like wildfire, since they struck Roger's enemies numb with fear.

Since the death of Guiscard in 1085, no duke of Apulia had probably aimed to make himself master over all Apulia as seriously as Roger now aimed to do. His determination to obtain respect there united his enemies against him. In 1127, when Honorius II took the lordship of Troia he called on all the great men of Apulia (*universi Apuliae ... magnates*) to pursue a personal vendetta against Roger – to drive him away or kill him. Telese names Grimoald, prince of Bari, Geoffrey, count of Andria, Tancred of Conversano, and Roger, count of Oria, as joining the papal plot, together with Robert of Capua and Alife. In 1128, Roger's campaigns enabled him to take various strongholds, including Taranto, Otranto, Brindisi, one of Tancred's cities, and Oria before Honorius' confederacy broke up and Honorius decided to negotiate with Roger. The Apulians remained very disgruntled by the papal volte-

face. Though Roger was able to gain possession of Melfi and other ducal
cities (*ducales urbes*), Troia resisted his siege, and Tancred recovered
Brindisi and other places while Roger wintered in Sicily after his
agreement with Honorius in August. The following year (1129), when
Roger had tried to take Tancred's strongholds back again, he still faced
bitter resistance. However, the capture of Montalto castle, and then of
Tancred's city of Ruvo, had induced the rebels to reconsider their
position. Tancred, his brother, Count Alexander, Grimoald and Count
Geoffrey all submitted and were confirmed in their holdings; then they
joined in Roger's assault on Troia. At this point Troia appealed for help
to Robert of Capua, who thought better of intervention; the more
courageous Alife, who tried to succour Troia, was obliged to withdraw
when his own lands were threatened. Troia on its own could not defy
Roger. Its submission had confirmed his hold on all Apulia, where his
peace was proclaimed at Melfi in August 1129.

Despite this general recognition, rumblings of discontent were not
silenced. Roger continued to distrust certain magnates, such as Count
Roger of Oria and Count Geoffrey of Andria, who bought Roger's
goodwill only by surrendering castles or lands. Trouble broke out again
after Roger's coronation when Grimoald of Bari repudiated his commitment to the king and joined Roger's enemies. Roger besieged Bari,
and since Robert of Capua dissuaded Alife from assisting it, the city was
taken after three weeks. Grimoald was sent to prison in Sicily. It was this
fate which made such a great impression on Robert of Capua. Tancred
likewise thought it safer to sell out his interests in Brindisi and elsewhere
to Roger and leave for the Holy Land. For these reasons, Roger
probably concluded his troubles in Apulia were really over by the time
he sought the showdown with Robert and Alife in 1132. Their victory
in July not surprisingly put fresh heart into the still feckless Apulians.
The principal Apulian leader became Tancred, who repented of his
precipitate decision to leave and brought the counts Geoffrey and
Alexander back into the war-league with Robert of Capua and the
German, Lothar. Attempts were made to win over Bari, but when
Roger got wind of the danger, he offered Bari attractive terms to stay
loyal, in much the same spirit as he had so recently shown at Benevento.
But Troia again took up arms, and other places too seized the oppor-
tunity to defy the king–duke.

These rebels, like Robert of Capua, may originally have put much
faith in Lothar's intervention, but by the time Roger was ready to
unleash his Sicilian armies, both sides realised that Lothar would not in
1133 travel further south than Rome. Roger therefore felt that his
enemies were at his mercy, and in his fury and indignation determined

not to spare any count, magnate or knight, guilty of faithlessness to him. Count Alexander was so fearful of Roger's vengeance that he fled, leaving his young son Geoffrey in the castle at Matera, and taking refuge with Alife. This in turn provoked Robert of Capua to flee to Pisa in search of reinforcements. Telese's tally of Roger's vindictive triumphs in Apulia unfortunately fails to date any of them, though they probably began as late as June 1133 and were certainly concluded by September when the king arrived in Salerno. Many rebel places were retaken, and their lords despatched in chains to Sicily; this meant the total destruction of the houses of Andria and Conversano. The most persistent and resourceful resistance was put up by Montepeloso, which Roger found well fortified and expertly defended. Tancred himself fought stoutly, and Alife sent a detachment of knights in token of solidarity. Roger finally prevailed by using siege machinery, and both Roger de Plenco, Alife's captain, and Tancred were captured. Tancred eventually followed other magnates to a Sicilian gaol, but Roger was hanged, and Falco claims that Tancred was forced to act as his executioner. This macabre tale is not given by Telese, who nevertheless confirms the view that Roger took gruesome pleasure in getting his hands on Tancred, and goes to some pains to elaborate on the just punishment inflicted on perjurers by referring to Nebuchadnezzar's vengeance on the disloyal king, Zedekiah. Other rebel places then submitted without much further ado: Acerenza, Bisceglie, Trani and Ascoli. Finally, the king recovered the fortifications at Bari, tactfully conceded to the citizens some months before, at Troia repaired its defences, and obtained by exchange Sant'Agata from which he could dominate all Apulia. This time there was no offer of compromise with magnates known to be unreliable, and a new regime was in prospect. Alife, impressed and anxious, sensibly tried to make allies in Benevento and Naples, anticipating that Roger would soon turn in his direction. In fact, the season was far advanced. Roger posted some troops to keep an eye on Benevento and Capua, and returned to Sicily for another winter of rest.

He was still in Sicily in May 1134, but as soon as he returned to the mainland, events moved fast. Before the end of June he had taken several important castles, induced Nocera to surrender, and by occupying some of Alife's lands persuaded him to submit rather than lose everything. Alife had insufficient men to maintain hostilities, and his lord, Robert of Capua, preferred to take pleas for help in person to Pisa rather than take command in Campania. Roger offered him harsh terms for submission, with the threat that he would take the lordship of Capua for himself if he had not returned by mid-August. Count Hugh of Boiano (Molise) bought Roger's peace by surrendering his lands east of the Biferno river.

The commander of the Beneventan knights fled to Sergius of Naples, who alone still rejected Roger's demands for submission. After Roger had actually been received into the great city of Capua, however, even Sergius gave up resistance, did homage and swore fealty. Roger finally took the homage of the contingents of the Borrelli family, and turning on papal Benevento, took oaths of fealty from the citizens, who reserved their faith to Anacletus. It was all over. In the autumn he was back in Sicily. For the first time since 1130, Roger could feel himself to be undisputed king in Sicily, Calabria and Apulia, with his rights in Capua, Naples and Benevento all conceded. Moreover, he had shown his capacity to exact obedience, and the surviving magnates had been made to part with some of their lands to obtain his favour. No doubt his kingship was unpopular with some, but he had the power to overcome them, and many preferred to enjoy some prominence in his kingdom on part of their old properties than risk, by rebellion, death or a Sicilian prison.

The enemy Roger had not been able to defeat was Pope Innocent II, who had withdrawn to the security of Pisa by the autumn of 1133 and who remained there until 1137, irreconcilable and vituperative about his rival, Anacletus', chief political supporter. Innocent II was not obviously formidable. Even Lothar could not restore him to authority in Rome. Only the death of Anacletus early in 1138 enabled Innocent II to act as a pope to be reckoned with. In the meantime, Innocent attempted to revert to the policies of Honorius II and foment discontent on the mainland to undo Roger's monarchy. Just as Honorius II had put his faith in Robert of Capua, Innocent placed his, with more reason, in Rainulf of Alife. But one great leader was not enough. When Alife died at the end of April 1139, there was no one else to take his place. Events were therefore again to show, and more than once, that Roger's authority in southern Italy was not easily conjured away by papal hostility. Innocent II cannot be expected to have realised this in 1134, but Roger II probably did appreciate the political realities of his kingdom well enough. His political sense was not matched by any of his enemies, with the possible exception of his energetic brother-in-law, Rainulf of Alife.

Telese describes the encounters between Roger and Alife in 1134 when they were reconciled, and embraced before a public moved to tears by the emotional scene. Alife had, before the meeting, agreed to Roger's terms for restoring to him his wife and son, namely the surrender of her dowry and the permanent loss of all such lands as Roger had actually conquered. In the king's presence, he had then bent his knees to kiss Roger's feet. Roger had tried to make him rise to embrace him face to face, and Alife had promptly taken the initiative in sealing their agreement. Roger was asked from the heart to give up his indignation against him, to love him from henceforth as he entered into his service, and to take God as his witness of their pact. There is a certain virile pride about Alife's moment of self-abasement, and Roger's willingness to accept his terms contrasts strongly with the vindictiveness he showed to the Apulian rebels. In Campania, Roger still chose to act more circumspectly, and he clearly regarded Alife as a man to be wary of.

Alife had been a valiant fighter and loyal vassal to the prince of Capua, and there is no obvious reason why he should not have been able to serve Roger with comparable devotion and valour. To explain how he turned against the king, Telese insists on the effects of persistent rumours in the spring of 1135 of Roger's death, apparently prompted by the depth of Roger's grief at his wife's death in February which kept him out of the public eye. Robert of Capua was bold enough to bring a great force of Pisans into Naples, where Sergius received them without further scruple (7 April 1135). Alife was similarly encouraged to take advantage of the favourable moment to recover his lost land and take the city of Capua for his old lord. Rather to his surprise, Capua resisted. The king's officials, the chancellor Guarin and the emir John, set about defending the castles of Campania against a generalised rebellion under the triumvirate of Robert, Sergius and Alife. Though Aversa surrendered to the insurgents, the royalists showed firmness of purpose until Roger himself arrived at Salerno in early June. Once again the itinerary of Roger's vengeance, though detailed, lacks dates. Roger unleashed his fury on Aversa and recovered other places, including Alife itself; both Sant'Agata and Caiazzo soon thought better of defying Roger. The main opposition was concentrated in Naples. Roger began a siege, but for various reasons had to abandon it. Even after his departure, however, the city remained under blockade, and soon felt the need of supplies and reinforcements. Once again appeal was made to Pisa, and when a new force arrived, they used their strength to seize Amalfi and its castles, taking many spoils. Roger duly returned from Aversa to drive off the Pisans, and the remnant fled back to Naples. Robert, leaving both Sergius and Alife in Naples, returned to Pisa to ask for more help. At this point Innocent II, made desperate by Roger's success, sent the miserable prince on to Germany to beseech Lothar to return. The pope still saw no other remedy.

Lothar did not in fact reach Italy again until September 1136. Even then he was in no hurry to move to the South, so by the time he was ready to enter Roger's dominions in April 1137, Roger was hardly unprepared. In the meantime, while the rebels held out desperately in Naples, Roger set about governing his conquered kingdom. Effectively, Campania was now his as firmly as Apulia. There was no further need to show caution or consideration to powerful towns and barons unworthy of his trust. Robert of Capua had lost all local support, and his chief city had shown loyalty to Roger under strain. Even Benevento had rejoiced at Roger's return, and it was in Benevento that he made a political settlement as the approach of autumn made his departure for Sicily imminent. Without reference to Anacletus he raised his son Anfusus to the principality of Capua, which thus became a mere fief of his kingdom. With Benevento docile and only Naples still eluding his grasp, the kingdom had visibly settled down under his command. At the time of Anfusus' promotion to Capua, Roger had already provided for his two older sons by making Roger duke of Apulia and Tancred prince of Taranto, confirming that he regarded the former political divisions of the whole region, including the partition of the duchy of Apulia, effected after Guiscard's death in 1085, as still significant. Telese concludes his story of Roger at this point with the monarchy's own endorsement of traditional patterns of government.

The main source of information for the next five years is provided by the exiled Falco of Benevento. He concentrated his attention on his patron, Innocent, whose success alone could restore him personally to his dignities in the city. 1136 was a year he records only for papal–imperial negotiations, and Roger's own movements on the mainland remain a mystery. Nevertheless, during this year Roger settled on one lasting change of importance for his government. He dropped styling himself in his charters 'King of Sicily and Italy', and adopted the curious formula 'King of Sicily, of the duchy of Apulia and of the principality of Capua'. In the South, following Byzantine usage, 'Italy' was at the time used to mean Apulia; elsewhere, however, it was used of the peninsula as a whole, though Germans often used 'Italy' in the narrower sense to mean the Lombard kingdom of northern Italy. The decision to drop Italy from his title in 1136 may, therefore, have had the tactful purpose of reassuring Lothar that Roger did not aspire to the German's own Italian crown. His own multiple title also confirms how far from united he considered his own kingdom to be. The change of title consecrated the new regime he had inaugurated at Benevento in 1135.

When Lothar duly arrived in southern Italy in 1137, Roger is said to have tried to negotiate with him for recognition as king of Sicily and proposed that his son, Duke Roger, should do homage to Lothar for Apulia, as Count William had done to Henry III in 1047. Falco, a contemporary prominent enough to know what transpired during

Lothar's southern journey (May–September 1137), was unfortunately more interested in events at Benevento, where Innocent II's return made it possible for Falco himself to recover his office, than in Lothar's main enterprise, the recovery of Apulia from Roger, which accordingly gets very perfunctory treatment. He subdued Siponto and Monte Sant'Angelo with such effect, Falco says, that Apulia was frightened enough of him to make a general submission as far as Bari, where Roger's castellans nevertheless kept up resistance for forty days. Falco says that after the fall of Bari, Lothar busied himself with winning the loyalty of the maritime region of Taranto and also of Calabria. Nevertheless, Roger's main force was not defeated, and Lothar did not press on towards Sicily to deal with the king. Instead he turned back to Melfi, which he took after some days, and then moved on to Potenza where he passed nearly a month at the lodge of Lagopesole. By this time, only one place of importance on the mainland, Salerno, still held out for Roger. Lothar at first left the Pisans, Robert of Capua, Sergius of Naples and Rainulf of Alife to conduct the siege, but eventually Lothar and the pope decided to negotiate terms of surrender with Salerno directly. At this, the Pisans took umbrage because they had not been consulted about the conciliatory terms. Although the town surrendered, the *rocca* was still held for Roger II. Despite their successes, moreover, the triumphant pope and emperor disputed throughout August whether a new duke for the defence of Apulia should be appointed in the pope's or in the emperor's name. A compromise was devised which permitted both pope and emperor together to invest their candidate, Alife, with the standard; this achieved a merely theatrical effect, and showed that they had not really been able to concert their policy for the South. This settlement, in early September, was the first and only indication of how the pope and emperor expected to fill the gap created by their defeat of Roger. This was critical, for Lothar and the pope continued to withdraw northward, the emperor to die (December 1137) and Innocent to await (not long as it happened) Anacletus' death (January 1138). Roger had not been crushed; the castle at Salerno still held out, and Alife's authority had yet to be tested.

As soon as the emperor had departed, Roger reappeared at Salerno with a sufficiently impressive army to recover Nocera, Capua and Avellino. Both Sergius of Naples and the judges of Benevento, so recently dutiful to Pope Innocent, promptly made peace with him. Only Alife, undaunted, realised that there was for him no alternative; he strove to vindicate his authority. He summoned a great force of knights from Bari, Trani, Troia and Melfi, and inflicted another inglorious defeat at Rignano on the king, who fled to Salerno (2 October 1137).

Alife followed up his success by forcing other submissions. Roger's authority did not, however, melt away. He still seemed formidable, even to such a supporter of Innocent II as Bernard, abbot of Clairvaux, who had vainly tried to avert the bloodshed of the recent battle. Bernard then produced a plan for patching up the schism in the church, and actually held discussions with Roger, which continued into December, though Roger withdrew to Sicily before anything was resolved. Innocent's own emissaries at Salerno also put forward proposals. Since Anacletus' party still gave Innocent concern, Roger's political importance could not be denied by his bitterest enemy.

Alife nevertheless proved for twenty months to be a match for Roger, and Roger consequently developed a bestial hatred of his brother-in-law, as he showed by his treatment of Alife's corpse after his death in April 1139. If Lothar had reanimated Apulian disaffection, it was Alife who retained support in Apulia by his energetic action, military reputation and the noble mildness of his character. Roger significantly spent the summer of 1138 stomping about mainly in the west, making a show of strength, but sedulously avoiding battle with Alife. The future of Roger's kingship had also been seriously compromised by the death of Anacletus in January. After some uncertainty, Anacletus' family made their own peace with Innocent, who entered the Lateran as universally recognised pope. Roger himself duly proclaimed that Innocent should be recognised as pope in his dominions. However, Falco does not mention any new Innocentian vicar at Benevento, which seems rather to have been at Roger's disposal, and no peace was made between king and pope. At his Lateran council held in April 1139, Innocent excommunicated Roger and all his followers, still expecting, with Alife's help, to resume Honorius II's original policy of combating Roger's dominance. Alife's death at this juncture immediately exposed Innocent II's own inadequacies. Roger's tactics suggest that he was prepared to wait for his enemies to commit some expected imprudence.

With Alife dead, Innocent was actually obliged to bring his own army south of Rome in the summer of 1139. Roger attempted to parry this with a request for negotiations. Innocent's terms, that Robert of Capua be restored to his principality, though quite unacceptable to Roger, were discussed for eight days. Roger then tricked the guileless pope by pretending to break off discussions to deal locally with the troublesome Borrelli brothers. The pope, instead of daring to demonstrate what he might in the meantime achieve by a display of force, settled down to a desultory attack on the fortified point of Galluccio, where he was caught by surprise when Roger suddenly returned. The papal force fled, leaving many dead and prisoners. The pope himself was ignominiously led off to the victorious Roger. Falco says that Roger humbled himself beyond belief (*ultra quam credi potest*) to persuade the pope, his prisoner, to make peace and concord, but it still took Innocent several days to reconcile himself to the fact that in his impotence he could hold out no longer. On 25 July 1139, the king and his sons, Roger, duke of Apulia, and Anfusus, prince of Capua, swore fidelity to Innocent and his canonical successors, according to the traditional formula of Roger's forebears. Then the pope immediately invested Roger with the kingdom of Sicily by giving him a standard (*vexillum*), and his sons likewise, Roger with the duchy of Apulia, Anfusus with the principality of Capua. Falco describes the general rejoicing that followed in Benevento, the prompt submission of Naples to the king, and the fealty there offered to Duke Roger.

Before Innocent entered Benevento in style, he provided Roger at Mignano with a written title to his kingdom that shows how he had wrestled with his conscience. He professed to grant Roger the regimen of Sicily on account of the merits of the king's uncle, Robert Guiscard, and of his father, Roger I; he claimed that there was no doubt, from reference in the ancient historians, that Sicily had once been a kingdom; and that this grant of a kingdom, with the duchy of Apulia, had already been made by Pope Honorius II; to this Innocent now added the Capuan principality. For his part, Roger (and his successors after him) would do homage and fealty and pay an annual pension of 600 *schifati*. Innocent's concessions at Mignano, in effect, were nothing less than a public confirmation of Roger's existing position. Roger, to get papal confirmation, had given nothing, except a show of vassalage. He was not himself humbled by this submission to the pope. It was Innocent II who had to climb down. What Roger had wanted from Innocent, as he had wanted from Honorius, was the public acknowledgement of his status. With this the papacy withdrew its support for any challenges to Roger's rule.

Neither Innocent nor his immediate successors reconciled themselves to Roger's triumph, and as soon as he was dead, the papacy tried to deny his heir the fruits of Roger's campaigns. Boso, biographer of Innocent II, did not mention his humiliation at Roger's hands, or acknowledge his concessions to the king. Roger was therefore probably aware that he could not count on Roman acquiescence, and that he would need to keep up the pressure as occasion presented itself. Innocent II, back in Rome by October 1139, never left it again before his death in 1143 and gave no trouble, even when he deplored the fact that Roger's sons, bent on recovering all the lands of the Capuan principate, encroached on his own frontiers. His successor, Celestine II (September 1143–March 1144), did not ratify Innocent's recognition of Roger; Lucius II (March 1144–February 1145) asked for the restoration of an independent principality of Capua, and eventually agreed only to a truce in the incessant border-disputes in Campania and around Benevento; Eugenius III, obliged to leave Rome, even before his consecration, had no direct dealings with the king for some years. Innocent appears to have hoped for a third German invasion to help him out, but after his death, the plans for a new crusade diverted the attentions of the northern princes from papal problems, and Roger had therefore less reason to fear a repetition of Lothar's interventions. After 1139, and for some years following, the papacy ceased to be a major obstacle to Roger's government. But the papacy was simply biding its time until sweet revenge for its humiliations should arrive.

CONSOLIDATION OF THE KINGDOM

The end of Roger's conflict with Innocent II seems to coincide with a new attention to efforts for strengthening his political position at home, but the extent to which his forces remained committed to warfare should not be overlooked. After his son Roger had been received in Naples, the king himself arrived in Troia, where he vented unseemly spite on the dead Alife before proceeding to Bari. Here, astonishingly, especially for the pope, its citizens, under their own prince, Jaquinthus, continued to defy the king and his siege engines for most of August and September. At last, overcome by hunger and dissension, the citizens negotiated with Roger for the surrender of the city and the mutual exchange of prisoners, with their lives guaranteed. However, egged on by a soldier who had been deprived by Jaquinthus of an eye, Roger forced the judges of Troia, Trani and Bari to adjudicate on the alleged contravention of the terms. In this way he secured the judicial murder of Jaquinthus, his counsellors and ten others, the mutilation of ten more and the imprisonment of an unspecified number of others. Roger's violence, bad faith, and caustic pleasure in forcing others to do his dirty work for him could not have been more blatantly paraded in what are almost the last paragraphs of Falco's narrative. There was no magnanimity in the mopping-up arrangements. For Roger the wars were not over.

At the beginning of the next campaigning season in March 1140, the king sent Anfusus of Capua, and a little later Duke Roger of Apulia, both with impressive forces, to the province of Pescara on the border with the (imperial) kingdom of Italy in order to conquer it. No provocation for this aggression is referred to, but by seizing many well-supplied settlements (*castella et vicos*), taking spoils and setting fire to some of them, they created fear and subjected the province to their control (*imperium*). Falco reports that Innocent warned them off papal territory, but they pleaded in justification the rights of earlier princes of Capua. Negotiations with Rome were begun when the king returned to the mainland, but Innocent himself avoided any further direct contact with his vassals.

In these conditions, resistance to any further conquests could only come from local lordship. The excuse advanced for Roger's expansion was the alleged rights of the princes of Capua in Marsia. The extensive northern regions of the kingdom won in the 1140s were divided administratively by the Gran Sasso d'Italia between the principality and the duchy of Apulia. The campaigns represented the will of both Roger's sons to make effective the authority last exercised there in the 1070s by such remote predecessors as Richard I of Capua and Robert Guiscard. Roger's consolidation of his authority in 1134 had already led him to seek, and obtain recognition of his lordship in these parts, first from the Borrelli brothers and then from Hugh, count of Molise, in 1135. Roger's increasing influence in these regions, perilously close to the imperial duchy of Spoleto, had correspondingly provoked Lothar's own actions there. Lothar's recent visit had in particular disrupted the authority of the counts of Loritello, who had been the dominant force, at least on the Adriatic side, for three generations. In his triumph, Lothar took the fealty of Count William of Loritello; his departure correspondingly threatened William with the fate of other great men disloyal to the king when Roger recovered his power. With the Borrelli brothers once more submissive (1139), and Molise overawed, Roger's sons saw that the moment had come to define the kingdom's frontier still further to the north.

Roger's lordship could not have been established without some local support. The assault on Pescara, launched in March 1140, was encouraged by the abbot of Casauria who asked for the king's help against Count Robert of Manoppello. Roger duly replaced Robert with Bohemond of Tarsia from Calabria. Anfusus was also able to exploit tensions in the family of the counts of Teramo, replacing Count Matthew with his brothers Robert and William. The local ambitions of such counts gave further excuses for the princes to move into Marsia. This campaign was assisted when Roger II himself moved up the valley from Sora and forced the abbey of Monte Cassino to surrender the valuable properties it had been granted by the counts of the region. By November 1143 (after Innocent II's death), all the lands of Marsia had submitted to Roger, and the counts of Albe and Celano were offered lands to make it seem worth their while to remain loyal. The counts of Valva and Penne retained their holdings; new bishops were appointed at Valva and Chieti. Papal influence in the region was swept away.

The campaigns of summer 1144 induced Lucius II to welcome at least a truce, but the king only agreed to it after the death of Anfusus of Capua in October, on the more than acceptable terms of restoring papal territory in the Campagna, but keeping lands taken in northern Marsia almost as far as Rieti. During the truce, Roger held on to this position, and when Eugenius III returned to southern Italy, Roger quickly forced to a conclusion the siege of Rieti (which fell to him early in 1149) in order to strengthen his hand in the negotiations that began at Tusculum in April. But Roger's high hopes of a real settlement with Eugenius III were not realised. In July 1150, Eugenius refused to ratify Roger's new acquisitions and tried instead to recover the papacy's traditional rights over many of the bishoprics and monasteries of the region. The pope's plans to bring about the collapse of Roger's authority involved another German invasion of Italy, this time by King Conrad III. Even after the deaths of Conrad (February 1152) and Eugenius (July 1153), the new pope Anastasius IV still persisted in the same policy by encouraging the bishops of Valva, Penne, Teramo and Rieti to regard him as their lord. Roger II naturally persisted in his defiance, and added to his control of the region by subduing Ascoli and Teramo. Since there was no settlement with the papacy until 1156, the substantial gains made in the 1140s to round off the kingdom meant that it was by then considerably larger than it had been in 1139. It was hardly surprising that the unwelcome recognition Roger II had wrung from the defeated Innocent II should have been so steadfastly denied him by Innocent's successors. They found that instead of shrinking back into insignificance, King Roger grew only more and more formidable.

Although there were many who benefited in the northern regions from the firmness of his government and from the end of local bickerings, others remained restless. It is difficult to believe that the royal regime survived mainly because of the advantages it brought to those in favour of it. As a region previously much fragmented and without coherence, both ecclesiastically and in feudal terms, and on the frontier of the emperor's kingdom of Italy, it submitted to whatever pressures were strongest. In the absence of imperial intervention, it was inevitably drawn into Roger's own magnetic field. His energy, and the preoccupations of the Germans elsewhere, mainly explain Roger's success. None of his opponents in the region showed anything of Alife's qualities to hold the field against him. Roger was not animated by sophisticated ideas about consolidating his territory or authority, though his conquests would have made it easier to block the Germans' passage to Apulia by occupying the narrow mountain passes. He pressed against his neighbours to test their capacity to elude his clutches. He was expedient in the manner of his family; expecting in due course to make concessions for a settlement, he took every chance to enhance his standing while the going was good. None of his contemporaries faced their responsibilities in this spirit, for they were all defending traditional positions. He, as a newcomer, was constrained by no formula.

Nothing perhaps better illustrates the way Roger baffled his contemporaries than his management of the problem presented by Louis VII's decision to go on crusade, published at Vézelay in May 1146. Louis, and after him the German king Conrad III, were ostensibly carried away by religious zeal to venture to the Holy Land in its hour of need, but Roger had to weigh their new interest in Mediterranean affairs against his own concerns. Roger had, from the beginning of his rule, to maintain good relations with the principal states of the region who had maritime interests. These included the cities of Venice, Pisa, Genoa and Savona, the Count of Barcelona, various North African towns, as well as Egypt and the Greek empire. His approach had necessarily to be as pragmatic as it was wide-ranging, and no other western ruler of the time matched either his experience or his detachment. Faced with the prospect of the French king going to the east, there was no reason why Roger should think first of the noble cause for which the crusaders departed, because the movement of so many soldiers overseas had inevitable implications for his own position, whether he liked it or not. Just like the eastern emperor, he had first to assess the consequences for his own government. The Greeks were still confident enough in 1146 to believe that they could deal with the crusaders without danger to themselves, but Roger, not surprisingly, was more apprehensive; crusaders crossing his lands from the North were bound to have an unsettling effect on his newly conquered dominions, and the papacy, even had it been more friendly in the first place, could not be relied on to stand by him. Although the complexity of his reactions may be remarked on, they were not in fact so exceptional. His political assessments have their counterpart in those of Conrad III. He had been considering an expedition to Italy to deal with Roger, and his negotiations for a marriage alliance with Constantinople to be directed against Roger did eventually bear fruit. Constantinople also naturally hoped to turn the crusade to its advantage, both by strengthening the Christian position in the Holy Land, and eventually by finding western allies for campaigns of reconquest in Italy. This crusade, unlike that of 1095, was led by kings with political commitments, who perceived that their actions would have consequences. Roger had more to lose than the others, and saw how he might himself profit from the expedition. At the very least, to distract Conrad and the Greek emperor would give him further respite; at best, he might insinuate himself into the expedition to such effect as to obtain control in Antioch, where many men of Taranto and Bari had long-standing connections. Roger's ingenious and audacious mind made him seize the chance to win a friend in Louis VII by his prompt and positive response to a feeler put out in the summer of 1146; he offered to transport Louis' crusading force by water. This proposal was cautiously rejected by Louis in the spring of 1147. In retrospect this seemed a mistake, certainly by the time of Louis' return journey, but in 1147, Roger's contemporaries were not ready to put their faith in Roger's ships. Northern princes feared that dependence on Roger would spoil their welcome in Constantinople. It is also likely that Eugenius discouraged Louis VII from making friends with Roger.

Roger therefore found himself cold-shouldered by the northern crusaders when they set out in the early summer of 1147. By September, though his enemies Conrad and Manuel were certainly discussing him in Constantinople, Roger could at least take some comfort from their being too deeply committed elsewhere to give him trouble for some time. To keep Manuel on the defensive, Roger launched his own fleet from Otranto against the empire and set about occupying Corfu and Cephalonia, with further raids as far off as Euboea.

Roger's willingness to demonstrate his confidence at sea can still seem rather disconcerting. It might be considered more statesman-like of him to have concentrated at this stage on enlarging and rounding off his kingdom by military conquests. However, in a way he was reverting to an earlier mode of campaigning. Long before Roger had engaged in military enterprises he had, as ruler of Sicily, already launched naval operations, just as his Muslim predecessors there had done. For Roger, Pescara in his kingdom was further away from Palermo by water than Greek Corfu or Muslim Tripoli. The acquisition of distant coastal sites would not have seemed any more precarious and transitory than the capture of fortified places within the kingdom. They were not necessarily acquired with a view to using them as bases for the conquest of full-scale colonies. They served perfectly well in themselves as depots for trade, as strongpoints to shelter ships, or for surveillance of trade-routes. Such Sicilian outposts, however scattered, no more represented an unfinished empire than the curious enclaves of British or Dutch ports around the world in the days of great maritime empires. The island of Sicily was itself placed centrally within the system, and was able to maintain far-flung links across the waters. The vicinity of Africa had made possible the Muslim conquest of Sicily in the ninth century, and before this Sicily had been a linchpin of the Roman empire, linking Italy to both Africa and Constantinople. Roger was not striving to resuscitate a moribund tradition from the past, for he had inherited in Sicily a working system of maritime commerce with the Muslim world, and in southern Italy with the Greek empire.

These commitments were inescapable, and Roger had no reason to neglect any of his opportunities to exploit his advantages. Even without a crusading motive, he had himself long since engaged Muslims in combat. As late as 1127, Muslim ships plundered Patti, Catania and Syracuse on the Sicilian coast. Roger naturally retaliated by exploiting any quarrels in North Africa which gave him an opening there. Just as a similar raid on the Calabrian coast at Nicotera in 1122 had been promptly answered by Roger's attack on Mahdia in July 1123, so the insult of 1127 was repaid by the recovery of Malta. It was the need to claim the duchy of Apulia after William's death in July that distracted Roger. Once Roger thought he had mastered the situation in Apulia in 1134, he had again intervened to assist his Muslim ally Al-Hasan, the ruler of Mahdia, who wanted his help against his Muslim rivals. A Sicilian fleet sacked Gabes in the autumn of 1135, and after taking much booty, sailed back to sell off the captured slaves, leaving Gabes under a local client governor. Mahdia's dependence on Sicilian political support was accentuated by several years of dearth that made Roger's ability to provide grain from Sicily a strong economic argument. The main influence brooding over North African politics was the threat presented by the growing force of the Almohades in Morocco. Their greater fear of these fanatical Muslims persuaded some North African rulers to acquiesce in Roger's interventions.

Roger himself did not participate in any of the African expeditions, but while his sons concentrated on campaigning in southern Italy, Roger in Sicily was that much freer to plan his African policy. Here, Roger took the initiative and, thanks to the Muslim historians, this aspect of his policies is perhaps better known than anything else he accomplished in the second part of the reign. By 1141–2 he had secured his hold over Al-Hasan of Mahdia. Roger even had his own officials in the customs to guarantee payment for his supplies of grain. The trading quarter there developed in these years under the patronage of the king's admiral, George of Antioch, and Sicilian pressure along the coast had been stepped up well before the crusade was preached in northern Europe. A Sicilian fleet attacked Tripoli when it repudiated Al-Hasan's authority. Though it was driven off, it attacked Djdjelli, the property of the ruler of Bugia. Two years later a fleet ventured even further to the west at Bresk, near Cherchell, where slaves were taken. But by this time the Almohades were moving firmly east, which may have encouraged the Sicilians to concentrate their own efforts on the Gulf of Libya, where prospects for success were greater. Moreover, the ports of this region were the natural termini of the great overland Saharan trade-routes, and the rewards of success were correspondingly more tempting. Tripoli was attacked again in 1144–5, and its submission was actually secured in June 1146. George of Antioch guaranteed civil rights there in return for payment of the head tax (*gizyah*) to Roger. Sicilians were encouraged to go and settle in Tripoli, which prospered under an Arab governor and the Sicilian connection while famine raged elsewhere. Roger had therefore already acquired sufficient credentials as an enemy of Islam before negotiations with Louis VII were opened.

Roger's Islamic policy, unlike Louis', was, however, not conceived in a crusading context. When Roger felt less need of his puppet Al-Hasan, the island of Kerkeni was attacked in 1145–6. The following year, trouble in Gabes appeared to offer Roger a further African outpost. Unfortunately, the indispensable George of Antioch was not available (as he had been sent against the Greeks in the autumn of 1147), so this opportunity was lost. When George returned in June 1148, however, Roger at last obtained the direct government of Mahdia, which was weak with hunger. Within a few weeks Susa and Sfax also fell to him. Al-Hasan fled. In his place, local Muslim governors were appointed, serving under George of Antioch (who is described in Muslim sources as Roger's 'Vizir') until he died in 1151–2. Roger also received tribute money. In his own way Roger achieved a victory in 1148 for Christians, just after the crusaders in the east had retreated from the attempt to seize Damascus. Arab writers praised Roger's government for keeping the terms agreed in the surrender of these places. There were reasons of self-interest rather than of religious zeal to guide policy, and there were practical limits to what Roger could do, for example against the Almohades. After the Almohades had shown their strength by their capture of Algiers and Constantine, and by defeating their African enemies at Setif at the end of April 1153, Roger did send a force to attack Annaba, but it was not long before his Christian enclaves duly collapsed. The last of them, Mahdia, held on until 1159–60, and even after that the Sicilians still continued their attacks on places along the African coast. When Maio, William I's minister, concluded it was simply futile to continue hostilities, his policy was thought contemptible, not realistic, by many Sicilians.

While Roger's forces were sweeping all before them in the summer of 1148, many of the French crusaders were already returning, disillusioned and keen to refurbish their tarnished reputations. Louis VII himself delayed until the summer of 1149 before returning by sea, and his ship then fell into a Greek ambush from which it only escaped with the help of a Sicilian escort. His wife, Eleanor, was also rescued from the Greeks by Roger's men and brought to Palermo. Roger appears to have hoped at this time to secure Louis' alliance against his own enemies, Conrad and Manuel, with both of whom Louis VII now had, as he thought, old scores to settle. Roger had three days of talks with Louis at Potenza. Roger had every opportunity here of measuring the weakness of Louis' resolution, but even diplomacy served its purpose, for a proposal to launch another crusade, this time against the perfidious Greeks, offered Roger yet more respite and gave concern both in Germany and at the curia. Eugenius III feared that the only outcome of any such crusade would be to strengthen Roger and embolden him to extend his kingdom into both Tuscany and the Romagna. The papacy did not therefore soften its view of Roger, despite his successes against the Muslims and his power to charm the very impressionable Louis.

Given that the last decade of Roger's reign coincided with the revival of trouble for the papacy in Rome itself, Eugenius III could not always act as consistently as he might have preferred. In 1149, it even looked as though Roger's own assistance was indispensable for dealing with papal problems in the city, and after Rieti had fallen to Roger in January, discussions for reviewing the truce were revived. Eugenius certainly needed some military support if he was to hold on to the papal position in Italy, but believed it preferable, if possible, to obtain prestigious and intermittent help from the German king than to deal with the brash omnipresence of Roger. Roger, on his side, could see that any pact agreed between the unpopular Manuel and Conrad would necessarily be viewed by the papacy as an undesirable imperial revival of some kind in Italy. Roger's problem was that although he entertained hopes of welcoming a frightened pope into alliance, Eugenius and his successors appreciated only too well the consequences of finding themselves, like Innocent II, coerced into taking Roger's vassalage. Roger was given no chance to inflict another military defeat on papal forces. His only other hope of deflecting the papacy from its course lay in setting Eugenius at odds with Conrad. But Eugenius would not be so manipulated, despite Conrad's determined loyalty to Manuel.

Nevertheless, rumours of an agreement between king and pope circulated, or were deliberately fanned, by Eugenius' enemies in Rome, and a meeting between them was finally arranged in July 1150, when a temporary settlement was at last negotiated. The main witness for the terms agreed at Ceprano is John of Salisbury, who may at the time have been visiting the curia, though his account is somewhat confusing. Eugenius declined to accept Roger's homage or renew the privilege formerly granted to him by the schismatic Anacletus II; what he did concede was only meant as an alleviation of the difficulties, particularly regarding the churches. According to John, Roger gave up his powers of making appointments to churches, and allowed the pope to scrutinise the elections already made. There was little proof that unsuitable men had been promoted by the king. As a result of this limited settlement, Roger ordered his archbishops and bishops-elect to be consecrated by the pope; this was accordingly done four months later at Ferentino. Eugenius III also granted Archbishop Hugh of Palermo a pallium as a sign of his acceptability, but refused to confirm Anacletus' grant of metropolitan status over other bishops because there was no canonical authority for this. Roger's substantial authority over his prelates was not, however, seriously compromised, nor were Eugenius' powers of intervention much strengthened as a result. It is a measure of the determination of both sides to get something for their diplomacy that such an unsatisfactory settlement was thought worth making. There had been no reconciliation, and the papacy remained weak. Eugenius skulked around Rome for the next two years, unable to regain admission there.

Events were to prove how great was the papacy's desire to continue believing that Roger's kingdom could be wished away in propitious circumstances. The papacy never willingly changed its attitude. It experienced no sincere change of heart. If Roger was disappointed not to have won confirmation of his kingdom from Eugenius, he did not allow this to deflect him from his course. His real authority in the kingdom did not actually depend upon papal blessing. Once Roger's bishops were consecrated, he did not find himself constrained by any 'treaty' obligations. At Easter 1151, he had his only surviving son, William, consecrated co-king at Palermo, without other authority than that of Archbishop Hugh's pallium. This provided for the succession in the traditional way of the French kingdom. After William's coronation, little is known of Roger's activities for the nearly three years that passed before his death. At the end of 1152, Eugenius III re-entered Rome; he and his successors were usually there until the spring of 1155. The popes in Rome and the kings in Palermo were not apparently in touch with one another.

Papal policy is plain in its determination to persist with plans to bring the compliant Germans back to Italy. After the death of Conrad III, his nephew and heir, Frederick Barbarossa, agreed to an alliance with Eugenius III against their common enemies – the rebellious Romans, King Roger and the Greek emperor. However, before Frederick actually arrived in Italy at the end of 1154, Roger and Eugenius, as well as Eugenius' successor, Anastasius IV, were all dead.

The new kingdom looked most vulnerable in the two years after Roger's death in 1154. There was a general expectation that Roger's kingdom, won by his conquests, would not survive him, and some great men sustained an understandable enthusiasm for reverting to the political arrangements of nearly thirty years earlier. None of his principal enemies had changed their minds because of the many demonstrations of Roger's abilities; they were the exiles who had conspired to bring about the collapse of the kingdom since the 1130s: Alexander, count of Gravina, Barbarossa's envoy to Constantinople, Robert of Sorrento, prince of Capua, and Andrew of Rupecanina, nephew of Rainulf of Alife. But the part taken by Robert II de Bassavilla, the king's cousin, came as a surprise. His county of Conversano had passed into his family as a reward for service to Roger in the 1130s, and his loyalty was so much taken for granted that, as late as 1154, he was also granted the county of Loritello by King William I. As count of Loritello, Robert acquired those responsibilities which had made his predecessors there quasi-autonomous. Although the proven loyalty of his family in the past commended him for the post on the northern frontier, he himself was quickly suspected of treachery, rightly or wrongly. When the king's suspicions came into the open, he fled, seeking first the help of Frederick and then of Manuel. The rebels of 1155–6 were reviving the troubles of Roger II's reign in the highly respectable company of both emperors and the pope.

These interventions from outside lend some coherence to the various dissatisfactions, and certainly secured for them the attention of chroniclers. Quite apart from the contribution made by Manuel's men and money, some exiles, confident that Frederick was on his way south to clinch their triumph, hastened to reclaim their ancestral lands, while the king was too embarrassed by the rebellion of others to oppose them. The initial problem was in the North, where Roger II had so recently pressed the implications of his kingship as far as Rieti. This region naturally took its first opportunity, on his death, to try and throw off a suzerainty so lately imposed. The relationship of kings and vassals was, by its very nature, personal; vassals were, of necessity, bound to test their new lord's reactions by seeing how far they could go before knuckling down to the new regime. They were further encouraged by the attitude of the new pope, Adrian IV. His biographer, Boso, claimed that he was asked by the counts, barons and principal cities of Apulia to come to them as principal lord of the land, which was known to belong to St Peter, and receive their homage. The timing of all the stages of the revolt are difficult to pinpoint exactly. William I attempted to deflect Adrian by making proposals for a peace-treaty. Since Adrian was by then expecting Frederick's arrival in Rome, and confident of his success, he scornfully sent back a message in which William was called mere lord (*dominus*) of

Sicily, not king. Adrian IV did not leave the matter at the level of verbal rudeness. According to William of Tyre, he immediately set about rousing the kingdom and its enemies against William.

Frederick and Manuel also agreed that the time had come to blot out Roger's achievements when the little-known William took his father's place. Fearing Frederick's arrival first, William attempted to make peace with Manuel in order to break up his alliance with Frederick. Manuel, however, who had recovered Corfu in 1149, was determined to complete his revenge against Roger's heir. To counter this threat from across the sea, William therefore negotiated a treaty with the Doge of Venice, Domenico Morosini (who died in February 1155); the king of Hungary, who had been fighting Manuel, was also in this alliance. William himself then arrived in Salerno early in February 1155 and ordered his troops to invade the papal lands and invest papal Benevento. Adrian IV countered by excommunicating him, and the siege of Benevento was abandoned. But Adrian could not do more. Until Easter, he was having difficulty in Rome itself with Arnold of Brescia's supporters, and was then detained by the negotiations that culminated in Barbarossa's imperial coronation at Rome on 18 June.

Frederick, however, did not then take the road south; he left his allies to overturn William. The Pisans had, with his encouragement, prepared a fleet to renew their attack on the kingdom; Greek forces arrived in Ancona and were greeted by Frederick on his way back north. Emissaries conveyed his approval to the rebels in Apulia. William's future remained uncertain. Though the Sicilian fleet, returning from an attack on Tinnis in the Nile delta, fought with the Greek fleet in August, the kingdom's coastal defences proved to be vulnerable on the other side of the peninsula when the Almohades sacked Pozzuoli. William's army was also demoralised; one of the two commanders, Count Simon of Policastro, was accused by the other, the royal chancellor Aschettin, of being in league with the rebels, and was sent back to prison in Palermo. When William himself fell sick in September 1155, rumblings of discontent burst into open hostility throughout southern Italy.

In October, the pope at San Germano took the homage and fidelity of the returned prince of Capua, Robert of Sorrento, and of other nobles, before moving to Benevento. Meanwhile, the Greek fleet arrived at Vieste. In the next six months the army, under John Ducas, took charge of the whole Apulian coast from Vieste as far south as Brindisi. The cities of Apulia that received Manuel's forces probably did so more from fear or cowardice than from any spontaneous rejection of King William I: Bari, for example, did not immediately and joyfully welcome the

Greeks. The towns cannot have reckoned to gain or lose much either way by preferring the Greeks to the king.

On the other hand, counts and other great men had very close personal relations with the king; it made a great deal of difference to their estimate of themselves and their standing in the kingdom if they were confident of royal favour. If this was withheld, they looked without scruple to other lords who valued their support and advanced passable claims on their allegiance. The baronage had already found William to be a king little to their taste. He left the management of affairs to his recently promoted minister, Maio of Bari. The baronage felt cut off from access to royal patronage and from the chance to give him counsel. Maio is said to have feared that his pre-eminence was threatened by the very worthiness of such great men as the constable Simon of Policastro, Robert of Loritello and the count of Squillace. Even if Maio did not deliberately plot their destruction, there can be little doubt that many barons blamed Maio for what they felt was the slight consequence they enjoyed with the king. So, quite apart from the appeal of separatist aspirations in the border regions, further trouble arose on account of the situation in Palermo. Both the chronicle of Romuald and the *Liber de Regno* blame Maio in particular for fomenting discord between the king and Loritello. Both sources agree that open disturbance began in Apulia, and the *Liber* offers as explanation the rumours of the king's death which began to circulate because he was not seen in Palermo during his grave illness of 1155. The unreliable Apulians (*inconstantissima gens*), desiring to recover their lost liberty, took to arms, organised pacts (*societates*) and fortified castles. When the Greeks intervened, the unrest spread to the Terra di Lavoro, as the principality of Capua came to be called. All the same, the author has little time or sympathy for these incidents: his main concern is events in Sicily, where he puts Maio at the heart of a plot to have the king killed so he could take the crown himself.

All this is difficult to credit. Maio is said to have lured the prominent count Geoffrey of Montescaglioso into the assassination part of the plot, but Geoffrey, suspecting Maio's real intentions, arranged with others in Palermo to murder Maio as soon as the king had been killed, intending to pose as his avenger. Nonetheless, Geoffrey too hated the king for his tyranny. These plottings were overtaken by events. Open rebellion was suddenly declared at Butera, where the fortification was seized and used as a base for raiding the countryside and rallying supporters. Count Geoffrey himself fled there from Palermo. When the king sent another prominent noble, Count Everard of Squillace, to find out why Butera was being held in defiance of his authority, the rebels professed total loyalty to the king, but alleged that Maio, and Archbishop Hugh of

Palermo, were plotting to seize the kingdom from William. The king was totally astonished by the allegations and lost no time in marching on Butera, taking with him the constable, Count Simon, who was released from prison. After a brief siege the rebels surrendered on condition that they were allowed to leave the kingdom without harm. With Sicily pacified, William decided to cross to Apulia and do real battle with the Greeks.

Boso reports that the Greeks were trying to make a very ambitious deal with the pope when Maio started fresh negotiations with Adrian to salvage something for the king. But Adrian was still so confident that William's kingdom would collapse, that he turned him down flat. Six months later this proved such a serious mistake that Boso, anxious to absolve Adrian from the ensuing criticism, claims that Adrian himself had been willing to accept William's submission and had been made to reject it because most cardinals (*maior pars*) would not agree. This seems highly unlikely. The importance of the negotiations at Salerno at the end of 1155 lies not in what they achieved, but in what they prove about William's situation by December. He tried to buy off the pope's enmity by offering total freedom (*plenaria libertas*) to all the churches of his lands, and three *castra* to the papacy: Paduli, Montefusco and Morcone. In return he expected the pope to receive his homage and fidelity. In retrospect at least, Boso says that these terms offered the basis of an honourable agreement with the papacy, yet if in his extremity William had not been prepared to surrender more than this, it is hardly surprising that the cardinals saw no reason to negotiate; they preferred to hope soon to be altogether rid of this tiresome king.

In the early part of 1156, William I was therefore obliged to re-establish his authority by strictly military means. Although Greek reinforcements had been moved into Brindisi, William, showing himself, like his father, decisive under pressure, secured the capture of the port and its commanders. Then he turned on Bari. With Apulia retaken, he advanced to Benevento where Adrian was now trapped and, like Honorius II and Innocent II before him, obliged to negotiate a binding settlement. Adrian was represented by the cardinals Ubald, Julius and Roland (later his successor Alexander III); the king was represented by Maio, great admiral of admirals, himself a pious layman, and by four prelates, the archbishops Hugh of Palermo and Romuald of Salerno, Bishop William of Troia and Abbot Marinus of La Cava. William was formally invested by the pope with the kingdom (Sicily, Apulia and Capua) in return for liege homage, fidelity and an annual *census*. He had no objections to the pope's desire to preserve the distinctiveness of the kingdom's three parts, and accepted separate investiture with each by a banner, though there were not, as there had been in 1139, three separate individuals to be invested as king, duke and prince. The pope also specifically abandoned to him Naples, Salerno, Amalfi, Marsia and other holdings which the king claimed beyond Marsia, while William restored to the papacy certain conquests on the northern fringes of his kingdom. The agreed frontier riveted the territorial interests of the papacy to those of the kingdom. Any invasion of the kingdom by papal allies would immediately invite reprisals into papal lands. The kingdom and the papacy were given an incentive to act together as southern Italian powers against the North, which in the twelfth century meant the western empire. To what extent there was awkward bargaining about the definition of the frontiers cannot be known. From the number of the ecclesiastical negotiators, however, it seems likely that the most contentious issues remained the royal rights over the churches. In 1156, the king was in too strong a position to give way over these. For this reason, there can be no doubt that the treaty represented a confirmation of William's victory, whatever else he gave to the pope to appease him. Thus the pope obtained the right to hear ecclesiastical cases on appeal from Apulia, Calabria and other territories bordering on Apulia, as well as the right to make consecrations, visitations and send legations throughout the mainland, but he gained nothing whatever in Sicily.

With this settlement at Benevento, the kingdom devised by Anacletus II in 1130 had finally won recognition from the papacy and, thereby, recognition in the eyes of western Christendom. The last showdown with the kingdom's enemies only came after Roger's death, because though thwarted by him, they had cherished hopes of at least defeating his mere successor. William's victory was therefore more than a personal demonstration of his ability to defend his father's creation: it proved that the kingdom itself was more than one man's adventure. The kingdom turned out to make better sense than anyone outside it had been prepared to imagine.

William's striking military successes, in Sicily, against the Greeks and against the pope, almost immediately restored tranquillity to most of the kingdom. As the finality of the new settlement gradually sank in, the rebels gave up their resistance, one by one. In 1157, Andrew of Rupecanina renewed his assaults on the kingdom, gathering reinforcements from the city of Rome, invading the principality of Capua and the county of Fondi, even defeating a royal army sent against him at San Germano in January 1158. Then he suddenly abandoned his conquests, apparently because his support from Frederick and Manuel was cut off. This exile did not find local loyalty itself sufficient to secure his restoration. By the Treaty of Benevento, the pope had secured terms allowing Robert of Loritello to leave the kingdom. In 1157, he too had renewed his attacks in the diocese of Penne; his constable, Richard de Mandra, was actually captured by the royal army. Loritello escaped, but continued on suitable occasions to renew hostilities. When the kingdom was shaken by another conspiracy in 1161, he penetrated far to the south before William could re-establish his authority on the mainland in 1162. Even though Loritello was obliged by military means to leave the kingdom and take refuge with Barbarossa in 1163, he continued to enjoy some credit with his vassals, dependants and relations. His importance was conceded by the monarchy itself. He was eventually recalled and restored to all his estates by the regent in 1169. Strange though it may seem, this persistent opponent of William I was never properly punished.

Creating the kingdom over twenty-five years had demanded persistent efforts from both kings. These are intricate to chronicle, but simplifying them can only distort the true character of the challenges to be met and defeated. Despite all the opposition, the new kingdom survived and continued in one form or another until the suppression of the Bourbon kingdom in 1860. Roger II's kingdom, however oddly put together, therefore proved to have enviable resilience. It is difficult to believe that royal will-power alone sufficed for this, and it is still less plausible to invoke any national sentiment, even amongst the comparatively small number of leading Normans. Yet there was sense in the new arrangement. The kingdom offered southern Italy a formal framework for its development, the lack of which in an earlier period had done the region much harm. Under the monarchy, its separate pieces, however disparate, discovered what they all had in common – a relationship with the central Mediterranean basin which the united monarchy promised to dominate in the general interest. Recognised by Rome but not much beholden to it, freed from fear of German emperors, and released from Greek and Muslim shackles, the kingdom was at last given the chance to make its own destiny.

PART II

THE KINGDOM

3

THE MATERIAL RESOURCES OF THE KINGDOM

·

The territories ruled by the Norman kings covered an area of about 100,000 square kilometres, slightly more than Scotland and Wales combined, or about three quarters of the size of England. Estimates as to the size of the population depend on some imperfect information about late thirteenth-century taxation which yielded an unexpectedly high figure of about four and a half million. Given the proportion of mountain and pasture-land in the South, some districts must therefore have supported impressive numbers of people by then. At the time of the Norman conquests, however, these lands were not overpopulated and efforts were made to attract settlers, particularly to improve cultivation. Colonists were found not only from outside the kingdom, but tempted from one region to another. Overall, the lands of the southern kingdom had a well-established reputation for fertility, and contemporaries all took their wealth and prosperity for granted. Although there is now little hope of providing an objective description of the kingdom's prosperity, a high proportion of the thousands of documents surviving from this period if milked for information, create an impression of general economic well-being, despite the occasional occurrence of natural calamities like earthquakes, volcanic eruptions, years of poor harvests and disease.

Unlike the northern Norman kingdom, the lands of the southern monarchy did not form a compact whole. From the Tronto river in the north to the southern tip of Sicily, the distance is about 500 miles; from Marsala in the west of Sicily to Otranto, the most easterly point of the mainland, is nearly 400 miles. Much of the territory is mountainous, divided by nature itself into several distinct regions, which make its fragmented past understandable. However, most regions of the kingdom had an exceptional relationship with the sea. Edrisi's geographical treatise, the *Book of Roger*, itself concentrates on the coastline, naming every bay, river, anchorage and port around Sicily and the mainland. No part of the territory was more than fifty miles from the coast. Before the Norman conquests, these facts of geography had given advantage to those who commanded the seas – the Muslims of North Africa particularly in the Tyrrhenian sea, and the Greeks across the Adriatic. Sicily's prosperity derived from its place in the Mediterranean commerce carried on by the Muslims. The wealth of the mainland had itself been concentrated in the ports: those of the Adriatic on the traditional routes from Rome to Constantinople, while western towns like Amalfi and Naples had kept up their own longer maritime links with Constantinople. The Norman conquests did not change the facts of connection, but thereafter, instead of being subjected to pressure from such outsiders, Norman Italy reversed the charge. Roger II raided and occupied cities in North Africa from which earlier Muslims had attacked Italy. The kingdom used its own naval resources to inhibit foreign aggression. This political success actually brought some economic disadvantages through the weakened power of both the Greeks and the Muslims. Though the monarchy was not solely to blame for these, it certainly played a major part in challenging the authority of the Greek empire. About the same time, the Muslims lost their own commanding role in western Mediterranean commerce, with unrest in north-western Africa and the contraction of Muslim power in Spain. Such disruptions all helped to compromise the kingdom's long-term chances of building up its commercial supremacy in the central Mediterranean. But after a century of Norman occupation, Sicily itself still seemed to Ibn Jubayr comparable only to Andalusia for its fertility and wealth. The Normans had not frittered away its potential: on the contrary they provided the region with able and effective leadership. Their ability to dominate the southern part of the peninsula and to hold it with Sicily may be contrasted with the situation in Sardinia and Corsica, islands also obtained from the Muslims about this time by the efforts of the Pisans and Genoese, both encouraged by the papacy. These islands were geographically further from the mainland, and it is understandable why it was the maritime states, rather than any military power, that challenged Muslim occupation. Unfortunately for the islands, the Pisans and Genoese were inveterate rivals who disputed for supremacy throughout the twelfth and thirteenth centuries. The same fate would certainly have befallen Sicily had the Normans not forestalled Pisan intervention and kept the northern Italian merchants under close supervision. Like the other islands, Sicily under the Muslims had been disrupted by internal disputes, and could easily have fallen prey to the attentions of rival merchants and colonists. Instead the Normans provided a stable form of government which, as in twelfth-century England, must have helped contribute to its increasing prosperity and a rise in population.

The well-being of the kingdom's own maritime cities was clearly dependent on the export of local produce overseas, rather than on the import of foreign goods. The creation of the kingdom helped to break down barriers to commerce from one part of the kingdom to another, but before 1130, many commercial links seem to have been with places outside the kingdom altogether, since the different regions found the best markets for their surpluses not so much with their neighbours, as with the populous cities of North Africa and the east. The most important export was the hard grain which Sicily had been famous for growing since antiquity, though other regions of the kingdom such as Campania and Apulia also produced it in sufficient quantities to export some. The South was able to export seasonal fruits such as hazelnuts, walnuts and chestnuts, as well as timber and oil, especially to Egypt. There were in fact many exportable products. Sicily was valued by the abbey of Santa Maria Latina in Jerusalem as a source of food such as bacon, tunny and cheese, but also for lamb-skins, rabbit-skins, ox-hides, wooden bowls, hemp and both linen and woollen cloth. Edrisi comments on the kingdom's rich pine forests, used as a source of tar and pitch, both exported for shipbuilding to many countries.

The most enterprising merchants of southern Italy in the eleventh century were those of Amalfi, who had been able to consolidate their own small but independent duchy. Amalfi was isolated and protected from its greater territorial neighbours by impenetrable mountains. This security gave it the possibility of carrying on valuable trade with Muslims as well as with the east, where it had depots both at Constantinople and in the Holy Land. Papal attempts to place embargoes on trade with Muslims could be resisted, and no scruples deterred them from even supplying Muslims with western armour, helmets, swords and lances. As a result, it did not suffer from Muslim raiding. The Amalfitani in their small territory could never amass enough to provide for their exports, so they engaged in local trade throughout the South to accumulate stocks large enough to make export worthwhile. The complexity of operations required the setting-up of agents in many local centres who inevitably dealt not only in grain, but also in other produce. The merchants used their profits in North African markets to buy local oil, honey and wax for sale in Egypt, where luxuries could be acquired

for the home market. The demand for these provided the incentive for
the production of marketable goods, mainly raw materials, apart from
the linen cloth made at Naples. Amalfi initially had only the Venetians
to fear as rivals in the markets of Constantinople, but their success
inevitably encouraged other enterprising merchants of the west to break
into their markets. The Pisans in particular attempted to acquire a foothold in Sicily, even before the Normans conquered it, and in North
Africa by the raid on Mahdia in 1087. Pisa served as the port of
flourishing Tuscany. Its main rival, Genoa, commanded the resources of
Liguria, and could count on a reservoir of potential buyers for its goods
in the lands bordering the Rhône valley. When Amalfi lost its independence and became part of the kingdom, the Pisans and the Genoese
naturally expected to take advantage of this for themselves.

The apparent prominence of Genoese and Pisans in the kingdom's
commercial life has created the impression that these merchants were
able to subject the kingdom to a colonial role, but this is misleading.
Sicily, unlike the crusading states, did not depend on Italian merchants to
throw it a life-line. These merchants were eager to buy the kingdom's
products, and they traded with the kingdom on terms acceptable to the
kings, who could cut off the trade if it suited them. Moreover, the
intrusion of northern Italian traders buying for northern clients did not
inevitably depress the commercial activities of the southern towns. The
merchants of Palermo, still predominantly Muslim at the end of the
twelfth century, traded with their coreligionists throughout the Mediterranean; the Amalfitani adapted their commerce to the new political
organisation. Messina was, in the twelfth and thirteenth centuries, a
deep-sea port, frequented by all contemporary merchants. The history
of Naples in this period is somewhat obscure, but by the early thirteenth
century, it was already in many ways considered the leading city of the
kingdom. On the east side, if Bari and Trani faltered, Barletta and
Brindisi prospered as bases for departures to the Holy Land; when
Siponto declined, its place was quickly taken by the new port of
Manfredonia. The monarchy cannot be shown to have stifled southern
commercial prosperity before 1266.

It is necessary to remember in what manner commerce was carried on
in this age, and not ascribe anachronistic concepts to governments.
Roger II's approach to such questions may be glimpsed in the terms
negotiated with the loyal city of Salerno, which alone had resisted the
claims of the German emperor in 1137. One of the favours the king
offered was to get the trading tenths (*decatias*) and other merchant dues
paid by Salerno at Alexandria reduced to the same level as those enjoyed
by the merchants of Sicily. Roger had therefore no aims to devise a

single commercial policy for all the merchants of the kingdom as a whole. The royal interest was at best engaged to secure particular advantages for special interest groups with some claim on royal intervention. Trading was conducted by groups of merchants acting in partnerships (*consortia*) of fellow citizens like those of Amalfi, who had their own quarter at Palermo and negotiated on their own behalf in the crusading kingdom. Great cities had to rely for their successes not on the royal government, but on the initiative of their own citizens. The most striking instance of this is the initiative of the band of sailors who brought St Nicholas' body from Myra to Bari in 1087 without authority or initiative from higher up. What we understand by economic life and enterprise in this period was not driven forward by the ambitions of rulers, and there were of course no economic theories to influence policy at any level.

The kingdom throughout the twelfth and thirteenth centuries played a key role in the traffic between northern Europe and the Holy Land; the Norman presence in southern Italy was itself one of the results of this. Though the French crusaders who left for Constantinople in 1147 eventually settled for the overland route, later expeditions invariably prefered sea-crossings. If they set sail at Marseilles or Genoa, they were bound to pass through the straits of Messina. Benjamin of Tudela regarded Messina as the point of departure for the best crossing and claimed it was a voyage of only twenty days from there to Damietta, though Ibn Jubayr took much longer on the return journey in bad weather. Pilgrims assembled and waited there for the Jerusalem journey, and its gardens and plantations helped to provide for its transient population. The combined forces of the kings of France and England were supplied there for six months in 1190-1. Although the Messinesi were roughed up in the process, this itself indicates that they had lost no money by the affair.

When Roger II offered to transport Louis VII's crusading force to the Holy Land in 1146, he obviously expected to be able to muster an adequate flotilla of ships from his own kingdom. Edrisi comments on the building of ships in several places of Sicily (San Marco, Messina) and the mainland (Gaeta, Sorrento, Bari), and there were probably many ship-building yards of only local importance, given the great number of anchorages and ports he mentions. Both the Greeks and Muslims, quite apart from the maritime republics (Amalfi, Naples), were experienced in naval operations before the Norman conquests. The Normans kept up this tradition with hardly any pause, except apparently in the 1160s. The twelfth-century kingdom showed every sign of appreciating the advantages of its maritime situation and exploiting its economic potential and political opportunities. The ports and markets of the kingdom, which attracted foreign merchants, sailors and adventurers, gave the government exceptional possibilities to profit for itself and not, like the crusading states, be beholden to foreign traders.

However, the arrival of northerners by ship depended on the availability of transport in the ports of Provence and Liguria. Numerous small vessels ploughed their way from port to port and around the coasts. For the French, the Genoese were the most reliable source of transport, and not only from north to south. When Peter of Blois had to run from Sicily in a hurry, he was lucky enough to get passage with a Genoese trader, laden with *tappetis, culcitris et mattis* (which amounts to comprehensive domestic furnishing such as wall-hangings, cushions and floor-covering), all very typical products of oriental craftsmanship produced in Sicily or North Africa.

Information about Genoese trade with the kingdom can be extracted from the treaty negotiated in the kingdom at Palermo in November 1156 and ratified in Genoa the following January. It reflects the different interests of the king and the Genoese themselves. The initiative was taken by the latter, who sent Ansald Doria and William Vento to obtain from William I not merely a confirmation of the customs (*usus et consuetudines*) which their citizens had enjoyed throughout the cities of the kingdom in the time of Roger II, but also a statement in writing of what they were. In a second document, the king issued letters of protection for the Genoese on land and sea within royal jurisdiction, except for pirates and those acting in concert with the king's enemies, particularly Manuel Comnenus, the Greek emperor. He is specifically mentioned in the written record of the oaths taken by the four consuls of Genoa and three hundred of the chief men, which was the guarantee the king required for the observance of the treaty. Two of the king's principal ministers, Richard Palmer, bishop-elect of Syracuse, and the master-justiciar, Rainald de Tusa, went back to Genoa to witness this ceremony. To what extent the king needed to threaten the Genoese with suspension of ancient uses to persuade them to abandon any political alliance with Constantinople can only be surmised. The Genoese must have realised after William's agreement with the papacy in June that they would be required to give some assurance about their political reliability if they were to resume trade in the kingdom on the old terms.

The information about trading given in the Genoese treaty may have been incidental to its main purpose, but has become primary for historians. The Genoese traded at Salerno and other cities of the kingdom, but only for four cities of Sicily (Messina, Palermo, Agrigento and Mazara) were the kinds of merchandise and the imports specified.

The king had not tampered with the old customs of the turbulent mainland in his first two years, but his grip on Sicily enabled him to adjust the rates in the island, possibly not so much for reasons of political blackmail against the Genoese as simply to raise more money. The main exports of the island were grain (from all ports), cotton (from west Sicily), wool and lamb (Palermo), bacon (Messina) and skins of various kinds (Agrigento and Mazara). The only import specified is woollen cloth. There are not only variations in the duty rates in each place, there are also differences in the weights or measures used; though the royal curia was to supply the Genoese with a standard measure (*cristo*) at Messina, they were allowed to use their own measures amongst themselves. The treaty purports to set out the old customs, so that these variations should not be regarded as attempts by William I to use duty rates to promote economic growth. Nevertheless at Agrigento, the duty on exported cotton bought in the towns was only half what it was on cotton bought outside, so that the king seems to have deliberately favoured Agrigento middle-men against (Muslim) cotton farmers. The old customs may themselves have signified an earlier attempt by Roger II to manipulate indirect taxation, but it is just as likely that they represent traditional dues and the continuing influence of local factors now beyond historical recall. At Messina, if the Genoese arrived direct from their home-city, they paid a due of one *solidus* on each *man*; at Mazara, each *merchant* paid ten *tari*. Variations like this do not smack of royal subtleties, but of the survival of local customs long observed.

The economic basis for the kingdom's prosperity was clearly not provided by the existence of a few great ports on the network of international trade, but by what could be produced and cultivated in the kingdom. The rural economy of the South cannot have been uniform, but its full complexity can never be grasped. Most of the documents available relate patchily to the affairs of Apulia, or to a few monasteries like Cassino, La Cava and Montevergine, and even these have not yet been adequately studied. The fertility of the soil and the industry of the population readily provided surpluses for the market. The network of domestic trade throughout the South brought these surpluses to some main centres. Markets in grain, nuts, oil and wine were certainly matched by those dealing in more perishable food such as vegetables, meat and fish which did not travel so far. Some contracts to encourage the cultivation of vines and olives involved long-term planning; the availability of surpluses was not merely fortuitous but contrived. The part played by small proprietors in all this needs stressing. Leases or sales of property which precisely describe estate boundaries commonly reveal that they were surrounded by many other small properties, and the process of fragmentation went on under the monarchy. Some property, for example, was still traditionally held in community by brothers, but when they came to marry, separate households were set up and the land divided. In much of the South, the rights under Lombard law of women to dowries and marriage-portions from their husbands helped to fragment landownership. This also made it easier for property to change hands. Just as rural properties were fragmented, so there were in southern Italy, if not in Sicily, numerous small cities and burgs boasting of city status, and acting as local market centres for produce.

These conditions were very general throughout the kingdom. So far as can be seen, there were no important differences of wealth between one region and another. Under Frederick II, for example, the tax burden was distributed in such a way as to suggest that the legacy of Count Roger I to his great-grandson was worth about a third of the whole kingdom; if the value of the other territories taken from the eastern empire is included, together they constituted nearly seventy per cent; this left the lands of the former Lombard princes and the counts of the Abruzzi to meet the rest. Within these regions there could have been much variation; nevertheless, it needs to be remembered, for example, that in this period Calabria had not yet suffered from its later impoverishment. Under contemporary conditions, Calabria still benefited from being the bridge-head into Sicily. It would be wrong to read modern poverty into the South at this time.

The importance of a market for grain underscores the central role of agriculture in the economy. Ploughing was clearly basic to Campania, and to the principality of Capua, later called *terra di lavoro*. The Norman princes calculated their financial liability to their papal overlord in 1059 according to the pairs of oxen under their jurisdiction. Judging from his grant to the bishop of Troia (1081), Guiscard appears to have also obtained actual produce – corn, barley and wine – from all his ploughmen (*ex omnibus nostris aratribus*). If surplus produce was regularly sold, its money value would have been generally familiar. It is impossible to say what proportion of their revenues from ploughed lands the Norman princes had been prepared to assign in 1059, but it is unlikely to have been more than a tenth. This would mean that their own annual revenues on each pair of oxen amounted to at least ten shillings. At Troia in 1128, it seems to have been assumed for taxation purposes that local men would each have a pair of oxen. In the late twelfth century the plough, now with four oxen, was still regarded as a basic unit in Campania.

The basis of the kingdom's prosperity was peasant cereal cultivation rather than organised seigneurial exploitation. The greatest monasteries themselves, such as Cassino and La Cava, owed their own wealth to numerous small estates scattered across the kingdom. Most monasteries had more modest endowments and only local reputations. Bishoprics likewise, within their narrow diocesan limits, cannot have generally counted on a large landed endowment. Such grants of whole estates with their tenants to the churches by counts and others, which prove the existence of the southern equivalent of northern lordships, did not necessarily involve the adoption of collective husbandry by dependent labourers. A grant made by the abbot of San Nicola in Troia of lands in his *casale* of *Ponte Albaneto* shows that at least part of it was leased out in sections to individuals to be ploughed, possibly by sub-tenants. Documents record contracts for cultivation by a few individuals and their families, and there are even references to middlemen. The abbot of San Modesto Benevento granted two of his properties for life to two knights and their men to have them cultivated. The terms envisage that the knights, or their men, or their agents (*missi*) would negotiate in their turn for some of the land to be ploughed by others, so that the monks would get produce both from their own tenants (two sevenths) and from the sub-tenants (one quarter). The monks had to send along their own agent at harvest time to measure their share, though the tenant accepted liability for delivering the grain to the monks' barn. The monks also got half the grapes and a third of the nuts, chestnuts and acorns, and some money presents at Christmas and Easter.

Short-term contracts for putting uncultivated land to good use were so common that they did not even need to be put in writing since the terms were settled by custom. If there were disputes, as recorded in a document of 1157, witnesses of an earlier verbal contract were brought in to testify to the original terms. The informality of possible arrangements is suggested by another record, made in 1145, when the rector of San Pietro paid 100 *tari* to get a confirmation from the seigneurial court of Paternopoli of lands he had held for a long time (*quieto jure*) by grant of an earlier lord made *partim pro anima* (that is to say, for the masses sung for the lord's spiritual welfare) and *partim* for a pair of oxen given him so that he could plough and establish his customary tenure. A surprising number of texts show clergy themselves taking on property with the obligation to cultivate it, and not always in connection with the ministry of a church whose land it was. The bishop of Ravello made a contract in 1100 with a new priest in the church of St Matthew, which specified not only his spiritual duties, day and night, in the church, but also his obligations to cultivate the church's property and make it fruitful, paying over a quarter of all the produce to the bishop. This system was not therefore considered an abuse, but a legitimate means of providing for the bishop's own support. There were enough priests, who did their own ploughing and were for this reason excused payment of tithes, for the abbot of Sant'Elena to make a distinction between them and those priests who got others to do the ploughing for them and paid tithes accordingly, when he confirmed customs of Roger II's time at Monte-calvo in 1190. If some priests ploughed as part of their duties in their churches, others had lands of their own to be cultivated.

Many documents of this period stem from a society with mainly family properties without seigneurial obligations. Clergy themselves acquired estates not only by lease, but also by inheritance; even some church property was still in family hands, proving the importance of proprietary sentiment which church reformers had not been able to destroy. In such a society, individual arrangements for cultivation were negotiated to suit the parties concerned. In 1152, the monks of Monte Vergine made a contract with one man who agreed to help out a day a week with manual work (*opera ad brachia*), and who paid over half the grain and wine crop from his holding. The royal *curia* itself did not dispense with such piecemeal arrangements. It granted an estate to John de Benedetto for ploughing (*ad laborandum*), spelling out precisely the dues in kind and cash. After his death, the estate passed to his wife and children, who were put into the care of a guardian. He complained when royal officials demanded contributions for the king's war with the Greek emperor, and an investigation established that there was no liability because the contract did not specify it. Here the legal liability depended strictly on the contract: ploughmen as such were not at the mercy of either lords or kings. Such contracts imply the availability of men able to enter into them without impediment by claims of lordship, and without fear of losing status by the performance of ploughing duties.

Cultivation throughout the kingdom therefore depended on many small proprietary estates, and on cultivators able to find lands available for lease. Some of the greatest landowners of the kingdom had tenants of this kind. One of Cassino's priors made a list in 1157 of the renders of his church from various properties – twenty-two separate holdings in ten distinct chestnut groves. After consulting the village elders of the estate (*veteres nostri*) about what had been paid before Vesuvius erupted in 1138, he set down for each place what was due, usually in the form of half the produce above ground, one tenth of what was underground, all straw, payments or duties with regard to the water supply from the *cisterna* and the repair of mill-stones, some hens and unadulterated wine (*vinum mundum*). All the shareholders (*partionarios*) had to provide meals when they pressed the grapes (*quando pisant palmentum*) and when they shared out the chestnuts. There were some money payments, but the monks got mainly produce. They may have had trouble in finding suitable tenants, but they were spared the burden of managing large-scale agriculture by themselves.

Documents referring to the goods sold out of the kingdom show too that animal products such as cheese, salted meat and leather were as much sought after as grain, wine or oil. These may have been of uneven importance in the kingdom; only in some regions was the king, for example, entitled to dues on cheese. Anyway, evidence for the pastoral economy is necessarily poor: shepherds were even less in need of written documents than cultivators. A rare reference to the important movement of stock from winter to summer grazing is provided by a concession from Henry VI in 1195 for the abbey of Corazzo to pasture two thousand sheep at *Buchafarim* in winter, and in the Sila in summer. Royal herds of grazing animals must have been enormous: Frederick II refers in passing to the thousands stocked in royal pastures. The then bosky slopes of much of the kingdom's terrain, not being suitable for the cultivation of crops, may have supported impressive numbers of animals belonging to many different owners. Exemptions from dues exacted for the passage and the grazing of these beasts alone hint at the value of the dues and the importance of the privileges. However fragmentary the evidence, their importance to the economy can hardly be overlooked.

Access to pastures was strictly controlled, and unless owners of animals had local customary rights, or enjoyed special privileges, payments were demanded for grazing in fields, fattening from acorns (*glandaticum*) and the provision of water. The Normans could have derived special advantages in their early days in Italy from their ability to restrict access to these wastes, mountains, marshes and woodlands, since their own guerrilla-like activities against the Greeks and Muslims gave them possession of secure hide-outs in such zones. However, there seems also to have been a clear understanding that the public power had general responsibility for controlling the use of natural resources. This emerges clearly from a statement of the customs of Atina (near Cassino), officially confirmed by Roger II in 1140. The king was expected to protect the roads, mountains, woods and water-courses for the benefit of the citizens, except where there were private inherited rights in wood and water. There were further provisions protecting access to the river banks for animals coming to drink, as long as there was water in the stream; rights to pasture, wood and cattlepens were held in common, though forest trees belonged to the owner of the land; hunting within the bounds of the city-authority was allowed by turns with neighbours. The Atina customs show that some woodland was in private hands, and

Roger II himself is known to have made a gift of woodland to reward service, though its bounds were very exactly described. But it seems likely that there was not actually much private woodland, and privileges suggest that access to supplies of wood was normally vested in the public power.

The supervision of water-rights by public authority was also already established on the mainland before the Norman conquest. An early Norman example is found in 1089 when Duke Roger of Apulia categorically confirmed for the monks of La Cava a right to take water within reason and make it flow by aqueduct (per ... arcaturiam) for the irrigation of their cultivated land. At the end of his life, the same duke renewed the rights of the monks to take water from nostrum aquarium, which sounds like a ducal reservoir. Valuable rights over water could be granted away without formal documents, even by Roger II, which seems rather insouciant of him. Not surprisingly, the consequence was litigation. One such dispute between the cities of Sessa and Teano lasted over twenty years. The case is of exceptional interest because the formal record made for the successful Sessans sets out the judicial formalities observed in the master-justiciar's court when it sat at Maddaloni in 1171. The bishop, judges, knights and citizens of Teano complained that the Sessans had diverted water to their own city, and the Sessans, also represented in court by their bishop, judges, knights and some citizens, replied that the water had been granted them by King Roger, as two witnesses then present could testify. Disputes between Teano and Sessa had already arisen twice previously, and a compromise had been proposed. But Teano tried to reopen the issue by denying that Roger had in fact made the grant to Sessa at all. Witnesses then recalled how Roger, standing at the window of the palace in Castro Sessa, had authorised them to take water from Rocca Monfina and channel it into the city. Teano could do no better than accuse the Sessan witnesses of false testimony, but when they offered to prove this by battle, the judges declared this an inadmissible procedure. The Sessans were allowed their water but warned not to interfere with Teano's supply.

Other documents also show how much precaution was taken to define rights over water. In 1185, for example, the bishop of Patti was induced to allow three brothers and their heirs to lease the sluice on the church's river at Modica for an annual rent of fourteen tari. Under the terms, they could conduct water from the river bed right across Modica to their own property, where they could do with it what they pleased, using it for their mills and machinery (de batinderiis). Apart from the rent, they agreed to mill all the grain needed for the (bishop's) house at Modica and to let the church's water run freely every Saturday from dawn until noon (*ad horam none*) in time of shortage (*cum necessitas incumbit*). Water-mills frequently feature in the records and gave rise to many disputes. The construction of new mills seems to have been active at this time and needed to be publicly authorised. The ownership of suitable sites proved to be a valuable asset and proprietors had to be able to guarantee access to the water-supply. The gift of a mill in 1205 records that it had been built by the donor's father on land bought from Greeks near Messina with rights to water on Fridays from the *flumarii de Caminariis*, which filled the wetland (*viridarium*) of the mill. For this water, the new owners had to supply the royal warehouse with one *salma* of corn and one of barley every year, as specified in the official deed (*sigillum*) of the *regie duane maioris quod . . . grece et saracine scriptum*. The royal interest was no doubt some security for the owner, and an offering in flour indicates the main motive for the construction of so many mills in the twelfth-century kingdom. The expense and difficulty involved in building mills could also be a bone of contention. An interesting agreement was made at Salerno by the abbess of San Giorgio with the abbot of Santa Maria in 1160, whereby the nuns lent money for the building in return for getting their grain milled without paying dues (*dazii*). The agreement actually foresaw the possibility that a build-up of silt, or the force of the water, might make it necessary to change the site of the mill. Although there is no early specific information about how the mills were run, later mills were managed either directly by the owners, or leased for payment of a duty on the grain milled; the miller did not necessarily work on his own and might have another man working to fill the sacks. Twelfth-century records about mills are mainly licences for favoured churches to build without further liability. Regular supervision of waterways is suggested by a document of 1171 in which the bishop of Agrigento needed royal permission even to rebuild a ruined mill. The potential value of such rebuilding is measured by a grant at the end of the century, in which Henry VI commuted his annual obligation of paying for the monks' clothes at the priory on mount Etna by simply authorising the prior to rebuild a ruined mill.

Inevitably, the records more often reveal disputes than agreements. The use of water by any party was bound to have implications for others. In 1156, the *camerarius* of the count of Lesina summoned the abbot of San Giovanni in Piano to answer a complaint that his sluices on the river Caldoli held back water from the abbot of Tremiti's mill lower down the river. Tremiti conceded that the water belonged to the other abbey, but claimed that even so it could not deprive the other mill of water without legal authority (*sine legali judicio*). At Salerno, difficulties arose when water was taken from the river Irno for the irrigation of the

gardens of the cathedral and others, because Luca Guarna (a royal
justiciar) tried to increase the annual levy due to him as water rights; his
claims appear to have been bought off by negotiation, so that he had the
use of the gardens in the period of irrigation for taking vegetables, citrus
fruits and cucumbers (*olera, citrolis, cucurbis*).

Water also provided abundant supplies of fish from the sea, lakes and
rivers. In some cases, grants of fishing were conceded in the form of the
right to keep a boat; in others, the beneficiary was allotted the services of
a fisherman. In a very detailed settlement reached in recurrent disputes
about fishing rights in Lake Patria ten miles west of Aversa, Duke Roger
gave judgement on behalf of the prince of Capua in 1098. The lake,
which is just to the north-west of the Phlegraean fields, must have been
considerably larger and more important than it is now. The Norman
princes of Capua inherited the rights of their Lombard predecessors to
underground caves (*cripta*), six named ports (*portum*) and exclusive rights
(for their men) to fish on Wednesdays and Fridays. On other days, the
prince got two big fish for all those caught each day (or their equivalent
in small fry), one for the prince, the other for his official (*gastaldus*);
twelve shad (*alose*) from each trap and twelve fish from each skerry; the
prince had three fishing places reserved for himself and the monks of San
Lorenzo of Patria. In addition, those who wished to buy and sell fish in
these ports had to contribute to an annual payment of 800 *tari* offered to
the prince by the consortium of fishmongers every year. The precision,
even the pettiness, aptly indicates the nature of princely taxation and the
importance of custom, not principle.

Reserves of natural resources could be of several kinds – marsh or
woodland, upland or plain, if not cultivated and apportioned. Thus, a
division of property concerning the lords of Sermoneta in 1183 left in
common the woods and marshlands (*silvae aquae pantani et paludes*)
where there were no individual properties but only rights of access and
use. Over such lands the public authorities exercised important rights
that left valuable powers and resources in their hands. The Norman
kings of England enlarged their forest jurisdiction steadily throughout the
twelfth century. In southern Italy, the public authorities had extensive
powers over uncultivated land from the beginning. The fertility of the
South, which nourished the local population, depended on respect for
these reserves which were protected by many public regulations. These
gave the public authorities important sources of revenue, but also duties
which emphasised their responsibility to look after public property (*res
publica*). These responsibilities depended on the public, rather than the

monarchical, power's awareness in each locality of what was required, and the ability not only of princes and counts to enforce custom, but of local communities through their elders (*boni homines*) to pronounce on what they were. The kingdom's greatest asset was its population.

4

THE RELIGIOUS COMMUNITIES OF THE KINGDOM

The inhabitants of most twelfth-century European kingdoms derived some sense of their common interest from sharing the same religion. In earlier times, English Christians had, for example, drawn together politically when confronted by the pagan Vikings. This southern kingdom could not count on common religious sympathies, since there was in the island a numerous population of Muslims, and also many Christians of the Greek rite scattered in various densities across its territories. The confessional 'problem' was not of equal importance in all parts of the kingdom. There were no real precedents to guide the Normans in how to treat Muslims or how to govern Christian subjects of another tradition. The Normans had to feel their way, though it was certainly part of their strength that they arrived as Latins determined to establish Latin ways in both secular and ecclesiastical matters. This did not make them impatient persecutors of alien traditions, though they could from the beginning deal harshly with both Greeks and Muslims. The Greeks immediately lost their ecclesiastical autonomy when their bishops were obliged to recognise Roman claims in southern Italy, though there was no attempt to change Greek rites. Many Muslims were obviously brought under alien domination, even if parts of Sicily seem to have remained predominantly Muslim and the practice of religion continued without a break. The Normans, with their Lombard allies, themselves operated in a Latin tradition, and in the long-term, Norman hegemony involved the eventual emergence of a dominant Latin church. By the thirteenth century, already, the very survival of other traditions was under threat.

MUSLIMS

In the Christian kingdom, the Muslims were a distinctly unhappy community, suffering from the misfortune of living under the rule of unbelievers. Before the Norman conquest they had been governed by local emirs who had not only fought one another, but had also been prepared to use Norman allies in their conflicts; the Normans had advanced their own cause by making separate terms with different Muslim leaders. Some of these arrangements must have survived under the monarchy, especially in western districts of Sicily where, by 1130, the density of Latin settlement still remained very slight. Muslim settlement itself since the ninth century had developed unevenly, the north-eastern third, Val Demenna, remaining very Greek. Only one in six of the leading centres of the island in the twelfth century had names of Arabic origin, and some continuity of life in most places suggests a high degree of intermingling between the Muslims and the existing inhabitants. In the late tenth century, a zealous Fatimid visitor found the country inhabitants so seriously compromised by inter-marriage with Christians, that their religious practice, their speech and their social behaviour had all been affected for the worse. If such conditions had once made it easier for the Muslim rulers to impose their own authority, after the Norman conquest, the rural population would have found it correspondingly harder to resist pressure the other way.

There is regrettably little detailed information about relations between the Muslims and the Christians under the monarchy. One of the most particular accounts of the Sicilian Muslims is provided by the Spanish Muslim Ibn Jubayr, who returned from the east through Sicily in 1185. His visit lasted less than four months, and his contacts with Muslims were all made along the north coast between Messina and Trapani. In Messina he met a high-ranking royal official who had chosen to protect himself by concealing his Muslim faith; in Palermo, a respected Muslim leader deplored his own condition to the point of regretting that he had not been sold away in slavery to a Muslim country. Ibn Jubayr comments, however, both on the royal favours accorded to Muslims and on the toleration and politeness shown by ordinary Christians to the Muslim population. Yet we know that on occasion, when royal power was impotent, Christian tolerance was not sufficient to prevent terrible massacres. Ibn Jubayr also contrasts the favourable situation of Palermo Muslims, who had many mosques with teachers of the Koran, were allowed the public call to prayer, practised as merchants, and had their own *cadi* for the settlement of their legal disputes, with that of the Muslims who worked on Christian lands, paying dues twice a year. The position of the Muslims was actually precarious, since they depended on royal or seigneurial protection and were at risk from basic Latin antipathy. Muslim parents had difficulties in coping with children who could throw off parental restraints by embracing Christianity. Muslims wanting official posts had to change or conceal their faith. Ibn Jubayr does not report that Muslims resented Christian persecution or intolerance. Rather, he was astonished that Muslims could practise so much of their religion and rise so high in government. He shows that some Muslim styles were even adopted by Christians, at least superficially, as with those Christian women at Palermo who used the same kinds of jewellery, make-up and perfumes as Muslim women.

Underlying tensions between the Christian and Muslim populations were real, and threatened the future good order of the whole kingdom, precisely because some crypto-Muslims came to occupy crucial posts in its workings. Such men did very well out of the monarchy. Achmet got three *casalia* from Roger II for his services, though such patronage, as in this case, may also have played a part in encouraging favourites to accept baptism. Achmet left his lands to Palermo cathedral, which is why his story is known. Some powerful Muslims were well connected with the court at Palermo, and others of Muslim origin served in royal offices, both in local government and in the ports, even if to obtain responsible positions, baptism was probably indispensable. Ibn Jubayr reports that wealthy Muslims were active in the work of buying back men enslaved for their faith, but they did not or could not do much for their co-religionists in the countryside whose lot seemed to him thoroughly pitiable.

The most detailed evidence about rural Muslims comes from a dozen long rolls of parchment (*jaraida* in Arabic, *plateia* in Greek) listing the names of the dependants assigned to landlords. The earliest rolls were composed when Count Roger parceled out the defeated inhabitants of Sicily after the completion of the conquest at a meeting with his barons at Mazara in 1093. Lists of the Muslims assigned to himself and his barons were drawn up. None of these have survived, but two years later, similar rolls were completed for the cathedral of Catania, one of which survives in the original.

The purpose of the listings after 1093 was clearly to eliminate arguments about which estate held which named individuals once the completion of the conquest put an end to the probability of Muslims escaping to still independent districts, or profiting from disorder to slip away to other lordships. Even so, other documents granting lands and Muslim labourers to some churches at this time, as at Agrigento and Mazara itself, do not name names, but award one hundred Muslims in round numbers. Elsewhere, careful description of the diocesan boundary provided an alternative way of separating the church's dependants from those of other landowners. Although it is not clear why some secular lords had their dependants listed by name, the most likely reason is that their holdings could not easily be separated geographically or by boundary markings. This seems clear in the case of Catania, where the church needed lists in 1095 because of its experience, or its fear, of lords with lists taking men it claimed itself. When the church of Catania was originally founded as a monastery, Roger granted it all the Muslims who had once lived there, even those who had fled in fear of Norman occupation, and their children, wherever they had since settled in Sicily. A charter describing the boundaries and assigning the Muslim population resident within them would therefore have been useless to Catania: the exodus had been on such a scale that the church could not have cultivated its estates with the labour of the remnant. The record shows that on one estate at Aci alone, it claimed over five hundred men. This situation was special and cannot be used to generalise about conditions elsewhere. The only early information about Muslims in the west comes from another list of tenants on an estate (*casale*) south of Piana degli Albanesi, in a document granted to the cathedral of Palermo by Count Roger, probably in February 1095. The names of seventy-five Muslims owing renders in money, wheat and barley twice a year (in winter and in August) are written in Arabic and followed in Greek by another twenty names of Muslims who had become heads of new households. This shows that the earlier names had been taken from a record made somewhat before 1095. Although this has been interpreted to mean that the Normans made use of Muslim administrative documents compiled before the Norman conquest of 1071, this is held to be unlikely, since under the Muslims, only Christians and Jews would have been liable for poll-tax. After the Norman conquest when the Muslims themselves were subjected to this tax, a new register would have been needed. The Palermo record must therefore have drawn upon that.

These early lists give only names and no boundaries to the estates in question. Lords obviously did not assume that all the Muslims living within their own boundaries should be their dependants. Only certain Muslims were 'enserfed', and the lists which defined the lord's claims necessarily protected unnamed Muslims from Christian appropriation. Rights over Muslim serfs were valuable, and some squabbling about ownership was inevitable: there was no limitless pool of Muslim labour available to all the Norman masters. The only evidence about them now comes from the archives of Christian churches.

Grants to other churches occasionally concede either named, or numbers of, individuals, and the use of such lists to establish ownership is proved by a lawsuit of 1159 when two Muslims, apparently brothers, were claimed by both Gisulf de Siclis and Robert Brittus. Robert claimed that they were registered on his list, which he had acquired as one of the title deeds to his *casale* of Bessana; Gisulf produced his own *plateia*, in this case the more recent, and had the better of the legal argument. In the 1159 suit, the two brothers themselves were not at fault; the dispute was between the lords who both claimed them. If the labourers themselves slipped away or denied their obligations there seems to have been no easy way to recover or coerce them. Some Muslims must have been able to flee to western parts of the island where Muslim communities still lived independently of Christians. An Arabic deed recording the declaration by one Muslim of his true status as a serf of the church of the Magione, suggests that the church had no better way of establishing its rights to him.

The majority of Muslims lived as cultivators either, as in the west, in their own communities or elsewhere in notable groups, perhaps alongside Christians or under Latin lordships. Some, probably most, had lands of their own held by customary arrangements. Some were obviously introduced landless by the conquerors, as slaves or as colonists from North Africa; others were perhaps fugitives from other districts or estates. The Muslim peasantry was not reduced to a common level throughout the island. They were most vulnerable where they were few or subjected to particular Christian lordships, and strongest where their traditional communities survived more or less intact, as in the west. In lordship they were 'registered' and paid a share of their crops, but not labour services, since lords did not keep sizeable demesnes needing cultivation. In traditional communities each district paid capitation tax to the king. William II's grant of thirty named Muslims to a monastery at Palermo notes that the *servitium* due from Calatrasi, the district where they lived, would be reduced proportionately in the future. The best information about the Muslim peasantry in the late twelfth century is provided by the rolls (*plateia*) compiled for the royal monastery of Monreale in 1182, when four whole districts (Iato, Corleone, Battallaro and Calatrasi) of about 1,200 square kilometres were transferred from royal to monastic ownership. Nearly 2,000 individuals were listed, living on 126 estates (*casalia*) in over 500 places. A recent study of these personal and place-names has provided a persuasive account of how the Muslim communities managed to maintain their traditional style of society. They practised mixed farming, probably with sufficient success to provide marketable surpluses. Some Muslim groups had their own mosques and were able to provide for religious instruction; some also had *cadis* and respected seniors able to adjudicate their disputes and speak up for the communities. By 1182, there may have been few of these semi-autonomous Muslim districts left. It is probable that the establishment of the monastery at Monreale, which provided closer oversight of the Muslims, was actually planned in part to speed up the process of their conversion and ultimate assimilation. In fact, this foundation seems on the contrary to have provoked unrest. By the end of the century, all the remaining Muslims in the countryside were up in arms against the Latins.

Apart from the rural population, the importance of Muslim inhabitants of towns must not be overlooked, though pathetically little evidence of their activities under the twelfth-century monarchy now remains. After the suppression of their communities under Frederick II, there can have been no further motive to preserve Arabic documents of sale, lease and contract, which must have been numerous in the twelfth century. In Palermo, Muslims originally had their own *cadis*. In 1123, a *cadi* gave evidence in court of an Arabic deed of sale. Before 1198, however, some deeds of sale relating to Saracen villeins were made in both Greek and Arabic by William de Partinico, who was described as *magnus justiciarius* of the royal great court and also *archadius sarracenorum*, so that by then Muslim *cadis* were subordinated to Latin authority. Urban Muslims were not necessarily all high-ranking merchants and officials. In the coastal districts some were traders and sailors. In the twelfth century they also exercised many valued artisan skills. In Messina, where Muslims were not normally allowed to settle, an exception was made for indispensable artisans. Some of their more specialised work, for example the decoration of ivory, commanded sufficient admiration for such objects to be prized throughout Christendom. They surely also made traditional pots and pans, fishing tackle and agricultural implements. They were certainly employed in Christian buildings as bricklayers or carpenters, and the majority of the building force is likely to have been of Muslim origin, or trained by those with experience of Muslim architecture. The new churches retained such features as cupolas, decorations of intersecting arcades, or techniques like polychrome brick patterning. Muslim detail in Christian churches is not found in the thirteenth century, either because the Muslim element in the work-force had by then been eliminated, or because the tradition had simply broken down after a century in the hands of mere labourers.

Sicily was not famed in Islam for its schools or learning – on the contrary, it was considered rather unorthodox before the Norman conquest. Nevertheless it had its own savants and poets, and such figures were inclined not to stay, but to leave for Spain or North Africa, which indicates that the right kind of opportunities were not available in a

Christian kingdom for Muslims proud of their own cultural traditions. They naturally preferred to make their careers in Muslim countries. The island became increasingly unattractive for devout Muslims as Latin settlers came in from other parts of Christendom, bringing with them anti-Muslim sentiments. Already there were disturbances in the reign of William I, and these probably helped to accelerate Muslim withdrawal from certain towns and regions; it could for a time have encouraged the concentration of Muslims in areas where they felt less vulnerable. Nevertheless, as late as 1183 in the list of ten *villani* and their holdings granted to Cefalù, only three had converted to Christianity from Islam. In eastern Sicily, enquiries conducted in 1172 by the master justiciar in Val di Noto still found respected Saracens in Syracuse to come forward and give evidence about land boundaries made some twenty years earlier. Yet in Catania, by 1179, the mosque was already abandoned and was converted into a church dedicated to Becket. There, it had taken about a century of Norman occupation for the Muslim presence in the city to fade away completely.

The break with the authorities from the 1190s is in marked contrast to the situation which had prevailed for most of the twelfth century, when tolerable relations between the Christian and Muslim communities could generally be taken for granted. The Muslims were not the only peasants in lordship or liable to arbitrary exactions. In some places Muslims and Christians lived together in the same villages. It was their religion, rather than their social status, that distinguished them, and it is known that when for whatever reason royal protection of them was powerless, they became liable to persecutions unleashed by the Latin newcomers who did not share the tolerant attitude of the government to these infidel subjects.

JEWS

The notable Jewish minority of the kingdom lived in scattered communities, so far as is known, exclusively in towns. The curious Jewish chronicle of Oria written in 1054 has no bearing on the Norman period, though its reference to the part played by the author's grandfather in managing the finances of the prince of Capua earlier in the century proves that they had not been kept on the margins of public life at that time. When Benjamin of Tudela travelled through the kingdom over a century later, he found Jewish communities in most of the principal cities he visited along the route, a few hundred strong at best, under respected and often learned men whose worldly occupations are not given, except for the dyers of Brindisi. Other references to their involvement in dyeing and their monopoly of it in the time of Frederick II certainly encourages the idea that they were active in this part of the cloth-making industry of the kingdom. They are also said to have traded with Genoa in leather from Mazara. Records from the Geniza in Cairo illustrate their commercial dealings with North Africa and Sicily. Comparatively few in number, pious Jews naturally preferred to live in communities large enough to maintain their own synagogues, which is why they are found only in towns: at Trani, they had more than one synagogue. They paid some kind of protection money to the lords who, on occasion, made over these rights to favoured churches. The Jews probably found towns safer, and may generally have lived together in particular districts of the town. Some Jews of Trani lent money, and a few documents hint at involvement in rural commerce. Their presence in the kingdom was no doubt of longstanding, since they are attested to in Muslim Sicily, imperial Apulia and the Lombard principalities. It is difficult to regard them as anything but fully acceptable in local society, not withstanding their legal and religious distinctiveness, qualities they shared with others at that time. Benjamin of Tudela made a point of noting in the account of his journey the size of the Jewish communities he visited, and whether the Jews had suffered any serious disabilities; he is not likely to have neglected to say so, or to have concentrated on describing the kingdom's amenities. His admiration for the beauties of Palermo would surely have been qualified had the 1,500 Jews of the city suffered persecution there.

GREEKS

The Greek peoples of the kingdom were numerous in Calabria and in the Salentino peninsula; they could be found along the Adriatic coast as far as Andria and north of Taranto round Gravina and Matera. Beyond the range of the eleventh-century empire, Greeks were found too across the Cilento as far as Salerno. There was a well-established Greek colony in Naples. In Sicily, the main area of settlement was the north-eastern third, the Val Demenna. In the west, Greek pockets of settlement were hemmed in by the Muslim majority. The position of the Greeks in the kingdom was very different from that of the two groups discussed so far. Nowhere could they be considered a 'subject' people. In Sicily, before he became king, Roger II issued most of his official documents in Greek; even after 1130 he signed his own name in Greek on Latin ones. Greek was the language of culture and administration, and Roger had no motive to despise or belittle the advantage this gave him. The Greek population of the island had a tradition of approval for the Normans who had overthrown the Muslim domination; it had nothing to gain from disaffection. On the mainland, the Norman conquest of Calabria from the empire can not have been equally popular, but the imposition of Latin ways proved very slow. Though the Greek bishops had to accept papal jurisdiction, monks kept open their links with Constantinople and Mount Athos. The variety of Greek groups found in the kingdom makes it unwise to think of them initially as a specific 'racial' or religious community. They blended with their neighbours in various ways according to local circumstances. Whereas the Latin bishop Maurice noted with satisfaction how eagerly a Greek abbot brought some of his monks to pay his respects to the body of Saint Agata when it was brought back to Catania, the Greek bishop of Bova in Calabria recalled with vengeful satisfaction the bad end of a Latin knight who had repressed and persecuted Greeks.

Though some Latin newcomers had resented or despised Greeks, it was not until after Roger succeeded his cousin in Apulia and became king that the Greeks began to slip from their prime place in Roger's government. If, like the Muslims, they were eventually edged into a position of inferiority, this took time, and for most of the twelfth century they could not have felt particularly threatened. Unlike Muslims, they were not descendants of recent immigrants, and took satisfaction in knowing that their ancestors had occupied these lands for centuries. They have left much more evidence than the Muslims of their activities, for many of the Greek monasteries preserved legal documents or religious works such as saints' lives and sermons, which all incidentally cast some light on the social life of the Greek communities.

In the Val Demenna, where they were numerous, though living in small scattered settlements, the king's local administrative official, the *strategus*, worked with Greek-speaking judges and wrote his documents in Greek. In Sicily and Calabria, considerable numbers of minor officials, as well as some senior ones, were also Greeks. In both regions there were, at the time of the Norman conquest, already many Greek monasteries in areas of densest Greek settlement, for even throughout the Muslim period, many Greeks had remained faithful to the Christian religion, and the well-being of the church had clearly rested with monks rather than on diocesan organisation. Although Roger I and his family became patrons of the monks, it was probably traditional Greek support, rather than the patronage of the Latin conquerers, which was responsible for the very flourishing condition of Greek monasticism in Roger II's dominions. However, early Greek monasteries, though numerous, had not been well-endowed or institutionally very durable. The Norman conquest put them at the mercy of another alien lordship, but subjected the Greek monks to closer supervision and discipline. This did not necessarily imply sectarian disapproval of their level of monastic observance, and for a time it may have produced notable results. But the effects were not beneficial in the long run. Since the new Latin ecclesiastical structure could not itself provide the necessary oversight of the Greek monasteries, other means had to be found. The Normans appear to have concluded that many small monasteries would not be viable unless they were amalgamated to provide adequate resources. This concern opened the way for an important change in the development of Greek monasticism in the kingdom. Roger II decided to appoint the head of his father's foundation at San Salvatore in Lingua Maris at Messina, as archimandrite of a congregation of about forty monasteries in the island and in Calabria (1131). This new system, possibly modelled on Mount Athos, was introduced on the advice of Saint Bartholomew of Simeri (d. 1130), founder of the famous monastery of the Patir at Rossano, and it was from this house that the king appointed Luke as the new archimandrite at Messina in 1134. The king and the bishop (later archbishop) at Messina left the archimandrite to watch over the monasteries of his congregation and check on the monastic heads (*higoumeni*) chosen by each community though, as in the Greek tradition, the king was expected to confirm these appointments. San Salvatore became one of the great religious establishments of Sicily. Many documents and manuscripts from its library demonstrate its effectiveness as a religious centre under the monarchy. Under William II, a similar congregation was established for Basilicata at Sant'Elia de Carbone: the experiment had been successful and the Basilian monks were now organised in the kingdom from regional centres.

To some extent, the delegation of responsibility to leading Greeks indicated that Roger as king was already losing his personal interest in the communities' own religious activities as he took on the foundation of Latin religious communities in Sicily. The Greek monks continued the tradition of cultivating their own property, and though Norman patrons gave them dependants and seigneurial duties, the monks remained psychologically much closer to the Greek populations than to the Latin ecclesiastical establishment. Greek monasticism itself drew no inspiration from fresh Western ideals and, unable to experience reforms from within, it was liable to succumb to some Latin innovations. Thus the Cistercians, who also had an ideal of working monks, eventually acquired some Greek monasteries; Santa Maria de Ligno was suppressed as early as 1188 for the benefit of the new Cistercian house at Palermo. Several Greek houses were absorbed into the order founded by Abbot Joachim of Fiore after he broke away from the Cistercian order. In the eleventh century, the example of such famous Greek monks as Saint Nilo had helped to shape notions of the monastic ideal in the Latin church, but after 1130, western reform movements ceased to respond to Greek ideals. Greek monasticism came to play a part only in the life of the Greeks, themselves a minority, and not in the ecclesiastical life of the whole kingdom. The continuing attractions to the Greek community of the ideals of Greek religious life should not be underestimated. There were even new foundations, like those for men and women established in 1163 by the *secretus* Roger and his wife, both prominent in Messina. Willingness to accept the obligations of direct cultivation by the monks is also attested: as late as 1247, a monk of a monastic dependency is recorded to have sweated (*in sudore sui corporis*) to improve the monastic property. The system continued to allow individual monastic vocations and small communities, but it approached monasticism in a very different spirit from that common to the great privileged houses of the western traditions. It also permitted the Greek social community, even as it was losing its political pre-eminence, to retain its grasp on its own spiritual traditions.

In the twelfth century, Greek peasants may have become more reluctant to alienate family-holdings for religious purposes, unless they were childless. As the numbers of the Greek working population declined, it may also have become more difficult to get monastic land cultivated: in 1168, the monks of San Filippo di Fragalà received royal permission to graze up to two thousand sheep, one hundred mares, two hundred cows and five hundred pigs on the royal domain, which points to a pastoral rather than an agricultural economy. Some Greek monasteries were certainly provided with dependent labourers, not all of whom were Muslims: there were Greek serfs too, as on Latin monastic estates. At Greek Agrò, they owed twenty-four days of sowing and other services in digging and reaping. At Latin Lipari, where the tenantry was predominantly Muslim and Greek, the abbot conceded more favourable terms, which nevertheless required of them one day a week for sowing, one day for ploughing, three days for grape-gathering and an extra forty offered in good will!

The most specific listing of peasant services comes from the end of the century. When, for example, the abbot of Santa Maria di Valle Giosofat wished in 1196 to construct a new *casale* in Sicily near Palermo, he brought over a (Greek) work-force from his property in Calabria. Each was assigned individually eight *salme* of land for ploughing from which the tithe was due; from the vines and olives they rendered half the produce to the monks. But they also did one day a week as *angaria*, and three times a year, for sowing, hoeing and reaping, they owed a block of three additional days, called (from the Greek) *paraspolario*, a service apparently peculiar to Calabria. The position in Sicily had by then probably changed because of the greater difficulty in retaining Muslim labourers. However, Greek communities were also being influenced by the prevalent practices of Latin lordships. 'Villeinage', for example, came to be acquired by the acceptance of servile tenures. This is illustrated from a case at Messina in 1195. Here, several properties held under various legal arrangements had been assembled by a monk, Leontios, who was made to acknowledge himself as *villanus* of the nuns of Santa Maria. On his death the properties passed to a relation and his four sons, provided that they too recognised themselves to be the convent's *villani* for the properties. This involved them paying dues in money and hens and carrying out such orders, including *corvées*, as they were given. In effect they inherited 'villein' tenures and recognised their obligation to do the services required, whatever their previous social status. On the other hand, the family had claims on the villein-tenures which the lord would not disregard. These notions of obligation have been adopted into a Greek religious and tenurial situation from a basically western system. Royal patronage and the conferment of seigneurial authorities both tended to nudge Greek monastic establishments towards the norms of Latin ones. Simply living in an increasingly Latin world inevitably altered general understanding of the nature of social obligations and the status of individuals. This insistence shows that from the Greek point of view, the right to take up family property mattered most, and that if this involved some nominal diminution of status at law, this was not itself so important.

LATINS

Most of the inhabitants of the kingdom were Latin Christians, and because they were not a religious minority, they cannot be defined simply by reference to their religion. Yet a surprisingly high proportion of our information about them relates to matters of religious import, and helps to establish important aspects of southern society. One striking feature is the self-confidence of Latin laymen in the religious sphere, probably because the clergy were not the only, or even the best, educated persons in the kingdom. Even the senior clergy were at a disadvantage. There were so many bishops that the office inevitably carried much less cachet than it did in Normandy. Anyway, bishops had neither the lands nor the privileges that made their northern counterparts so powerful. On the other hand, the plethora of clergy shows how thoroughly saturated the kingdom was with religion. The ruthless chief

minister of William I, Maio of Bari, himself wrote a commentary on the
Lord's Prayer for his son. The laity were not at odds with the clergy. All
took for granted a commitment to religious practice characteristic of a
society without doubts, confident of maintaining a tradition of continuous Christianity since the earliest times. Paganism was far more
remote in the minds of the people than it was in the North. For the same
reason, there seems to have been little commotion generated by the
eleventh-century 'papal' reform movement. Though in the South this
aimed to re-establish Roman authority over the churches, it did not
involve a challenge to secular abuses, for there was no Carolingian or
feudal system in place. There are signs that some bishops became critical
of the tradition of married clergy, but there are no indications that they
were successful in eradicating it. In the Greek church it was taken for
granted, and this may have made it more difficult to change in the Latin
church too. The churches of the kingdom do not seem to have been
caught up in the religious enthusiasms found elsewhere in the twelfth
century. The Cistercians, for example, made little headway here. This
may suggest that southern churches were complacent or decadent, but
the truth rather is that they belonged in quite a different religious context
from, say, Normandy itself, and should not be judged by inappropriate
criteria.

Interesting as an example of southern peculiarities are the churches set
up by the collaborative efforts of laymen, who retained the property
rights for themselves and their heirs without apparently exciting the
disapproval of the bishops. It is not possible to say how widespread this
custom was, but it seems to have continued at least into the thirteenth
century. In the late eleventh century, the bishop of Bisceglie dedicated a
new church which over a hundred named individuals from *Cirignano*,
Priminiano and Zappino had built at their own expense, and to whom
the bishop assigned the joint patronage. They had the right to appoint
incumbents (*abbates, rectores, presbiteros* or *monachos*) and, provided the
priests obeyed the bishop, he renounced his right to excommunicate or
evict them. This church had no parochial rights, and was only a private
venture over which even the bishop had minimal control. Another case
illustrates the kind of legal problem that might arise from family rights in
churches. In 1161, the sons of a Barese sailor sued their father's brother,
himself a knight, for what they claimed was their inheritance in the
church of Saint Eustratus, which their father and uncle had held jointly
as *socii*. The uncle protested that the church was not held in common, it
was his own; when the boys' father had married, he and the uncle had
divided their joint property. Though the matter was all settled amicably
in the end (and without reference to the Church), the principles invoked

are those of secular property and family law. Nor were all such ecclesiastical property owners necessarily of high social standing. At Aversa in 1095, the four owners of a church were described as *villani* when they were granted away with their *hereditates* and things to the church of San Biagio in Aversa, with the consent of the prince of Capua. The system was not seriously changed in the twelfth century. In 1202, the prior of San Leonardo at Siponto obtained the rights of patronage to a church in Andria from the previous owners, four priests, two knights and ten other persons, none apparently related, though the simplest explanation for their common interests would be that the property had been divided equally between two siblings in four successive generations. Ownership of church property was settled legally according to secular precedents. Multiple ownership of such a discreet unit of property as a church certainly suggests that the origins of the rules go back far into the Lombard past when legal ownership was still shared or collective.

Tangible benefits of a different order could be provided by the churches. A dispute between the monks of Angers, installed in a former Greek monastery at Naples, and the porter, John, was eventually resolved in 1100 when he abandoned all his claims on them, except his right to a banquet on the feast day of St Sebastian. Feasts were apparently quite an important part of southern religious life. Bishop Constantine of Minori was distressed by their frequency, and following a precedent set by his predecessor, tried to cut back on the dinner-parties given by his priests (1127). He thought it particularly unseemly to have general feastings on Good Friday, for Christ's death should be commemorated with sadness, not with banquets and drinking sessions (*illicitibus potationibus*). Good living in the South was also remarked upon by John of Salisbury, who visited the kingdom on two separate occasions, both convivial. He was invited to drink wine with the king's English chancellor, Robert of Selby, and along with his friend, John of Canterbury (later archbishop of Lyons), attended a fabulous banquet given by a rich man of Canosa, where the delicacies of every levantine country vied with the native produce of the kingdom's own regions. Clergy and laymen were clearly at one in their appreciation of good food, drink and company. Lavish hospitality probably helped to make visitors enjoy their southern travels.

A more predictable concern of laymen in their dealings with the church was to make appropriate provision for their burial in the place of their choice with masses to be celebrated for them after death by preferred clergy. Specific contracts show what was wanted. The bishop of Minori sold land for a 100 shillings of gold to a widow and her sons in 1094 so she could make a tomb (*sepultura*) there for her late husband,

The kingdom

covered with a marble *cantarum*, where her descendants, male and female, would be laid to rest without further hindrance, provided a fixed tariff was paid every time the vault was opened. About the same time in Bari, the new church of St Nicholas bought out a layman's half-share of a church where he had probably intended to be buried. Apart from cash, the vendor also got two seats in the new church, one for a man and one for a woman, and two burial places, one, a *camera* or a *pesculum* to be made by him where he liked in the courtyard (*atrium*), and the other, *sub terra* wherever he chose in the churchyard; all this in addition to food, clothing and footwear for life so that he should not suffer hard times. A little later, a usurer made a will requiring his executors to spend up to 100 good *michalati* on building a *camera* in the monastery where he could be buried. The wish to be buried in or near a church where prayers and intercessions were constantly being made is often expressed. A widow recovered the body of her husband killed in battle in 1137 and secured burial for him at Monte Vergine. Southern churches seem to have been quite accessible to people at all levels of society.

Concern with death in the South struck some contemporaries as exaggerated. Bishop Luke of Bova wrote a discourse deploring displays of excessive grief for the dead, which he blamed rather oddly on Muslim traditions, perhaps to strengthen his campaign of disapproval. Falco reports the grief at Salerno when Duke William died in 1127, and the *Liber de Regno* gives a very elaborate account of the lamentations made in Palermo on the death of King William I. The mourning was ostentatious: three days of public grief when noble women, especially Muslim, with their attendants dressed in sackcloth and their hair unloosed, roamed through the whole city wailing to the beat of drums. Apart from individual occasions, there may in the early days of the monarchy have also been a public commemoration in Sicily of the heroic dead who had restored the island to Christianity. Roger I founded in their memory the church of St George at Tricala (Caltabellotta) in 1098.

Public and collective religious activities mentioned in these texts most notably included processions. On some special occasions the bodies of the local saints were borne through the streets, but processions were anyway an ordinary part of the liturgical year with street-marching for traditional display of group solidarity, as familiar as the celebrations of the liturgy and needing no commentary. The importance of lay participation in church services in the Lombard south can be further demonstrated by reference to the surviving Exultet rolls. These illustrated texts of the Easter-eve celebrations were unrolled before the assembled congregation and designed to co-ordinate their responses. As such, they serve as a reminder of other differences in the liturgical practices of the South when compared to the North.

In their enthusiasm for acquiring the bodies of wonder-working saints, southerners were second to none, and here laymen even surpassed the clergy. In this respect, the theft of the body of St Nicholas from Myra by sailors from Bari (1087) was outstanding. Nicholas' reputation in the west had grown steadily during the eleventh century, and the Normans were early devotees of the cult. The popularity of Nicholas then (indeed to the present time) immediately made his new burial place at Bari a flourishing centre of pilgrimage, and it is hardly surprising that the sailors were promptly recognised as public benefactors. According to reports, the sailors had encountered some Venetians at Antioch who alerted them to a Venetian plan to seize the body of St Nicholas from Myra, and the sailors had promptly decided to forestall their rivals. This they did, not so much for their own glory and honour as for the advantage of their own country (*totiusque patriae nostrae decore et ornamento*). These sixty-odd sailors accordingly became men of standing on their return, and when a new church was built as a shrine for the body, the sailors formed a society and were given special privileges – a place of burial outside the church but up against its walls; two seats in the church (*sedile*) for themselves and their wives; a place in a church without further offering if any wished to become a clerk; proper care if they fell on hard times; and a share in the oblations made at the feast of the translation every year. Although these privileges were already being denounced by 1105 as unlawful on the grounds that laymen had no rights to church property, the sailors' descendants did not willingly give up their privileges. Calixtus II ruled in council in 1123 against sharing out the annual oblations with laymen, but as late as 1207, a husband and wife could still release to the poor a mere third of what this nautical inheritance was worth to them.

The cult of St Nicholas provoked a spate of stories about his wonder-working powers. These spread throughout Europe, and like other tales of the miraculous powers of saints provide the most vivid descriptions of every-day life. They serve to show how even the most ordinary events might be interpreted as wonders. In 1136, when only one of three ships of pilgrims returning from the Holy Land survived a terrible storm, a madwoman (*daemoniaca*) provoked the admiration of the crowd simply for greeting each of the survivors, whom she had never seen before, with the words: 'You are certainly of the number of those whom Nicholas has saved for us.' In the same simple spirit, Bishop Maurice of Catania was happy to regard as one of Saint Agata's miracles the failure of the wind, or the carelessness of the child-attendants, to extinguish any of the candles in the procession formed to carry her body on the stony path from Aci to Catania for reburial.

The holy bodies so much treasured in this period were not frequently treated with respect. Nicholas made it clear to the faithful by miracles that he did not want his body to be dismembered; in compensation, a wonderful balm oozed from his body which could be taken away by the faithful in phials. The body of Saint Agata, which was venerated at Catania, had, however, been stolen at night from a church in Constantinople by a couple of enterprising body-snatchers, who unceremoniously chopped it up and wrapped the pieces in various small parcels to facilitate export without detection. Really extraordinary events occurred on the journey to Sicily, particularly at Taranto. They were credulously reported by the bishop of Catania, who repeated what he was told when the brokers secretly informed him about the availability of the body. He and his monks made no difficulties at all about accepting that what they were offered constituted the relics of the martyred virgin. The recovery of the body, exported for safety to the east at the time of the Saracen conquest, put the seal upon the restoration of the church in the island. The miracles performed by the saint in the first ten years after her return cured in general very humble people suffering from blindness or epilepsy. The passing references to their occupations and humdrum concerns leaves no doubts about the social realities, even if the bishop fails to convince modern readers of the miracles themselves. By the end of the century, Saint Agata too had acquired an international reputation. The English chronicler who passed through Sicily in 1190 thought it was her intercession that had stilled Etna's eruptions for more than forty years.

Miracle stories which incidentally established the wonder-working virtues of the saint are direct indications of what pious Christians wanted from religion in this period. Religious feelings and excitement apart, they wanted help with the difficulties of life, such as sickness or travel. The sailors who were devoted to St Nicholas did not scruple to bargain with the ecclesiastical authorities for a share in the material advantages that accrued to the church from their action: a share in the annual dividend, or insurance if they fell into want. Scattered throughout the surviving documents are regular indications that the laity expected practical help of all kinds from the churches they patronised.

The interest in acquiring relics of great saints was itself not new. In the ninth century, many relics had been hastily removed from Sicily to save them from the Saracens. Both the Lombard capitals of Benevento and Salerno had also managed to obtain the bodies of apostles for their cathedral churches. Disinterring the mortal remains of much less famous saints was a more hazardous religious investment. Accounts of how these discoveries were made, and how the bones, properly validated, were translated to shrines worthy of their sanctity, give the impression that dreaming alone might be sufficient to alert the pious as to their whereabouts. When discovered, such bodies were rarely those of saints already venerated, and their identities had in some mysterious way to be revealed. In their own way, these stories show contemporaries rediscovering the Christian origins of their own places and practising the traditional Italian art of tomb-robbing as they stumbled upon the considerable physical remains of ancient Italy. There may have been more argument than is known about the naming of these bodies. Celestine III backed the disciplinary action taken by the bishop of Sulmona against the tiresome people of his diocese who insisted on treating the relics of his saintly predecessor, Pamphilus, as those of Saint Pelinus, bishop of the neighbouring, but abandoned, see of *Corfinium*. Most accounts stress the fragrant odours that proved the sanctity of bones in contrast to the normal smell of decay. Any doubts could be allayed by submitting the bones to the test of fire (in accordance with a canon of the council of Zaragoza). At Aquaputrida, the archpriest took charge of the recovery of the bones of St Priscus, a Greek 'confessor', beside which a stone with that name on it was conveniently found. The bishop of Frigento instructed a fire to be lit before the altar, where a piece of the cranium, when put to the test, immediately extinguished the flame. A passing comment in the narrative explains that the location of the body had been known some years before it could be dug up, because while Leo, son of Peter, was called 'papa' (Anacletus II), they had miraculously not been able to move the stones.

Comparable events are recorded in Apulia. At Trani, the archbishop deliberately deferred the translation of the body of St Nicholas the Pilgrim into a fitting resting place until the political disturbances of Apulia were resolved and he could be assured of assembling many clergy and people for the ceremony so that the merits of the saint of Trani could be really proclaimed. This Nicholas had been a strange Greek youth who abandoned monastic life in Calabria in order to wander barefoot round southern Italy carrying a cross, singing God's praises and, not surprisingly, pursued by a swarm of mocking boys, to whom he handed out apples bought from the alms he had received. Treated as a madman in Trani, he told the archbishop that he simply obeyed divine orders. He died quite suddenly in June 1094, and his sanctity was almost immediately established by miracles and promptly endorsed by Urban II. What was known about him was written up straight away for Archbishop Bisantius I. When the body was translated by Bisantius II, his deacon, Amandus, wrote a more extended account of his life and attendant wonders. Trani was exceptionally lucky to have gained possession of a contemporary saint so immediately recognised and so well known, which redoubled determination to give him both an architectural and a literary monument.

The deacon Amandus eventually himself became bishop of the suffragan see of Bisceglie, where in 1167 he celebrated the discovery and translation of the bones of three holy bodies, each of different colours, when a sarcophagus was dug up in the field of a local oratory. This was in response to the dream vouchsafed to a youth from Acquaviva, south of Bari. The saints, Maurus, Pantalemone and Sergius, are not otherwise vouched for, but Amandus went to considerable lengths to establish three separate justifications of sanctity, and the proof of putting the bones to the test of fire coupled with the miracles placed the issue beyond doubt. The bishop was able to whip up sufficient enthusiasm to get an oratory built by volunteer labour within two months, and to assemble a fine number of local bishops to participate in the ceremony of consecrating it. He rather oddly explains that the two archbishops of Trani and Bari could not attend, since one was on a royal embassy to Constantinople and the other on royal business in Palermo. The curious blend of the matter-of-fact and the extraordinary reveals only too clearly the willingness to read the miraculous into the fortuitous.

These stories give the impression that bishops were expected to be on call in their local sees when wonders were reported, able to rush out with a crowd of enthusiastic clergy and laymen in a suitably impressive processional style. Bishops may indeed have been eager to respond to initiatives taken by others, and their participation was always eventually necessary to authorise popular cults. The stories consistently emphasise the spontaneity of lay enthusiasms: the first stages in discovery of sanctity could be taken by persons without any direct connection with the approving church; the miracles themselves were frequently acts of mercy to the humble, women, children or the old. Frequently the cures by miracle followed years of wasted effort and money squandered on medicine. Invariably, the stories relate to persons from adjacent towns, with a sprinkling of examples about passing travellers, and often include examples of scornful incredulity properly silenced. There are the ever-popular stories of miraculous escapes from disaster, and descriptions of the horrific deformities that defied medical skill. In search of cures and exculpations, the devout travelled to places of great repute. But as the archdeacon of Bari stopped to explain in his account of St Nicholas, the physical cure was not so important as the spiritual benefit of accepting humbly what God willed. Another writer told the story of how a schoolmaster of Bari composed canticles in praise of St Nicholas to win the favour of a pious lady he was in love with, and eventually had a dream in which the saint reproved him for his lip-service while his heart was elsewhere. How much the spiritual element touched the throng of onlookers cannot be known. Tolerance of popular credulity did not stifle appreciation of profounder religious feelings, and recognition of the desirability of validating relics is noteworthy.

Sicily seems by contrast to have felt a want of adequate relics. It proved very difficult to recover the holy bodies exported for safety in the ninth century. Admittedly, the Greek *Life of Saint Marina* claimed that Sicily was richer still in relics of martyrs and of saints, riches that never decay, than it so manifestly was in various and delightful earthly goods, but even so the Greek community of San Salvatore at Messina purchased relics in 1141. If the Greeks at Messina felt inadequately supplied with relics, it is not surprising that the Latin church was in need of them. In the western part of the island, the rebuilding of the churches was not accompanied by any revival of local cults. At Agrigento, the early twelfth-century bishop Gerland himself rapidly came to be regarded as the cathedral's saint: in the west, the history of the pre-Saracen church could not achieve desirable tangibility. Even the east was unlucky. Syracuse claimed that St Peter had appointed its first bishop, his disciple St Marcian, but his body had been taken to Gaeta for safety in the ninth century and could not be recovered: only his arm had remained on the island. For this, Bishop Richard commissioned a new silver reliquary – but when he was translated to Messina in 1182, he took the reliquary with him.

This interest in death and dead saints did not mean that contemporaries were indifferent to examples of living holiness. The southern churches did not obviously have much impact on the religious life of the rest of Christendom, but this is no reason to minimise its vitality, even its originality. In the eleventh century, St Nilo from Calabria extended his influence on monasticism to the gates of Rome. The revival of Monte Cassino, particularly in the time of Abbot Desiderius, drew many monastic communities and lay rulers into its orbit. The appointment of Cassino monks to local bishoprics diffused a new piety and idealism outside the cloister. Some bishops of the period themselves obtained at least local reputations for sanctity. Most of them came from indigenous families, but the Normans too played some part in setting up holy bishops. Apart from the famous teacher Gerland, who was brought from Besançon and appointed at Agrigento, the Normans put the saintly Gerard on the see of Potenza. Given the large number of sees in the kingdom, evidence about episcopal activity is rather sparse, but what there is obviously indicates activity rather than neglect.

Not much attention has been given to the Latin religious life of the kingdom, partly because the monarchy itself is usually presented in strongly secular terms. The Norman leaders had in fact very little impact on southern religion. Their concern for religious reform was confined to the setting-up of metropolitan authorities, and to paving the way for the resumption of Roman jurisdiction in former parts of the Greek empire. Only in Sicily did Roger I and his successors create an entirely new diocesan system. Although most of the Christians in the island were Greeks, the new bishoprics were all decidedly Latin. How they coped with their responsibilities remains rather a mystery. Under William II they had a reputation, even in England, for being politicians who neglected their dioceses, but it must be remembered that Latin Christians were originally not numerous and not in need of much pastoral attention. Moreover, several sees were provided with resident communities of monks (Catania, Lipari, Monreale) or canons (Cefalù), so their parishioners were not entirely uncared for. It is also probable that like Greeks, Latins drew most religious sustenance from the monastic communities. It could have been observation of the importance of monasteries in the island that encouraged the Latins to provide regular communities for four of the nine bishoprics, though the English precedent may have been known too. The main religious problem in the island was the presence of so many Muslims. Some became Christian converts, but how they were won over and in what proportions the sources do not say. Since the Greeks and Muslims had long been neighbours, converted Muslims would probably have found it easier to be absorbed into Greek rural communities. Only with the royal foundation of Monreale does it become certain that the Latins assumed responsibility for predominantly Muslim districts.

MONASTERIES

The Normans brought with them from Normandy an enthusiasm for monasticism, and the idea that social eminence required the exercise of benign monastic patronage. Most members of the Altavilla family in southern Italy proved generous patrons, and founded new monasteries to serve the religious requirements of their fellow Normans, recruiting both monks and abbots from their homeland. On the mainland, the Normans encountered many well-established and famous monasteries with their own long-standing patrons. The Norman foundations did not set higher standards than the old; nor did they change the character of local monasticism. The best established, such as Monte Cassino and La Cava, secured new Norman patronage in the eleventh century, but for the most part the old and new communities appear to have catered for different social groups.

The Benedictine tradition insisted on the autonomy of each monastery. To that extent it might stifle curiosity about what was happening beyond the range of the monks' own properties. England, nonetheless, produced some notable monastic historians, and in the deep south of Italy, the Norman Geoffrey of Malaterra, monk of Sant'Eufemia, wrote up the achievements of the Altavilla family in a spirit that was far from parochial. On the whole, however, the established monasteries of the kingdom apparently took little interest in the Normans, particularly after the creation of the kingdom. The friendship of Abbot Desiderius of Cassino for the Norman conquerers after 1058 prompted Amatus to write a detailed account of their successes, but he did not establish a tradition; historical writing at Cassino resumed its traditional form of concentrating on the monastery's own affairs. Cassino often found itself in the front-line of the kingdom's fortunes, and its relations with the kings precluded any hopes of remaining aloof, yet the chronicle record remains disappointing. In the thirteenth century, Abbot Stephen actually had to encourage a lay notary, Richard of San Germano, to compile a chronicle. Richard's first version indicates the narrow geographical range of his interests and mainly ecclesiastical preoccupations – the royal government impinged too little to concern him. The major twelfth-century monastic chronicles written in the kingdom are modelled on the type produced at Farfa in Sabina about 1100, where a register of title deeds was complemented by a chronicle as a form of commentary. At the ancient monastery of San Vincenzo al Volturno, the monk John compiled a single chronicle-register for his abbot Gerard in the early years of the century before the kingdom was founded, and continued it after himself becoming abbot in King Roger's time. Since the later part was lost, or possibly never completed according to plan, it is not possible to know whether the abbot modified his original programme in the new circumstances of the kingdom. It is precisely at the point where notice is first taken of the Norman successes at Capua in 1058, that the surviving text of the chronicle becomes fragmentary, as though the author could no longer cope with the complications. The main interest of this work for the culture of the kingdom lies rather in the line drawings that illustrate the text; however significant in their own way, they confirm an impression of comparative indifference to political concerns. A comparable illustrated chronicle-register was compiled at the Casauria monastery in Pescara in the late twelfth century by the monk John of Berardo for Abbot Leonas; oddly, this record also peters out in the mid-twelfth century.

Monastic influence on the religious life of the kingdom could not, however, be confined to the cloister. Several monasteries acquired possession of country churches, possibly in the expectation that they could provide services there, by setting up a small priory. The bishop of Lucera actually complained in 1099 because a benefactor and the monks had utterly disregarded his formal rights of jurisdiction over the parishes. It is implied that the monks at Monreale had churches served by monks in 1198. Giving monks oversight of the Muslim peasantry itself suggests that the monks were intended to build and serve churches as centres for converting the infidel. La Cava, the parent house of Monreale, also had many churches. It is said to have been patron of twenty-nine abbeys, ninety priories and about four hundred churches. Significantly, it was found necessary at Barletta in 1167 to forbid monks to perform baptisms or bury the dead, and they must therefore have exercised some parochial functions at times. Still in 1180, when Archbishop Rainald of Bari took the abbey of Sant'Erasmo Acquaviva into his protection, he confirmed that they had a cemetery at the church of St Peter in Valenzano and were allowed to baptise, celebrate marriages and hold schools and processions; the monks here retained a whole range of parochial responsibilities. In the kingdom, twelfth-century monks probably played an active part in stirring religious sensibilities outside, as well as inside, the cloister.

The most original monastic movement in the twelfth-century king-dom was that connected with St William of Vercelli, founder of Monte Vergine. The phenomenal expansion of his community probably consti-tutes the most important evidence in the South of the vitality of spontaneous enthusiasm for living individuals regarded as holy. The site of the community at an altitude of 1,270 metres drew converts up the mountain away from crowded settlements. Even priests joined the community of hermits. Rather against his own inclinations, William had allowed the building of a great new church, dedicated by the bishop of Avellino in 1126, and the priests of the community soon pressed their claims for a more clerical kind of life. William found their presumption in his own house so intolerable that he appointed his disciple, Albert, to the headship and slipped away to resume his wandering life of asceticism in inaccessible places. In time, he was of course trapped by more disciples into further religious foundations. The ascetic ideals of the monks inspired the gift of a great many small properties offered by quite humble patrons, and in time the community spawned a number of dependent priories. The nature of the far-flung congregation recalls the earlier pious traditions of Camaldoli and anticipates the later appeal of the Franciscans. Unfortunately, the many surviving legal deeds and the somewhat legendary lives of the founder-saint are rather unreliable guides to the spiritual history of the congregation and its religious impact on the district.

It seems that from his orphaned childhood, William had roamed. After going to Compostella, he had projected a visit to Jerusalem. Meeting John of Matera, some years his senior, who encouraged him to find his own religious path, he had thereafter defied the traditional forms of piety, except by his mortification of the flesh which in his case required him to wear perpetually a military breast-plate and a helmet (*cophia*) on his head. It was said that it was only to avoid tiresome arguments with the priests who had joined him in the wilderness that he consented to their demands for the right to live decently as priests and not spend all their time cultivating the lands as though they were no better than rustics. William himself however remained utterly indifferent to organised religion and rituals. He was no preacher, but when pressed by the learned and articulate he could confound his critics; he pursued holiness for himself and did not willingly undertake to censure others. After his death in 1142, the whole movement not surprisingly became organised by more conventional figures. When the papacy took it under its protection, the hermits agreed to live according to the rule of St Benedict. The early life of the saint makes only too plain the nature of the spiritual tensions involved, but William's originality could not be altogether disavowed by his conventional successors.

William's *Vita* recognises the influence on him of St John of Matera, who is a much more shadowy figure. His *Vita* gives little precise information, but claims that John ran away from a good home at an early age and tried religious life in a community at Taranto before making his way to Sicily where he lived for some time on his own as a hermit. Although in William's *Vita* he is made to seem quite a kindred spirit, his own life appears to stress a much greater interest in seeking direct confrontation with the irreligious people of the world. When he returned to the mainland, his preaching in Bari provoked accusations against him of heresy and blasphemy. Eventually he settled down at Pulsano, building up a great congregation of houses for both men and women. He soon had to contend with outraged parents who objected to his admission of their children into religion without their consent. He clearly thrived on opposition. In his congregation, the traditional Benedictine expectation that monks would cultivate their own fields was strictly observed. John did not have the same reluctance as William to assume pastoral responsibility for his growing congregation. This presumably made easier the task of holding it together after his death (1139).

The self-sufficiency of these orders isolated them from the religious life of others, so they are best known from the accounts preserved in the communities. Here, however, memory preserved only what seemed most important for the less experimental monastic life which eventually took shape, and this inevitably minimises the religious novelties actually found in Roger's kingdom. These novelties were not those of the North, and the main interest of them now is their uncanny resemblance to the later aspirations of Francis of Assisi.

The southern Italian abbot who had the greatest impact on the later Franciscans was Joachim of Fiore. Quite possibly of peasant origin, Joachim passed his youth, like several other famous religious figures of the kingdom, wandering far and wide as an ascetic. At last he entered the Cistercian order at Sambucina, daughter-house of Casamari; from there he was elected abbot of Corazzo. Formed intellectually as a Cistercian, he took advantage of the opportunities given by the order to rustics of Latin speech for a life of religion. In the end he proved dissatisfied with the order and broke away and established an independent monastery in the Sila, at San Giovanni in Fiore, which itself became in his lifetime the head of a small congregation, later much enlarged. Since his aim was to found an even more austere community high up in the Sila, where there were already several Greek religious communities, some closer affinity on his part with ancient Calabrian traditions of monasticism seems to be involved. The rigours of monastic life did not preclude even there a high degree of learning and literacy, and the compatibility of Fiore with Greek traditions is confirmed by the later incorporation into the Fiore congregation of several Greek houses. Joachim also succeeded in a worldly way by obtaining confirmation and gifts from both King Tancred and the emperor Henry VI, and was in some ways encouraged by popes, both as a commentator of scripture and as a monastic reformer.

Yet there is regrettably little certain information about Joachim and his disciples. The main direct source is a brief memoir written by Luke who acted as Joachim's amanuensis at Casamari, returned with Joachim to the abbey of Corazzo, of which Joachim was then abbot, and later became abbot there himself, ending his career as archbishop of Cosenza. Not surprisingly, he makes little of Joachim's break with the Cistercians. Joachim's new followers at Fiore seemed reluctant to promote his cult, perhaps deterred by the condemnation of some of his theological teaching at the Fourth Lateran Council in 1215. Memories of him that survived until the sixteenth century before being written down are hardly trustworthy. Joachim's reputation grew out of his fame as a biblical exegete which spread right across Christendom, not necessarily by dissemination of his written works. Originally it was his striking interpretation of parallel passages in the Old and New Testaments that struck contemporary scholars. Amongst laymen, his gift of prophecy stirred greater interest. In this context, however, Joachim's importance lies in what his life reveals of the intellectual and religious interest of the southern kingdom.

Only in the present century has Joachim been rescued from the exclusive attentions of would-be prophets. A fuller understanding of the elements on which he drew for his work must await further study of the intellectual history of the kingdom. Calabria, after the arrival of the first Cistercians, offered a unique environment in western Christendom for such an awkward, uncompromising figure as Joachim. He drew from the sources to hand for his understanding of the course of human history. The Trinitarian emphasis of his exposition, rather than the incarnational theology of the Cistercians, points to Greek influence. The Cistercians must have helped him formulate his ideas more cogently in Latin terms. He cannot be considered typical of Calabrian spirituality. It is the coexistence of two monastic traditions, perhaps even some rivalry of esteem between them, which helps to situate him most convincingly.

The Latins in the South, whatever political advantages they derived from the Norman dominion, found their religious inspirations locally. The nature of our sources – saints' lives, miracle stories, sermons, letters – are not unusual, but the details they reveal show how distinctive the kingdom's religious enthusiasms were by twelfth-century standards. If the saintly figures stand out most prominently, they are set against a background of popular piety, itself made up of forceful, individual characters. The ordinary folk of the kingdom are most vividly revealed to us by their own particular religious contexts.

Potentially the Christian kingdom could draw upon spiritual, as well as material, resources of exceptional quality. Foreign visitors of the period were impressed by what they saw and not, like those of later times, depressed by evidence of poverty, superstition or degradation. The South did not at this time pose a problem: it presented itself as a promised land.

5

INTELLECTUAL AND ARTISTIC ASPECTS
OF THE KINGDOM

·

The mixture of religions and cultures found in the twelfth-century southern kingdom has excited the interest and admiration of the modern imagination. Attention has been focused on such extraordinary buildings as the royal palace–chapel in Palermo, where the talents of craftsmen from different artistic traditions were put to work for the king's glory. Contemporary visitors to the kingdom, who found their own reasons to marvel, did not, however, comment on the attractions offered by a cosmopolitan society. Those who actually lived in the kingdom were more aware of the mutual antipathies of the various groups than of the potential advantages of a cultural mix. The Latins had the political mastery; in time the culture of their group prevailed throughout the kingdom. Muslim culture in Sicily not surprisingly went under first, for difference of religion made Muslims unassimilable in the long term. By the end of the twelfth century, they felt sufficiently alienated to take to open rebellion against Latin authority. Frederick II dealt ruthlessly with Muslim rebels and deported many of them to Lucera on the mainland, and at the end of the thirteenth century, the last surviving community was broken up and sold off into slavery. The Greeks were never persecuted in a comparable way: as Christians who accepted Roman ecclesiastical authority their differences could be accommodated. In the end, however, they too were submerged in a predominantly Latin environment. The multicultural dimension of the southern kingdom was therefore only a transitory phenomenon, and it is unlikely that there was ever any genuine interest in fostering intercultural relations or protecting minority cultures. On the other hand, since there was no deliberate policy to impose uniformity, it only came about as an indirect consequence of increasing self-confidence on the part of the Latins. Little by little their numbers grew, and the royal government itself built up its own establishment of officials, craftsmen and clergy; slowly but inexorably 'non-conformists' were forced to the margins. It is not possible to chronicle the process of cultural imperialism over the centuries, but the points at issue are clear enough.

Quite apart from differences of religion there was the potentially divisive factor of language. In the case of England, the closest parallel, French became the language of government, law and culture, and had a marked influence on the development of English. Nevertheless, its dominance was not permanent. English remained the speech of the majority and in due course recovered its cultural dominance when it became a medium for polite literature. One of the strengths of English that had helped it survive the Norman conquest was its own literary tradition. There was nothing comparable to this in Lombard Italy. In the South, it must have been accepted long before the Normans came that there would be a great variety of speech patterns; there was probably widespread facility in the use of more than one language. French was just another tongue to be spoken there. Though it was spoken at the twelfth-century royal court at Palermo, it was not obviously used throughout the system of public government. The French-speakers may themselves have been too few to impose their ways. Perhaps they found it easy to pick up the local tongues. It is not possible to prove with certainty what French words were adopted into Italian at this stage, but it is assumed to have been fairly easy for Normans and Lombards to communicate. They did not belong to distinctive language groups. No one vernacular prevailed, and even in court circles there is no evidence for the cultivation of any vernacular literature until the appearance of the poets associated with Frederick II, who used the vernacular in the so-called 'Sicilian' form. For official and legal purposes, Arabic, Greek and Latin were all written by professionals. The likelihood is that the spoken languages in use were many but remained little-influenced by government or education. The Greeks in particular appear to have skilfully translated Greek works into Latin, and to have made accurate transcriptions of Arabic. From the first they played an important role as interpreters and middlemen. The Normans may themselves have been gifted as linguists, since they won a reputation for practising clever deceptions on their enemies. Guiscard, specifically, appears to have been a persuasive speaker in more than his own tongue, but it may have been a talent cultivated deliberately by other rulers. Ibn Jubayr reports with some admiration that King William II himself spoke Arabic. It is in this tradition that should be read the observation of Giovanni Villani that Frederick II spoke five languages.

The polyglot kingdom could have seemed particularly welcoming for travellers and individuals in search of prospects. Much travel at the time was ostensibly for religious purposes, and most of those who came so far south were bound for the Holy Land and did not intend to spend long in the kingdom. The shrine of the archangel Michael on Monte Gargano had attracted pilgrims from as far away as northern Europe since the early eighth century, and had been boosted by Greek patronage. King William II visited it in 1172, and it may have continued to act as a powerful draw as a centre for pilgrimage in its own right. Many of those who came to Rome on business had perforce to seek out the *curia* at Benevento on many occasions, so that they too caught a glimpse of the kingdom. Others, like Archbishops Anselm of Canterbury and William of York, found refuge there as exiles, some being able to take advantage of family connections. But even religious visitors discovered other matters to interest them in the kingdom, and they left travellers' impressions of some diversity.

One of the most persistent interests seems to have been the links established between southern sites and the classical literature known to northern visitors. Conrad, bishop-elect of Hildesheim, for example, wrote about his visit to Virgil's tomb in Naples, and Gervase of Tilbury reports that Virgil's bones had been found and reburied there during the reign of Roger II. The importance of literary tourism emerges even from some notes on maritime sites from a twelfth-century guide-book incorporated by Roger of Hoveden into his chronicle-account of the journeys made by the kings of England and France on their way to and from the Holy Land in 1190–1. On the summit of Cape Circeo, the guide pointed out a pirate castle; off Gaeta, the island of Pontius Pilate; Ischia was volcanic and always smoking; but at Baia the reputation of the baths was enhanced by attributing the foundation to Virgil. In Naples, at San Gennaro, King Richard himself actually went to see another literary museum piece: the four mummified sons of Aymon (heroes of French poetry) standing in furs and bones in the crypt. The miscellaneous variety of things thought worth seeing is remarkable – flying fish at sea; a beautiful room underground where Lucan had been in the habit of studying at Scalea; and, further south at Mileto, near the abbey, a wooden tower stormed by Guiscard. Once the party reached Sicily, Richard's political problems became the main concern of the chronicler, but the description of a frightening thunderstorm in December which sank one of Richard's galleys dwells in particular on the globe of fire seen over the pinnacle of a church, more light than heat, as another remarkable phenomenon of nature said to be frequent on such occasions. The greatest of human wonders for Richard I and his entourage turned out to be the venerable abbot Joachim, who was brought from his abbey of Corazzo to expound his interpretations of the book of Revelation to a somewhat sceptical audience. Richard offered his own views about anti-Christ and waxed sarcastic about Joachim's. The problems of the Holy Land gave some urgency to this concern about what the future held for them all; nevertheless, it is not without interest that it was in Sicily that they found someone prepared to tell them.

Joachim's biblical exegesis had by that time already won him some fame, though he is not known to have attracted northern disciples. What may have excited more general interest in southern learning was the availability of ancient books of prophecies that explained the past and prepared men for the future. One of these Sibylline prophecies, the Erithryaean, was translated from Greek into Latin by Eugenius, a scholar who became an important official of the government in the late twelfth century. Unfortunately, no manuscripts of this translation older than the thirteenth century have survived, and these show that the version was up-dated and reinterpreted in the light of Joachim's own prophecies, at that time at the height of their popularity. Joachim clearly drew upon a strand in the kingdom's intellectual tradition that went back to the Greeks, and in a sense was an intermediary for the transmission of such ideas to the rest of Christendom. A belief in the possibility of obtaining foreknowledge of the future may have also been reinforced from the learning about the stars circulating freely in the Muslim world. Although the royal court kept its own astrologers for advising on the right time for action, there is no evidence for schools of any kind of scientific learning as such in Sicily.

The South was, however, a place where northerners could find unfamiliar treasures if they wanted to. Judging from the books available in the library of Monte Cassino, for example, southerners had access to classical Latin texts of Varro, Tacitus, Apuleius and Seneca not available or read in the rest of Christendom, but copied because still valued in the South in the eleventh and twelfth centuries. This may give some clues about the continuing 'humanistic' interests of educated southern Latinists of the day. Appropriately enough, a students' introduction to this literary culture was written in the late eleventh century by the monk Alberic at Monte Cassino. This *Breviarium de dictamine* was formerly considered the forerunner of the new manuals for teaching formal letter writing in twelfth-century Europe, but this is now disputed and northern Italian teachers at Bologna are given credit for this innovation. Alberic's manual thus represents the older tradition of learning. It is notable that this had no influence on northern education. Northern scholars did not even appreciate that southern literary culture might be more versatile than their own. If John of Salisbury picked up a few refinements of interpretation of a text from a bilingual Greek, there is no evidence that he thought it worth studying with any southern teacher. Peter of Blois knew a grammarian, Master John of Naples, but was not much impressed by local teachers, one of whom, Walter, later archbishop of Palermo, he thought particularly contemptible. Peter, instead, boasted of his own role as the king's tutor in superior literary studies. By northern standards, classical education in the South, however distinctive, did not seem worth emulating.

Other kinds of learning peculiar to the South proved to have stronger attractions for northerners. The scientific interests of Adelard of Bath, for example, are believed to have been extended by his familiarity with Muslim learning. Where did he acquire this? His earliest work is dedicated to William, bishop of Syracuse, whom he praised for his knowledge of mathematics. This work provides positive evidence of Adelard's links with Sicily. It has also been argued, from mistakes in Adelard's translation of Al Khwarizmi's astronomical tables, that he had a better knowledge of spoken than written Arabic. This might be because he spent some time in Sicily, though it would also suggest that he had not pursued any scholastic studies with Arabic teachers, but relied more on conversation with local savants. Adelard himself, however, refers only to scientific conversations he had with a learned Greek on leaving Salerno, and this itself indicates the informality of his studies in the South. It does not help to clarify the nature of any Muslim scientific learning available to him in Sicily.

The school of medicine at Salerno promoted something more than opportunities for casual learning. Its reputation as a place for studying practical medicine had already spread north of the Alps by the early eleventh century. The tradition of medical learning there was originally Greek and based on compilations from various writers of the past; to this was added, from the later part of the century, some knowledge of Arabic medicine. Alfano, archbishop of Salerno, who himself had medical knowledge, encouraged Constantine, who arrived from North Africa *c.* 1077, to make translations from the Arabic of several popular medical texts. Though Greek learning was slow to appreciate how it might benefit from other traditions, by the late twelfth century Salerno was at its peak as a centre of medical knowledge. It attracted a number of scholars from northern Europe like the Magister John Anglicus *medicus*, described as a citizen of Messina in 1211, who had decided to stay on in the kingdom after completing his studies. Some 'scientific' manuscripts –

compilations, commentaries on them, translations or collections of scientific questions and answers – refer specifically to Salerno. Several manuscripts of works ascribed to the teacher, Urso of Calabria, are found in England, which confirms the far-flung reputation of such authors. These works show the range of learning in natural philosophy, as it was then known, at the end of the twelfth century. One of the questions concerns a spring of water near Salerno that ran in summer but not in winter, for which King William was able to provide an explanation. This royal involvement in the scientific curiosity of the day reflects the same kind of interest taken in the natural world by Frederick II, William's nephew. Rulers can hardly have avoided contact with practitioners of medicine anyway. William I needed the services of Romuald, archbishop of Salerno, as physician on his own final sick-bed, and the emperor Henry VI was not surprisingly attended by doctors from Salerno when he was taken ill at the siege of Naples in 1191. Peter of Eboli described how the king himself reassured his visitors by asking them to feel his steady heart-beat under his clothes, however weak his voice while he was sick in the grip of fever. His doctor Gerard kept his servants quiet, and saw that in sleeping and sweating nature herself aided recovery by these hopeful signs of health. The desire to control medical quackery in the kingdom also resulted in the publication of a royal decree that medical practitioners and pharmacists had to be approved and registered, as some safeguard for the health of the general population. This reform was presumably enacted with the strong backing of the professional medical fraternity.

Another piece of evidence about the southern reputation for health comes from Pozzuoli, where the thirty-five baths known in ancient times were recovering their popularity in the late twelfth century. Benjamin of Tudela mentions about twenty hot-water springs where men bathed for improving their health. Some twenty years later when Gervase of Tilbury visited Naples, he refers to the legend that Virgil was responsible for building the Roman baths then being used, which seems to have enhanced their reputation for cures, at least with the erudite who wrote about them. Frederick II, when taken ill in 1227, went to the baths to assist his recovery. Local tales about the curing qualities of each bath had formed the substance of the lore committed to the Latin verses of Peter of Eboli which he had presented to Frederick some years earlier.

Medical students in the South became alert to the possibilities of enlarging their scientific understanding, not by frequenting other schools, but by taking advantage of the availability there of other rare books. A preface in one manuscript of a Latin translation of Ptolemy's *Almagest* explains how the translator, while studying medicine at Salerno, heard

that the Sicilian envoy to Constantinople had been given the Greek text
of it by the emperor Manuel. (A manuscript now in the Marciana
Library in Venice may be this very copy.) The medical student was so
eager to read the book that he set out overland to find the envoy
Aristippus, archdeacon of Catania. He tracked him up Mount Etna
where he was making scientific investigations. Aristippus was therefore
himself of scientific bent, a learned Greek beneficed in the Latin church.
When the student himself set eyes on Ptolemy, however, he realised that
he would need to study Euclid and Proclus before he understood the
difficult subject matter well enough to translate it. As a result, he may
have completed his task by translating these two authors as well. His
translation of the *Almagest* is known from four manuscripts. Only one of
them is complete, which puts this translation's influence on western
astronomical studies in doubt, particularly since the (later) translation
made by Gerard of Cremona from the Arabic in 1175 was very popular.
The circumstances of the Sicilian translation need to be noted. A
northern scholar, possibly German, who happened for other reasons to
be in the South, recognised the value of the book and mastered enough
Greek to set about translating it *c.* 1160. There was no tradition current
in the kingdom for making Greek and Arabic works accessible to Latin
scholars. The manuscript itself had arrived somewhat fortuitously in
Sicily; it formed no part of an existing scientific library. The only scholar
there known to have helped the foreign translator was not Aristippus,
but the learned Eugenius, who had himself made a Latin translation from
the Arabic version of Ptolemy's *Optics* a few years earlier *c.* 1154. This
does appear to have been highly valued, for twenty manuscripts of it are
known. There is, however, evidence that the works of some other
ancient writers on science, such as Hero of Alexandria, were also
available in twelfth-century Sicily, and the library at Syracuse is said by
Aristippus to have been rich in scientific works. Several important texts
of scientific interest seem to have reached the west through Sicilian
contacts with Constantinople. What is lacking is any evidence of a
flourishing scientific culture in Sicily, or of any manner of making such
texts systematically available to Latin scholars, either from the kingdom
or from outside. Nevertheless, translations from works available in the
South show that one of the consequences of creating a Norman
dominion there was to improve access by Latins to the cultural treasures
of the Greeks and Muslims. These were not all strictly scientific. The
versatile Aristippus had at the beginning of William I's reign made
translations of the theologian Nazianzenus, and of Diogenes Laertius'
lives of the philosophers. A little later, he dedicated a version of Plato's
Phaedo to an unnamed scholar returning to England. He had begun it, not

on demand, but to while away the tedium of the siege of Benevento in 1156, though his other translations were done for King William, for the royal minister, Maio, and for Archbishop Hugh of Palermo. His scientific interests probably explain his familiarity with Aristotle's *Meteorology*, and his translation of its fourth book into Latin proved to be popular and circulated quickly. The cultural interests of the court circle are notable, but should not be mistaken for evidence of scientific schools.

Eugenius is an enigmatic figure in twelfth-century culture. He translated fabulous and serious works from both Greek and Arabic, and was certainly a poet. Miss Jamison (see later chapters) believed he was also the author of the political history *Liber de Regno*, though she did not convince others of this. His twenty-four short Greek poems, which survive in only one defective fourteenth-century manuscript, show that he wrote rather unexceptional verse in the manner of his contemporaries at Constantinople. A few pieces give some insight into his relations with the king, perhaps William I, and Greek religious figures at Brindisi and Messina; one lament on his captivity in Germany, after being accused of conspiring against Henry VI, relates his personal fate to the evils of the present time, and the philosophical tone prevails. These poems indicate the level of literacy and learned culture to which the kingdom's Greeks could attain.

Another puzzling piece of evidence about the intellectual milieu of the kingdom's Greek community is provided by the copy of John Scylitzes' chronicle in Madrid, which has only recently been recognised as having been written in the twelfth-century kingdom. Its most extraordinary feature is the abundant illustrations (nearly 600 pictures surviving out of many more) attributed to nearly a dozen different artists. It is now believed that the illustrations were not modelled on an earlier exemplar made in Constantinople (where the chronicle was written in the late eleventh century), but must have been devised in the kingdom itself, though initially by artists familiar with the techniques of Constantinople. Some of the illustrations, however, show the artists to have also been conversant with Muslim artistic conventions. This points to cross-cultural influences in the visual arts. Looking forward, the style of the chronicle's illustrations of such scenes as court-life or siege warfare bears a strong resemblance to the illustrations found in the (unique) Berne manuscript of Peter of Eboli's verse chronicle, written for Henry VI at the end of the twelfth century. These two manuscripts point, therefore, to the development in the kingdom of skills in illustrating secular, historical works in both Latin and Greek, possibly building on the artistic experiences of southern Italy, where several monastic chronicles are illustrated with drawings, though these are not painted. The Madrid manuscript was formerly at the Greek monastery of San Salvatore in Messina, but it is not established that it was written there. Two scribes of the text have been identified: one, the notary who wrote a royal document for Patti in 1142, the other, the transcriber of a Greek medical text, now in the Vatican, possibly from Reggio di Calabria. Some scholars have wished to interpret this evidence to mean that the chronicle was commissioned by Roger II himself, since he knew Greek and was interested in Greek history. The Madrid manuscript, however, despite its importance, is not exactly what one would expect of a text prepared and adorned for a king such as Roger II. The use of two different scribes and several illustrators who did not even finish their work would at least indicate that, if the king commissioned the work, it can never have been presented to him.

If artistic traditions could be interchanged, the same does not seem to have been true in matters of religion. There is little evidence of Latin interest in Greek religious studies, though it is just possible that the Greek Septuagint version of the Bible stimulated textual criticism of the Vulgate. In this connection, a Vulgate psalter written before 1153 is notable for containing an interlinear Arabic gloss, which could indicate a concern for opening up the Christian scriptures for Muslims. There is also a text of the Gospels in Greek and Arabic to support this conclusion.

Whereas in modern times the racial, linguistic and religious variety of the southern kingdom in itself seems to have constituted an environment favourable for cross-fertilisation, it is clear that Sicily proved to be rather less important than Spain in helping to diffuse Muslim learning in the Latin west. Cordova had, however, formerly been one of the great intellectual centres of Islam, and until the end of the twelfth century, Islamic scholars and *savants* kept up their activities in Spain. In consequence, Christians wanting to be informed about Islamic science, ancient philosophy and even the faith of Islam itself went to Spain, particularly Toledo, for the books, contacts and interpreters necessary for their requirements. Sicily had, however, been only peripheral to Islamic culture. It was famed for its gardens, its fertility and its wealth, not its schools. Even its orthodoxy had been impugned. After the Norman conquest, Muslim scholars increasingly preferred to abandon the beautiful island, perhaps with regret, but realistically recognising that they could no longer share in the intellectual traditions of Islam under an alien regime. Similarly, the Greeks had remained culturally in the shadow of Constantinople. Surprisingly, the Greeks seem to have experienced something like a revival of their culture in the Norman period, after the political link with Constantinople was broken. Some monasteries took the lead here. The fact that the Comneni emperors recognised the need to take the Normans seriously also meant that diplomatic relations were conducted at a higher level in the twelfth century, and the Greeks could profit on their own account for a time. But apart from the royal court itself, there was no forum where the different cultural traditions of the kingdom could meet as intellectual equals. The cultural eclecticism which made the court, rather than the church, the focal point of the kingdom's intellectual life probably enhanced interest in matters of secular curiosity.

The exoticism of the South was not only remarked on by travellers: the inhabitants had to live with it. Aristippus may have been able to investigate Mount Etna, but it was not always placid. A document which records the eruption of Vesuvius in 1138 is a reminder that natural calamities afflicted this kingdom, as nowhere else in Christendom. The impact of the Sicilian earthquake of 1169 was both physical and psychological. The *Liber* gives a precise circumstantial description. The earthquake swallowed up fifteen thousand people at Catania, bishop and all, on 4 February, at the first hour of the day. Other places as far as Reggio were shaken; new springs of water gushed out and old ones were blocked up; the summit of Etna, seen from Taormina, caved in; the famous limpid fountain of Arethusa at Syracuse became agitated and took on a taste of salt water, while the fountain of Taius was dammed up for two hours and then burst out, coloured like blood.

The author of the *Liber* thought the savagery of nature perfectly matched the character of the local inhabitants. He explains at the beginning that dreadful political dramas were hardly news in Sicily, where *Fortuna* turned her wheel more rapidly and with less compunction than elsewhere. For him, the inhumanity of the island was not mainly revealed by such physical disasters as earthquakes, but by the treachery of the people who fawned on those they hated and would murder, and by the power of rumour that ran through the people exciting changes in the public mood. This sinister aspect of the island's life was noted by other authors such as Peter of Blois. The *Epistola ad Petrum*, written in 1194 by an author who was fundamentally charmed by the beauties of Sicily, also alludes to it. Though he regarded Sicily as outstanding among kingdoms for its endowments and virtues, it was fated to be torn apart by those it had brought up, just when they reached their full strength. This enigmatic statement has been interpreted as referring to Roger II's daughter Constance, his ultimate heiress, rather than to the population in general, but either way a sense of impending doom for the island is evident. For him, the potential hatred created by tensions between Christians and Saracens particularly threatened to overwhelm the kingdom in the emergency opened by Tancred's death.

This author, however, takes a mental trip round the great maritime cities of the island in turn, which creates a more positive impression of the island's virtues. Messina is praised and held responsible for inflicting great damage on the Greeks, in Africa and in Spain, by its piratical activities; Catania is praised for its resilience in surviving so many natural disasters; as is Syracuse, where philosophy and poetry once flourished. Last of all he treats the splendid city of Palermo itself. The writer claims words are inadequate for this, but cannot restrain his desire to express his admiration: the site itself; the buildings, particularly the royal palace complex, its textile workshops singled out even ahead of the fabulously ornate royal chapel; the three main streets of the city; and finally the abundant fertility of the cultivated area round it, its irrigation-wheels, vines, vegetables, fruit trees, sugar-canes and date-palms. Palermo impressed even the great traveller Ibn Jubayr. It is not hard to explain why those who found themselves in the kingdom were generally astonished and delighted. Many visitors stayed on. The sour note struck by Peter of Blois is most simply explained by his disappointment at being obliged to leave the kingdom in a hurry, when his patron, Stephen of Perche, was overthrown by a *coup d'état*. Peter's brother William obtained the favour of the queen-mother, and became a mitred abbot in the kingdom, though he is best known to scholars now for the lubricity of his Latin secular works.

The romantic environment of the South suitably provided the setting for a long French epic poem, the *Chanson d'Aspremont*, focused on the mountain of Aspromonte in Calabria. This is known from several thirteenth-century manuscripts (including some from both England and Italy). There is even a version of it in Old Norse. Appropriately the cast is recruited from all over the known world. An English king called Cahoer is presented as a vassal of Charlemagne, and the epic has been plausibly assigned to the 1190s, about the time when Richard I visited the kingdom and was forced to recognise the lordship of the emperor Henry VI. In the poem, Charlemagne fights the Saracens in southern Italy. This historical inaccuracy did not prejudice its popularity. One of its important characters was the familiar Burgundian hero Girart, who here holds Gascony and Aquitaine as an allod. Did this enhance the interest in the poem of the people from the Plantagenet empire? As a penance for his brutal life, Girart joins Charlemagne in the holy war, a feature which has been said to reflect contemporary efforts to recruit even the reprobate as crusaders. Though the Saracens are, of course, in the end defeated, they are not all contemptible: one noble adversary is converted to Christianity by arguments, and another gives proof of extraordinary fortitude in death. The Saracen king Agolant is buried in a tomb that can still be seen, the author says, in a place near a pillar. This attempt to vouch for the truth of the tale certainly relies upon a common fact of experience for travellers in the south – that there were many tombs as relics of ancient times. Some of them, it was thought, must certainly be those of well-known individuals, and gossip about them was designed to please visitors. Contemporaries who expected all the material remains of the saints to be available for inspection, thought it only natural that fictional heroes of the imagination should leave equally tangible proofs to satisfy legitimate curiosity. This tale, set in the southern kingdom, actually had recognisable points of contact for English, Burgundian, Gascon and German knights who passed through. There is even a king of Hungary brought in at the end of the tale, which makes more sense than it would seem at first sight, since the rulers of Sicily traditionally took the kings of Hungary as allies because of their common antipathy to the Greek empire. The kingdom may be thought of as open to all comers. In medieval terms, it was already a land for high-class tourists.

How did the native inhabitants react to the presence of foreign travellers in their midst? They should not be thought of as dependent economically on big spenders from abroad. They had their own tradition of travel to far-away places. Their economic and governmental interests had long since obliged them to acquire knowledge of, and maintain links with, their Mediterranean neighbours. The merchants of Amalfi had established their hospital at Jerusalem before the first crusade, and it appears that early eleventh-century Norman pilgrims to the Holy Land were already using the southern ports. Both the Greek and Muslim communities supported contingents of sailors, who might be pressed into the service of the Normans. With the first crusaders a southern company had set out and in due course established a colony at Antioch under Prince Bohemond. Communication between the kingdom and the Holy Land was closer and faster than for any other western kingdom. There cannot really be any doubt about the depth of the local inhabitants' commitment to enterprise overseas and the acceptance therefore of the continuous movement of both goods and persons across the territory. We know that both the Jew, Benjamin of Tudela, and the Muslim, Ibn Jubayr, found no difficulties in passing through the kingdom. There is even some evidence that travellers went from the kingdom to Spain: a prospective pilgrim to Compostella prudently made his will at Molfetta in March 1148 before setting out.

Modern views of the kingdom are not derived entirely from travellers' tales, but given the lack of other evidence, it is mainly from surviving private documents, such as wills, deeds of sale, marriage contracts and legal settlements, that any native impressions of life in the kingdom must be drawn. They are still remarkably numerous in comparison to northern Europe, and they must have once been even more abundant. Nearly all the Muslim documents have perished, though during the twelfth century Muslims, at least in the cities of the island, would have made regular use of written records. Writing was in fact widely used for everyday purposes throughout the kingdom. It was not confined to ecclesiastics. In this respect too, the South stands in some contrast to northern Christendom, if not to other parts of Italy. How literacy was provided for is, however, rather a mystery. Over the mainland, there were a very great number of bishops' sees, and it is reasonable to suppose that in each of these there would have been some kind of school available, so that elementary learning need not have been relatively inaccessible. Many of the clergy were married and could have taught their own children. The documents themselves provide ample evidence for the availability of professional notaries, even if there is no indication of how they acquired their basic competence not merely in calligraphy, but in a level of legal understanding indispensable to their calling. There seems to have been a form of public endorsement for such professionals, intended to prevent unqualified persons from practising, and to guarantee that the kingdom was adequately supplied with competent drafters of acceptable legal deeds. Since all kinds of legal transactions, even amongst men and women of modest fortune, were confirmed in written documents, notaries enjoyed a prominent place in the management of everyday affairs. Although some of them were clerics, chiefly in the lower ranks of the major orders (sub-deacons or deacons), the number of laymen amongst them tended to rise in the twelfth century. Literacy amongst laymen had not been uncommon in Lombard, Greek and Muslim areas, but the established writing traditions of the kingdom were not so strong as to resist the influence of French writing styles brought in by the Normans. These became so familiar that by 1220, Frederick II actually insisted that documents should no longer be written in traditional scripts of notaries in Naples, Sorrento and Amalfi, but in the more generally current forms modelled on the French miniscule. From the same period, the peculiar scripts of Lombard Italy as cultivated at Benevento and Bari, and in such monastic communities as Cassino, fell into disuse. How these practices had changed cannot be dated precisely or explained, but they go to show that whatever the strength of established ways, they were not immune from change and could not thwart Latin innovations from the North.

From these documents can be sketched the character of literate culture in the South. There is the plain importance in each place of respect for local customs, coupled with the regular recourse to men knowledgeable in the law and experienced in its enforcement. The legal form of documents in the kingdom naturally varied from one cultural region to another. Custom may have developed somewhat differently in areas where Lombards lived under Greek imperial law from those where Lombards themselves ruled. In Sicily, where the Muslims and Greeks maintained their own legal customs, the skills of continental notaries were not so much in demand by the new Latin population. Study of the problem is inhibited by the fact that notaries are not often named in Sicilian deeds. Latin documents were, however, not written in the developed calligraphic styles of the mainland, and the notaries must have been less important to the island's cultural life.

From the mainland comes a variety of documents, written in both Lombard and Greek Italy, which demonstrate the character of civil society. Apart from documents regularly drawn up in connection with marriages, or to make testaments, there are formal records, such as adoptions of sons, emancipation of sons from the father's control or the divisions of property carried out when brothers married and no longer lived in common. The sheer accumulation of detail from one deed to another brings a vanished world back into view. People are described in the texts as they move by water from one port to another, or along ancient established routes with their mile-stones or boundary marks. The towns have their more opulent market squares and districts for special trades or minority groups. The houses have courtyards, balconies, communicating roofs; some have piped water supplies, others wells. There are regulations about not fouling or blocking communal entries, which disgruntled neighbours try to get enforced. The assignment of marriage portions by Lombard law involved extensive inventories of household necessities and luxuries, and are more informative even than lists of ecclesiastical vestments and furnishings to indicate the great range of artisan activity.

The abundance of artefacts mentioned in the texts brings to notice another important group of southerners, the artisans, who made their mark on the cities in particular. The best evidence of their skills is now provided by the great ecclesiastical buildings, and in particular by their spectacular embellishments. Apulia had a powerful tradition of stone-carving. Astonishing proofs of its mastery and versatility, already in the eleventh century, can still be seen: bishops' thrones, pulpits, lecterns, candelabra, as free-standing objects, quite apart from the decorative features of the main fabric, the portals, window-embrasures and corbels.

Artists of comparable accomplishment were brought to Sicily by William II to work on the cloister at Monreale because Sicily had no sculptural tradition of its own. Apulian sculptors probably drew upon a continuous local tradition of figurative sculpture and absorbed its respect for line and simplicity. Somewhere in these former Greek provinces Frederick II found the designers of his augustalis coin, struck at Brindisi, with its classical portrait-profile and the clear image of the imperial eagle. These craftsmen may not appear in documents, but the evidence for their importance is unmistakable. They serve to represent the phalanx of artisans whose products were in constant demand but whose role has been overlooked because their goods were made of less robust materials.

The growing refinement of the metal foundries may be illustrated from surviving objects larger than coins. Southern appetite for skilled metal work had been satisfied in the eleventh century by foreign imports, such as the bronze doors acquired by merchants in Constantinople for the churches of Amalfi and Monte Cassino. A century later, however, comparable doors could be made in the kingdom itself. Doors for Trani, Ravello and Monreale were all made in the decade 1175–85, by Barisano at Trani. They share a common technique and decorative programme which combines both religious and secular subject-matter. The secular subjects draw upon eastern as well as western sources of inspiration, particularly Greek or oriental designs imitated from fabric and small chests whose decorative charms enhance the religious themes. It is not known how long these skills had been cultivated in the kingdom. The bronze doors used in Bohemond's mausoleum at Canosa were not of southern manufacture (c. 1111), so Barisano's mastery looks like proof of a very rapid development of a new industry. There is no evidence that the acquisition of the required knowledge from the lands of the empire awaited a royal initiative. Artisans were quite capable of finding patrons or clients locally.

Attention should also be drawn to another aspect of church decoration: the art of the pavement-makers, now best illustrated by Otranto cathedral, where inscriptions explain that it was commissioned by Archbishop Jonathas in the years 1163–5 from the priest Pantaleone, who also worked at Trani and Brindisi. In this region, where the Greek emperor's forces had so recently been defeated by the king, loyalty to William I is affirmed not only by the reference in the inscriptions to him as *magnificus* and *triumfator*, but also by the depiction on the pavement of *Alexander rex* (a well-known symbol of the Greek empire) who aspired to fly up into the sky and whose pride was humbled by literally being trampled upon by the worshippers. Pantaleone decorated the pavement with many lively figures and stories from the Bible, as well as secular literature: King Arthur, for example, is shown astride a goat, being startled, and then throttled, by a leaping cat. In this corner of the kingdom, with its old Greek affiliations, the design can nevertheless accommodate a new character such as Arthur (who had only appeared in French literature in the previous generation).

The cultural position of Calabria and Sicily under the monarchy differed from that of the provinces to the north. Here, Latin settlers and culture were necessarily novelties, forcibly grafted into alien societies, so northern European influences may have been greater. Understanding the full force of the Norman impact there has, however, been prejudiced by the decline of Calabria after the War of the Sicilian Vespers, and the accumulation of neglect over centuries which obliterated much of its history in the great days of the twelfth and thirteenth centuries. Only very recently have local historians begun to put the record straight and show how the Latin occupation of Calabria marked an important stage in the assimilation of northern influences, as in architecture, before the better-known buildings of Sicily were erected. Several great cathedral churches were certainly constructed just before the monarchy was founded. Of these, the only visible remains are at Gerace which, when new, was one of the biggest and most beautiful of the region. This taste for big buildings derives from the North. From Calabria it reached Sicily. Roger I took two early Sicilian bishops, Stephen of Mazara and Ansger of Catania, from the monastery at Sant'Eufemia, and they probably planned their cathedrals in the new French style. Points of similarity have even been noticed between the surviving Norman cathedrals of Sicily and England. The length of the naves, as at Palermo, the frontal towers of Cefalù, and certain decorative details in the arcading and grouping of capitals can all be matched by English examples. These may be most simply explained as the result of English craftsmen coming to work in the island, though not in gangs since the survival of local building traditions also points to the use of local labourers.

The availability of skilled artisans in the southern kingdom was of course much more extensive than the surviving evidence indicates, for much of their work has inevitably perished. From the palace silk workshop in Palermo, only the magnificent cloak made for Roger II in 1133–4 may still be admired at Vienna. There are also other gold and silver ornaments and enamel ware, inspired by the styles of both the Limousin and Constantinople. The demand for skills in working precious and semi-precious materials probably developed most notably in the twelfth century. Abbot Desiderius of Monte Cassino had had to import most of what he needed for his new abbey from Constantinople, and attempts to train native workmen were still recent when the kingdom was founded. Palermo already had a sizeable number of skilled craftsmen and the kings, if they encouraged immigrant craftsmen, were not above importing them by force, as when Roger II seized silk-workers at Thebes in 1147. The extraordinary diversity of skills so quickly cultivated in the kingdom owed much to the talent assembled from many nations, but southern Italians must also have been quick to profit from these opportunities. The kingdom was not just a northern colony set up by domineering Normans amongst people deemed primitive and inferior. There were indeed Norman innovations, but these were grafted into a living organism with plenty of vitality, originality and energy of its own.

6

THE ORDERING OF SOCIETY

•

The exotic impression carried away by foreign visitors to the kingdom has been reinforced by many modern accounts of the twelfth-century kingdom. A moment's reflection is enough to recognise what difficulties for society and government were created by bringing together peoples of so many diverse traditions in one political unit. Even the creation of the (Norman) monarchy did not immediately impose the authority and *mores* of a coherent governing group, as happened in England. Roger II himself tempted capable persons from different cultures to come to his service, not finding in the kingdom all the talents required. Throughout the twelfth century, the kings encouraged men from northern Italy, Spain, France and England to serve them; merchants from Pisa, Genoa and Venice established colonies to promote their trading interests. The governing group, which was itself permeable to new elements, accepted the need to recruit foreign extras throughout society, mainly, but perhaps not quite consciously, in order to strengthen the dominant Latin elements in the island, where all the Latins were immigrants. Manpower was, as such, also limited, and some deliberate efforts were made to attract labourers and add to their number, even by enforced deportations from Greece and North Africa. To the original diversities were therefore added others. If in the long term, all these elements would be submerged by the rising Latin tide, in the short term, local diversities were accentuated and not forced to trim their eccentricities. All this makes it difficult to envisage the state of the kingdom according to the simple criteria devised to meet the comparatively homogeneous cultures of modern western Europe. In Catania, Bishop John offered all four peoples – Latin, Greek, Muslim and Jew – the benefit of their own laws, as if the king himself had laid down no statute for the personality of law. There may have been expectations to this effect, but what happened in practice depended on local conditions.

COMMUNITY

There is a sufficient body of information about both rural and urban societies to illustrate the variations within each place, and the importance attached by the local inhabitants to preserving their own traditions. The evidence generally takes the form of confirmations of local custom by the lord of the place, who appears to be graciously conferring a benefit. In fact, however, the customs were confirmed at the insistence of the local communities, and showed their ability to confront their lords and defend their own distinctive patterns of life against any attempts to introduce novelties. The communities owed this recognition of their liberties to their own strength, shown particularly no doubt at times when their lords tried to subvert custom or were in need of cash support or recognition. Lordship was, however, by its very nature an innovation in the South and dependent on local goodwill. Even when it appeared to be taking the initiative, as, for instance, in organising defensive settle-ments called *castella*, the lords' powers to set up fortified villages to protect cultivation from marauders like the Saracens of the tenth century and the Normans in the eleventh century actually depended on the availability of potentially war-like cultivators able to defend their settlements. Such communities, called into being by lordship, essentially owed their character to the local inhabitants. Local autonomy was not a consequence of lordship, but of the facts of geography and the exper-iences of history.

The oldest surviving statements of local customs come from some eleventh-century Cassino deeds. In a document of 1061, Traietto is pompously called a *civitas*, but it had some very rustic characteristics. At Suio (1079) there was collective concern about property, service in arms with horses, local judges and daughters' marriages, in a community where some men there also owed three *opera*: one day each, sowing, reaping and in the vineyard. Suio was not therefore just a community of free citizens. The definition of rights and duties, however different within each place, shows how the judge and chief men secured general terms for all. Despite differences of obligation, in certain respects all the inhabitants, however humble, benefited from common rules of prop-erty. The burdens of service were evidently light and the sense of family rights strong.

The standing of the local community in its dealings with its lord may also be illustrated on the island, where the Normans as conquerors had not acquired the power to subjugate the inhabitants, including the Latins they had established there. At Patti and Lipari, agreements were reached in 1095 by Abbot Ambrose with all the men (*omnes homines*) in both places who were prepared to settle and cultivate, provided they were not liable for dues to others. The terms were specified in writing and chirographs made so that the men could have a copy for themselves. By 1133, the men of Patti had unfortunately lost their copy in a fire and had to consult the church's copy. However, the implications of the formal arrangements used are that the communities were in principle capable of keeping a communal archive and had some capacity for acting together in legal matters, independently of the lord himself.

One of the fullest statements of local custom comes from the late twelfth century at Corleto, where the men complained to the king because their lords were demanding unwarranted dues and services. Having obtained royal intervention in their affairs, they got their traditional customs officially recorded in punctilious detail, and despite the differences within the community, they acted in concert to secure their collective advantage. The royal government's particular concern was to protect the feudal tenants there, and as a result of the enquiry, the lords lost their claim to powers over the *feuda* and other royal dues. The feudal tenants were not the only ones to benefit. Also confirmed were the rights to free alienation of other property, the exemption of the priests and clergy from all dues to the seigneurial *curia* (apart from Christmas and Easter *salutes*), and exemptions from all payments of widows and of orphans until they came of age. There were rules about the succession to estates, particularly where there were several brothers to share the inheritance. Even those under the lord's own protection were declared to be exempt from all other renders and services, once they had paid long-standing dues to their lords; and after their deaths, their sons and heirs became liable only for the same renders as their fathers, dividing the sums amongst themselves. Those owing services to the *curia* got quittance or alleviation of other dues, so that if, for example, a man sent his ass to curial service, he was pardoned all his *angaria* that week. If he had debts, his pig was not to be taken away in part-payment. The men of Corleto were allowed to buy and sell there without paying market dues to the Corleto *curia*, and litigants able to find pledges did not have to give surety from their property; those who could not find pledges would have the due penalties assessed by the judge and the elders (*boni homines*). Nor would men of Corleto owing court service be obliged to leave the territory, except for journey service (*viaticis*) or on royal service. Further protection allowed them to dispose of property at death, and leave it to an adopted son; the lord's steward (*baiulus*) was not allowed to distrain any debtor's beasts if he had anything at home worth taking. Churches built on the elders' property (*in patrimonio bonorum hominum*) remained in the lordship of the builders, subject to ecclesiastical law; anyone wishing to take ecclesiastical orders could do so on the recommendation of the archpriest, judges and other good men, unless he was liable for *angaria* (a variation of the rules elsewhere ascribed to royal assizes).

The interests of particular groups within the community were also protected. Knights were not obliged to do service for their patrimonies, only for their *feuda*. Men were required to pay corn tax (*terraticum*) and wine-dues according to agreed measures. If husbands were adjudged to forfeit their property, the wife's goods, namely bed, clothes and bed-linen (*cooperimenta*), were protected, even against the *vicecomes* on the look out for something to distrain on. Whoever had inherited property in Corleto from father or grandfather had the right to plough it. There were magistrates (*mannenses*) owing only a fixed pension to the *curia*; the knights, the judge and the priests were by right exempted from payment of market dues (*plateaticum*). The community's concern for traditional rights to pasture extended to the forest (but not to fell timber); they could keep what was hunted, provided a quarter of the bears, pigs and stags taken was offered to the lord (*curia*). No ban (*bannum*) could be proclaimed without the consent of the good men. As to fixing dues, alien merchants paid a fixed percentage (6.25) on each transaction; merchet (*capistragium*) was paid by men, other than knights, who married their womenfolk outside the territory; the fee for notaries writing documents for sale of property was fixed at half a *tari* (though the judge and witness got something too). As to other matters touching military obligations, a meadow was provided for grazing horses and proper equipment for *servientes* sent to the host by the lord's command, which included a pack-horse and groom as well as the replacement of arms lost in combat. The men were liable for aids (*adjutorium*) according to the king's assize, and the rates for pasture (*herbaticum*) fixed at one animal in forty and for pannage (*glandaticum*) at one pig in thirty. Despite the occurrence of buying and selling, Corleto was obviously a rural community, able to defend its various interests against its lords, and differences of rank, tenement and standing did not prevent co-operation at a local level. The minute particularities almost lovingly reveal every detail of local importance to the community. Its life was regulated by local customs, and there is surprisingly little reference to any specific laws of the kingdom in which the community found itself implicated.

Other documents also show how much custom crystallised in local communities. The sense of belonging in a particular place was characteristic of the kingdom and did not depend on lordship for its articulation. In each place, various categories of men, and for different traditional reasons, owed several different money payments. Lords had to defer to strong family sentiment even in the lower ranks of society. The rules were defined separately for each community which naturally had as the focus of its collective life the court where its customs were declared by its own *boni homines*. Although next to nothing is known about the 'good men', each village must have taken for granted that it would have its own council of trusted elders.

If rural communities were capable of securing written confirmation of their specific customs, it is hardly surprising that townsmen also took advantage of suitable occasions to get them. The towns had their own range of social ranks from knights to rustics. Coastal towns were never so commercial as to be without animals and pastures. Some documents incidentally give details about houses, in the legal concern to keep sites near the walls clear or control building in the market-place; complaints about the nuisance caused by stagnant water call attention to the awareness of the public interest, and can be matched by references to individual water supplies and baths. The state of the urban fabric may reflect dilapidation caused by warfare or clearances for the building of new churches. The spotlight is on the minutiae of town life, but though there is little information about the formal arrangements for governing the communities, the very composition of private deeds takes for granted the existence of law courts and the need for written documents as formal proof.

For a few cities, there are charters that open up the urban community and its collective preoccupations for scrutiny. The city of Troia founded by Boiannes, the Greek Catapan, in 1018, played a notable part in the history of the kingdom until the thirteenth century when it was finally overshadowed by Foggia. At the end of 1127, when Honorius II was trying to build up his alliance against Roger II, he confirmed the city customs to get the city's support, the terms of which show the citizens' outrage at recent infringements of their liberties. These had apparently not previously been put in writing, but the concessions imply that Troia had a coherent, long-established community living under its own law, even if the bishop and the three monasteries had the lordships of their own men, and the knights of the town had their own customs (*usus*) and law. Somehow or other not specified, the body of citizens could be consulted, and the pope promised that no one should be forced to go and fight, except for the town's own advantage and with the advice of its betters (*sanior pars*). He also gave assurances that the town would not be sub-infeudated to a third party, and that no governor should be appointed without its consent. No fortress (*castellum*) should be built in the town or in the neighbourhood.

Most of the clauses deal, however, with respect for the city's laws, and the very first gives a promise that no man or woman of Troia should lose life or limb or be detained without legal process by the pope or any of his subordinates, and that property (*praedia*) seized from them should be restored. They were clearly concerned about the importation of alien customs, such as the ordeal in place of Lombard custom, or taxes – *dazii*, aids or public works (*angaria*). Rights of inheritance and bequest were confirmed even for travellers, pilgrims and bastards. Judges were to be local men and law-courts were not to be held outside the city. They were allowed to build on their own property in the public squares, provided that free circulation was not impeded; they acknowledged liability to pay market rights (*plateaticum*). Those Trojans who ploughed might on certain conditions be excused payment of the corn levy (*terraticum*). Trojans might have slaves, men or women, but these are only mentioned in case they committed thefts with or without their owners' knowledge. There is little about the occupations of the individual inhabitants. The charter nevertheless gives an idea of Troia's sense of its own identity.

Bari was one of the greatest cities of the kingdom and sufficiently independent to establish its own principality in the Norman period (1117) and to defend it persistently against Roger II until 1139. Even under William I it was drawn into opposition to the monarchy by the Greeks in 1155, for which the city was razed to the ground by the triumphant king. No statement of customs has survived, but the terms negotiated by its *juratores* with Roger II for its surrender in 1132 indicate sufficiently clearly the issues of greatest concern to the citizens. Roger swore not to touch the relics of St Nicholas; to respect the archbishopric; to receive the *fideles* of Bari (with six named exceptions); and not to impose *dazii*, aids or public works, exact military duty (*expeditio*) or introduce the ordeals of iron, *caccarum*, battle or water.

After Roger II's experiences with Bari in the 1130s, it is hardly surprising if kings took care not to allow cities to maintain their own defences. Just what independence towns and cities continued to hanker after under the monarchy remains obscure. Certainly not all cities resented the monarchy. The great Lombard capital of Salerno remained faithful to Roger even against Lothar in 1137. To reward it Roger II offered not institutional concessions, but such financial ones as exemptions from exchange dues (*mediaticum*), or the *plateaticum* due from ships coming from other parts of the kingdom (Calabria, Lucania (Basilicata) or Sicily) and on their own catches of fish, or the duty on liquid measures. He also ordered royal officials to drop the practice of taking their animals for public service.

The ambitions of the kingdom's towns probably did not all run along the same lines or necessarily in the direction of autonomy. What appear to be the best indications of them come from the terms of the charters conceded by King Tancred to a number of towns between April 1190 and July 1193. These charters were not honoured by his successors and can be represented as a serious renunciation of treasured royal prerogatives, at a difficult moment for the monarchy. Even so the towns did not or could not exact any terms at all. The original splendid charter for Barletta still survives as a record of the reward for its fidelity – to be attached forever to the royal domain. In particular the citizens wanted the privilege of not being cited in pleas outside the city without special royal authority. Their judges were to be from their own city. There was to be no trial by battle except for charges of treason or for crimes punished with life or limb. One clause dealt in detail with the validity of wills made by travellers (*peregrini*) of whom there were always many in Barletta, particularly when the only evidence for them came from the oral testimony of the master of the lodging house where the traveller died. The citizens were allowed free pasture in the marsh between Barletta and Trani, provided that it was not wasted.

Older and greater cities had many more requirements and more leverage, and retained their distinctive institutions. When Tancred met a deputation of the citizens of Naples in June 1190, both recognised how indispensable Neapolitan naval strength would be for the king's survival. Naples too was offered perpetual royal lordship, and the king offered to repair the city walls for its greater security, but it was to be ruled nonetheless by its own *consulatus* who, with the citizens, were to exercise justice. This was important. Neapolitans would not normally have to leave the city for judicial purposes, unless called for legal matters reserved to the crown, and the king's own justiciars were not allowed to hold court in the city. The king renounced all royal claims on the property and goods of the citizens, alive or dead, and pardoned all debts due from citizens, barons or knights for any fee, church or contract. Barons and knights had half their due service remitted, and could not be forced into service in the king's fleet. The city was also allowed to strike its own silver coinage. Other concessions, though much less extraordinary, deal with the familiar grievances about dues exacted by the officials at the city gates, in the ports, or the imposition of military services, or the pressing of sailors into the fleet and galleys. Sailors who served voluntarily were guaranteed wages of an ounce of gold and corn for subsistence. Most striking of all, Tancred condoned the recent Neapolitan seizure of royal properties outside the city of Aversa and confirmed the property of thirteen individuals with fees in Aversa and houses in Naples, taken after William II's death the previous November. In return for this, Tancred was allowed to appoint a Neapolitan as his own *baiulus*, answerable to the royal *dohana* for the revenue he collected.

These terms may be compared with those granted to Gaeta the next year, when Tancred confirmed ancient customs going back to his grandfather Roger II. Gaeta was also made part of the royal domain; the Gaetani could choose their own consulate, and judges, though these needed to be approved by the royal *curia*. They were allowed the use of the king's office (*camera*) in Gaeta for holding their own courts (*curia*). Here too the king had his own *baiulus*, who was to be from Gaeta, but might not be either a consul or on the council (*consiliarius*). The consuls were confirmed in their custom of striking small bronze coins. The city and commune was granted the local dye industry. The judges gave judgments by local custom; civil pleas, as before, were to be settled in Gaeta. Criminal business was, however, to be judged in Palermo *in magna regis curia* (and without trial by battle), until such time as a new prince was appointed at Capua, when it would be judged there. Matters of treason would go to Palermo, with due safeguards for false accusations. The city was given two *castella*, formerly in the county of Fondi, for the service stipulated in the official records (*quaterniones*), and the king renounced his right to one of the two armed galleys owed as royal naval service, except on such occasions as the defence of the kingdom required it. Sailors were paid at the standard rate for the principality of Salerno. Matters of trade and tax took second place to the predominant concern about justice and security. Gaetani were confirmed in their rights over the ports and islands (the king reserving only his hawking), and in the privilege of taking wood as far as Cuma. Except when a general ban was in force, they could export corn from Sicily to Gaeta itself and not be obliged to carry corn or other victuals to Sicily, unless there was urgent necessity. They had to pay a due called *falangagium* on the coast from Gaeta to Palermo, but those coming from North Africa, Sicily and Sardinia were excused the levy called *catenacii*. Property rights in shipwrecks were protected. Tancred confirmed William II's remission of the dues payable for crossing the river Garigliano between Lazio and Campania. Variations in such charters necessarily make plain how impossible it is to generalise about conditions in the cities, and reveal the point of greatest importance to contemporary citizens: the desire to secure confirmation, not of urban privileges as such, but of the traditional customary practices of their own city.

The cities of Sicily, even the great ones such as Palermo and Messina, had no traditions of urban independence to match those of such mainland cities as Bari or Naples, and their mixed populations must have added to the difficulties of developing a sense of civic community and identity capable of institutional expression. Messina had a mainly Greek population and was already a lively port in the twelfth century. Ibn Jubayr commented on its deep harbour where ships could be drawn up alongside the quays, and certainly regarded it as the main city of the island, even if Palermo was more beautiful and could claim primacy as the seat of royal government. The Messinesi were easily stirred into taking bold action for their own ends, though their piratical enterprises must otherwise have made them valuable members of royal expeditions overseas in North Africa and in Greece. The Norman conquest had given Messina its opportunity, for it commanded the indispensable crossing to Calabria. Most journeys from the island to the mainland and back were made through it, and the security offered by the kingdom drew into the straits the traffic of all northern traders like the Pisans and Genoese bound for the east. The city was throbbing with vigour and audacity; and its wealth naturally made it the focus of ambition and greed.

Its influence in the kingdom may be gauged from the part it took in the disturbances that brought down the chancellor Stephen of Perche. Stephen originally came to Messina in November 1167 with a reputation as a reformer which secured him a welcome there. He rapidly improved his position by getting the king to grant a charter of privileges gratis, and by having the *stratigotus* condemned on the many charges of oppression, corruption and abuse of office advanced by the citizens. Yet before he returned to Palermo after a five-month stay, Stephen had become the object of a plot against his life. When the conspirators were apprehended and imprisoned, he blithely thought it safe to return to Palermo, little realising how hated his party had become or how much sympathy the Messinesi had acquired for his enemies. The new *stratigotus* failed to calm sedition in the city, and when the royal court at Palermo, hearing of the troubles, sent a soothing letter to reassure the citizens, they became suspicious of the chancellor's own loyalty and took matters into their own hands. The condemned conspirators were released by force from Reggio and Taormina; Stephen's chief agent in Messina was captured, tortured and killed; then the Messinesi prepared to descend on Palermo, where the unrest in Messina had encouraged the revival of earlier plots against the chancellor. Though Stephen's downfall had already been secured by the time the galleys arrived from Messina, there can be no mistaking the decisive effect on events of the actions taken by the Messinesi on their own initiative, and the utter inability of royal officials, or indeed of the great men involved in the conspiracies, to manipulate the citizens. The men of Messina might be fickle, but they were determined to be masters of their own fate and, thanks to their intervention, the royal government of the whole kingdom was changed.

Although the actions of the citizens are described in some detail by the historian, nothing is said about their organisation. The *stratigotus* was the royal official and had no popular support in the city. The royal letter was addressed to him, the judges and the people of Messina; the leading citizens are referred to as *majores*, but just how the citizens were brought out in arms or their galleys made ready is never explained. The charter offered gratis by William II in 1167 restored city privileges conceded originally by Roger II, but later withdrawn. Although no texts survive of any authentic charter from Roger to the city, King Manfred's judges examined such a privilege in 1262, and concluded that the *stratigotus* was not allowed to exact anything, or take penalties or merchandise without the approval of the *judices ordinarii* of the city, if any matter arose touching the constitutions and the customs of Messina. The only other early royal charter to survive is that granted by William I in May 1160, which reduced the port rates due to the royal *dohana* from ten to three per cent, exempted victuals from port dues, forbade *baiuli* and other officials to take horses for public service by force or to oblige citizens against their wills to buy slaves (*servos ... et ancillas*), cloth or other things belonging to the government. The expenses of any envoy service (*missaticum*) were to be met not by the citizens, but by the *curia*. Lastly, the legitimate sons of fee-holders killed on royal service should inherit the fees, provided that in the case of minors, the services due from the fees should be performed for them until they came of age.

The great city of Messina with its city walls clustered with turrets proved to be equally truculent with Richard I when he stayed there in 1190–1, though his chronicler believed that the king succeeded in humbling the intolerable arrogance of the Greeks. In the mid-thirteenth century, the Messinesi armies in Calabria threatened to emulate northern Italian cities in acquiring their own dependent territories. The Messinesi can hardly be described as meekly subservient to royal authority, and the monarchy had not succeeded in deflating their self-importance before the end of the period.

Cultivated writers and officials probably always found Palermo a more attractive city, with its beautiful site, its gardens and the handsome buildings erected by the kings to embellish its natural advantages. No

Panormitan eulogist has been identified, and foreigners may have been more easily impressed by its superficial beauties. The author of the *Liber de Regno* creates a very jaundiced picture of the population, not given to spontaneous violence, but deceitful and treacherous. The capital city, *prima inter alias Sicilie*, as Alexander IV called it flatteringly in 1255, had not only the king, but also the claims of the archbishop and the Muslim traditions of most of its inhabitants in the early days to thank for a notable lack of institutional coherence. In 1200, when a charter was issued in the name of the six-year-old King Frederick, the *cives*, as a reward for their fidelity to the crown, were given exemptions on all *gabelle* on the port and gates of the city, except on the export of such victuals as required special royal permission, and on merchandise exported from the kingdom, for which rates were fixed. They could import freely victuals and other goods from all parts of the kingdom; rates for wine and oil imports by sea were duly fixed. The Panormitani also wanted free pasture for their flocks on the king's land in Sicily, and freedom to take timber, green or dead, from the royal domain. Their legal right was to be spared the duel, except *de crimine majestatis* and other crimes. In a later privilege, however, Frederick renewed older customs going back to the days of William II, not otherwise authenticated, which protected citizens from being cited in courts of law outside the city, and from an official device of holding general or special enquiries (*inquisitio*) against one or more citizens and imposing penalties in person or by money when the perpetrators of crimes could not be found. The rural interests of citizens received further protection from royal officials in 1243 over an ancient right to cut canes in the sugar plantations for use in their vineyards and pasture for their tamed bulls, provided they were properly attended, did not come in droves (*in armentum*) and no hunting was done. Alexander IV used fine words in 1255 when claiming to release the city from its vile subjection to the emperor, but gave little specific guidance as to what had to be restored to make it honourable again, apart from its traditional customs (*rationabiles consuetudines*) and the mint (which had actually been lost at the end of the twelfth century).

The sources therefore encourage us to think of the kingdom as a mosaic of distinctive communities in both town and country, concerned with local rights and conditions, all generally geared to rely on themselves, rather than on any distant ruler for government. The just ruler confirmed good old local customs. Innovation was the work of those who abused their actual power to impose uncustomary exactions. For many local communities, these novelties were associated with the Normans, such as the use of new ordeals at law or new financial levies claimed for military tenures. Against these bad uses, the communities expected royal help for themselves, not solidarity with Norman lordship.

In a society of intensely localised loyalties, the Normans, as original immigrants mostly of military profession, were not easily assimilated, except as lords and protectors. From the beginning they had been inserted into the South through the favours of the existing public authorities, and they had consolidated their grip, if necessary, by intermarriage with prominent Lombards. Little by little they had come to supplant the established holders of public office, and by the first half of the twelfth century, Normans were clearly the dominant force throughout the governing order of the South. The leaders surrounded themselves with supporters of their own kind in government, church and military organisation. Granted their political importance, they are singularly elusive from the historical point of view. A recent attempt, using very strict criteria, to identify all the Normans mentioned in eleventh- and twelfth-century sources produced a list of only 375 names. It also revealed that nearly a third of these names anyway indicated an origin from some French province other than Normandy itself. That such low numbers grossly misrepresent the extent of Norman, and indeed of French, immigration is hardly disputable. Nevertheless, the enquiry indicates the limitations of what can ever be known about the specifically Norman elements in the South and notably fails to give any lead as to the relative numbers of these military immigrants and their families. With Domesday to help, English historians still do not know how to estimate the relative numbers of Normans and Englishmen in 1086. In the South, it seems probable that the French contingent must have been considerably smaller in both absolute and relative terms, but whether they were as many as one in twenty or as few as one in a hundred or even one in a thousand is unknowable. However, it seems unlikely that after, say, the year 1100, many Normans continued to send to Normandy for wives. Increasingly the descendants of Norman soldiers were born into mixed marriages, or to parents long domiciled in Italy. The commitment of these 'Normans' to the traditions of their fathers' family and homeland, however conscientious, must have steadily lost credibility. Some of them will have been more quickly assimilated than others, without necessarily dropping out of a local aristocracy. This was itself anyway changing. What must have kept this governing group together socially was not so much the common French origins of its members, as the status of their families at the upper end of the political order. This included surviving members of the old Lombard governing families and was dominated by those with Norman connections.

The largest and most powerful of the Norman families was the Altavilla, to which Roger II himself belonged. In the twelfth century it was vastly extended, and its members can be found at most levels of royal government, though it would be misleading to think of the kings as deliberately promoting their kin to strengthen their authority. According to Geoffrey of Malaterra, the Norman Tancred of Hauteville had twelve sons by his two wives, most of whom made their fortunes in the South. Count Roger I was the youngest of them, and Roger II the last of his sons. By Roger II's time, there had been tremendous opportunities for the immigrant brothers and their children to spread themselves round southern Italy. Any original fraternal support tended to be forgotten as rivalries and new family connections came to the fore in succeeding generations. The Altavilla were not in Roger's time a powerful clan as such, even if the progeny of twelve brothers had multiplied throughout southern society. There is no reason in principle why many other Normans in the South should not have established themselves as surely, if less conspicuously. By virtue of their own prominence, the Normans were condemned to competitions for dominance. This made them eager to attract and keep faithful followings. For them, the creation of the monarchy had an immediate effect because it set up a lordship that not only overcame all its challengers, but insisted that royal vassals respect their oaths or suffer accordingly.

Roger II owed the acceptance of his lordship to the great men; without them, the monarchy would have meant nothing. Just as he expected the prince of Capua to acknowledge his kingship, so he had comparable expectations of the counts within the kingdom. Individual counts who proved disloyal after 1130 were imprisoned or driven into exile, but their counties were not broken up. New counts from loyal families could be appointed, as at Conversano after 1133, or officials put in charge of them until the old counts returned to make their peace with the king. Charters show that Roger II's counts added to their titles the phrase *gratia regia*, but significantly they retained in first place the established form 'by the grace of God' as well. The king only acknowledged therefore the authority they had from above. It is not possible to follow the fortunes of all the many counts in the kingdom. From the little that is known, it is hardly justifiable to construct a royal policy for dealing with the counts in general. The problem was really one of securing the loyalty of individuals. Some of them married into the Altavilla family, as in the past, which should have helped to link together the great men of the kingdom by ties of kinship. This itself should not be regarded as a plan to absorb the counties into one great royal estate. The monarchy also had a political interest in winning over established families and broadening the basis of its support. The monarchy accepted that the counts formed part of the ordinary structure of government and did not try to diminish their authority.

The basis of the count's strength was his military command of his knights. The count of Loritello defended against the king's chancellor his right to command his own men. The county itself was definable not so much in geographical terms, as in terms of the count's lordship of vassals and their estates, which carried with it judicial responsibilities and financial advantages. The counties of the kingdom developed according to no one model. Some of them, such as Amiterno, Penne or Valva, were of Lombard origin and retained their identity within the kingdom, at least to judge from the *Catalogus Baronum* (see below). Several other counties traced their origin back to the Norman settlement of Apulia in 1042. To judge from its twelfth-century records, the original Norman county of Aversa, which had no count of its own after Count Richard became prince of Capua in 1058, preserved something of its distinctiveness. Counties were clusters of lordships and could be assigned as parcels of rights and held in plurality. Queen Margaret's acquisitive brother Henry, for example, obtained both the county of Monte Scaglioso and the county of the Principality. To conciliate the nobility during the period of the regency Margaret thought it politic to recall three exiled counts (Acerra, Avellino and Loritello) and appoint eight new ones. Some of these were appointed to fill vacancies in such established counties as Molise, Loreto, Fondi and Albe. The monarchy did not find, or did not take, the opportunity to suppress the office altogether, and counts continued to muster the military strength of their vassals and articulate their views of the monarchy.

To be count was not, therefore, mere enjoyment of courtly rank: it continued to carry power and consequence, as surviving charters can prove. The count of Marsico, whose county was unusually carved out of the former county of the Principality in 1150, disposed in the traditional way of rights to pannage, pasture, timber and water. In 1161, the count of Conza gave the clergy of the church there the church of Sant'Andrea with all its men, exempt from all secular service, subject entirely to the jurisdiction of the clergy of Conza, who were given the right to make vineyards, gardens, houses and other buildings, to enjoy pasture, water, and timber as other men of Conza, to use water-ways within given limits, and to build mills. Similarly in 1179 William, who had succeeded his father as count in the new county of Marsico, founded a church dedicated to St Thomas of Canterbury and gave it on his own authority eight named *villani* not paying tallage, and seven subject to *angaria*. He also gave the right to enroll (*affidandi*) sixty-five men and their families and to buy inheritable property (*heritagia*) from all men except the most burdened (who nevertheless were assumed to have *heritagia* potentially for sale), namely those exempt from tallage, the *extaliati* and the *angarii*. The church was exempted from dues on markets and other obligations (*foresteria et bando*). The count reserved no powers for his own steward (*bailus*) or forester, and considered himself able to grant away wood from his forest and bestow a mill. The count's rights acknowledge no powers reserved for kingship; it is as though the count himself disposes of favours as sovereign.

The full force of the count's authority may be assessed in the terms of a settlement agreed between the count of Fondi (Richard de Aquila) and the local bishop in 1178 near the kingdom's boundary with the papal state. The count agreed not to capture clergy or their servants, beat them, or try them in his courts over claims to traditional dues on markets, pastures, woodlands, water or animals: such cases would be tried in the bishop's court. The two parties agreed about how the ban (*bandum*) would be enforced. It is not that the king was ignored, for the count specifically recognised the king's right to *adjutorium* for his expeditions (though even so the count was involved in collecting it). He was himself entitled to *aids* for the marriage of his own sister and daughter, as well as predictable services for sowing, keeping vines and reaping on each holding. For most practical purposes, therefore, the king was treated as a remote overlord. Real government locally came from the count. It was he who authorised freedom of bequest, marriage and the rebuilding of the bishop's mills. If he did all this, what exactly was the scope of the king's government in his county? Some counts are actually described as justiciars in their counties, as in Molise. Though this suggests that as delegates of royal justice they acquired judicial powers in addition to their comital ones, it cannot be shown what precisely counts could do as justiciars that they could not do as counts. Counts were, however, clearly far more than mere titular officials of the monarchy. They were persons of consequence in their own right, of good family, with their own vassals and a sense of their place in the kingdom and their right to be heard.

Barons also must have been very numerous, and the Norman term probably covered all major lordships. The presence of royal barons to give dignity to local courts of law is fairly frequently attested, and it may have counted as part of their baronial duty to the crown to participate at sessions of the justiciars. Some counts had barons of their own, so barons were not necessarily tenants-in-chief. No doubt the important require-

ment was that barons, as lords, had jurisdiction and not merely a holding
of land with military obligations. In his court, the baron enforced his
rights and dues. Contemporaries clearly understood the meaning of this
term without choosing to define the obligations more closely, probably
because variations depended on local circumstances and kingdom-wide
definitions were inappropriate. Very occasionally barons appear as
beneficiaries of the churches, also disposing of sovereign powers over
water, wood and pasture, rather like small-scale counts. Adequate
allowance should therefore be made for their local importance too
throughout the kingdom.

The information available about the great families of the kingdom
may seem to leave them with only peripheral roles in government. Yet
interest in trying to explain their significance is comparatively recent,
and if preconceived ideas about the nature of royal government are set
aside, it is clear that there was considerable scope for the great families to
exercise their influence locally. Because of the poor documentation,
many questions about them will, however, never be resolved. To what
extent did the Norman lords marry into local power? Did they take
over many Lombard vassals or absorb Lombard tenures into their own
military provisions? The Normans were certainly not numerous enough
to displace the prevalent laws of property and, as they did in England,
lay the basis for a new common law of military tenures protected by
royal courts that would in time establish new norms. On the contrary,
Lombard legal customs survived and Frankish rules which applied
mainly, but not even then exclusively, for military tenures were the ones
considered anomalous.

Quite apart from the numbers involved, the process of Norman
settlement was so long drawn out that there can be no question of
discussing the matter in terms of one man's policy at a given period of
time, as happens in the otherwise comparable case of England. Roger II
was the first 'Norman' ruler able to supervise all forms of Norman
landholding throughout the kingdom, and he had acquired arrangements
devised by many different leaders under several different regimes in the
previous hundred years.

Surprisingly little information can be squeezed out of the documents
about how the Normans were actually established as landowners in the
South before the monarchy. The Norman settlement had begun at
Aversa in 1030, exactly a century before Roger II became king. The
chronicles may record part of the process whereby the Norman leaders
got 'official' recognition of their status; they do not show the leaders
parcelling out their conquests or reallocating existing lordships. Before
1059, both Guiscard and Richard of Capua had reserved some lands for

themselves and granted away other lands to their Frenchmen (*ultramontani*), but the sources do not show what they conceded or what services they reserved. Robert Courtenay, a Norman, who received a vineyard as his holding from his lord, Count Geoffrey of Conversano, disposed of it by sale to three brothers, as though it were his personal property. Under the monarchy, Roger II introduced a new law to forbid the alienation of property held of the crown, including military fees, without royal permission, but the very need of such a rule itself implies that in normal circumstances property would be legally alienable. Villeins themselves could sell their tenures. In these circumstances, it was not possible for such military tenures to become the new feudal norm of free tenures. The sense that rights of property were immemorably ancient emerges in a document of 1253, in which Conrad IV renewed without demur a concession of feudal property: the holder claimed it had been in his family since the times of the Goths. As against this natural trend to treat fiefs like family property, Roger II had to insist on a different rule – that the landholdings of military men were of a special kind and subject to an exceptional control of alienation designed to preserve their capacity for military duties. How did he actually enforce his new conception of feudal lordship? There is very little guidance about this provided by the sources. The *Catalogus Baronum*, which set down all existing military obligations in writing, apparently for the first time, was not a register of fiefs since it was not just concerned about knightly tenures. It also shows that existing military obligations were not considered as a Norman innovation, and that the monarchy made no attempt to standardise military services. Some *feuda* in it were stated to owe no service to the king (*feuda plana*), and such fees had not disappeared even by Frederick II's reign. Military lordships had remained unsystematic even under the monarchy.

When Roger II became king, there were already several different groups of *milites* in the kingdom. Apart from Roger's own knights, others were at the disposal of the great lords, and there were some in the cities. In general, knights were equestrian soldiers and men of standing with their commanders. Then, as later, they may have been expected to meet the ordinary expenses of their military service from their own properties. The extent to which Norman or other lords themselves had already assigned benefices to their vassals in order to obtain knightly service by 1130 is not knowable. Certainly, in turbulent districts near the later northern border, well before the monarchy, the bishops of Teramo and Chieti already had certain properties assigned as knights' fees. A bishop of Chieti bought the *castellum* of San Paolo and undertook to provide one armed knight from it to serve in Le Marche for forty days a year, if Count Robert made an expedition there. Though this apparently reveals a current notion of liability from (certain) estates for military service, the bishop could have discharged this obligation by sending a member of his retinue to serve; he did not necessarily have to enfeoff a knight for this purpose.

Some allowance must be made, at least in some places, for the extent to which military obligations had to be met in terms of earlier arrangements. This would also help explain why some established religious houses carried military burdens. There was no attempt to blame the Normans or the monarchy for these. The abbot of Torremaggiore, whose military liability is defined in the *Catalogus Baronum*, already owed service in 1116, when the customs of the castrum of San Severino referred to the obligation to supply men for the army (*in hostem*). Such men could be described as *milites*, and their holdings may be considered for that reason as fees. Under Frederick II, the abbot accordingly sent three knights to help the king at the siege of *Mensane*, as part of the service he owed for his estates.

Roger's own ability to re-shape both feudal and military arrangements was limited to specific occasions. Falco says that when Naples finally accepted Roger II as king in 1140, he provided each existing Neapolitan knight with five *modia* of land and five *villani* to cultivate them. This seems to show that by 1140 there was a generally accepted assessment of what a knight needed in land to provide for his upkeep, though there is no proof that such an assessment was due either to King Roger specifically or to the Normans in general. If by the mid-twelfth century there was a common expectation that 'knights', as at Naples, should be men of some standing with property sufficient to be cultivated by five tenant cultivators, the figures provided by the contemporary *Catalogus Baronum* do not support this equation, since over half of 160 holdings, where the numbers of dependent villeins are given, had less than five. Nevertheless in more general terms, the *Catalogus* confirms the idea that knights were landholders with dependent cultivators. Of 8,620 recorded knights, only forty-seven are described as very poor, and eighty-four as having no land at all. Knights may therefore be considered a kind of gentry group, even if not of comparable size and importance to the enfeoffed knights of Norman England.

The generous scale of Roger II's own possible provision for knights is illustrated by his enfeoffment of Deutesalve, who does not appear to have been a Norman. The document was made in Greek, though it survives only in a later Latin translation. Roger, at Palermo in September 1144, granted his *fidelis* and *familiaris* Deutesalve about fifty men in serfdom (*ad servitudinem*), and various pieces of property – a *tenimen-*

tum called *Pilatta*, a *cultura* called *Pretura*, three mills in the river Simeri, and some pieces of land held by Deutesalve's ancestors in Simeri with various rights. In return for all this he owed service *in capite* in Calabria for one month a year at his own expense, and if necessary for longer, in Calabria or elsewhere with the remuneration normally allowed to the *curia*'s knights. Deutesalve, if only as *familiaris*, may have obtained specially favourable terms, but the miscellany of his holdings, the importance to him of privileges over water and marketing, and the reference to the customary stipend of curial knights all throw some light on the situation of others. His holding of fifty tenants seems exceptionally lavish. They were obliged to pay him not only the dues vassals (*homines*) normally owed to lords, but also, and therefore exceptionally in his special case, dues on herbage, pannage and *indicamentum*. In return, they were allowed, like him, to graze their sheep, oxen and pigs in royal pasture without charge. In addition he was allowed to gather all outsiders (*extrane*) on royal lands not in *plateia* or royal *quaterniones*, unless they were named in some other lord's *plateia*. He was not explicitly given any jurisdiction over his tenants. They must have expected to make standard payments for the knight's military upkeep. Frederick II still took it for granted that fee holders exacted contributions from their tenants for the costs of their maintenance and the burdens of paying reliefs on succeeding to their fees. Though knights may not have acquired jurisdiction of their tenants, they might exercise responsible functions of some kind in their districts. Three knights, for example, occur amongst the witnesses to an official document issued by the *camerarius* of the Val di Crati for Corazzo in 1180, two of whom claimed to be both *miles* and *judex*.

There were, however, recognisable limits to the authority of feudatories over their tenants. The king himself met complaints about prelates, counts, barons and knights who exacted aids (*adjutoria*) at will from their tenants by insisting on moderate rates, and specified the occasions. For seculars these were: for raising ransom money if captured in royal service; for the expenses of knighting their son; of marrying a daughter or sister; of buying lands for royal service or military obligation; and for meeting the expenses incurred for entertaining the king (corrody). Aid was, however, only one of the rights exercised by feudatory lords over their tenants, and defined because its inherent vagueness exposed it to potential abuse.

Royal supervision of military estates would normally have been more concerned about making sure they were able to render the services due, than with protecting tenants from impositions. Twelfth-century royal edicts, for example, dealt with the problem of fee holders needing to provide dowries. Barons or knights with three or more fiefs could make over to the wife one of the fees, even a *castrum*, provided it was not the one that gave its name to the barony or county. If they had fewer fees, the dowry had to be in money. Brothers who had no movables or hereditary lands for the dower of their sisters could assign parts of the fief, provided the king had approved the marriage. This policy of supervising feudal marriages must still have been a novelty when it provoked resentment in the 1150s. The problem of dower did not affect the king alone. Other lords were concerned to get assurance from dowered widows that they would do the royal service (*servitium curie*) when summoned (presumably by proxies), or risk disseisin.

One reason for the complications of feudal obligation under the monarchy was that most fees had not been freshly created according to norms devised to suit the monarch. From Roger II's point of view it was not providing *milites* with estates adequate to their obligations that gave most concern, but actually winning the loyalty of the many landlords with military potential who became his subjects after 1127. They had acquired their holdings by inheritance, or from lords who might themselves have rejected royal lordship. Roger can have neglected no opportunity to secure the allegiance of lords with strongholds. In 1129, before becoming king, he had already taken oaths of fealty and published a ban on private warfare. Roger II considered himself legally entitled to impose forfeiture on disloyal military vassals, whatever might originally have been the nature of their property rights. Unfortunately it is not possible to demonstrate how this policy was implemented and, oddly, the only evidence of royal supervision of fees does not show it to be as forceful as might be expected. The document is cast in the curious form of a personal declaration by John fitz Geoffrey, *Maleconvencionis*. For his fee of the *castellum* of Calatrasi, south of Palermo, he had owed the service of eleven knights to the *curia*. However, when he was called to Messina to help William I destroy his enemies and traitors, he could only equip three knights. According to him, he was advised by the *familiares* of the court to beg the king to receive back Calatrasi, and grant him instead other lands in Sicily from which he would be liable for only three knights' service. Eventually, by the influence of his friends in high places, he was able to put his pleas to the king in person. Before the magnates of the court and other barons, John renounced the fee of Calatrasi and swore with his two brothers to give up all claims on it, receiving instead a *casale* at Iato as a fee of two knights, and another *casale*, Cellario in Sciacca, as the fee of one knight. Six of the witnesses to the deed were bishops; one count and two constables are also mentioned; three others may be fellow barons. The initiative for the change in obligation came from John rather than the *curia*, which seems to have resisted change and wanted to exact full penalties for inadequate service. By 1162, anyway, land liable for military service had already been cut up into units of such prescribed obligation that there could be no question of obtaining a reduction of service for Calatrasi itself. The exchange depended on the availability of three vacant fees.

It is difficult to say how the king, or others, used their feudal forces for military purposes. On the borders of the kingdom, Abbot Leonas of Casauria took eighty gold coins (*bisanti*) from Mallerius de Palena in 1161 as payment for a grant to him and his son of an inalienable military holding. The various services specified included help when needed for the defence of the land in the monastery's local *castella*, and two knights with arms and horses in Teramo and one knight for the abbot's service. The needs of the royal army are not mentioned, and the arrangement seems to have been made mainly for the abbot's benefit. A later concession by the lord of Pratella in March 1197 set up Matthew fitz John in fourteen properties for him and his squires (*scutiferi*), their horses, horse-shoes and nails (*claves*), and involved five days' active service (*in hoste*). How this force was constituted and assembled is nowhere indicated by the sources. As long as military duties were supervised locally, there can have been little chance of uniformity about the arrangements, and during the twelfth century, the military forces of the kingdom were often in practice still under the effective jurisdiction not of the king himself, but of some local commander.

Even in England by 1130, the Norman lordship was becoming domiciled, though without losing its *esprit de corps* and its characteristic social forms. In southern Italy, however attenuated, the military establishment retained under the monarchy an aspect that can be called Norman. At the king's court in Palermo, Greeks and Muslims were not necessarily more influential than royal kin, the families of the queens or the kings' trusted ministers themselves, taken from French lands or northern Spain. The monarchy was another of those Frankish states of the twelfth century found between the Holy Land and the British Isles; it was accepted and recognised as such. As everywhere else, the Franks and Normans adapted themselves to their new situations. In the Lombard south, the Normans had married their way into influence more than had been possible in England. Even so, their dominance in Lombard, as in the former Greek and Muslim territories, was achieved by the development of lordships which gave them political mastery. For them the monarchy was a logical culmination of the order they had introduced. The indigenous population, which preferred autarchy, had no ambitions to create a larger political order, but the Normans, who belonged in no particular place but only to one another, respected greater lordships, provided they could prove their strength. Though not all the Normans realised it immediately, the monarchy could also help them to consolidate their hold on the South. Without it, since their own individual lordships were confined in space, isolated Normans would eventually have been absorbed into local cultures, for on their own they could not have resisted Lombard and Greek pressures on them for long. The monarchy helped the 'Normans' to establish a new coherence for themselves throughout the kingdom, as a new governing order with social and political advantages.

In thirteenth-century England, an important legal distinction came to be drawn between those whose persons and property were protected by the royal courts and those who were unfree, that is subject to lordship. Frederick II, in his constitutions of 1231 (III, 4 ii), similarly claimed that those directly under the king's protection (*nullo mediante*) should be considered free (*liberi censeantur*), even though in the context of this law he was attempting to recover dependants of the royal domain. It is possible that in Frederick's kingdom, from its beginnings, many considered themselves free enough to appeal to the king for justice, even if they were in lordship: the king's court inherited the responsibilities of all the public courts formerly held by the king's predecessors as duke of Apulia, prince of Capua and others. Frederick II himself still allowed appeals to his courts from *villani* under lordship, calling them his *fideles* and investigating their complaints about lords claiming uncustomary dues and services. Faced with the prospect of royal supervision, lords may have wished to define their own rights over dependants more exactly, so that only those classified as 'free' would retain the power to invoke royal protection. The monarchy itself may therefore have played an important part in focusing attention on the nature of legal freedom.

The creation of the monarchy left the counts and others with some of their former powers intact. In effect, the monarchy endorsed the existence of lordships with jurisdiction. There is no way of establishing to what extent such lordships were already in place before 1130. Some favoured bishops and monasteries certainly provided courts of their own for tenants. There is no evidence about the powers of secular vassals within the counties and principalities. Recent arguments that lordship was not as common in the kingdom as was once supposed would, however, seem to leave the majority of the population still subject to the local public authorities for justice, and the monarchy continued to provide for this. At the same time, the monarchy also needed the support of its great men and was in a position to make exceptional grants of jurisdiction as favours. The monarchy might therefore be pulled in different directions.

Information about such things is only episodic, and it is unwise to draw firm conclusions about policy. The situation may only be illustrated by examples. The *Liber de Regno* gives passing reference to a problem touching the townsmen (*oppidani*) of twelfth-century Sicily. Some of them complained to the king about the way they were treated by their new lord, a Frenchman, John of Lavardin, who, thanks to the influence of the new French chancellor, Stephen of Perche, had been granted property formerly held by the conspirator Matthew Bonell. French-style, John thought he could demand half of his tenants' chattels on the grounds of custom, but the men argued that the citizens (*cives*) and townsmen (*oppidani*) of Sicily had freedom (*libertas*), and were therefore exempted from renders and exactions (*redditus, exactiones*), bound only to make voluntary offerings and give their lords services if in urgent need. Only Saracens and Greeks, they said, were *villani*, obliged to render produce (*redditus*) and annual rents (*pensiones*). This complaint was exploited politically by opponents of the chancellor, who stirred up the xenophobia of the Sicilians because French lords were allegedly attempting to subvert native customs and impose conditions of servility such as they had in France. It is highly significant that the servitudes of France were known about in Sicily and were unwelcome. However 'Norman' the governing class, it was hostile to 'French' influence. The *oppidani* themselves did not deny that they were in lordship; only that the limits of lordship were set and had to be honoured. These *oppidani* were not making appeals to any ancient, pre-Norman past, for all Sicilians, except Greeks and Muslims, were Latin immigrants introduced by the Normans. The ideas of the Sicilian *oppidani* could have been influenced by the traditions of their places of origin in Italy. Northern Italians had settled in the Madonie, at Aidone, Polizzi, Petralia and Sperlinga. Roger II's mother, Countess Adelaide, who came from northern Italy, had encouraged such immigration. Genoese too had settled, as at Caltagirone. But the *oppidani* alleged local Sicilian custom and did not recognise that Norman settlement might have established a seigneurial regime as such. Since the Normans' main purpose had been to foster a Latin hegemony in the island, these Latins obviously expected the king's government to protect their freedom.

This protest also reveals how much the issue of status mattered in the kingdom. There is more than a hint of 'racial' prejudice about the claims that only Greeks and Muslims were *villani*. Such a sweeping statement

ignores differences of degree in their societies, and seems designed to
relegate all the autochthonous inhabitants to an inferior level, if only to
enhance that of the Latins. The latter may have been concerned not only
to evade certain kinds of payments to their lords, but also to challenge
the new implications which were beginning to be attached to 'villeinage'
itself. One of these became sufficiently important to require formal royal
edicts: the rights of *villani* to obtain priestly ordination, as opposed to
their lords' right to prevent it.

Before the twelfth century there was clearly no impediment to the
ordination of *villani*. In Sicily itself, many Greek priests were drawn
from *villani* families. On the mainland too, some priests were the
dependants of others. In 1111, Count Robert, son of Count Ranulf,
gave to one priest at Sant'Angelo ad Acquaviva the public dues (*de
publica parte*) rendered by another priest, John, and his son, Caro, with
their inheritance at *Pollari*. If *villani* had been traditionally free to
become priests, and the hierarchy raised no objections, lords who tried
to prevent this in order to protect their own interest gave offence both to
the church and to the men concerned. Roger II was clearly pressed to
issue an edict designed to protect the lord's rights adequately by insisting
on his prior approval for the ordination of *villani*. Lords were forbidden
to sell their consent in return for money, which had presumably become
a common way of claiming compensation. The church could not allow a
practice so obviously tainted by simony. There is, however, an instance
of such a transaction recorded in 1134. William de Gutzulinus actually
received thirteen *michalati* from one of his men, *qui est clericus*, the son of
a priest. Though this payment was allegedly in return for granting him
his liberty at Nardo, this itself might have been a preliminary to his own
ordination.

Roger's edict proved to be inadequate. William I modified it by
resorting to a formal distinction between *villani* bound by their persons
and those only bound by their tenures, which must have been difficult to
apply in practice and there is no example which fits exactly into these
categories. The problem can be illustrated by reference to the baron of
Barletta, who in 1185 exercised his customary right as a baron (*more
baronum*) to recover the holding of a former *villanus* who had become a
priest and had stopped paying his tribute money. This *villanus* had been
bound by his tenure, but had obviously not abandoned it to the lord on
becoming a priest. His holding was in effect resumed only because as a
priest he tried to evade payment of his renders. William I's law also
prescribed that priestly ordination, which emancipated the priest, should
not have the same effect on his children. They remained *villani*. This
rule, however, effectively protected the sons' customary rights in their

father's holding. The law seems by intention to be conservative rather than reactionary.

The need for royal legislation on such an issue points, however, to the pressure of secular lords on kings to defend their (common) interests against the church, whereas the church itself favoured even more liberal terms. These the kings could not endorse. The law which confirmed rights of sanctuary, for example, specifically exempted from its terms any serf (*servus, colonus, servus glebe*) who had fled there from his lord. Lords were in fact very reluctant to abandon all their claims on *villani* who did manage to get ordained. Although priests were explicitly exempted by another royal law from obligation to perform personal services to anyone, one version of this text refused to extend the privilege to deacons and clergy in minor orders, while releasing them from other menial obligations (*ab obsequiis sordidis*). There was obvious reluctance to admit all clergy to the privileges accorded to priests.

Lords were trying to establish their rights in a field lacking definitions. William I's law on the distinction between *villani* by tenure and by person protected the lords' rights to jurisdiction of bondmen and over villein tenures. The existence of such tenures meant that those who acquired them, whatever their own legal status, became *villani* subject to lordship. This has been described as a typically Latin interpretation of custom which threatened to establish a man's standing in terms of his holdings rather than his family. At the end of the twelfth century, this notion, introduced by the Normans into Sicily, had already begun to affect the tenures and obligations of the Greek peasantry too. Latin lordship gradually established a new norm for the kingdom.

If the church took a more liberal view of villeinage, this is not necessarily because it was itself introducing new concepts, but rather because it endorsed an older view of villeinage still current. The term *villanus*, already in use before the Normans, originally meant nothing more precise than country dweller, a man living in a village or on a villa. It may have suggested in particular a cultivator. In 1104, Count Tancred of Syracuse, for example, made a grant of fifteen *villani*, one smith or farrier (*ferrarius*), and one fisherman (*piscator*) where the occupation of the *villani*, rather than their status, appears to be indicated. Documents of this period frequently record the transfer of small numbers of *villani* by counts and princes into private lordship. Count Roger of Sicily gave the monks of Catania four *villani* in Messina, two Christians and two Muslims, in 1091; the approval of Prince Richard of Capua was apparently required for a grant, made to the nuns of Aversa in 1095 by a married woman, of four *villani* along with their church of Santa Juliana and other lawful property and chattels, as well as three *curtisani* and their goods. Not all the men granted away in such charters are described as *villani*, and the precise signification of the different terms used is elusive. Nevertheless, it is clear that men of various qualities and occupations were being granted away from the public sector so that they should discharge their traditional obligations to the benefit of the beneficiary, and did not lose either dignity or rights by the transfer. The loser was the public authority. Thus Richard of Capua gave the monks of Aversa in 1100 a *fabricator* called Constantine, with his sons and all their property, to be their *servientes* for ever, paying in the future all the *servitium, census* and *dationes* which they had formerly rendered to the prince *parti publice*. In 1103, he gave them five men (*homines*), namely two families of brothers, with their sons, daughters, houses, possessions and all their property formerly held from the prince in fee (*in fevo*) now transferred in perpetuity to the monks. They were to receive all that had previously been due to the state (*respublica*): various dues listed as *servitium, censum, dationes, publicalia* and *scaditiones et alia omnia*. Another early grant of two brothers (*homines*) with all their property *in loco Octaianu* to a church in Naples (1113) also spells out a comparably miscellaneous set of obligations, *angarias, servitias, pensiones* and *tributa*, as rendered to the Norman donors, Richard de Venabile and his son. Though the grant apparently needed the approval of their lord, Geoffrey de Medania, Richard himself seems to have been a baron of some importance with officials and a financial office (*camera*) of his own. These brothers were certainly under his 'jurisdiction' at the time of the transfer, doing him service and paying him various dues.

Willingness to grant away into private lordship men who would otherwise have discharged their obligations to the state (*respublica*) was on the increase, though it had not begun, in the Norman period. Earlier public authorities had occasionally made comparable grants of traditional services, but lacked the obvious motives of the Normans for making such concessions. The Normans in the South not only looked as vassals to lords for authority to act, but also became complacent as lords about granting away public rights to their followers or to churches they patronised since this consolidated their governing group. The gift of a few *villani* may not have always involved the acquisition of exclusive jurisdiction over them, but when extensive numbers of men or properties were granted, the new lords would have necessarily acquired jurisdiction as part of the arrangement. Count Roger I of Sicily, for example, recognised that the monks of San Filippo di Fragalà were entitled not only to collect *herbaticum* and *angaria* from their *villani*, but also to judge them and collect fines imposed as penalties. If this could be regarded as an acceptable way of providing for the local government of a

Greek peasantry, it is, nevertheless, only an early example of what is also found later when Roger II himself generously conceded as many as eighty of his domain *villani* at Mesagne to the nuns of Brindisi in 1133. He also defined their profit first: 140 *michalati*, 100 *milarenses*, a quarter of the olive crop and the *musti* from the vines, with *herbaticum* on their lands and pannage from grazing flocks. But the nuns also got in perpetuity the jurisdiction (*lex* and *placia*) of these men and their descendants as, the document notes, they held it over their other men and *villani*. The implication of this is that lordship as such involved jurisdiction. In the thirteenth century, this was glossed to mean that the nuns had the right to appoint officials at Mesagne, who could settle the civil disputes in personalty and realty of the convent's men. Although the men were in lordship, they were still entitled to their own law, and were expected to have legal disputes about their own property. In a sense, where communities existed, they proved a match for lordship itself. Kings could only transfer communities from one lord to another.

Effective lordship, as far as individuals were concerned, did not necessarily await formal concession on the part of the public authorities, for men and families could themselves withdraw from their original communities and seek protection from lords of their own choosing who were strong enough to guarantee it. In such cases, however, the local community itself would certainly attempt to counter the influence of lordship, since any diminution of its own numbers or resources risked putting a greater burden on the rest of the community. This concern of rural life may be illustrated by a dispute of 1159 involving Scafati, a priory belonging to Monte Cassino. The prior thought it wicked of men in Lauro to tell the local public official, the catapan, that about half-a-dozen men there did not belong to the priory, since the catapan had promptly concluded that if they were not in lordship they must be liable for public duties, namely twelve *tari* in *adjutorium* and the performance of *angaria*, as other 'public men' did. When the men duly complained to the catapan's deputy (*vicecomes*) that neither their fathers nor their grandfathers had done this, he was quite unimpressed, and distrained on their oxen to induce them to submit. This forced them to seek the prior's intervention. He persuaded the catapan to come to Lauro where the status of the reluctant taxpayers was examined in the local court of knights, judges and elders (*veteres homines*). When a local chaplain repeated the testimony given by his own father in a previous enquiry made by the lord of Lauro, it became clear how lordship had been established. The family's grandfather had been brought up in the priory and the monks had found him a wife and made him a freeman of the monastery. In the next generation, the family suffered such insults from the knights and men of Lauro that they had sought the protection of the lady Sarracena, widow of the late lord of Lauro, then married to her son's guardian, and paid ten *tari* to be under her protection (*defensa*), to keep themselves and their animals safe from everyone, including the *vicecomes*. The catapan bowed to this evidence. By securing exemption from their public obligations, the men of the family had to acknowledge in return that they were subject to the prior's justice, owed him gifts, services to help with his animals, work on his water-supply and a contribution (*adjutorium*) from their legumes (*legumina*) and flour.

The development of lordship in the twelfth-century kingdom cannot altogether be explained in terms of seigneurial initiative or royal favours. It responded also to the willingness and ability of peasant cultivators to seek better conditions for themselves, if only by migration from one place to another. Lords were actually competing against one another, as well as against the public authority, that is the king himself, in order to obtain tenants whom they could only keep by blocking any public claim for services. This points to a general shortage of peasant cultivators in the kingdom. Various devices for dealing with this problem on any proper-ties held in lordship were tried. Some churches were able to obtain privileges which ran counter to general custom. Duke Roger of Apulia, for example, allowed the monks of La Cava in 1110 to claim as *servi* of the monastery all the offspring of both *servi* and *ancillae* who married freely. There was no legal or customary barrier to 'mixed' marriages as such, and it would have frustrated the purpose of the privilege if it had actually inhibited mixed marriages thereafter. But the privilege proves that in Campania, custom had normally treated the children of *servi* in mixed marriages as free. What La Cava required was the power to retain all the descendants of its own tenants in subjection, notwithstanding local custom.

How successfully lords enforced such privileges is arguable. William II and Frederick II both believed that many of their own peasants eluded their supervision and found more congenial lords. Attempts to control flight from settlements included the listing of tenants by name, but named peasants also fled elsewhere. Some attempt to prevent lords taking on any peasants who presented themselves seems to be involved in the requirement that lords obtain a formal privilege from the public authorities before they could accept new settlers on their estates. Privileges of *affidatura* are known before the monarchy and do not therefore seem to be Norman innovations. Local variations about the terms agreed were standard. William II in 1172 granted *affidatura* as a favour to the bishop of Giovinazzo, but only within the framework set by local custom, restricting the right to twenty-five men. The terms offered by the abbot of Conversano were set out in 1172 when he got permission, not this time from the king, but from his local count, to adopt two *coloni* from the Terra d'Otranto to bring his property at Castellana back into profitable cultivation. The terms cover the use of water, the sowing of corn and the planting of vines. If the *affidati* had no oxen, they were to be offered the use of the monks' own for eight *provensini* per annum; if they had their own oxen, they were liable only to pay the tithes due. Those who made wills were to leave a quarter of their property to the monastery; if they died intestate, the monastery would take their property anyway. If women married outside the estate, the monastery was entitled to a fine of one *solidus*; priests would owe nothing except one pound of wax a year. Castellana had its own judge and bailiff, so that however shaky, the community had its own legal identity and unique customs. Although *affidati* entered into a personal dependence on the lords, they must have been in a position to haggle about terms. Some men were certainly drawn from other parts of the kingdom; some brought their own plough-beasts; such men were therefore free in their native districts to move away, or at least could actually abscond from disagreeable lordship; others could well have been independent cultivators with inadequate holdings, eager to find better conditions for themselves and their plough-beasts. The weakness of a lordship anxious to get fresh colonists encouraged bargaining for whatever terms could be arranged.

Cultivators of whatever social rank were important assets to lords, and they drew no important distinctions which would place false emphasis on social rank. When the abbot of Cassino made concessions in 1162 to encourage men to return to the abandoned *casale* of *Castellione* near Troia, he expected to be able to coax knights by offering to relax all the dues for one year, except the tithes on fields, vines, gardens, olives, pigs, flocks, lambs, wool and cheese; lesser men were not however subject to notably worse terms, though they paid two extra customary offerings (*salutationes*) a year, at Christmas and Easter, as proof of their subject status. The comparative unimportance of social barriers in the kingdom is suggested by a document from Cosenza of 1180 where a knight (*miles*) stands as guarantor (*fideiussor*) for a *nativus* who had negotiated an exchange of lands with the monks of Corazzo. It must also be recognised that *villani* would certainly be still expected to contribute as members, to the military protection of their local communities. Many twelfth-century knights were probably drawn from the ranks of the *villani*. Even under the monarchy, the *Catalogus Baronum* notes that the service due at Sicignano and Muro Lucano by its lord was performed by *villani*, though this was by mid-century an exceptional arrangement.

Nevertheless, the fact that *villani* could do military service is a useful reminder that there could not as yet be a deep social divide between *villani* and others throughout the twelfth-century kingdom.

The strength of the peasantry in the twelfth century is also suggested by the story of how the enslaved peasantry of Santo Stefano de Bosco improved their position. Abbot William was prepared to alleviate the servitude of his perpetual villeins by precise definition of their obligations. On the strength of this, the *villani* by the 1220s were able to appeal to Frederick II against attempts by Abbot Roger to impose unjust burdens on them, and hoped to make use of this royal intervention to limit lordship still further. In the course of the ensuing litigation, the story was set down of how their ancestors had been condemned to death by Count Roger I for their part in a conspiracy on his life at Capua, and had their sentence commuted to perpetual villeinage through the intervention of St Bruno, founder of the original convent on the site. These Greeks had all originally been free; some were artisans, others sailors. If the memory of their families' origins played some part in shaping their subsequent aspirations to recover status, it cannot explain the attitudes of either Abbot William or King Frederick which reveal how well-disposed these lords were to the peasants.

Written evidence about the peasantry's conditions of work by its nature defines and limits obligations, so that even though such documents emanated from lordship, they must have benefited the workforce. There is no way of knowing anything at all about perpetual villeins whose terms of service remained undefined. Even the extent of perpetual villeinage in the kingdom is unknowable. The case of San Stefano del Bosco seems to suggest that it was sufficiently unusual to require explanation as punishment for the atrocious crime of treason. What does seem to emerge from the little information available about working conditions on seigneurial estates, is that all of them comprised tenantry with differing kinds of obligation. The peasantry was far from uniform. Enquiries in 1249 into the value of *casalia* revealed at Santa Lucia in Sicily that, of 118 families, sixty-eight had no oxen and did two days' service a year, one at sowing and one at harvest. The fifty with oxen also did two days' service a year, one for ploughing and the other for sowing, paid corn dues (*terraticum*) on their own cultivated lands, ploughed the lord's demesne (*cultura*) and contributed to the mill payments. The oxen-less peasantry had no heavier service burden and must have been mainly occupied in the vineyards. On the estate of Sinagra, about twenty miles away however, the wine and corn were much less valuable. There were sixty-one families of *villani*, only ten with oxen. The others owed *angaria* and *charissia* for sowing, hoeing, garnering and tending the vineyards. There were also twelve townsmen (*burgenses*) here, who paid a collective levy (*assise*) and owed sixty-six days' work a year in the vineyards. Twenty-eight *angarii* were more heavily burdened: 207 days' sowing, hoeing and other jobs were required, as well as twenty-eight working days in harvest time. The tenantry here did heavier services than those at Santa Lucia; they paid dues in cash as well as hens and eggs and other renders in kind. These tenants were of different categories, but some *villani* had oxen, others not; some were *burgenses*, some *angarii*. Between the two estates there is a marked discrepancy in the proportion of men with oxen. The prosperity of the whole kingdom was closely related to the possibility of growing good grain, and this made villeins with their own oxen fundamental to the kingdom's well-being. The categories specified (*villani, burgenses, angarii*) were all traditional, though the *burgenses* were presumably descendants of the *oppidani* who had entered Sicily only in the wake of the Normans. Their status was expressed by the payment of a modest tax. However, their daytime work at Sinagra was more burdensome than that of the oxen-less *villani* at Santa Lucia. The record makes it clear that while only about a quarter of the families at Sinagra were called *angarii*, more than twice as many *villani* there without oxen also did *angaria* and *charissia*. The main difference seems to be not so much in the number of days service owed, but in the liability of the *angarii* to do other services where required. Given the great variations from one estate to another, revealed in these examples, it is obviously unwise to try and generalise about the working conditions of all the peasantry in the kingdom.

To be *angarius* by the thirteenth century seems to have been regarded as the lowest of all social states. Frederick II decreed that no *vilis villanus* or *angarius* could become a judge, though it is interesting that he considered it might otherwise happen. (In fact, Frederick II had an imperial justiciar in Sicily called William Villanus, which suggests his humble origin, if not his personal status.) *Angarii* were liable for performing personal services at their own expense, such as providing horses or carting when required. The details of their obligations are never given, and the social standing of those liable cannot be described. They could not all have been of the same legal status, since Richard fitz Richard, baron of Flumeri, says explicitly in his grant of 1136 to the monks of Monte Vergine that any *angarius* of his, serf or free (*servus sive liber*), might offer himself to the monastery, presumably to discharge whatever obligations he was under to the monks instead of to the baron. Originally these services had all been owed to the public authority, and may in consequence have seemed no more demeaning than paying other dues or taxes, though it seems likely that the services expected of free *angarii* differed from those expected of serfs. There are no acts imposing new burdens, so *angarii* presumably became rarer, as individuals were granted away out of the public service and whole categories of persons, such as priests, were exempted from such burdens.

At the very lowest level of southern society were the slaves, who occur in the documents mainly as domestics. Their numbers are incalculable. It was not acceptable to make slaves of Christians. All slaves were therefore acquired by purchase from abroad, and one of the chief sources of supply in the kingdom must have been through acts of piracy. Before the Norman conquests, Muslims and Jews had kept slaves, probably also as domestics, and though they were later forbidden to keep Christian slaves, this did not prevent them from continuing to purchase blacks or other pagans from North Africa. Some slaves may have been employed in market gardens around Palermo. The king himself kept Muslim slaves, perhaps generally acquired from abroad rather than from Muslims in Sicily. Some of these rose to positions of responsibility, not only in his household, but inevitably in his government too, such as the *gaitus* Peter, only emancipated by William I's testament. This pious act has parallels in some surviving private documents, where the testator liberates his personal slaves. In those for Bari, a formal ceremony in church gave publicity to the fact of manumission. In a dispute about one man's legal status, witnesses testified that his mother was Bulgarian and Christian, which meant he could not be a slave, since it was only lawful to take slaves born of 'Slav' or pagan stock. Even if such slaves received baptism, this was not itself apparently sufficient to secure their freedom, though manumission at the death of the owner may have been considered normal. A woman left her *servus* to a priest on condition that after five years' service day and night (*die et noctu*), he should be formally manumitted (if he had not fled in the meantime). As isolated individuals, employed as servants, the lot of a slave may in practice have been no worse than that of other domestics. A widow of Amalfi discharged a debt of four gold *tari* in 1090 by assigning her daughter to a man and his wife to serve them all their life, day and night. Although the mother stipulated that her daughter should be well treated and provided with food, clothes and shoes according to their ability, she also foresaw that her daughter might abscond, since it was agreed that the master would have the right to recover her, even if she ran home. However, in compensation, when the master died, the girl was to receive eight *tari* and a trousseau to equip her for marriage.

Some female slaves were certainly concubines, in practice if not by intention, who bore their masters children. Some marriage contracts obliged husbands to drive any *ancilla* from their house before the marriage was completed, which even as a legal formula makes its point. Wills often made provision for such women and their children. The monks of Monte Vergine received a legacy in 1198 on condition that they allowed their benefactor's natural children by his *serva Rocca* to hold property at a fixed rent of two *tari* per annum. In wills which mention slaves, the benefactor shows consideration and care for individuals who had been of service.

Although a Messina charter refers to the abuse of royal officials forcing men to buy slaves, there is no other evidence of how slaves might be acquired. Here the most likely explanation of the reference is the attempt to secure an immediate return on captives taken in piratical raids abroad. The private sale of an *ancilla* and her baby daughter by a Calabrian Greek at Bari in 1121, insists that she was slave-born (*ex genere sclavorum*), and as usual in such cases, her child became a slave like her mother. These two changed owners in 1121 for nearly one gold *uncia*. In another instance, a Slav woman was sold for three and a half gold *unciae*, in Barletta. The evidence for slavery in the kingdom is strongest for Apulia and Sicily, where the tradition of keeping slaves had probably still flourished under the Greeks and Muslims. Wealthy Lombards in other parts of the South may also have been able to acquire slaves for their households, but it seems very unlikely that the majority of the population of small peasants and craftsmen did so. Had slaves been numerous, they would surely have been mentioned more often incidentally in the varied materials available, even if they had not been able to leave records of their own. To be a slave was a very miserable but unusual condition which followed some calamity: war, crime or bankruptcy. In the kingdom, the expectation was that the king's men were free. Though they lived according to their own laws, they expected the king to defend them from oppression, even that of their lords, the king's own vassals.

PART III

THE MONARCHY

7

THE KINGS IN THEIR KINGDOM

Twelfth-century European kings on their accession normally entered into an acknowledged kingly role; Roger II was different in that he had to define and make his own way. The idea of the king who sets out to shape the destinies of his subjects has appealed to historians since the Enlightenment made royal innovators attractive. It is, however, unlikely that Roger II either appreciated his opportunity or gloried in his powers of innovation. If anything, he preferred to play down novelties and win respect by claiming ancient precedents for his monarchy. To take root, the monarchy needed to establish itself by disturbing existing authorities as little as possible, dealing with avowed enemies, but not provoking new ones. The very title assumed by Roger and his successors, 'King of Sicily, of the duchy of Apulia and of the principality of Capua', signalled that older entities had been united by the monarchy, not submerged.

In Roger's lifetime, his sons were assigned the titles of the former mainland rulers and discharged the responsibilities that went with them. The oldest of them, also Roger, was made duke of Apulia. He issued documents, held courts, received the submission of Naples in 1139 and waged war in the 1140s. Though he died before his father in 1149, he left a (bastard) son, Tancred, who did eventually become king. By 1149, the only one of Roger II's sons still alive was William. He in turn became duke of Apulia. The idea that the duchy was the 'apanage' of the king's heir was maintained throughout the rest of the century. William I granted the duchy to his eldest son (also Roger), and on his death to the next son, William (later king). When Tancred became king, he made his heir (Roger) duke of Apulia, and married him to a princess from Constantinople. These later dukes were promoted as children, and signs of their political activities are wanting, but even if titles were granted only as a sop to local sentiment, this would be worth noting. In the parallel case of the principality of Capua, the autonomous tradition was initially maintained under the monarchy by the existing prince, Robert II. After Roger II broke with Robert, Roger's sons, first Anfusus, then William, became princes at a time when the distinctiveness of the principality could not be ignored. In the disturbances of 1155–6, Robert II was still remembered; he was recalled and recognised again as prince for a time in some places. Later, William I made his younger son, Henry, prince of Capua. Only when he died in 1172, forty years after the kingdom was founded, did it become necessary for the royal government to assume direct rule of the principality. The sense that it might still be managed separately did not, however, disappear immediately. In 1191, the men of Gaeta looked forward to the possibility that another prince with local powers would be appointed.

The princely title of Bohemond was also at first retained by Roger II for his son Tancred at Taranto. It must have lapsed mainly because kings did not have enough sons to go round. Interestingly enough, William I is said to have revoked Roger II's testamentary concession of the principality to his own bastard son, Simon, because it was unseemly: the great titles were reserved for sons fully royal. From the reign of William I, because William's own sons were not of age, the king's government must anyway have taken over effective control of the duchy of Apulia and the principalities in a way not open to Roger II. This did not necessarily involve changes of substance, for it must have been assumed that royal princes nominated to these offices would live to an age when they could take on the responsibilities for themselves. Had they done so, the kingdom could have remained as composite in structure as twelfth-century France, or the dominions of Henry II of England. The future of the kingdom would have then depended on the forcefulness of the kings keeping their relations in order rather than on any centralised structure of government.

The Norman kings, Roger II, William I and William II, have, nevertheless, acquired a modern reputation for ruling an authoritative centralised state, unique in western Europe for its forward-looking bureaucratic organisation and its sense of purpose. Attempts to scale down this estimate of the kingdom's modernity have not carried much conviction in Italy. There is admittedly rather little evidence about how the monarchy actually functioned, so differences of opinion about it are difficult to settle conclusively. Yet it is surely safer to assume that the monarchy was in most respects similar in character to those of contemporary, neighbouring states, unless very persuasive evidence of its precocity can be advanced. Moreover, the real difficulties of creating the kingdom and getting it accepted must not be minimised. Roger II had to start from scratch. Unlike Henry I of England, he did not have behind him a tradition of monarchical government and an administrative structure that brought the local authorities of shire and hundred into contact with the royal will. Roger II had to improvise his government even while also more or less constantly at war. Many of his contemporaries clearly considered that this dominion depended on his will rather than on political structure, and though they were mistaken in thinking that the kingdom would crumble away on his death, it seems to have been saved mainly by the military competence of William I, not by new habits of respect or the effectiveness of bureaucratic management. It was not necessarily a disadvantage in the long term for the survival of Roger II's form of government that it had been created at short notice, without any pre-existing foundation, but at the very least, for it to become second nature to the kingdom's inhabitants would take time. How long would be necessary? Roger's own reign as king of twenty-three years seems too little, but even the next thirty-five years up to the death of William II is a brief enough period for the consolidation of any monarchy, still less one supposedly constructed on innovatory lines. Finally, if this type of monarchy expected the ruler to exercise so much authority, it is highly singular that of these three kings, only Roger II has left evidence of his own forceful character. Although William I was a capable soldier, the principal historical record of the reign claims that he preferred when possible to leave government to others. The Ferraria chronicler refers to him in more personal terms: his frightening black beard and his formidable physical strength. He could, for example, bend a couple of horseshoes with his bare hands, and he was nicknamed 'strong-arm' by his father because on one occasion he was able on his own to bear the weight of a laden pack-horse which had slipped from a dilapidated bridge. This unexpected glimpse of William I shows that although he created a strong impression on his subjects, it was as a person rather than as a ruler. After Maio's death in 1160 he did not come into the limelight: the last years of his reign are almost a complete blank. William II is an even more shadowy figure. He left no reputation as a soldier, nor even as a diplomat. The surviving records make it difficult to form any clear idea either of his personality, or of the nature of his contribution to government.

Modern historians of the twelfth century are disinclined to believe too much of what chroniclers report unless their hearsay can be confirmed by reference to official documents. The twelfth century was a period when governments made ever more extensive use of writing for expediting business. The English royal government kept annual account rolls from the second or third decade of the century and, by 1200, also kept regular 'memoranda' rolls for separate kinds of official business. The records of papal decisions on controversial points of law were being collected by jurists from mid-century. By the end of the century, the papacy had compiled a register of its rights to land and dues (the *Liber Censuum*), and under Innocent III (1198–1216) itself regularly maintained file-copies of outgoing correspondence. For preserving bulky government records it was desirable to have a fixed seat of government, and it is generally agreed that the kings of Sicily, who kept residence in the royal palace at Palermo, were well placed to accumulate and preserve a government archive. There are, however, no surviving records of any regular government business, financial, judicial or executive. There are certainly allusions to royal records, such as books of estate boundaries and lists of serfs on royal and baronial holdings. The government therefore compiled registers for its use. One such record of military obligations (the *Catalogus Baronum*) was somehow preserved until modern times. It shows signs of revision within twenty years of its original composition. However, the revision was not completed, and the fact that even so it was thought useful enough to be re-copied in this form nearly a century later in Manfred's reign surely rules out the likelihood of any subsequent attempt to bring its information up to date. At the most, in the mid-thirteenth century, its information was supplemented with the results of an enquiry of *c.* 1175 into knights at Arce, Sora and Aquino. There is thus no proof at all that officials regularly kept their records up to date. In itself this may not prove very much, but it is at least necessary to bear in mind when trying to establish the nature of the kingdom's government in the twelfth century.

Without a sequence of government records to use or infer from, historians have to make do with the surviving royal *acta*, mostly, as is normal for such records throughout western Europe, preserved in ecclesiastical archives. A scholarly edition of these *acta* is only now in the process of being published. Under Roger II, it has been estimated that at least three quarters of all the documents issued by the royal chancery were written in Greek. Thereafter there was a dramatic decline in their number. By 1200, Greek was no longer even in use as an official language of the chancery. Most of the Greek documents known were granted to the Greek monasteries of the kingdom. More will become known when the archives of Messina, transported to Spain in the seventeenth century and recently rediscovered in Seville, become available generally for study. Proper assessment of the importance of the official Greek elements in the kingdom will have to be deferred until the publication of all the relevant documents in modern editions. At the moment, only fifty Greek texts are known, though there are thirty-nine others surviving in Latin translations made at various times since the twelfth century. From all these, only sixteen are originals, from which reliable criteria for proving authenticity have to be derived. Arguments dependent on documents of Greek provenance need therefore to be treated with care, certainly more than some historians have shown.

A critical edition of eighty texts of Roger's Latin *acta* was published in 1987. Only about fifty of these have come down to us without unofficial amendment. Quite apart from the problems presented by interpolations in these texts, there is the matter of their very small number. When all the *acta* of the Norman kings are eventually published there will still be only about 400 available for the study of royal action in government before 1189. (In England, for nineteen troubled years of Stephen's reign, there are over 700 surviving texts from Stephen himself to be read alongside an impressive body of chronicles; even so, interpretation of his reign remains controversial.) It is a singularly daunting task therefore to write the history of these three southern Italian reigns from the meagre store of their documents. This may seem a mere matter of bad luck: Professor Brühl, who has edited Roger's Latin documents, comments that the survival rate for Roger II's documents is worse than for the ninth-century emperor Louis the Pious. But his own estimates of how many documents Roger II's government ever issued (925 Latin privileges in twenty-seven years, 1127–53) would still only make an average of thirty-four a year. (This is less than the *survival* rate of charters for King Henry I of England.) From this it seems safe to conclude that the issue of written documents under royal authority must be a highly misleading way to measure the activities of royal government. The documents cannot be dispensed with, but to interpret them as evidence of their own day they have to be set in a context.

The historical context of the monarchy was the fragmentation of authority in the South and a mixed cultural tradition. Although official documents were issued in both Greek and Arabic, relatively speaking they declined in importance over the twelfth century, whereas Latin increasingly came to be the principal language of government. This means that the kings cannot have deliberately shaped their government along the lines of the government of Sicily before 1127, when Greek- and Arabic-speakers formed the majority of the population. Whether the late preponderance of the Latin element was due to the influence of procedures adapted from the mainland traditions of the kingdom, or to the employment of northerners like Robert of Selby and Richard Palmer, or to the kingdom's susceptibility to the general currents of western European practice, cannot be categorically settled. But it certainly makes it less likely that the kingdom derived more than residual benefit from its Greek and Arabic inheritance. In other words, the inspiration of its government was not Greek, but western. If anything was borrowed from Constantinople, it was its Roman core, not its Byzantine shell.

Professor Ménager is the most distinguished scholar to advance a view of the kingdom's political structure that stresses its French and feudal elements. This interpretation, though regarded as 'novel', actually stresses the conventional wisdom giving the Normans themselves credit for the political acumen found in both the Sicilian and the English monarchies, and even traces some of its features back to the Norman duchy. For all their virtues, the Lombards, Greeks and Muslims had not succeeded in creating a single kingdom in the region. It was the Normans who fashioned the blocks from which the monarchy was built. Roger II's contribution to the enterprise confirmed how Norman it was. In one document he is represented as referring to those who had despoiled a monastery of property as *nostri Normanni*. Roger II himself treated Greeks as his principal enemies and forced Muslims in North Africa to recognise his lordship: he was no friend to these peoples, even if he wrote his name in Greek. His closest 'Greek' adviser was from Antioch, the Norman principality which itself resisted imperial claims.

To insist on Norman qualities does not force the Sicilian kingdom into the same mould as Normandy or England: there is no one Norman mould. It does mean that comparisons with these other states can be considered legitimate, which would not be the case if Roger II's monarchy were modelled exclusively on Constantinople, or considered a unique prototype of the modern state.

Like other western kings, Roger II and his successors came to the royal office by a ceremony of coronation. Roger II insisted on obtaining for the archbishop of Palermo, where his royal state was kept, a grant from the pope of the pallium, which authorised him to crown kings. Not only did he obtain this for himself in 1130; he also secured from Eugenius III the pallium for Archbishop Hugh before having his last surviving son, William, crowned co-king with him in 1151. This procedure he plainly adopted from the custom long-observed in France, and also appreciated in England in the mid-twelfth century, of providing for the royal succession. John of Salisbury reports that on this occasion in 1151, Roger required William to swear an oath to do his duty as king, that is, to observe peace and justice, show honour to the church, and respect his father as his lord all his life. This underlines how conventional Roger's kingship was, even though John chose to represent Roger's behaviour as an intolerable defiance of his papal overlord.

The precise form of the coronation in the kingdom has been disputed. A Cassino manuscript of *c.* 1200, which gives a form of ceremony ultimately derived from a German model, also shows variations apparently designed to adapt it for Roger II's kingdom. If Roger accepted a coronation ritual deeply rooted in the western tradition, this itself indicates where he felt his affinities to lie. The coronation ceremony comprised several different parts. A question was put to the king:'Do you wish to hold to the holy faith, to be the defender of the church, to rule the kingdom justly?'; another to the people (*populum*): 'Do you wish to submit yourselves to this prince and obey his commands?' After this came the anointing of the king's hands, head, breast and both shoulders; the girding of the king with the sword, as the means of establishing equity and opposing iniquity, helping widows and orphans; then the vesting of the king with *armillas*, *pallium* and ring; the sceptre was put in his right hand and the orb (*regnum*) in his left hand; the crown was placed on his head by the presiding archbishop. At the end of the coronation mass, the great men, duke, prince, counts and magnates kissed the king's feet as he sat on his throne. When the ceremony was over, the occasion was concluded with a great feast in the royal palace. The order of the parts and the phrasing of the questions may sometimes be uncertain, but the contrived interaction of the king with the clergy, the people and the magnates was designed to emphasise that the king received his royal commission from God, and that there were clear duties and obligations that he took up; in return for what he undertook to do for them, his people acknowledged him as their ruler.

Some royal vestments of this period have remarkably enough been preserved. There are also surviving images of royalty. From these it appears that the royal crown (*diadema*) had lateral pendants studded with pearls and gems and was similar in form to those worn by the Lombard princes (as shown on their coins). Since this type is ultimately derived from the style of a Byzantine imperial crown in use as far back as the sixth century, the Sicilian kings' use of this diadem has been interpreted as evidence of their own imperial aspirations. This isolates one element of the coronation symbolism and gives it a false emphasis. The form of the crown itself is less important than the ceremony in which it was conferred.

The coronation promises are often taken by historians of the twelfth century as formal expressions of contemporary expectations of good kingship. Professor Ménager had therefore good reason to invoke them in the case of the Norman kingdom. He also noted that, according to Amatus of Monte Cassino, Guiscard (who was not crowned king) had already consoled the helpless, judged justly but mercifully, and honoured holy church. He may therefore be considered, *ante rem*, the very embodiment of royal virtue as required by the coronation ceremony. Guiscard's brother, Roger I of Sicily, and his son, Duke Roger of Apulia, left comparable reputations for discharging these princely duties. In this sense, royal coronation stressed the conventional virtues of rulership. Documents connected with Roger II regularly insist on the king's concern to defend the church, succour the weak, guarantee peace and justice for his people and eradicate evil customs, restoring all things to their best state (*cuncta in meliorem statum reducere*). The coronation ceremony only endorsed established uses, and monarchy did not create totally new expectations in either king or people. The major difference was that Roger did not allow anyone in the kingdom to evade obligations to his monarchy. Sovereignty and majesty became uniquely 'royal'. A document of December 1129 already threatened those who offended Roger II's *majestas* with the heavy fine of 300 gold pounds. However, the price to be paid for such an offence, like the term *majestas* itself, must have been decided by the royal notary not the king, for a later notary dropped all reference to majesty when warning those who dared violate royal privileges and thought twenty gold pounds sufficient penalty. After the early 1140s, all references to money penalties for defying the royal orders were dropped from royal documents. By the 1140s, Roger II's majesty had been thoroughly vindicated. Buying off royal ire had not so much become cheaper, as beyond price.

Roger had dealt mercilessly with the noble rebels of the 1130s because his own political future was at stake, but this did not make him in principle hostile to the baronage or incline him politically to despotism. Some of his authentic documents show him surrounded by his barons, on several occasions apparently completing public business while engaged in that favourite Norman sport – hunting, where not only did his great men share in the pleasure, but suitors could also expect to find the king in good humour. Although William I did not apparently ever enjoy good relations with his barons, after his death, Queen Margaret certainly aimed at reconciliation with estranged nobles and did not seek to persist in any hostility. When William II began his personal rule, there is no reason to believe that he considered ferocity to them indispensable. This was not necessarily a sign of weakness; it points to the nature of the southern monarchy. Unlike Henry II, who had many more interests than the English kingdom, William II was kept fully occupied as king at home, where he did not need to aim at more than retaining general respect of his rule. For the most part, his kingdom ran itself. The king's political role was to retain the loyalty and attention of the great men, and make use of their talents. The king's subjects in general expected him to see that good old customs were observed; they had not consented to monarchy in order to get government cast in a new form. It was the kings, not the people, who got the kingship established, and kept it going, but to last it had to fit in with the people's expectations.

THE KING AS SOURCE OF PEACE, JUSTICE AND LAW

Any development in contemporary ideas about royal authority and how defiance of it should be punished can only be illustrated in a very casual way. To make good this deficiency, Professor Delogu analysed the opening *arenga* of royal documents and argued, from the differences found in them under Roger II, William I and William II, that a quite original conception of royalty can be seen developing in Sicily. Under Roger II, it seems as though the monarchy began modestly to defend the exercise of royal power in terms of its duty to protect the church and preserve justice (as in the coronation procedure). Under William II, the monarchy is described as a virtue in itself, the summit of generosity and clemency. Delogu showed, however, that the grand phrases of William II's monarchy coincide with the dominance in government of the king's former grammar teacher, Walter, archbishop of Palermo, and do not survive his death. If the explanation for the rhetoric of monarchy lies with the secretariat rather than with the government, it cannot have had much substance. This is an important conclusion because many scholars who have been impressed by some equally grandiloquent passages from the royal 'assizes' attached significance to them simply because they supposed 'laws' carried more weight than charters. In both cases, however, the forceful language may rather be designed to create an impression of authoritativeness. The 'assizes' which are most elaborate are also profuse in exhortations to show mercy.

It is regrettable that there is so little hard evidence about how the government actually enforced its will to set against such documents. What appears to be the only example of how breaking the peace was dealt with is recorded for 1180 when the lords of Montemiglio were accused of various acts of violence *contra pacem domini regis* and cited before the master-justiciar, Tancred of Lecce. This certainly induced them to make their peace quickly with the abbot of Monte Cassino, and spared them further trouble. Would Henry II in England have tolerated an administration of justice that winked at the offence to the king, just because the injured party allowed himself to be bought off? But royal justice in the southern kingdom was only fifty years old in 1180, whereas Henry II operated in a tradition of government which had punished treason against the king with death since the time of Alfred.

Roger's assumption of the responsibility to keep the peace throughout his lands had been proclaimed, even before he became king, at his meeting with the great men at Melfi in September 1129. All the counts, bishops and abbots of Calabria, Apulia, Salentino, Lucania and Campania were present, and all the *optimates* had to give up warfare against one another and swear henceforth to see that the peace was kept; they would not protect men who practised theft and robbery, but would bring them to justice, apparently in courts set up by Roger, to whom they swore loyalty and obedience. Telese is unfortunately not more specific about how Roger's courts functioned, though he is ecstatic about the continuous peace Roger obtained by this measure, and about the fear he inspired in evil-doers. It came as no surprise to him that God had allowed Roger to subjugate all these lands to such good effect. The abbot does show, however, that peace was a particular blessing for ecclesiastical persons and their property – archbishops, bishops, abbots, monks, clergy, ploughmen, villeins and all the native peoples of Roger's lands, as well as for pilgrims, travellers and merchants. These were the 'unarmed' men for whose protection the Truce of God had been originally designed, and the abbot clearly saw Roger's edict at Melfi as a proclamation in the tradition of the 'Peace of God'. How much Roger himself knew of earlier attempts to keep the peace is unknown. The original inspiration for the peace movements had been ecclesiastical. After Guiscard's death, when popes moved freely in the South, the Truce of God had been intermittently proclaimed, as by Urban II at a council in Melfi (1089), and Paschal II, for three years, at Troia (1115). Roger's peace was permanent and not dependent on ecclesiastical censures, but on the judgements of his own courts. Telese is convinced of Roger's effectiveness, and the Salerno chronicler, noting several events of the years between 1139 and 1148, confirms that Roger established perfect tranquillity in his kingdom, appointing *camerarii* and *justitiarii* in all his land to keep the peace (*pro conservanda pace*). The chronicler again did not enlarge on how these officials worked, but later evidence suggests that since *camerarii* tended to see to the administration of the civil law, criminal cases fell to the justiciars. In the twelfth century, however, some of the great men, if not all, exercised the powers of justiciars in their own lands (it was Frederick II who forbade this), and it is therefore possible that when in 1129 Roger II secured oaths from his magnates for the keeping of the peace, he intended to make them part of the enforcement procedures. A passage inserted later into the Salerno chronicle, but drawing upon authentic information, says that the counts swore at Melfi not to allow or connive at theft and brigandage in their lands, which would seem to have left them with some real responsibility for keeping the peace in their own lordships. If the judicial machinery used cannot be described better than this, there can, however, be no argument about the result. Rebellion apart, the kingdom was a land at peace. The threat of judicial action on a charge of breaking the king's peace was sufficient to frighten off men of violence.

The ordinary business of the lawcourts in the kingdom is better documented, particularly for disputes about property, for which legal judgements became important evidence of title. On the mainland, when Roger II became duke, he stepped immediately into the shoes of his predecessor at Salerno, Duke William. William's reign of eighteen years has not been studied, but at least one document of 1124 shows him active in judicial matters. In a dispute between the abbey of Elce and the lord of Bisaccia, the abbot had complained to the duke of injustice. After listening to the abbot and inspecting his privileges, William compelled the lord to do justice to the abbot; though the lord professed to do so from fear of God rather than by human compulsion, his own document recognises that the duke's intervention had brought the matter to a head. The earliest example of Roger II's part in justice on the mainland shows him playing a role comparable to William's. The abbot of San Nicola of Troia took advantage of Roger's presence there in November 1129 to sue for the recovery from La Cava of property at *Fabrica* which he claimed his monastery had been given by Robert Guiscard. On inspection, La Cava's privileges turned out to be older still. Roger took advice from the archbishops of Palermo and Salerno, the bishop of Troia, the archbishop-elect of Siponto and others, including three men called the duke's judges. They failed to resolve the matter by law, but sought to reach a compromise. The formulae are typical of many other recorded settlements throughout southern Italy both before and after Roger II became king. Even in Sicily, Roger II often negotiated a settlement rather than pronounced formal judgements, perhaps because cases brought to him were either too complex for simple resolution or concerned persons too eminent in the kingdom to be offended by adverse judgements. In what appears, for example, a very minor problem of disputed ownership over a single Greek *villanus*, the widow of William de Craon and her son were only induced to abandon their claims to the bishop of Agrigento because of Roger's special insistence (*consilio atque . . . precibus*), not by his judgement.

Surviving documents from bishoprics and monasteries show prelates applying to Roger II for justice, because they enjoyed his special protection. The extent to which the clergy accorded the king a role in the settlement of their affairs may be demonstrated by the willingness of the monks of Tremiti to grant a life-lease of property on the mainland to Count Bohemond of Manoppello in order to obtain his help, if by any chance they should ever have any lawsuit (*placitum*) before the king. If he were not able to attend in person, he was bound to send one of his barons; if he were ever to leave the kingdom on royal service, the monks would recover the holding while he was away. These monks sensibly cultivated friends in high places and accepted that they could not dispense with royal justice. The king for his part treated his bishops as his *familiares*, and they returned the compliment by bringing him their problems. The royal court must likewise have provided justice for the barons, though there is only one record of this: the account in the *Liber de Regno* of the trial of the count of Molise. Whatever its importance, there are no indications as to how regularly the king's court met, how it was constituted, and what kind of judicial business it dealt with.

The creation of the monarchy did not involve any fundamental change in Roger's existing judicial administration in Sicily, for Roger II's authority as king did not differ noticeably from what it had been as count over the previous twenty-five years. His new absences on the continent did not make it desirable to appoint a viceregal 'justiciar' to act for him while he was away. Whether suitors were content to await his return or pestered him on the continent with their affairs, there is no way of knowing.

The king was normally resident in Sicily, and Roger II is found presiding in important lawsuits there, but after his death, there is scant notice of any royal part in the doing of justice anywhere. There are only two instances recorded of William I dealing with judicial disputes. Both come from early in his reign and from the mainland, when he held court at Salerno with his counts and magnates (*cum comitibus et magnatibus regni*). In the first, the abbot of Monte Cassino made five distinct charges against Hervey de Bolita, in his capacity as lord of Rocca Guglielma rather than as royal justiciar. Hervey's official standing no doubt made it imperative for the abbot to take his case to the highest authority. The king's part in the proceedings was confined to ordering that the boundaries of an estate, defined by his father's order to his officials, should be respected, in spite of Hervey's objections, until such times as Hervey had proved in court that they were unjust and unreasonable. Otherwise the pleas and counter-pleas were assessed by the *curia*, which pronounced on the correct procedure or settled points of law in passing. Likewise, in the second, a dispute between the bishop of Melfi and the abbot of Monte Vulture about churches and mills, the legal decisions were taken by the archbishops, bishops-elect and other princes. The king only ratified their verdict and issued a document to provide a permanent record.

Much later in 1178, when two bishops from the mainland (Marsi and Segni) sought resolution at Palermo of their difficulties with Oddo de Celano, another royal justiciar, there is no reference to any meeting of the king and his great men in a court. Instead, it was left to the *familiares*, the archbishop of Palermo, his brother Bartholomew, bishop of Agrigento, and the vice-chancellor, to provide justice, but they did not constitute a formal court. As Roger II had sometimes done in the past, they played the part of honest brokers in bringing the parties to a settlement. The mainland bishops had been advised by their friends to draw the attention of the authorities in Palermo to their problem, probably to put pressure on Oddo to accept a settlement. The king's *curia* itself did not arbitrate. It only set the seal on the *concordia* negotiated by the parties themselves who presented it for authoritative confirmation from the seat of majesty (*dum in solio majestatis suae resideret feliciter*). Four years later, when a new bishop of Marsi went to Palermo with a complaint against Gentilis de Palearia over a monastery in his lands, all he got from the government was a mandate instructing the *magister justiciarius* on the mainland to give judgement. The apparent withdrawal of the king from judicial proceedings, both on the mainland and in Sicily, is most simply explained in William I's case by his apparent dislike of public life. During the minority of William II it would also be understandable if the regent, Queen Margaret, regularly delegated royal responsibilities in such matters. In this way, justice could have slipped inadvertently out of the king's personal charge.

The most revealing example of the great men managing royal interests in justice during William II's minority is provided by the *Liber de Regno*, which describes the trial of Richard, count of Molise. This had some of the characteristics of a political frame-up, and the authorities could even have exaggerated procedural formalities to cloak what might have otherwise seemed like blatant injustice. In its own way, however, the account paints a rather impressive picture of the politically prominent acting together to keep the government on course. Molise was accused of conspiracy against Chancellor Stephen in 1168 by the young Bohemond of Tarsia, a staunch supporter of Stephen. This charge was on the point of being resolved, as normal, by a judicial duel, when another accusation was levied by Robert, count of Caserta. He alleged that Molise had acquired Mandra in Apulia and towns near Troia improperly from the crown. The count defended himself by claiming to have received them

from authorised officials, but one of them, the *camerarius* Turgis, denied
any knowledge of it. This charge was not resolved by a duel, but by
deliberation: all the *proceres* (except the curial *familiares*) were orderd to
retire and reach a verdict. These 'jurymen' were 'peers' of the accused:
five counts (Monopoli, Caserta (the accuser), Avellino, Sangro, Gerace),
the son of the count of Tricarico, together with high-ranking officials –
the master-constable (Roger of Tiron), with Florius de Camerota, Judex
Tarentinus and Abdenago fitz Hannibal *qui magistri erant justiciarii*. They
decided that, although Molise had received Mandra properly enough
before the *gaitus* Peter had fled, he had thereafter continued to hold it
secretly and had not informed the *curia*, so that he had in effect been an
intruder. The count of Monopoli, *vir eloquens*, as chief juryman, judged
that in consequence all Molise's lands should be in mercy. This judgement
was unimpeachable. When Molise complained that the sentence was
unjust, he was immediately accused of offending against the king's majesty
by impugning the judgement of the royal court. This further charge
involved another change in the procedure. It was put to the archbishops
and bishops present and they declared that for this offence, according to
the kingdom's laws (*constitutiones regum Siciliae*), Molise was himself in
mercy in life and limb, as well as his lands. There are many special features
to this trial, including a political element. Nevertheless, at every stage it
obviously proceeded according to well-established judicial norms. The
majesty of the king's court is the ultimate value, and its honour did not
have to be vindicated by the king or a viceroy but by the royal *familiares* –
here all ecclesiastics, who appealed to the kingdom's constitution
(apparently, but not necessarily, in written form).

The passing reference to *magistri justiciarii* reveals the existence of some
'professional' judges; other sources indicate that they were considered
members of 'the great court'. The key word here may be *magistri*,
meaning that they were masters or learned judges attached to the king's
court as professional advisers. These master-justiciars and the great court
do not appear outside Sicily (except incidentally in Calabria), and it is
possible that their learning and competence had some specific relation to
the written law in use amongst the Greeks. At Messina in 1172, when
William II, still under age, was present with his barons (*proceres*), the
archbishop was accused in the king's court by Leo Chelones of
appropriating a field due to him by inheritance. Leo is said to have
previously pursued the archbishop's predecessor in the *magna curia*, and
had obtained there a judgement for the recovery of his property by
reference to the definition of bounds made before a group of Greek and
Latin *proceres*, headed by George of Antioch (that is before 1152). In
1172, Leo wanted this judgement implemented. This issue of civil law

was delegated for judgement to John Burdon, Bartholomew de Piazza and Jodicus Persicus (*megaloi kritai . . . megales kortes*). A few months earlier, John, Bartholomew and Judex Tarentinus (*magistri justiciarii magnae curiae*) are recorded in a Latin private document to have arranged settlement of a family dispute about inheritance, so they did not only function within the royal court. Although in both these cases they acted in threes, there are other instances of individual master-justiciars passing judgements or presiding, alone, as in disputes about boundaries. Some doubts must arise about what precise meaning should be attached to the phrase 'great court'. Does this literally mean the king's own court? Or was it more like a 'high' court with specific functions? A privilege granted to the royal monastery of San Salvatore Messina in 1177 implies that it dealt with matters of a particular kind (*que specialiter ad cohercionem magne regie curie pertinarent*), but gives no details.

There is no reference at all either to the great court, or to master-justiciars until the reign of William I. Rainald de Tusa, only a local justiciar in 1145, was called *magister justiciarius* when he went as royal envoy to Genoa in January 1157, and in 1159 when he held a sworn inquest over boundaries by royal order, and on a mandate issued by Maio he was called *magister justiciarius magnae curiae*. The nature of the surviving evidence makes it difficult to be categoric either about these justiciars, or about the great court itself. Several of the records in which they appear were not themselves official. They could obviously be drawn into legal cases without royal instigation, as though they were known to provide a conciliation service. This seems at variance with what would normally be expected of the king's supreme tribunal. Its normal role in government is perhaps established by a case in which the bishop of Cefalù complained to it because the countess of Golisano had forbidden him to use the pastures or hunt on her lands. The great court then sent instructions to the justiciar Roger Buxell to examine Roger II's charter for Cefalù and see that its terms were properly enforced. Such cases must have been brought to the attention of the great court not so much to secure judgement, as to force distinguished defendants to answer suits. If, however, it was necessary to use the great court for this purpose, local justiciars' tribunals in Sicily cannot have been able to secure attendance of the great men at their general sessions without special summons.

Royal justice on the mainland

A king resident in Sicily would have had few difficulties about exercising his judicial functions in person had he wished to do so; on the mainland

the position was different, and there can have been no general expectation of his doing so regularly. A royal representative was needed. The
preoccupations of the kingdom's leading politicians in Palermo with the
problems of obtaining a commanding role in the management of affairs
in Palermo itself, ruled out any interest they might have had in the
acquisition of such a great office on the mainland. The people of the
mainland were anyway considered unruly and unreliable, no doubt as
much a basic prejudice of the Sicilians against Apulia as a judgement
derived from actual experience of Apulians as the subjects of Roger II
after 1127. Appointments made for the mainland, if they were to be
effective, had to be acceptable there. What was needed was not an
obedient puppet but a dependable viceroy. In the early years of the
monarchy, Roger's sons obviously exercised real authority over military
and judicial matters. After William I became sole king in 1154, the
situation had to change. Gilbert de Balvano, who had commanded
Roger II's army against the emperor Lothar in 1137, seems to have
exercised a supreme military command as master-constable of Apulia
with general powers. He must have been succeeded from early in 1155
by the seneschal Simon, brother-in-law of Maio of Bari, whose
influence over appointments was thus affirmed so early in the new reign.
The *Liber* calls Simon master-captain of Apulia and Terra di Lavoro.
Three years later, a mandate was issued by Stephen *amiratus*, master-
captain of Apulia, presumably Simon's successor. Stephen was Maio's
own brother. These appointments need to be borne in mind when
considering the disaffection of the mainland to Maio's government, but
are difficult to interpret given the paucity of information about how the
office was exercised. There is then no further reference to such officials
until 1171. During this period, royal government on the mainland had
been anyway disrupted by rebellion, and a document from Naples
showing that King William II dated his lordship there only from 1169
indicates that the restoration of the royal administration must have been
slow. By 1171, a new system was in good working order under great
men from the mainland itself. In that year, Robert, count of Caserta,
was described as *magister comestabulus et justitiarius Apuliae et Terrae
Laboris*. The variations in title (master-constable, master-captain, and
master-justiciar) may seem to indicate some earlier irresolution and
confusion, but in practice these men all exercised the military and
judicial functions of the absent king. In 1172, Count Robert had a
colleague, Richard de Say, count of Gravina. Thereafter, two master-
justiciars were in office at the same time in the combined regions of
Apulia and Terra di Lavoro. In 1182, Robert told the monks of Casauria
to apply in matters of justice to himself or to Tancred, count of Lecce,

by that time his colleague, as though either was equally competent. No clear-cut division of responsibility between them, say on a geographical basis, can be detected.

In Calabria, where Roger II never delegated any of his responsibilities to his sons, he may nevertheless have appointed a deputy as early as 1140, when Roger, son of Bono *magnus justitiarius Calabrie et magne curie*, made a gift to the monks of Santo Stefano del Bosco. This presumably indicates some special eminence amongst other Calabrian justiciars, such as those mentioned with territorial titles for the Val de Sinni and Laino in 1140, and for Calabria and Val di Crati in 1150. Another example occurs before 1168: Count Hugh of Catanzaro is described as *magister justitiarius et comestabulus totius Calabriae*. Under William II, therefore, it seems safe to conclude that both the main parts of the mainland recognised officials called master-justiciar drawn from the best families of the kingdom who acted as the king's representatives.

Nothing is known of any of their military activities, except that in this capacity Tancred commanded, with Roger fitz Richard, count of Andria, the forces massed on the north-eastern frontier to oppose the imperial armies under Christian, archbishop of Mainz, in 1176. There are only occasional glimpses of other activities. Stephen, as master-captain, authorized the royal *camerarius* in Salpi to permit the building of an oven there in 1158, and Count Robert of Caserta likewise gave orders to the *camerarius* of the principality of Salerno in 1182, as though he was his normal superior. Some barons accused of breaking the peace in 1180 were cited before the court of Tancred as master-justiciar.

Most of the references to the master-justiciars of the mainland connect them with legal business, mainly in the regions of Apulia and Terra di Lavoro. Robert of Caserta was in office in 1171, and served until his death in 1183. In 1172 he and Richard of Gravina, together with the *camerarius* of Terra di Lavoro, were ordered by the king to ascertain whether some monks of Sora had been endowed by Roger II with the rents of four churches. Richard is not mentioned again as master-justiciar, and was apparently succeeded by the king's cousin, Tancred, who from 1176 also held the combined offices of master-constable and master-justiciar. Robert and Tancred acted jointly in a court at Capua in 1182 on royal instructions brought by the bishop of Marsi, who had difficulties in enforcing his episcopal rights over the abbey of San Bartolomeo di Avezzano, because of the backing given it by Gentilis de Palearia. Given the distinction of the protagonists, the master-justiciars may have thought it advisable to act jointly. Although in 1180 Tancred held court in Aversa at the bishop's palace to settle a dispute over property claimed by the monastery of Santa Sofia in Benevento,

Tancred normally presided in Apulian courts. After Robert's death, Tancred, with his new colleague Roger of Andria, sat at Barletta in another case brought by Santa Sofia. Although the master-justiciars did not divide up their duties geographically, it is true that Tancred seems to have operated at Bari, Barletta or Troia, while Robert of Caserta is found in the west, near Caserta, or at Capua and Aversa. The litigants who came before them both included the greatest subjects of the kingdom: the bishops of Marsi (1182), Teano and Sessa (1171), the abbots of Cassino (1180), La Cava (1171, 1177, 1182), Venosa (1176) Benevento (1180, 1185), Bari (1181) and Troia (1183).

To judge from these records, the courts of the master-justiciars were especially grand occasions, with many prelates and royal barons present, as well as regional justiciars and local judges. In a case heard at Bari in February 1181, the monks of St Nicholas produced a royal mandate addressed to Tancred, written in Palermo in May 1180, instructing him to examine their complaint about disseisin by Geoffrey Gentilis. In this case, the court was required to inform the king of what the enquiry revealed so he could make the final decision. The case turned out to be contentious, for Gentilis was not easily overawed. At first he declined to appear in the master-justiciar's court at all, on the grounds that he had been summoned to Sicily on the king's service. Then it transpired that he was the legal heir of his father-in-law and had been given the *castellum* of Toritto by the king, which he considered adequate justification for the alleged disseisin. The court ordered Gentilis immediately to reseise the monks with the property in dispute and resume the pleadings when he returned from royal service. The monks did not, however, settle the matter to their own satisfaction until 1196.

Another difficult case was finally resolved by the master-justiciars at Barletta in November 1184; it too had been initiated by a royal writ obtained many months earlier in January 1183. The abbot of San Nicola Troia complained to the king when he was at Capua about men from Ascoli who were ploughing land belonging to his monastery and who had beaten and forcibly detained him at Ascoli. Tancred was expected to conduct an investigation together with the *camerarius* of the principality of Salerno. For a long time the latter was unavailable, but when he left on business for Palermo he sent a representative to Apulia so that the abbot's case could proceed. The abbot's claim depended on a grant made by the count of Loritello (who had died in 1182); the men of Ascoli replied that since the count had no rights in their land, his grant could not have included their fields. The first stage of the enquiry required a perambulation of the boundaries of the respective estates. After this, the men of Ascoli were still dissatisfied, and produced documents issued by

Duke William to support their claims. The court then had to decide between two sets of privileges, and came to the conclusion that Troia had deeds of greater authority. This was still not the end of the matter. Both sides nominated fifteen men to swear to their rights. Ascoli accused the Troia group of perjury and challenged them to 'battle'. Because an impasse had been reached and the dispute touched the king, the judicial duel was allowed, and since both the principal witnesses were old and infirm, champions were used. The field was marked out at Barletta; the champions took the oath, and the Ascoli champion was vanquished. The court ordered the abbot to be formally seised of his land, and Tancred's notary recorded the proceedings. The monks of Venosa claimed similar rights over this property as the men of Ascoli. However, at the time they had no abbot and could not plead, though they were allowed to reserve their rights for settlement at some later date.

Just as the *magna curia* in Sicily might order local justiciars to see justice was done, so too the *magistri justiciarii* on the mainland could delegate responsibility for judging suits. Tancred sent a mandate in November 1176 requiring the bishop of Bitonto, the abbot of Monopoli, two royal justiciars, two *camerarii* and several of the king's barons to settle a dispute between the abbot of Venosa and men of *Casavetere* who refused to recognise his seigneurial authority. Tancred's colleague, Roger, count of Andria, was responsible for seeing justice done in another way by instructing the regular court of Avellino to ensure that two brothers who had been deprived of their patrimony without due process (*sine judicio*) by Count Roger of Avellino should recover their rights. The two brothers had already taken their complaint to Palermo and obtained a royal mandate in their favour addressed to the count of Avellino. However, he had ignored it; for how long is not known. Although Palermo was obviously not left out of the process of mainland justice, its normal reaction was to send instructions back to the local justiciars there, and the vagaries of these the petitioner had already experienced.

When the king did appear on the mainland the opportunity was certainly taken to try and secure more direct action. Abbot Leonas of Casauria, for example, is said to have actually managed to get William Morello, a local baron, to appear in the king's court at Salerno where, according to the royal mandate, the abbot obtained authority by *judicio curiae nostrae* to remove his own men from William's *castellum* of Ripa. Appropriate instructions were accordingly despatched from the court to the local justiciars: to be effective, justice had to be administered on the spot. Later in William II's reign, when the same abbot made various complaints to the king about other lords in the Abruzzi, he got no judgement, only royal letters ordering the lords to allow the abbot his rights so that there should be no further complaints. The king played his part in getting justice done, but there is little sign of his sitting in judgement in person.

The use of royal mandates to secure the doing of justice locally was obviously a regular procedure, but there is no way of knowing how common it was for grievances to be effectively resolved by invoking such machinery, and it is certain that some powerful men could evade royal instructions. Justiciars may not always have been confident of their authority. On occasion, the king had to encourage them to do justice notwithstanding social rank. William II, for example, sent a judicial mandate to Florius de Camerota, William de Rocca and Roger de Duna authorising them to summon Abbot Nectarios of the Patir monastery at Rossano to come to their court to answer a complaint of unjust disseisin. These justiciars declared that it was their right to do justice where it suited them, and because the king's justice was the same everywhere, the abbot was not entitled to get justice done in his own district.

Royal edicts

Some evidence of the king's part in doing justice can be read from royal legislation. In an exceptionally expansive edict issued by William II, he recalls how complaints were brought to him as he was travelling in Apulia, and it is reasonable to suppose that on such occasions, however unusual, the king would have rectified wrongs as well as drafted new rules. The complaints about the abuse of pasture rights by officious foresters, not only of the king, but of local counts and barons, came from owners of grazing animals, including those in transit from one district to another, and from men with mules and pack-horses who were fined for taking twigs from the trees, probably for their camp-fires. The king reckoned to solve these problems by changes in the law itself, restricting the number of foresters in each district to reduce the level of harassment, and by ordering that damage caused by animals should be assessed by honest neighbours.

The issue of a royal *constitutio* as a remedy for abuses brought to royal attention reveals one of the ways in which kings could be induced to take reforming action. They were on occasion expected to override established rights in order to advance the just and peaceable interests of the kingdom as a whole, though how far the king could push this concept against the interests of his own great lords is not demonstrable. Yet in some matters concerning feudal tenures, William did give rulings about provision for dower or the exaction of aids that ran counter to seigneurial pretensions, presumably by virtue of his own superior lordship over his vassals. There must have been some general acceptance of his powers in this respect; unfortunately there is no evidence about their effectiveness in practice.

Norman kings issued 'assizes' as legal enactments. The eleventh-century Lombard princes are not said in the chronicles to have published laws, but the role of earlier Lombard kings as law-givers was of course widely recognised on the mainland. In other parts of the kingdom, law-giving was certainly regarded as a normal duty of government. In the lands of the Greek emperor, for example, the rulers' *novellae* had been enforced, and Roger II, who succeeded to their authority, duly issued a *novella* in 1150 when he instructed the judges of Calabria and Val di Crati about how property should be divided amongst heirs. The text of the law survives, and provides indisputable evidence about how Roger legislated when required. It does not, however, follow that all his subjects expected royal 'legislation' to amend existing laws. Even less certain is the idea that Roger, or his successors, took for granted any right or duty to legislate for the whole kingdom as an ordinary attribute of their sovereign power.

That the king issued edicts, gave rulings and modified laws when abuses were brought to his attention by aggrieved subjects, is undeniable. More contentious is the idea that the Norman kings published a code of law, as Frederick II did at Melfi in 1231. Since, on his return to the South in 1220, Frederick had already immediately promulgated a sheaf of twenty laws known by the French term *assisiae*, some of which specifically refer to earlier kings, it looks as though he knowingly revived earlier procedures. Unfortunately, the evidence for comparable law-making in this way under the Normans is not so conclusive. According to Falco of Benevento, Roger II issued an order for the circulation of the new royal coinage at Ariano in 1140. Some historians believe that it was at this time that he issued laws relating to peace and security as mentioned in the chronicle of Romuald; it is also often said that a text of them is provided by a manuscript now in the Vatican. At least one other similar text exists at Monte Cassino in an early thirteenth-century manuscript, to which a later hand has confidently added a title, *Assise regum regni*. These laws are on no better authority frequently referred to as the Assizes of Ariano. It would not be strange if the monks of Cassino, and others with powers of jurisdiction, appreciated a collection of royal instructions or assizes. It does not follow that all these 'assizes' were issued at one time, and it is still more arbitrary to ascribe them to Roger II's assembly at Ariano in 1140.

That the Cassino text contains laws not only of Roger II, but, towards the end, of other kings, is suggested by the fact that two of them which

Frederick II included in the *Liber Augustalis* were there attributed to William II. The title of the Cassino manuscript, however apocryphal, indeed emphasises that it contains the laws of kings, rather than of only one king. In the Vatican manuscript, a *Proemio* refers to 'our predecessors in making and interpreting laws', which on the face of it rules out Roger as sole author. Neither manuscript of these texts gives any indication of the time or place of issue, or claims any authority or consent from an assembly for publishing laws. After the proem, the Vatican text has forty-three chapters of variable length, importance and elaboration. The texts were mostly cobbled together unsystematically from a variety of sources. Most of the laws are succinct instructions without any verbiage, and two thirds of them are in substance not original at all, since they are derived either from Books 1 and 9 of Justinian's Code, or from Book 48 'On Public Judges' of the Digest. The sequences of clauses from Book 1 related to ecclesiastical matters with which many clergy of the kingdom would have already been familiar. Officials involved in administering law in ecclesiastical courts could have found use for a collection of authorities from civil law suitably amended to fit the times. In most respects, these borrowings from Roman law do not demonstrate any royal interest in learned law, still less any plan to make it an instrument for enhancing royal authority. Its emphasis is undoubtedly ecclesiastical; in the case of sexual offences, it relates to matters claimed for the jurisdiction of ecclesiastical courts.

However, an important part of the Vatican text looks more innovatory. In clause 34, for example, judges are warned to give appropriate sentences in lawsuits involving court officials (*curiales*), according to the dignity of the persons involved on both sides and to the degree of temerity, because offences against such men touches not only them, but also the royal dignity. Several other clauses are concerned with the respect due to public authority, or social order and dignity. On the other hand, there is also a perhaps underestimated insistence on the desirability for all those in authority in the kingdom, from the king down, to show mercy and consideration to those subject to their jurisdiction. These chapters tend to be somewhat prolix, and this underscores their exhortatory character.

The chapter that shows most influence of Roman law spells out, impersonally, a law of treason which was one of the two cases invariably reserved for the royal courts. It would not be surprising if Roger II had felt the need to frame such a rule. In fact, the chapter 'On Majesty' enlarges on the basic feudal promise not to harm the lord's life and liberty or betray his counsel, though it also counts as 'treason' any plots to kill the distinguished men of the royal council and consistory. The punishment was execution, confiscation of goods, disinheritance for the sons and invalidity of all legal actions from the date of the crime. Nothing is said about where such heinous crimes might be judged, though a charter for Gallipoli in 1200 specifically assigns jurisdiction over *lèse-majesté*, like homicide, to the local justiciar. The confirmation of privileges issued for Palermo, also in 1200, specifies that although the citizens might not otherwise be subjected to trial by battle (*duellum*), this privilege would not be allowed in cases of *lèse-majesté*, or indeed for any of the serious crimes for which the penalty was death or mutilation. Thus accusations of treason were dealt with by introducing Norman, not Roman, procedures, and the treason law was treated as part of the new criminal code the Normans had imposed. Another important chapter designed to protect the royal interests declares that whatever belongs to the king (*regalia*) cannot be given, sold or alienated, or diminished in whole or in part, by anyone holding anything great or small of regal rights and properties. The essence of this rule was certainly known in Roger II's reign, for there is a charter claiming that a gift made by a royal *baiulus* was invalid because no *baiulus* had authority to alienate royal land.

The fact that kings published laws does not make it more likely that they also issued a 'code', texts of which were somehow preserved in the Vatican and Cassino manuscripts. Law-giving under Roger and his successors appears rather to have involved the issuing of individual instructions or orders as occasion required. The most plausible explanation for the two manuscripts is that in the second half of the twelfth century, an ecclesiastical institution with legal jurisdiction, such as Cassino or the archbishopric of Salerno, itself made a collection of legal rulings from various sources thought to be authoritative and useful for the conduct of its own courts.

The monarchy undoubtedly stimulated a more systematic approach to doing justice in the kingdom, but it needs to be remembered that southern Italy was not immune from legal influences from other quarters than the monarchy. The publication at Roncaglia of the imperial decrees on the recovery of *regalia* in 1158, though directly applicable only in northern Italy, cannot have passed unnoticed in the South. Barbarossa was himself engaged in cultivating friends and vassals in the kingdom, and considered the kingdom itself to be properly part of his empire. Imperial patronage of law studies at Bologna, at a time when the kingdom had no established schools of jurisprudence of its own, meant that southerners in search of schooling were drawn north. Such pursuit of learning was regarded by one contemporary philanthropist as deserving as much support as pilgrimage to Jerusalem or Compostella. Trained lawyers returned, not necessarily as advocates of the emperor's rights, but certainly better prepared to propound the rights of the public power. A *magister legista* occurs at Foggia in 1164, and a notary from Bari made his will in 1180 in case he should die while he was away studying in Bologna. The kingdom was not therefore isolated in a legal time-warp of its own. Allowance must also be made for the influence in the kingdom of canon law. The matter of Sicilian customs, resolved at Benevento in 1156, no more cut off the church in the kingdom from the effects of ecclesiastical legislation and justice than the Constitutions of Clarendon were to do in England. Relations between William II and Alexander III were quite uncomplicated, and Alexander spent much time in the papal enclave at Benevento where he heard many legal cases. The limited evidence now available for papal interference in the kingdom does not rule out the probability that ecclesiastical lawyers, here as elsewhere, had a strong impact on the kingdom's development of greater legal subtlety, stricter formality and system. If southern laws were in some senses different, they were not immune from the pressure for general change in western European law procedures.

THE KING AS PATRON

Kings did not need to give all their energies to government to play an important role in stabilising the expectations of their subjects and in building up confidence in the monarchy. Their personal interests, as far as may be detected, must have helped to make the royal court itself the heart of the kingdom. The kings certainly gave free rein to their taste for culture and pleasure, in particular by indulging a personal enthusiasm for building: churches, palaces and secluded pavilions set in gardens and parks. This interest was already evident under Roger II. Romuald of Salerno himself records Roger's construction of the royal palace at Palermo, some of which can still be seen, and the building of a retreat at Favara near the sea beside a specially-stocked fish-pond for use in winter and Lent. Having enclosed with a stone wall a great park planted with fine trees round the hills and groves outside Palermo, for keeping roe deer and wild boar, he built yet another residence, the 'Parco', a thousand feet above the Conca d'Oro, with its own water supply, where he could relax at the chase in summer. To these amenities, William I added 'La Zisa', also provided with beautiful gardens of fruit trees and water channels, on which he is said to have spared no expense; its name comes from the Arabic meaning 'glorious'. The Arabic inscription indicates that William II completed the work after his father's death. 'La

Cuba', surrounded by water, is known from its inscription to have been William II's own foundation.

Romuald proceeds, immediately after the description of Roger's pleasure palace, to list the clever men he called to his service from all parts of the world. The royal court as a place for appreciation of poetry and learning receives acknowledgement in a number of places, most movingly in the prologue to Aristippus' Latin translation of the *Phaedo*, where William I's court is praised. The importance of a cultured court to William I may be measured by the care taken with the Latin education of the king's children. Peter of Blois was engaged to help with the education of the young William II, and though Peter later wrote rather spitefully both of his pupil and of William's grammar teacher, Walter, later archbishop, even his unfavourable comparison between the king's learning and that of his father-in-law, Henry II of England, shows that Sicily's kings were in the front rank. The kings are well known as patrons of learning. Roger II certainly gave Edrisi a commission for his geography, and William I is said to have commissioned a translation of Nazienzenus, the Greek theologian, from Aristippus. It is less certain that William II asked John Tzetze to write the commentary on the martyrdom of Saint Lucia of Syracuse. Some works must have been dedicated to rulers in the hope of preferment and reward, like Peter of Eboli's eulogy which, when presented to Henry VI, secured for the author the grant of a mill. This was surely a reward for his panegyric; it is to be hoped that such a work was not admired as poetry.

Not all 'royal' culture has to reflect the kings' personal characters, for some of it was also affected by contemporary fashions. It has been argued that because the kings chose to be buried in porphyry tombs, they must have had pretensions to imperial status. But Pope Innocent II, as well as other Latin rulers of the early twelfth century, are now recognised to have had a similar weakness for imperial porphyry. The Norman kings lived, moreover, in an alien context which presented them with problems of a special kind. They had not only to please themselves, but to consider what persons of other traditions might think. One of the most intriguing aspects of the Norman kings in the South, for modern taste, seems their readiness to embrace oriental cultures, whereas other northerners have hardly ceased yet to look down on the effeminate and luxurious peoples of the eastern Mediterranean. The Normans, unlike transient visitors from the North to the Holy Land, settled and ruled in the South. The kings made the best of their opportunities, in much the same spirit as their non-Norman contemporaries in Spain or the Holy Land, with the one important difference that their lands soon ceased to be in constant fear of resurgent Greeks and Muslims. The Norman kings did not therefore borrow any exotic trappings from their enemies, but from their own subjects. The Normans had brought no visible images of royalty with them, and anyway Norman respect for kingship depended on the capacity of their rulers to impose themselves by military and political might. It was for the majority of the king's subjects who had less direct contact with rulership that efforts were made to impress them according to standards set in the Mediterranean world by the Greek emperor at Constantinople.

Speaking Greek gave Roger access to the culture of the Greek empire, but it is necessary to remember that in the twelfth century, the emperor at Constantinople was not thought of as the ruler of Byzantium, but of the Roman empire, the living representative of a continuous cultural tradition. The Greeks, in Roger's kingdom as elsewhere, calculated the passing of time, not by their rulers' years, nor even by years since the Incarnation, but from the very beginning of the world (5508 BC). Roger did not see himself as dressing up in alien clothes, but as appropriating a legacy that was his by right, and restoring to the west after centuries of decadence what chance had preserved in the east.

Given the nature of the surviving evidence, it is not surprising that royal interests can best be illustrated by ecclesiastical affairs. A treatise on the five patriarchal sees was written in Greek for Roger II by Nilo Doxopatrius, who spent some time in Palermo. It is dated 23 March 1143 and belongs therefore to Innocent II's last year, by which time Roger may well have become rather exasperated by Innocent's aloofness since 1139. Nilo showed how the jurisdiction of the Roman 'patriarchate' had once extended as far as Thrace, and how the sees of Calabria had been annexed to the patriarchate of Constantinople because of the contingent trouble from barbarians. He knew that Pope Gregory I had appointed a bishop at Agrigento in Sicily, and conveniently demonstrated that there had once been a metropolitan bishop in Sicily. His account of how Pope Leo III and Charlemagne had made a pact which destroyed the Lombard kingdom and partitioned Italy, assigning Tuscany to the emperor, while the pope took Longobardia, its neighbouring regions and Sicily, had obvious contemporary echoes: it would have reminded Roger II of the recent pact between Innocent II and Lothar which the pope was at that very moment trying to reanimate with Conrad III.

Roger's favour to Greek clergy may also be illustrated from surviving sermons of the famous teacher, Philagathos de Cerami. Well-read, but a popular, elegant and direct preacher, Philagathos appears to have been invited to preach in some famous churches both in Calabria and in Sicily, which are mentioned in the texts. He was certainly respected by Roger, and preached before him in the Capella Palatina. He also

preached in San Giovanni degli Eremiti, Roger's other palace foundation, as well as at San Salvatore, Messina, the Greek monastery lavishly
patronised by the king. The texts of two homilies delivered in the
Capella Palatina at least show what Roger heard. The more often
quoted begins with admiring appreciation of the chapel's rich mosaics,
pavements and ceiling, to prove that the genial theologian was himself no
enemy of art. The text then deals directly with the nature of Peter's
sanctity (appropriately for the chapel's dedication), but more pointed
allusions to Peter's actual representative at the time, Eugenius III, are
probably intended.

The prolonged difficulties between the papacy and the monarchy,
particularly with regard to the earlier papal influence in the South, make
it all the more noteworthy that there were no southern churchmen who
showed any interest in taking the papacy's part against Roger II, in
contrast to the position in England, where both Anselm and Becket
looked for and found papal support when opposing their kings.
Although there was no tradition of ecclesiastical deference to monarchy
in southern Italy, the southern clergy were as submissive to the king as he
could desire. In part, this is presumably explained by the fact that there
were no churches so heavily privileged or endowed as to be confident
enough to defy the royal will. They simply lacked those pretensions to
autonomy or consideration that made some northern churches so defiant
of monarchs. Furthermore, though southern churchmen had had their
own quarrels in the past with particular rulers, in general, their
affiliations with the local nobility and princes had made for good
working relationships. Nor had they been so well endowed as to stir
princely appetite. If the creation of the monarchy presented new
problems, there was at least no previous history of 'church–state' tension
to prejudice understanding between kings and churchmen. There was no
general expectation that there would be tension between papacy and
monarchy.

At the time of the creation of the monarchy, the other kings of
Christendom exercised by tradition influence in ecclesiastical appointments which the investiture dispute had everywhere challenged but not
suppressed. It is difficult to believe that Roger and Anacletus did not
discuss the possible implications of Roger's royalty for his powers over
the southern Italian churches, but what Anacletus conceded is unknown.
When Innocent II submitted to *force-majeure* in 1139 over Roger's
kingship, he made no concessions to the king over church appointments,
and Roger II presumably carried on as before. In 1142, Innocent is said
to have ordered Roger to refrain from choosing bishops, because he had
no right to do that (*non esset iuris sui*), but Roger replied that he would

not give up the *consuetudo* of his predecessors. This implies that he claimed no new powers as king, not even to extend any special rights of the rulers of Sicily to his mainland territories.

Until 1130, all the Sicilian bishops had been directly subject to Rome and were consecrated by the pope. By giving the archbishops of Palermo (1130) and Messina (1131) rights to consecrate the bishops of their provinces, Anacletus therefore surrendered most of his powers over them, leaving only Catania and Syracuse directly dependent on Rome. Although Roger duly planned to set up new sees at Lipari-Patti and Cefalù in order to give substance to Messina's archiepiscopal pretensions, the death of Anacletus ruined these novel schemes. Even the metropolitan status of Palermo was not fully confirmed by Rome until 1156, and only in 1166 did Alexander III similarly countenance the Messina archbishopric and allow the consecrations of new bishops for Cefalù and Lipari. The fact that the papacy eventually gave in shows the obstinate determination of the monarchs after 1130 to get their way, but also that they had no power to dispense with papal authorisations. Roger II and William I insisted on a second archbishopric, at Messina, and two suffragan sees along the busy north coast, but this long-cherished scheme of only two provinces was upset when William II pushed ahead with ambitious plans for his exempt royal monastery at Monreale. Alexander III, who authorised the setting-up of a bishopric there, declined to go any further, but his successor, Lucius III, who had been a papal envoy in Sicily, obligingly acquiesced in the king's desire to turn it into an archbishopric, with the distant Benedictine see of Catania assigned as its suffragan. This was unpopular at Catania, where previous bishops had received the papal pallium. In 1188, when Clement III surrendered Syracuse (also under papal protection) as well, the scheme was complete. William II offended many clergy to get his own way, but the episode goes to show that however much the papacy might drag its feet, the shape of the Sicilian church was determined in the end not by papal, but by royal policy, not to say whim.

The endowments of churches in Sicily after 1130 depended mainly on royal patronage. Since this only began in earnest after Roger's coronation, it may indicate that his interpretation of his role as king was to protect the church. Before leaving for the mainland in 1131, Roger set about the foundation of two new churches, both dedicated to the Saviour, one to be the cathedral of Cefalù, the other at Messina, for Greek monks. In both cases, Roger brought in clergy from Calabria to get the new foundations going: the Augustinian canons from Bagnara for Cefalù, Greeks from the Patir at Rossano for Messina. Roger II actually intended Cefalù to be his place of burial, but when the time came, this church was still not consecrated because of papal disapproval. The reasons for this must go deeper than pique about Anacletus. There was a profound unwillingness before 1156 to allow the king to design the diocesan structure of the island.

Roger II also set up other churches exempted from the ordinary episcopal jurisdiction at Palermo. The foundation charter (1140) of the palace chapel exults in Roger's victories and his distinguished ancestry, proclaiming his monarchy as a revival of an ancient one and the fruit of the conquests made by his father, Roger I, and his uncle, Guiscard. The only mention of the tiresome papacy is that his kingdom had been authorised by the Roman church. In July 1148, he decided to found a Benedictine monastery beside the royal palace and near the church of St George de Kemounia. This time, the very lavish material provision for this monastery was apparently matched by a grant from Pope Eugenius III, giving the abbot permission to use the mitre, sandals, gloves, tunic, dalmatic, pastoral staff and ring. The abbot, like other prelates of the kingdom, was to be a royal *consiliarius* and *familiaris*; more specifically, on feast days he was to act as the king's special *capellanus* and *confessor* in the palace chapel itself. The monastery was to accept for burial all the dead of the king's palace, except the kings themselves. This new foundation indicates that, in some ways, the palace chapel had not realised all Roger's original expectations and the need to supplement his earlier religious provisions.

Roger's forcefulness in church affairs in Sicily is undeniable, but as the 'pope's legate', he could not totally ignore papal wishes. John of Salisbury gave an account of how Roger negotiated with Eugenius III and confirmed the right to free elections in the kingdom. Since John reveals that ecclesiastical electors invariably swore that they were not swayed by the king in making their choice, and there was no proof of simony, it seems that Roger actually took pleasure in appointing worthy candidates. John objected to this, because Roger gave away churches as though they were palace honours. Yet John admitted that Eugenius had to be correspondingly careful not to accept favours from candidates for office. The papacy was not itself always beyond reproach.

A general settlement of outstanding problems between the king and the pope was postponed until Roger's son, William, extracted an agreement from Adrian IV at Benevento. These terms confirmed such considerable royal powers over the churches of the kingdom for the next forty years as to outrage Frederick Barbarossa, who did not enjoy anything comparable in the empire. John of Salisbury also regarded them with abhorrence as a deplorable precedent bound to encourage tyrannical rulers like Henry II into pressing for confirmation of their own customs. These comments by outsiders cast no light on the way southern clergy viewed the matter. After his martyrdom, Becket was venerated in the kingdom, but he had no imitators. The Benevento pact lays down the procedure for elections in terms that cover both those of bishops and abbots. The clergy responsible (*clerici*) were to agree on a suitable person, and to keep the name secret until the king was informed. The king would then give his assent, provided that the candidate was not a traitor or enemy of the king or his heirs, detestable (*hodiosus*), or if for any other reason the king could not accept him. This formula left the king considerable scope. Provided the formalities of free elections were observed, the papacy had no effective way to hinder royal control. The king was pleased to encourage popes to perform consecrations anywhere in his kingdom to get his prelates recognised. The papacy was also allowed to make visitations and to exercise its customary rights over the churches under its special protection everywhere. Some clauses sharply distinguished between the island and other parts of the kingdom. On the mainland the king allowed appeals to the Roman curia in disputes between clergy over ecclesiastical cases which could not be resolved by ecclesiastical courts in the kingdom, and permitted the Roman church to hold councils in any city (except those where the king or his heir was then present), as well as to send legates freely, with the proviso that legates had no rights to plunder the church's properties. The papacy was even allowed discretion in exercising the right to make translations of bishops in case of need, which meant when the king asked for them. In Sicily, however, there were to be no appeals and no legates, except by royal request. Although the papacy had the right to call away clergy, kings could retain those they wanted *pro christianitate facienda vel pro suscipienda corona*, opaque phrases that nevertheless gave kings enough authority over Sicilian prelates to keep them at court on royal business. When the pact of Benevento was renewed by Clement III for William II in 1188, the agreement was summarised as granting a fourfold privilege over elections, legations, appeals and councils. The interest in protecting the formal rights of the papacy to appoint legates, hear appeals and hold councils did not seriously limit royal power over the church.

The crucial issue was elections, and the king's 'rights' were not in doubt. During ecclesiastical vacancies, the king appointed *baiuli* to look after the church's property. William II granted the archbishopric of Palermo the privilege of having its interests at such times entrusted to three members of its own community. This later became a general rule throughout the kingdom: even so, there was still some scope for the king to name the commissioners. Royal influence in the process of selecting new prelates can actually be demonstrated in detail. When, for example, a new abbot was needed at Monte Cassino in 1174, the monks informed the king of the late abbot's death and asked him to provide a replacement. The king allowed them to do this, requiring them all to meet and agree secretly on a candidate from the community, loyal to the king and of reliable family, honest, religious, educated and competent; they were then to send three or four monks to tell the king whom they had nominated for election. If by any chance this nominee was not approved, the delegation of monks should have powers from the community to make another nomination in the king's presence (*in conspecto nostro*), which the monks at Cassino were bound to accept. In the meantime, the custody of the monastery was taken by the *decanus* of the monastery and not by the king's own officers. That this procedure was customary in the principal bishoprics and monasteries is confirmed by what is known of other cases. Even those directly under papal protection, as Cassino was, accepted the king's right to supervise new elections, as is shown by the further details available about finding a new abbot at Carpineto in 1181. The monks failed to agree on a unanimous nomination and proposed two names, neither of which the king would accept. He obliged the monks' delegates to find a third candidate, and then asked two bishops of the kingdom (Valva and Teramo) to check the validity of the election. Only when this had been settled to general satisfaction within the kingdom did the abbot-elect seek consecration from the pope, who had played no part whatever in the election process itself.

A revealing story of episcopal-election preliminaries came out of the enquiry into the allegedly simoniacal election of Bishop Maraldus at Minervino in 1178–9. The most striking aspect of this case is not what it uncovered but, once again, the fact that the enquiry was carried out on orders from the king, this time by the archbishop of Bari, the metropolitan, with five of his bishops. The case dragged on because of the bishop-elect's resourceful excuses. His exasperated accusers were reduced to threats to take the case not to the pope, but straight back to the king, if the tribunal continued to give in to Maraldus. In the end, three members of the electoral body confessed, but two were promptly reprieved on account of their poverty and great age. Temptation had been put in their way. The candidate had promised, if elected, to share out a third of all the tithes and oblations paid in as *iura episcopalia* and to expel two clerks from the cathedral. It is hardly surprising if other clergy excluded from the plot were outraged and made their accusations. Apart from what it reveals of very petty town jealousies and corruption, the case demonstrates a scrupulous concern to get to the bottom of the issue. It hardly produced evidence of very great wickedness.

By 1130, elsewhere in Europe, kings had not only a long history of monastic patronage behind them; the old Benedictine order had already been infiltrated by the enthusiasm for reform, with the Cistercians well in the lead. Roger's kingdom had no established monasteries long-since committed to the view of kingship as divinely ordered to protect God's church, and it had no reforming abbots eager to give rulers the benefit of their advice. Roger himself had not much experience of the old kind of monasticism. Before 1130, the only Benedictine monastery in Sicily still without episcopal status was Lipari, which had been selected by Roger's mother as her place of burial. Roger's idea of patronage was to realise his father's original project of making it an episcopal see.

Roger's non-commitment to monasticism stimulated the abbots of both Cluny and Clairvaux to try their arts of persuasion on him and secure patronage for their monks – neither with conspicuous success. Peter the Venerable wrote at more length and with more conviction about Roger's merits as a ruler who gave the peace and security required for the Cluniac type of monastery. Roger seemed a ruler of the traditional kind, and the charitable Peter became his champion with the pope, trying in the Cluniac way to foster concord between mighty kings and holy church. However generous in other respects, Roger gave the Cluniacs very little property in response to Peter's pleas. Bernard of Clairvaux, forced to change his mind completely about Roger after 1137, also found his mellifluous pieties had less than their usual persuasive appeal in Sicily. Compared therefore with their experiences elsewhere, the Cistercians had little impact on the kingdom; had it not been for the monasteries of the Roman Campagna, Casamari and Fossanova, and the changed relationship with the papacy after 1156, the Cistercians would hardly have established themselves in the kingdom at all.

Roger's own detachment from the traditional royal patronage of monks may be illustrated from the case of Monte Cassino. The only genuine privilege of Roger II, a routine offer of protection, was issued before he became king. Since Cassino still has one of the best-preserved archives of all the churches in the kingdom, this must be significant and an indication that Cassino remained out of favour after the foundation of the monarchy, probably because it was compromised by its traditional links with the western emperors and the princes of Capua. The monastery of La Cava provides something of a contrast. La Cava also has a well-preserved archive (though it still remains one of the least well known), but the monastery's role under the monarchy has not been much studied. Cassino had had to acquire a healthy respect for the princes of Capua; La Cava from the first (1025) enjoyed the patronage of the princes of Salerno. As their successor in Salerno, Guiscard inherited this responsibility. It was even more enthusiastically continued by his half-Lombard son, Roger. Roger II, who had been welcomed at Salerno as surely as he had been rebuffed at Capua, had no reason to repudiate his obligation. La Cava had Cluniac connections and made no problem about co-operating with monarchs. Abbot Marinus (1146–70) was one of William I's negotiators with Adrian IV at Benevento. It supplied an abbot for the Altavilla family monastery at Venosa under Roger II, and Roger's grandson borrowed the customs of La Cava for the new royal mausoleum at Monreale. All this suggests a special relationship that could be documented in detail.

MOSAICS AND THE MONARCHY

The most enduring examples of royal patronage in the southern kingdom were the resplendent mosaic decorations of the royal ecclesiastical foundations at Cefalù, in the royal palace chapel and at Monreale. Secular buildings of the monarchs were also lavishly decorated. Though too little of this survives to indicate the scale of royal extravagance, the 'Sala di Ruggiero' in the palace at Palermo is at least a reminder that mosaicists were not exclusively employed to hieratic effect. Though the art form is often associated now with majesty, it was in the twelfth century still capable of providing charming and naturalistic decoration.

Mosaic work was not altogether unknown in the South before 1130. Greek artisans had worked for Abbot Desiderius at Monte Cassino, and in Guiscard's new cathedral at Salerno, where Roger II had certainly seen mosaics when he was installed as duke of Apulia in 1127. This example may have influenced him when considering the adornment of his foundations in Sicily. The quality of the work there was exceptionally high. It prompted even contemporary expressions of admiration, as from the chronicler Romuald of Salerno. The Sicilian mosaics attracted attention. Richard of San Germano, a generation later, believed that William II had adorned his foundation, Monreale, to a degree unrivalled by any other king of the time in the whole world. The mosaics have continued to rouse admiration to the present day. Some critics have regarded them as proof not only of royal opulence, but of the kings' aspirations to an imperial grandeur to rival Constantinople itself. Modern criticism has, however, also drawn attention to the kings' dependence on foreign craftsmen to realise their programmes, and the failure to establish a lasting tradition of the craft in the kingdom: it remained a court art, too costly for others. This criticism can become a reflection on the nature of the Norman monarchy itself. Monreale, the

greatest of these churches, with 7,600 square metres of mosaic decoration
on the walls, instead of being seen as the pinnacle of Norman achievement, can be presented as the sepulchre, not just of kings, but of the
whole Norman era. These wonderful monuments have therefore
become very important, but ambivalent, evidence for the kingdom's
culture and the nature of royal patronage.

Royal interest in securing mosaic decoration for royal foundations is
only one aspect of the chequered history of their buildings. The
complications that beset Roger II's plans for Cefalù cathedral had their
impact on the decoration. Historical accounts of how work progressed
on the buildings depend essentially on close analysis by art historians of
the works themselves, and this leaves a lot of room for disagreement.
Moreover, art historians traditionally display a grasp of biblical texts and
theological doctrines that were not so obviously important to kings
themselves when planning their churches. Kings may have been more
concerned with commissioning splendour than with details, which
would therefore reflect the learning of their artists rather than their own.
At first, the kings must anyway have been mainly interested in the
buildings themselves, and it is not even always clear what specific
purposes, if any, kings had in mind when founding the churches. Unless
this is understood, the chances of interpreting the decoration aright must
be limited. Roger's new church at Cefalù, for example, is first heard of
in 1131, when a bishopric was set up as part of the scheme to create a
metropolitan archbishopric at Messina, but it was only by giving Cefalù
two porphyry sarchophagi in 1145 for his burial in the church that
Roger II indicated the nature of his personal interest in the foundation.
The acquisition of imperial porphyry for his interment by 1145 may be
explained by reference to the fact that Innocent II, Roger's enemy, was
buried just two years earlier in the porphyry tomb formerly used for the
emperor Hadrian. It is also worth drawing attention to the foundation at
Constantinople in 1136 of a great new church dedicated to the Pantocrator by the emperor John Comnenus and his wife, where John was also
buried in 1143. This church had a great mosaic of the Pantocrator above
the entry, and mosaicists working in Sicily in the 1140s would have
known this and probably used it as a model. Even so, why Roger II
planned a comparable place for his own burial at Cefalù in particular is
difficult to explain. Perhaps for this reason a story circulated from the
thirteenth century claiming that Roger had made a vow to found a
church dedicated to the Saviour if he were saved from a storm at sea.

The earliest datable mosaics put up for Roger are not those of Cefalù
but those in the cupola of the palace chapel, dated 1143 by a Greek
inscription which gives the year in Greek style, 6651. The decoration of a

cupola with mosaic follows a well-established tradition of Byzantine art, and the marked Greek accent in the chapel occurs even more firmly in the church of the 'Martorana', built about the same time by Roger's minister, George of Antioch, for Greek nuns very close to the palace. The evidence of the Greek inscriptions, the Greek iconography and the Greek saints depicted in the earliest datable decoration points incontrovertibly to the engagement of Greek workmen at Palermo in those years. To realise his ambition for visual magnificence, the king had no alternative but to obtain the men required from Constantinople. They must have included the masterminds who planned the decoration, the draughtsmen who sketched out the designs, and the craftsmen who actually applied the plaster and fixed the *tesserae*. Given the many workshops of highly prized artists in Constantinople about 1140, and the links between the Greeks in Sicily and great churches of the empire, Roger or his minister George of Antioch cannot have had much difficulty in attracting a respected master or masters to bring over workmen, and the Greeks who came are not likely to have found Greek-speaking Sicily particularly alien. They could have quickly settled down and taken on and trained local talent. What they certainly found was that Roger had engaged them to decorate churches already planned and in part built, so they had to adapt their techniques to buildings in some ways unsuited to their art. In this sense, Roger's patronage was not an act of servile importation of superior Byzantine art on its own terms. It was a proud insistence that Greek techniques be put at his disposal.

As work on the palace chapel continued, both in completing the decoration and in making adjustments to the original plans, it would be understandable if some of the new local artisans came to the fore; not all the work in the chapel was done by foreigners. The ornamental paving indicates that at least some of the workmen must have been Saracens, and the wooden ceiling appears to be of exclusively Saracen design and decoration. The kings took talents from wherever they could find them, either to urge forward completion more rapidly, or to achieve a more splendid effect by deliberately making use of several heterogeneous elements. Palace culture may have begun by exploiting what was available, but by being spread over some time went on to provide good opportunities for training a new generation of craftsmen.

Not a great deal can be known for certain about the building of Roger II's royal palace at Palermo. It had included a chapel establishment before the monarchy, but the royal foundation of 1140 was on a much more ambitious scale. Roger's coronation in 1130 had been performed in Palermo cathedral, where the archbishop had been deliberately provided with the pallium which gave him authority to crown the king.

All archbishops at Palermo must therefore have intended the cathedral to remain the proper place for royal coronations. Roger appears, however, to have subsequently decided that he wanted a place to exhibit his own royal glory, and the new palace chapel would have been designed for this purpose. In its foundation charter, Roger celebrated his monarchy in terms derived from the agreement with Innocent II in 1139, and the chapel may in this context be regarded as a monument to Roger's tenacity. It was dedicated to St Peter as the patron from whom Roger held the kingdom. The history of this new chapel can actually be traced back at least to 1132, when Archbishop Peter already gave the king formal permission to establish a parish church of St Peter in the royal palace, exempt from his own jurisdiction. This surely means that the king was already planning to make use of the palace-chapel as a small resplendent setting for his royal appearances. The scale of the establishment is revealed by the foundation charter of 1140. It was served by a college of canons, praying for the souls of Roger's eminent predecessors, his own family and all who had worked for the acquisition of Sicily. He incorporated into this royal chapel the endowment and establishment of an earlier chapel for two canons set up by his late wife Elvira, whose piety probably had some influence on the king's project. This made a total provision for eight canons in all. The staff of the chapel comprised both Greek and Latin clergy. There are Greek signatures on the foundation deed and Greek priests are known to have still celebrated in the chapel in the late thirteenth century. The practical importance of this royal peculiar, exempt from the archbishop of Palermo's jurisdiction, must have been enhanced for Roger II personally by the long period of effective vacancy in the archbishopric when his bishops-elect could not get consecration from Pope Innocent II. The very special role acquired by the chapel at that time may help to explain why the king insisted on such a magnificent ecclesiastical building within his own palace. He was effectively debarred from comparable displays in the established cathedrals of the kingdom.

The history of its foundation had implications for the building itself, as can be shown from a study of the chapel's decorative scheme. The conch in the apse of the south transept has a half-figure of St Paul looking down the nave aisle where scenes from his life are depicted. On the nave aisle walls of the north transept are scenes from the life of St Peter, but instead of Peter in the corresponding conch of the apse, there is a half-figure of St Andrew, Peter's brother. Originally there must have been plans to match Paul with Peter, particularly since the chapel is actually dedicated to Peter. In fact, he enjoyed no prominence at all in its decoration. There is also something odd about the decoration of the central apse. A Byzantine church with the Pantocrator in the cupola (as here dated 1143) would have normally had the central apse decorated with the celebration of the liturgy in mind, and it cannot have been any part of the original plan to provide it with another even more dominant figure of the Pantocrator, as here. The new figure was clearly inspired by the masterpiece at Cefalù dated 1148, and can therefore be confidently assigned to the period after the completion of the cupola (1143). Even this second Pantocrator was not the last: two more were put up later in other parts of the chapel. For whatever reason, St Peter, instead of being accorded special honour in this chapel, was demoted and overshadowed by one greater still. At some stage under Roger or his son William I, some striking modifications of the spiritual message to be read from the figures were decided on.

The great apse mosaics at Cefalù, which were finished and dated 1148 by inscription, must have been begun some time earlier. The eastern apse of this church had been built in the Romanesque style of Burgundy, possibly soon after 1131. It had been raised high enough to pass the level of the three *oculi* seen from the exterior before any decision to decorate the inside wall with mosaics can have been taken since, for this purpose, the *oculi* had to be blocked in and plastered over. The earliest mosaic work found at Cefalù had not, therefore, been planned from the start of the building. If the timber roof of the nave is also early (as comparison with the Palermo palace-chapel roof suggests), then the decision to add Greek-type decoration at Cefalù was a very belated decision indeed, and may plausibly be connected with the availability of the mosaicists recently brought to Palermo. At Cefalù, however, they were required to work on a project utterly unfamiliar to them – namely the decoration of a Romanesque church. Their most remarkable achievement was to compose a stupendous mosaic of the Pantocrator figure for the apse, a figure larger than any known in Byzantine architecture, and probably modelled on the figure in the great church of the Pantocrator in Constantinople just founded by the emperor John.

From the 1130s, Roger was clearly identifying the Saviour as his particular protector. The bust of Christ holding the book had appeared in 1140 on one side of Roger's new coinage, coupled on the other with the images of Roger and his son, with the king dressed in the vestments of the Greek *basileus*. An almost identical image appears on the king's seal used in 1144, where the king himself is shown with a full beard. This insistence on the king's relationship to Christ did not remain peculiar to Roger, for his grandson, William II, similarly had a seal showing Christ with the book on one side and the king dressed like a Greek emperor on the other. The Pantocrator at Cefalù was of exceptional size and quality, but this is not so much an indication of Roger's preference for the colossal as a consequence of its occupying a great space not originally planned with the idea of such decoration in mind at all.

Papal disapproval of the scheme to set up a bishopric at Cefalù had been made clear not only by Innocent II, but by both his immediate successors well before Roger made his gift of porphyry tombs, so that to do this in 1145 expressed his defiant commitment to the foundation. It is difficult to explain why Roger II remained so insistent on his burial there. He had already buried his mother (at Lipari), his first wife and some sons (in the Magdalen chapel of Palermo cathedral). When he assigned two porphyry tombs to Cefalù, he explained that he envisaged one for himself; the other was to be a mere memorial. Cefalù was not therefore planned as a dynastic mausoleum for the whole royal family. In fact, Roger's wish to be buried at Cefalù remained at risk from the papacy's persistent refusal to recognise the foundation and authorise consecration. As late as 1148, the church was provided with a proud inscription inviting the divine presence in the church Roger had lavishly adorned. However brave a face he put on, when Roger died in 1154 his body had to be interred, at least temporarily, in Palermo cathedral because Cefalù was still under papal ban. Though William I continued to take sufficient interest in Cefalù to add to its endowment (with the Benedictine monastery of Santa Lucia in Syracuse), he staved off requests from the canons at Cefalù for permission to re-bury Roger, at least until such time as the church might be consecrated. William I did not actually live long enough to see the bishopric of Cefalù finally approved by Alexander III (1166). William I, who built churches less enthusiastically than his father, in the meantime concentrated his efforts on getting the palace-chapel decoration finished. Not inappropriately therefore, when he died, his body was buried in the chapel crypt.

Papal confirmation of the bishopric at Cefalù inevitably encouraged the clergy to press for the realisation of Roger's project for his burial there, but they needed royal backing if they were to frustrate the understandable desire of the clergy at Palermo to keep Roger's body and to make the cathedral the normal place for the interment of the royal family. Too little is known about the cathedral before 1169 to illustrate in detail the attitude of the clergy there to royal policies. The new archbishop, Walter, had been the king's tutor, and in his long period as archbishop eventually became a prominent politician, but when appointed in 1169 he was not apparently a great favourite with the queen regent. She had plans to found a monastery of her own where she might be buried, and this, if realised, would have wrecked any surviving hopes in the cathedral that the royal family be buried there. At Cefalù, however, Walter seemed powerful enough to be held responsible for preventing the realisation of Roger's own plans. Walter cannot actually have had much to do with frustrating the hopes of the canons of Cefalù. He soon had to deal with an even greater difficulty than theirs. The young king decided to build yet another church as a mausoleum for himself and his parents, and where their souls might be more worthily prayed for than by the canons of Palermo. This project was carried through with speed and determination. Nothing went wrong this time.

The beginnings of William II's great monastery at Monreale can be traced back to the end of 1174, when the king obtained papal approval and protection for his foundation on the site of the former Greek archbishop's cathedral under the Muslims at St Kuriaca (the Sunday church). This removes any doubt that the king was already planning to revive a metropolitan see there and thereby diminish the standing of Palermo. Later legend attempted to see in this extravagant foundation an element in the downfall of the dynasty. Richard of San Germano, obsessed with the problems created for the kingdom by the failure of William II to leave a son, believed that the church, so richly endowed and adorned, had been designed by the king to win the blessings of the Holy Virgin on his sterile wife. This is pure fantasy: in 1174, William was not even married, and in his early twenties is unlikely to have been worrying about his lack of progeny. On the surface, it is rather the act of a young king asserting himself in the tradition of his grandfather, who had founded several churches. He was probably also influenced by his pious mother's foundations of two monasteries, one for men and one for women, and perhaps also by the death of his teenage younger brother Henry, prince of Capua, in 1172, which had recently reopened the question of where the royal family should be buried. Monreale is mainly remarkable for its lavishness. William wanted a bigger and finer church than could be found elsewhere, and one that would indeed become a fitting place of ultimate rest for all the members of his family. Such a building could not be accommodated inside Palermo. It was established within his grandfather's pleasure park, though on an already hallowed site. By drawing the monks of the church from La Cava, William came as close as he could from native resources to the Cluniac tradition. One hundred monks arrived under Abbot Theobald in April 1176 to buildings already prepared for them. The monastery was placed under papal protection, by which the king affirmed the royal alliance with the papacy; the regal standing of his community was expressed in the pension (*census*) of 100 gold *tari* a year paid to Rome. In return, Alexander III conferred on the monastery the full array of abbatial insignia, mitre, gloves, sandals and pastoral staff, and gave it complete independence from the bishop. William's privilege, published on the Feast of the Assumption 1176, still refers to it only as a monastery; by November, however, the first abbot, Theobald, was already styled bishop. Through his last years, William II added to the endowment and privileges, but the lengthy privilege of 1176 gives ample proof of the king's ambitions for the house from the beginning. In a charter of April 1177, Abbot Theobald produced no less than twenty-eight monks who were priests as witnesses. When he died in 1178, Prior William succeeded him. Lucius III did not long resist renewed royal pressure to make William an archbishop, expressing surprise and pleasure that the monastery had been built so quickly and so magnificently. To have two archbishops so close together at Palermo and Monreale, Lucius recognised, might be unusual, but since Monreale was anyway already exempt from Palermo's jurisdiction, he could see no fundamental reason why the king's taste for the grand gesture should not be indulged. The papacy went along with the idea; the running was all William's.

Unlike Cefalù and the palace chapel, Monreale was built and decorated in one tremendous expense of effort and resources within a comparatively short time. William II surely knew what he wanted from the beginning. His enormous church would be ready as a place of burial when the time came. He transferred the remains of his father there, and his mother was buried there in 1183. It was decorated throughout, in mosaic, like the palace chapel, but according to a unified scheme, planned by a single master and carried out to the last detail under his eye. The decoration was to be more extensive and complete than anything ever accomplished in Sicily, or indeed anywhere. The western-plan building was a relatively plain affair architecturally, designed essentially to provide great wall-spaces bearing mosaic pictures, like tapestries. No mosaic was placed in cupolas or vaults, their proper place in Byzantine architecture, for the roof was timbered. The western imprint is self-assertive throughout, and the relentless application of mosaic to the narrative sequences favoured by Latin taste in part explains why the work at Monreale, though technically assured, has not always secured the highest praise from modern critics.

William required, or received, bigger and better versions of the story sequences found in the mosaics of the palace chapel. The church was actually so big that it needed many extra figures to fill up the space available. Leaving aside biblical representations, all the Sicilian mosaics contain figures of those saints particularly honoured in the kingdom. The palace chapel itself found room for 138 of these. At Monreale there were 162. In fact, since as many as 72 saints were depicted there for the first time, a surprising number of those found in the chapel failed to hold their place in the royal pantheon. In general terms, the king wanted to have around his church figures of the saints familiar in the liturgical experience of the kingdom, whether they were of local southern Italian and Sicilian origin, or imported from Rome, France and Normandy. The oldest representation of Becket was installed prominently in the main apse: the latest addition to the honourable company of the saints. Greeks had little influence on the choice of figures, though it has been argued that Greek disapproval of the cult of Jerome must explain why he does not figure there. The general conception of the decoration at Monreale is certainly not the responsibility of any Greek Christian. William II may have taken some interest in the choice of subjects. He was given relics of St Castensis as a wedding present by the archbishop of Capua, and two stories from his life were depicted on the west wall of the church. Another person more likely to have assumed responsibility for the overall planning of the decoration was Archbishop William. Before succeeding Theobald in 1178, William had been Prior and as a monk at La Cava, he would also have been well prepared to accord honour to the saints shown to be in favour at Monreale. The mosaics were almost certainly completed while he was archbishop. Little enough is known about him personally. He died on crusade, but not before impressing Richard I sufficiently to have secured the king's recommendation of him to Canterbury as successor to Archbishop Baldwin. Baldwin's actual successor, Hubert Walter, chosen by Richard for the post, was by any standard a remarkable prelate, and if William of Monreale appeared to Richard to have qualities fitting him for Canterbury, he had perhaps comparable mastery to Hubert; the competence so conspicuous in the decoration could at least have assisted the planning, if it did not actually initiate the artistic programme. There is another and more substantive link between Monreale and England. William II was married to Henry II of England's daughter, Joanna, in 1177, and the depiction of Becket in mosaic shows how quickly William II was affected by the religious affiliations of his wife's family. Some art historians have also believed that there were links between the artists of the Winchester Bible and the mosaicists. According to Otto Demus (pp. 450–1), 'the attitude, the draperies and even more, the facial types . . . are more than echoes of the Monreale mosaics'. If this were generally admitted, it would still have to be explained. Since the Winchester Bible seems to have been illuminated earlier, could the artists have gone out to Sicily with Joanna? Could they have been assigned some part in designing the mosaics, a medium quite new to them? However improbable this may seem, the link, if accepted, would have to be established in some such way. Monreale has not yet yielded up all its secrets to the historian.

Monreale, William II's creation, became one of the wonders of Sicily. It survived disagreeable experiences after the death of its founder which effectively cut short its future as the religious focus of the Norman monarchy, as William II had planned it. For this reason Monreale was the swan-song of the Altavilla monarchy. William's cousin, Frederick II, did not leave his artistic mark on Sicily. His conceptions were even more self-consciously imperial than those of his predecessors, but it was Rome rather than Constantinople that stimulated his vision. Too much should not be made of this contrast. Roger II from the beginning brought Greek craftsmen to carry out his projects. Sicily was not, like Serbia or Russia, a cultural dependency of Constantinople. Greek mosaic was adapted in Sicily to adorn buildings of Latin significance; at Monreale, a great western church made use of Greek-type decoration, but on a scale with no precedent in Greek lands. The monarchy was fully confident of what it wanted and how to achieve it; it was far from living in the shadow of Constantinople. By emphasising its exotic elements, historians may play down the real importance of the whole Norman enterprise which brought all these southern lands firmly into the same religious and political order as northern Europe. As part of that complex of interests, the monarchy was bound to come to terms with both the papacy and the western empire, and it is not surprising that both of these attempted to draw the kingdom into their affairs. Until 1189, the monarchy treated the papacy and the empire with respect, but could keep both at arms' length. The royal mosaics, more than any other of the kings' works, exemplify this self-confidence of the monarchs, their power to dazzle, their drive, their accomplishments, above all in gathering talents together in order to achieve rapid results. However diluted their Norman blood, they are recognisable offshoots of the Norman world.

8

ROYAL GOVERNMENT AND ADMINISTRATION

·

The administrative coherence of the Norman kingdom was first described by Rosario Gregorio at the time of the French revolutionary
wars. He attributed to Roger II the formulation of a political structure
which reserved to the sovereign ruler sole responsibility for general well-
being and public order. He examined, but rejected, the idea that the
Normans erected the monarchy on the basis of any vestiges of Byzantine
or Muslim institutions, and insisted on Norman originality. He also
made several pointed comparisons between Roger II and William the
Conqueror, who could impose his new order at one sweep by virtue of
his conquest. Not content with recognising that the Norman conquerors
in Italy had brought their own legal customs with them, Gregorio argued
that Roger even willingly adopted some of the political institutions
devised by William in England. Feudal monarchy is here presented in
the garb of enlightened despotism.

The twelfth-century text which sheds most light on the inner
workings of the southern monarchy is the *Liber de Regno*, and it portrays
a kingdom where the kings count for less than their great ministers. Its
view of events in the 1160s could hardly be sharper. It would be easier to
assess if its author could be placed. No other Latin writer of the twelfth
century, or indeed of the middle ages, writes Latin with such classical
assurance, or of public affairs with comparable detachment or firmer
commitment to a sense of how they should be honourably managed. He
criticises all the parties, but with such self-effaciveness that even his status
as cleric or layman remains in doubt. Given that the Latin clergy of the
period constantly betrayed the prejudices of their calling, it seems better

to conclude that the author was a well-educated layman. He demonstrates a passionate dislike of 'tyranny' as a form of government but admits, nevertheless, the impossibility of governing effectively without calculated severities.

The text is, unusually for its period, conceived as a continuous whole, and cannot be conveniently divided either by episodes or by dates. It begins with a justification for history derived from Sallust, and gives a cool appraisal of Roger II's great qualities as a ruler before launching into its main subject, the misfortunes brought upon Sicily by his two unworthy successors. The book ends without peroration or climax, that proves it is unfinished. Although it is impossible to know to what point the author would have proceeded had he been able to do so, the text as it survives concentrates on two issues. The first deals with the plans of Maio of Bari, William I's minister, to take the throne himself. These were frustrated by a patriotic conspiracy of nobles that led to Maio's assassination (1160), but not to the restoration of the sound traditions of Roger II's government. The text then passes quickly to the second issue when some years later (1166), the queen regent, Margaret, entrusted the government to her young kinsman from France, Stephen of Perche, whose attempts to reform the management of government were cynically opposed by vested interests that ultimately secured his dismissal (1168). The picture of Sicilian government thus painted could hardly be more complete or more depressing, and it is difficult to believe that such an accomplished author had not achieved his main purpose. There are no irrelevant episodes, and the narrative passes from one scene to another with the confidence of a novelist. The author's quality shows too in the vivid character sketches, the sardonic anecdotes and the elaborate speeches he puts into the mouths of his characters. These are unlikely to have been written long after the events concerned. The author's sense of how political affairs are managed by men of different ambitions, backgrounds and integrity, and how admirable designs can be thwarted by the selfish interests of leading figures, gives his history an uncanny realism. There is some caricature in his pictures of William I's inadequacy and Maio's overweening ambition, but the melodrama of this section may not in fact be so untrue to Sicilian conditions. Even today, Sicilian ferocity can seem extravagant to outsiders. The text notices, as occasion requires, events on the mainland and in North Africa, but its focus is on Sicily, particularly on the court at Palermo as the author explicitly declares in his preface, where he claims to write from what he has seen himself or what he has learned from eye-witnesses.

The *Liber de Regno* takes for granted the rights and duties of the well-born and well-endowed in the kingdom to a share in the government, criticises William I for trusting such a low-born man as Maio, described (falsely) as the son of an olive-merchant from Bari, and shows Maio picking off one by one the great men, invariably counts, whose characters, independence or reputations could have challenged his supremacy. Their standing is confirmed by the presentation of Maio as dazzled by the distinction of the nobility, seeking to gratify himself with their women or to obtain matrimonial alliances with them for members of his family. The families of these great men showed some sense of solidarity in facing this upstart, and their fortunes were securely enough rooted to survive the imprisonment or personal downfall of individual counts. The entrenched position of the great families of the kingdom made them a power in the land that court intrigues at Palermo could not conjure away. By the reign of William I, noble families could claim a history of possession and political consequence in both Sicily and the mainland that stretched back several generations. If anything, events on the mainland between 1127 and 1140 had given Roger II greater opportunities than he found in Sicily to rid himself of those who were too independent, as well as to promote others well-disposed towards his monarchy: but they were not recruited from a different social layer. If the king's protégés in turn became difficult, it was not so much because of the inveterate instability of the Apulian nobility, as because a government in Palermo had perforce to leave much power on the mainland to those with enough status there to command respect. On their side, the ambitions of the nobles were to secure royal appointments, or at least confirmation of their own positions on the mainland, where their belief in their natural right to exercise their own lordships made them less concerned about the seemingly domestic offices of the royal palace and court. Accordingly they left palace politics to the ministers in Palermo. The *Liber de Regno* nevertheless reveals that the well-born resented the great ministers Maio and Stephen of Perche who held the monarchs on leading strings.

THE ROYAL MINISTERS

Both Maio and Stephen apparently became pre-eminent on being appointed to high office, Maio as emir of emirs and Stephen as chancellor. This focuses attention on these titles. Since both first appeared soon after Roger II's coronation, they may have been deliberately created to strengthen, or at least adorn, the new monarchy. Roger II promoted Guarin, his *magister capellanus*, to be chancellor sometime before August 1132. Guarin did not resign his earlier office, but how it had prepared him for promotion or helped him with the chancellorship is not known. Telese describes him as learned, most prudent, careful and attentive to worldly matters: the king's confidence in him was justified when he served on the mainland as the mainstay of Roger's government during 1135 and 1136. Though he is named in royal documents (1132–4), he had little to do with 'office' work. It was the professional notary, Wido, who probably single-handed coped with actually writing whatever official Latin documents the king required.

Until he ruled in Apulia, Roger II had issued mostly Greek documents modelled in form on those of the leading officials of the Greek emperors in Italy. Earlier dukes of Apulia had similarly issued some documents in Greek as well as more in Latin. With the acquisition of the principality of Salerno, Guiscard obtained the services and traditions of the Lombard princely writing office. Its standards were high: the parchment used is said to have been of even finer quality than that used by Roger II. The expertise of this office in drafting Latin documents became available to Roger II after 1127. The standard opening clause of the duke's solemn *acta*, invoking the Holy Trinity, was characteristically changed by Roger to an invocation of the Saviour. Other improving touches were introduced into the royal writing office, and it constantly modified and polished its procedures into the reign of William II. It borrowed from the papacy the device of the 'Rota' as a proof of authenticity; other minor changes were adopted from Byzantine practice. In the early days it is hardly surprising if experiments were tried. The surviving original documents of the king are too few to demonstrate all the developments of the office in detail, but they are sufficient to prove that from the beginning of the monarchy, the king's new responsibilities and dignities encouraged the clerks in his service to work at finding expressive formulae for them.

Guarin the chancellor and Wido the notary both died early in 1137. Guarin's two offices were now separated. Both passed to English Normans: Robert of Selby served as chancellor until his death in October 1151; Thomas Brown became *magister capellanus*, and as such played an important role in office work. Robert, like Guarin, served the king on the mainland. Roger II's need to attract competent officials from far away to his service and promote them to the highest posts shows that there was no adequate machinery already in place and that he did not expect to be able to enlarge the scope of his government after the creation of the kingdom without injecting new blood. It is possible that the death of Henry I in England in December 1135 released several able men, and Roger's attractions for men of the Anglo-Norman realm would be understandable. They would not lack friends to introduce them to the king. This phase was comparatively short. After Robert of Selby's death, Maio took his place, first only as vice-chancellor, then as chancellor (sending Thomas Brown back to England in disgrace at the beginning of the next reign); Maio was, eventually, raised to the even higher rank of grand emir, or 'emir of emirs', by the new king William I, before June 1154.

Whatever satisfaction Maio took in this last title, there can be no doubt that he had actually built his reputation through his services in the royal writing office. The development of this office throughout the 1140s indicates one of the ways by which the monarchy sought to improve the effectiveness of its authority. The fact that Maio was from Bari may point to the influence of a local tradition of well-oiled bureaucracy there. Though Greek imperial administration had collapsed as far back as 1071, the city retained its former eminence in Apulia, and had been capable of keeping its own principality going for over twenty years. Maio was the son of the royal *proto-judex* of Bari, installed there after the city's submission in 1139. Maio was not the only Barese to reach Palermo at this time, since several of them were deported in 1144, presumably in connection with efforts to pacify the city. Maio began his public career in the novel post of archivist (*scriniarius*), which he already held in 1144 when Roger issued an edict requiring all ecclesiastical and secular persons in the kingdom with old privileges (*antiquitus composita*) to show them to the king and get them confirmed.

The motive for this review of privileges is said to be the king's dutiful concern for better order, especially to strengthen the liberties of the churches. The review comprised the submission by the community at Cefalù of the king's recent grant of 1133, but most of the privileges confirmed were much older, especially those of Roger's father, issued in the 1090s when provision was being made for ecclesiastical endowments. Only one secular privilege is now known to have been concerned. The review looks like an attempt by those experienced in established administrative traditions to scrutinise privileges issued in less punctilious times by less professional scribes, most of them in Greek, though there are a few in Latin for some of the Calabrian monasteries. Since few original royal Greek documents survive and Greek privileges, in the Byzantine manner, named no scribes, it is difficult to estimate the number of Greek scribes needed in 1144–5 to complete the work of confirmation. But there can be no doubt about the meaning of this evidence for better office organisation. Ten years later, the *Liber de Regno* refers to the royal employment of many notaries. The king's writing office had become a power in the land.

The title 'emir of emirs' (together with that of 'archon of archontes') had first appeared in February 1133, when it was assigned to George, former *strategus* of Iato, in Greek documents for the bishop of Patti–Lipari. In two gifts he himself made in 1143, George signs his documents in Greek as 'archon of archontes' and 'emir'. This explains why in Latin texts he is referred to as *amiratus amiratorum*, which summed up his true position of eminence amongst the leading men of the kingdom. The first indication of George's importance to the king occurs however in 1131 when, almost immediately after Roger's coronation, he was sent in command of a fleet to secure the submission of Amalfi. He was described by Telese as most experienced in secular affairs. Originally a Greek Christian from Antioch, he learned his business from his father, whom some Muslim sources report to have been a financial expert in various Syrian towns and afterwards at Mahdia. From there, George came to take service in Sicily, where he served Roger II for nearly thirty years until his death in 1151. The stages of his career cannot easily be reconstructed. He is styled 'emir' in documents from 1124–5. He is particularly associated with naval expeditions, notably those against Mahdia which he knew well in 1123 and 1148, and in other parts of North Africa. His reputation as a financial administrator indicates that his services to Roger's navy were more than those of fighting captain, though Roger's confidence in him in that capacity was already high by 1131. George had probably proved his financial abilities before the foundation of the monarchy, but it is not obvious that he did so from within an office which itself had specifically financial responsibilities.

Since Roger at this time appointed to the new Latin-type office of chancellor, with military duties on the mainland, it would be neat had he decided to give an exalted title to a trusted official in Sicily with naval responsibilities. Certainly, the use of the Greek and Arabic titles 'archon' and 'emir' only made sense in Sicily, and on the mainland no satisfactory translations for them could be found, so a new Latin word was coined from the Arabic. George was not the only royal adviser to be called emir; the title 'emir of emirs' or 'archon of archontes' at least implies the existence of other emirs and archons at the same time, and 'emirs' were not necessarily of Muslim origin. The title of honour enjoyed by George of Antioch clearly implied such standing that Maio of Bari was determined to have it and considered it a promotion from the mere chancellorship. It is, however, not certain that he obtained with it control of a separate organ of government, which would have secured for him ministerial dominance. The best explanation for Maio's ambition is that in the previous twenty years, George had enjoyed unchallenged eminence as the king's right-hand man.

The promotion of Maio in Sicily, unlike that of George, was resented, and rapidly provoked a political crisis, probably in part because in Sicily he was a newcomer. Unfortunately, the *Liber de Regno* is neither impartial nor very coherent in its account of the plots of 1155. It jumbles together several unrelated elements: Maio's alleged treachery, Maio's unpopularity, the double-dealing of Count Geoffrey of Montescaglioso, and mysterious unrest at Butera, quickly settled when the king made a show of force. No link is established between the disorder that broke out in Apulia after Roger II's death and the intrigue at Palermo. There is even a basic incompatibility between them, as Sicily was obviously not infected by any nostalgia for the pre-monarchical regimes, as was the case on the mainland. The shortcomings of the *Liber*'s analysis are probably accentuated by being written only after Maio's death in 1160 and the even greater hatred he had inspired by then. Yet the facts of Maio's real importance by 1155, and the king's unpopularity with the baronage, are not in doubt.

Despite his unpopularity, Maio managed to rule the kingdom for nearly seven years before succumbing to the great conspiracy concerted to destroy him. This episode reveals the author of the *Liber* at his best. He claims that Maio had woven a very close web around himself, so the conspirators were quite unable to work upon any disaffection to bring him down. The assassin was Matthew Bonell, a young man of good birth, whom Maio had groomed as his son-in-law. This illustrated a favourite axiom of twelfth-century statecraft – beware the friend in your own bosom. No combined action was planned with restless barons and cities elsewhere; Sicily itself had no leaders willing to risk action. Palermo was, however, rife with rumours about how Maio had fallen out with his chief political ally, the archbishop. The author of the *Liber* gives detailed accounts of Maio's conversation with the archbishop, his hypocritical visit to enquire about the archbishop's health, the circumstances of his departure from the house after nightfall on 10 November 1160, and what happened when Bonell and his assassins confronted him in the street. If the historian was not an intimate member of Maio's household, he was a crafty inventor of plausible fictions. In the ugly situation that developed after Maio's murder, royal government did not, however, collapse, and the enemies of Maio's system were driven to devise yet another plot, this time to seize the king himself. This enterprise depended essentially on the treachery of the head warden of the prison (the *gavarettus*), who released political prisoners held in the palace prison since 1156. Their task was to arrest the king, which they did on Thursday 9 March 1161. The idea was now to replace the king with his heir Roger, nine years old, who was acclaimed as the new king and paraded round the city to reassure the people. They were not convinced by the arrangement. Things got out of hand, the palace was pillaged, and the Muslims of the city were set upon, murdered and robbed. The small numbers of conspirators involved and the unpopularity of their cause were rapidly exposed, and support flowed back to the king. By Saturday, the people of Palermo, doubting that their hero Bonell had any part in the plot, began to deplore the king's detention by a few desperate bravados. Forcing their way into the palace, they secured the king's release. For a time the balance of political interests made a show of reconciliation expedient on both sides. Bonell and other barons of the island briefly recovered the king's grace and favour, though some other conspirators left the kingdom for the papal patrimony or the Holy Land. Mavericks, like Roger Sclavus, whipped up sedition in the island and set on Muslims wherever they found them. The various conspirators thus showed their own political ineptitude. This stands in sharp contrast to the intelligent composure always shown by Maio, as even his outraged critic makes plain.

In the absence of alternative ministers and faced with a military problem, William I himself rose to the occasion. The disturbances in Palermo had inevitably had some effect in other parts of the kingdom, and the king perceived the sense of trying to rally the barons of the mainland, particularly after Easter 1161 when many of them joined Loritello (who had never been reconciled to the king) because they feared royal vengeance on their earlier fecklessness. There is a curious hiatus between the disaffection at Palermo and that on the mainland. The unrest in Palermo lasted four months (November–March) and proceeded without reference to the interests of the barons who never pinned their hopes on a palace revolution. The failure of the coup at Palermo released the king from constraints in Sicily. As soon as he recovered his resolution and crossed the Straits of Messina, the baronial opposition on the mainland promptly melted away. Only Taverna, where the countess of Catanzaro had taken refuge, put up much resistance. When it fell, Loritello was disconcerted. He had so little faith in his troops that he withdrew to Taranto and then northwards to his own lands. The king pursued him to Taranto and then turned on Terra di Lavoro, where he intended to make an example of Salerno by razing it to the ground, as he had done Bari in 1156. The other rebel counts (Conza, Fondi, Acerra and Avellino) all fled. William scattered his enemies in time. Rather like Robert of Capua in 1134, they had really been relying on the emperor to join them and break William's kingdom. Frederick I may actually have been less interested in helping them than they supposed, but anyway unfortunately for them, Milan did not surrender to Frederick until March 1162. By the time Frederick was prepared to move south on his own account, it was already too late to catch William while he was distracted. Although Frederick negotiated alliances with the Pisans in April and the Genoese in June to provide him with the fleets needed for his invasion of the kingdom, William I had confidently returned to Sicily without fear of trouble being renewed on the mainland. Frederick in fact abandoned his immediate plans for invasion. Without the stiffening Frederick alone could provide, the rebels, however numerous, were not prepared to withstand William's military onslaught. Not surprisingly, they generally preferred to flee than to fight; the comparative few who fell into his hands were mercilessly executed.

The lack of co-ordination between the rebels of the island and the mainland resulted from the still very different preoccupations of the regions in 1161. Though Maio was said to have been hated in Apulia, the rebels there were not so much interested in a change of regime at Palermo, as in recovering independence for themselves under nominal imperial lordship. Their confidence in getting this imperial support was, however, once again exposed as ill placed. This may have persuaded them from this time to reassess their major objective. The hated minister was dead and a new policy of seeking consensus could be pursued.

After Maio's death, William I did not take another chief minister, and it seems that the affairs of the monarchy were entrusted to a group of ministers working together. The full significance of this has been overlooked because in the early years of the next reign, the queen regent tried to advance her kinsman, Stephen of Perche, as sole minister, making him chancellor (1166–8) and promoting him to the archbishopric of Palermo. This move proved unsuccessful. In fact it turned out that the kingdom did not need a chancellor any more than it needed a grand emir. When Maio became chief minister, he was replaced as chancellor by Aschettin, archdeacon of Catania, but he only remained in office for about a year. Like Robert of Selby before him, he exercised his responsibilities on the mainland; he does not appear to have taken over direction of the department of notaries built up by Maio. Apart from Stephen's anomalous appointment, the kingdom then had no chancellor until 1190. It is possible that the very importance of the department under Maio and the degree of expertise shown there, for example by Matthew of Salerno (as vice-chancellor), made appointments to the chancellorship itself contentious. Stephen as an outsider was doomed since he was disliked in the writing office when he tried to cut down corruption there. The fact that there was no chancellor does not indicate that the writing office was itself unimportant.

A group ministry is more difficult to study historically than a minister in the limelight, because it is no longer possible to be certain of who is really responsible. Immediately after Maio's death, William I is said to have replaced him, not as emir, but as *familiaris*, with Henry Aristippus, another archdeacon of Catania and a man of learning in both Greek and Latin. His duties apparently required him to take charge of the notaries (that is, Maio's old office), and discuss the affairs of the kingdom with the king in private. This was not tête à tête; other *familiares* such as Richard Palmer, bishop-elect of Syracuse, and Silvester, count of Marsico, the king's cousin, now come to the fore. As *familiaris*, Aristippus was no great success; before long William became suspicious of his loyalty and imprisoned him. The monarchy continued to function without the need to find another mastermind like Maio. The king did, however, deem it necessary to find an executive minister. For this reason the notary, Matthew of Salerno, was released from prison. He had served under Maio and had acquired such a thorough knowledge of the *consuetudines* (traditional payments) of the kingdom that he alone was able to reconstitute the archives deliberately destroyed when the rebels pillaged the palace. These archives were *defatari* (called *libri consuetudinum*) and also *terrarum feudorum distinctiones ususque et instituta curie*, presumably registers of feudal grants with their boundaries and the *curia*'s own formula book. Matthew was indispensable to the functioning of government, but his ambition to become chief minister as emir of emirs, or at the very least chancellor, was deliberately thwarted for more than twenty years. Admittedly he ranked amongst the most influential *familiares*, but it looks as though the royal advisers deliberately eschewed individual political prominence during this period, perhaps warned by experience of the fates that overtook both Maio and Stephen.

The new arrangements of the group ministry after 1160 nevertheless emerged from traditions of ministerial effectiveness in government, already noticeable in the earliest days of the monarchy. George of Antioch, Maio of Bari and Stephen of Perche all exercised real authority in their own time. After Roger II's death, it looks as though the kingdom was more obviously ruled by royal ministers than by kings themselves. Although the *Liber de Regno* did not approve of this, it never pretended it was otherwise. If, after Stephen's downfall, no single minister dominated government, it is in a way even more remarkable that a small group of men were able to keep affairs in the hands of a junta and prevent the emergence of either a prime minister or the return of direct royal rule. Personal ambitions and antipathies must have been subordinated to a political calculation which put the stability of the kingdom or the continuity of the cabal first.

However important, this feature of government is puzzling, and reasons for it must be advanced with caution. It is probable that even at a time when there appeared to be a chief minister, too many decisions for the whole kingdom were being made at Palermo for any one man, even Maio, to have dominated affairs entirely on his own. The *Liber* itself presents Maio as feeling the need to find a political ally, and choosing Archbishop Hugh of Palermo. The latter could have extended his influence over William I thanks to Maio's support, but the queen regent's promotion of the chancellor Stephen to the archbishopric in 1167 surely suggests that by the reign of William II, the archbishop was himself expected to share in royal government. This made appointments to it of keenest interst to the politically ambitious clergy. These were numerous, and their influence grew in the period between 1169 and 1231. They included, in William II's reign, the Englishman Richard Palmer, educated in France, who was bishop-elect of Syracuse for at least twelve years before being consecrated; later he was translated to the archbishopric of Messina (1183–95). Political bishops-elect in Palermo aroused such jealousy and resentment that intrigues were mounted to force several of them to seek consecration at Rome which, it was hoped, would oblige them to take up residence in their sees and so secure their removal from Palermo. They were so notorious that in the letter Archbishop Richard of Canterbury wrote to Alexander III pleading for the papacy's tolerance of the English practice of having some bishops in royal service, he claimed indignantly that in Sicily bishops spent years at court away from their dioceses. Ecclesiastical politicians had not been prominent under Roger II. The *Liber de Regno*, which painted prelates in so unflattering a way, still certainly assumed that politics was properly a matter for laymen, and was probably written for lay readership; laymen named in it heavily outnumber the clergy. This makes it all the more surprising and notable that by the reign of William II, royal government relied so little on Greek laymen and owed so much to Latin clergy.

After the death of William I there was a break in the tradition of royal government dating back to Roger II. Responsibility devolved on the queen regent, Margaret of Navarra, who may have encouraged leading clergy as her advisers, since this was common practice in other Christian monarchies. By making her young kinsman, Stephen, archbishop of Palermo, she found a simple way of providing him (as she hoped) with an assured place in Sicily. Though Stephen himself did not last long, he was succeeded as archbishop by William II's former grammar teacher, Walter, and he clung to power for over twenty years. His source of political strength is not clear; he does not appear to have been English, as was once believed. He came to be called *protofamiliaris*, leading counsellor (hence his assumed English name, Offamil). His brother, Bartholo-

mew, soon joined him as a *familiaris*, and after a spell as bishop of
Agrigento, succeeded Walter as archbishop. The archbishop in Stephen's
time was an important public figure in the royal government in a way
uncharacteristic of Roger II's reign when his bishops-elect could not be
consecrated. The tradition, once established, proved lasting. Frederick II
found his archbishop, Berard (who outlived him), a tower of strength.

The emergence of leading clergy in royal government, if not their
dominance, naturally followed from the better relations with the papacy
which provided Sicily with the episcopal framework required by the
kings. Even so, episcopal pre-eminence became glaring by contemporary
standards, and other factors were probably at work. The development
of royal responsibilities in the kingdom, particularly for kings who
apparently travelled little round their dominions, meant that government relied extensively on communicating with its officials and subjects
by writing. Before 1127, the management of Sicilian affairs could be left
mainly to Greek laymen. Under the monarchy, the Latin element,
recruited initially from laymen born on the mainland, like Maio of Bari
and Matthew of Salerno, steadily improved its standing. From the ranks
of these notaries and their families were eventually recruited some of the
kingdom's leading prelates. The churches set up by the monarchy
provided admirable posts for government men, and were coveted as
perks of office. Thus, Matthew of Salerno's son, Nicholas, became
archbishop of Salerno itself. The episcopal duties of leading administra-
tors were never very burdensome and the monarchy found, here as
elsewhere, that ecclesiastical benefices made admirable stipends for the
highly educated officials needed in administration.

Authority for a variety of judicial, administrative and financial
business was, under William II, normally issued by three or four
familiares, such as Walter, Bartholomew, Richard of Syracuse, usually
with the vice-chancellor. These men constituted a kind of privy council,
recruited from a wider group of *familiares* which may have included all
the leading prelates and nobles, with others. Although the term itself
means no more than membership of the king's household, it had become
a term of distinction in the twelfth century, and was not applied to mere
household servants. Given the nature of our information it is difficult to
be more precise. One of the most striking features of this government
under William II is its corporate character. Mandates are always issued
by several *familiares*, not one alone. The king himself seems to be a mere
figure-head, and effective government depended on securing the political
consensus of the chief men. It is difficult to penetrate deeper into the
heart of power, though the *Liber de Regno* points the way with its
account of how Maio worked with others to achieve his purposes. The

careful way royal embassies to Genoa (as early as 1156–7), England (1176) and Venice (1177) deliberately vested authority in several delegates seems to show a similar recognition of the need to placate various interests.

A special group of ministers stand apart. Their role is difficult to assess from Christian sources since they became increasingly suspect to the powerful Latin elements in Sicily. The palace eunuchs, most of whom were called *gaitus*, a title of respect derived from the Arabic (*caid*), were ostensibly Christian but, according to the *Liber de Regno*, Muslim at heart (*animo saracenus*). This may be calumny, but it shows that the best witness of Sicilian political temper in the twelfth century was both hostile to these men and doubtful of their Christian conviction. They owed their influence with kings to their place in the royal palace, where they were brought up as castrated slaves in the royal service. Devoted to the king personally, they were not however civilian Janissaries, for they enjoyed the covert sympathy of the Muslim population of the island, and in Palermo they must have owed some of their training and their knowledge of Arabic to local Muslims. Any special advantages this gave them for rule in Sicily correspondingly prejudiced their chances on the mainland. Their political influence was chiefly exercised through offices connected with the management of the king's own household. There is less information about this than their importance warrants, but it is also necessary not to take advantage of our real ignorance to fantasise about the value of Muslim traditions of administration in the Norman monarchy.

THE *DIWAN*

The only office of central government that has been written about with some confidence is the so-called *diwan*, a word of Arabic origin. Latinised as *dohana* or *duana*, the word has given its name to many modern government customs and excise departments. What exactly the *diwan* did in the twelfth century is poorly documented. There is now more evidence of it from records in Greek than from any in Arabic, but there is no sequence of office documents to compare with the Pipe Rolls of the English Exchequer. Allusions to its records indicate that the *diwan* compiled and preserved descriptions of estate boundaries, lists of royal serfs and account books. There is no hint of any regular annual audit like that of the English sheriffs' accounts. The importance to any government of competent staff for managing its estates and revenues needs no stressing, but there are real problems about writing convincingly of how they worked in the twelfth century.

The term *diwan* occurs, apparently for the first time, in Arabic in the
1145 confirmation of the Catania serf list. Here it most obviously
translates the Latin word *curia*, then in general use not only to mean the
persons about the king (the court), but also the royal interests themselves, the fisc or state property. It appears next in a Latin charter,
ostensibly of 1148 but interpolated, in which the monastery of San
Giovanni degli Eremiti was awarded 2,552 gold *tari* for clothing and
necessities to be paid annually in August from the revenues of the royal
dohana in Palermo, where the word has already its modern connotation.
This phrase is missing from the confirmation of the monastery's
privileges issued by William II in 1167, where the *dohana* is referred to
only as an office of the palace which apparently doled out daily supplies
of bread. There is therefore no totally reliable Latin text of Roger II
which uses the word *dohana*. However, an important document of
December 1149 was issued in connection with a grant of property by the
king to the monastery of Curcuro (near Palermo), and this is the only
official document written entirely in Arabic to survive from the reign of
Roger II. It was authorised by the caids Barrun and Otman (both
Muslims), acting on a royal order granted in April which defined the size
of the donation in land and villeins from the royal estate of Rahl al
Wazzan. It was the caids' duty to send instructions for the holding of an
inquest at Iato in order to mark out the bounds of the plot given to the
monks. The determination of the jurors was recorded in writing, a copy
was assigned to the monks as a title deed, and (here we have it for the
first time) the bounds were also entered into the *daftars* or boundary
registers kept in the office. All this executive action necessarily involved
an understanding of Arabic witnesses, and competent staff in the relevant
office to deal with it. The final document was issued with the 'alamas' of
the two caids and the office motto of authentication. Four and a half
years later, immediately after Maio had at last obtained his coveted
promotion to the post of archon of archontes, he signed in Latin an Arabic
copy of the 1149 deed, on the grounds that the earlier document lacked a
seal and was not therefore sufficiently authoritative. This 'confirmation' is
odd because it gives a completely different set of bounds to a different
estate under the names of the same jurors as in 1149. Maio could not
himself have known enough Arabic to spot the anomaly. His eagerness to
supply the defects of the old deed seems to have something to do with his
new responsibilities as archon of archontes, though he characteristically
insists on chancery practice by stipulating the seal as proof of validity.
Maio's 'interference' in *diwan* business may in fact go further back than
this, since after George of Antioch's death, his signature appears on an

Arabic document of AH 547 (1152–3), that is, while he was still only chancellor.

These documents raise several interesting questions. One of the most important concerns the nature of the responsibility enjoyed by Arabic, even Muslim, staff in the management of the king's landed interests. Most of the surviving documents which contain any Arabic are mainly written in Greek. This seems to imply that the Muslims served in a subordinate capacity. The most likely explanation for this is that in the earlier part of the century, Greeks had already achieved dominance in the management of Sicilian affairs. The only early evidence of Muslim officials is provided by a bilingual mandate sent by Roger II's mother, the regent Adelaide, to Castrogiovanni (Enna), which proves that some local government must have been in Muslim hands. Another bilingual document of 1134 instructed the king's port and customs' officers to respect a royal grant of exemptions for Patti on the dues normally paid on the import and export of such goods as grain, butter and cheese, so it is safe to conclude that some port officials were Muslims. The royal mint at Palermo was certainly still managed by Muslims. It is probable that Muslim influence on Roger II was actually weakest in his earliest years, and only became stronger after Duke William's concessions gave Roger the sole lordship of Palermo in the 1120s.

There is now no document older than 1133 which contains work by a Muslim scribe in the professional *diwan* style of calligraphy: it recorded the result of a new inquest held to determine the boundaries of estates. The text is written in Greek, and the boundaries are given first in Greek and then in Arabic. It is worth noting that, although George of Antioch some years before as *stratigotus* of Iato had already established the boundaries by taking the oral testimony of local Christians and Saracens, a written record of them had not been automatically provided, any more than it had been when the estates were first given to the bishopric of Patti in 1111. This supports the idea that only at some later stage, perhaps only just before 1133, was a new policy of securing written records of estate boundaries introduced. For this purpose, professional Arabic scribes would probably have acquired new importance in the estate office at Palermo. It would also be understandable if they called the office where they worked the *diwan*, the Arabic word for government or authority. The same kind of professional calligraphy used in 1133 is found in the bilingual document of 1134 addressed to the port officers. In both documents there is more Greek than Arabic, and since their authenticity was guaranteed by Roger II himself, who put his own signature in Greek at the foot, this makes it difficult to resist the inference that Greek officials must still have been the more senior.

The only influential person who may plausibly be linked with the development of such an office as the *diwan* in these years is George of Antioch. Direct evidence of his own knowledge of the procedures used comes from his own grant for his foundation of the monastery of Santa Maria (dell'Ammiraglio) in Palermo (1143). It records Roger II's approval of George's grant of villeins given him by the king himself. Both George and Roger signed the grant in Greek; there is also a statement, in Arabic, of the king's consent, with the royal 'alama'; George signs and seals as archon of archontes and emir. This document is a model of its kind, and presumably exemplifies the recommended form for grants. On the assumption that George, together with Greek officials, was in charge of the office at the beginning, it seems reasonable to conclude that the *diwan* had become a responsibility of the archon of archontes and emir. After George's death, Maio himself sought to supervise it, so it was not until after Maio's own death in 1160 that a Muslim had the chance to emerge as its effective head.

Shortly after Maio's death, the king issued a mandate for the sale of property that had escheated to the fisc. It was implemented by the *gaitus* Martin and by Matthew and others of the royal *sekreton*, who sold the property to a Jew and recorded the cash-price in a *quaternus*. This is the earliest appearance of the Greek word *sekreton*, which was used as equivalent of *diwan*. (Greek documents always used *sekreton* and made no attempt to hellenize the term *diwan* itself.) Martin, who was certainly a Saracen converted to Christianity, governed Palermo during William I's absences on the mainland, and was one of the earliest Saracens in the kingdom's history to attain high office. It is tempting to see in Matthew the chief notary, though it is possible that another converted Saracen is meant. From 1161 until the 1190s, at least one of the two or three men found authorising *diwan* business was a Saracen, usually given the title *gaitus*, probably Arabic slang for lord or 'boss' (*caid*), as against the Greek title *kyrios*, lord. Martin is said by the *Liber* to have been the head of the *duana* in 1167; he is also described as *gaitus* of the royal palace in 1172. Even more distinguished later was *gaitus* Richard, whose role is cumbersomely explained in Latin as *magister regie duane de secretis* in 1169, *qui est super omnes secretos*. Richard was already *magister camerarius* when he commanded attention as one of the leading opponents of the chancellor Stephen, able to count on the support both of the palace eunuchs and of Abul Kasim, one of the richest and greatest of the island Saracens. After Stephen's fall, Richard himself joined the 'privy council' as *familiaris*. He remained active in administration until his death in 1187. He was not the first known *magister camerarius*; there may therefore have been an established bureau of cameral officials by his time. A predecessor, Peter, had been William I's slave, manumitted by the king on his death-bed, but he was more than a keeper of the king's privy purse. He was also so trusted by Queen Margaret as to fall foul of men powerful enough to scare him out of the island by their intrigues. Even before Peter's time, there had been a *magister camerarius*, Johar, who incurred the enmity of Maio and defected to the count of Loritello. The precise nature of the relationship between the *diwan* and the *camera* is not known, but both apparently provided fresh opportunities after the fall of Maio for men of Muslim origin, not only in administration but in politics as well.

Under William II, most available *diwan* documents were still written in Greek and Arabic. Though Latin was probably also being used with increasing frequency, only two Latin *diwan* documents survive, both issued, exceptionally, for mainland beneficiaries. Anyway, the office must have employed a mixed staff, and if it is not possible to describe its structure or hierarchy, there are some pointers to the situation. In an Arabic document of 1172, the 'sheik' Geoffrey de Centuripe is called head of the *diwan al tahqiq al ma'mur*; the parallel Greek text, with its less flowery rhetorical tradition, calls Geoffrey merely *sekretikos*. He and his fellows (John, son of Emir George, Nicholas *logothete* (official notary), and the *caids* Buttaip and Machluf) defined the boundaries of an estate on receipt of orders from the *archontes* of the great court. These were the *familiares* Archbishop Walter, Matthew the vice-chancellor, and bishop-elect Bartholomew. In 1182, the same Walter and Matthew, this time with Bishop Richard of Syracuse, ordered the office to provide Monreale with boundary documents extracted from their official Arabic *defetari*, together with a Latin translation of them. If this does not necessarily mean that the *diwan* only acted on the authority of the *familiares*, it certainly shows that the *familiares*, all Latins, took the important decisions and expected the office merely to carry out orders. Even when *gaitus* Richard himself went to Messina to investigate losses of royal property in 1171, he acted on orders from the *familiares*, and not under his own steam.

Documents of 1172 name several members of the office and give some idea of its organisation. Apart from Martin and Richard, there was Eugenius 'to Kalo', *magister duane de secretis*, and Geoffrey de Centuripe, *sekretikos* (or sheik), with his colleagues, who acted at Misilmeri. In a (Latin) document for Cluny, Geoffrey appears with another *magister duane nostre de secretis*, the Saracen, Abul Kasim. The *stratigotus* of Syracuse noted that his orders for assigning estate boundaries had been issued not only by the king and the lords of the *curia*, but especially by his immediate superior, *D. Gaufridi secretarii ad cuius baiuliam hoc pertinet* and *cui ego respondebam de baiuli mea*. This appears to mean that Geoffrey had special responsibilities in eastern Sicily, and it is therefore possible that his colleague, Abul Kasim, had comparable authority in the more Muslim west. Another document for the same year in which Martin acted on behalf of the archbishop of Messina is witnessed by a Roger, who could be yet another official. This makes a possible total of ten officials, all important enough to be named in connection with *diwan* business for 1172.

The responsibilities of the *diwan* at this period do seem to be focused on the management of the royal 'estate' rather than the control, collection or audit of royal finances in general. Obviously if the *diwan* sold and leased royal property, the money which was paid over and duly recorded in its account books presumably found its way eventually to the king's treasury. Richard is called treasurer in 1169, and could have been in charge of this department as *magister palatinus camerarius*. At the time there was no official with the title 'emir of emirs', and Richard might for that reason have been given general oversight of *diwan* affairs too. As to other possibly distinct departments, such as the mint or the customs, no particulars are known. *Diwan* business specifically concerned royal property, and it seems safer to conclude that it was mainly designed for this. The *diwan* was not therefore equivalent either to the treasury or to the exchequer.

The *diwan* nevertheless played a key role in the articulation of government. It gave local officials like the *stratigoti* and *baiuli* authority to act in matters of particular interest even to the greatest men in the kingdom. In 1168, the bishops of Cefalù and Malta obliged the *forestarii* of Petralia to assign bounds to a property by obtaining a mandate from the *archontes* of the *sekreton*, John and Abul Kasim; the bishops had applied to the office with the requisite coercive power. The same office may also have already become responsible for regular checks on local administrations as indicated for 1192, when Eugenius de Calo and John of Reggio were at Messina collecting demesne revenues (*ad exigenda dominica tributa*) as officials of the *sekreton*. While there, they authorised the building of a mill near Gerace in Calabria, and fixed the rent for it to be paid to the local *baiulus*, as though this was also part of their regular duties. Four years later, direct evidence of the subordination of *baiuli* to the *duana* is provided by Constance's mandate addressed to Eugenius de Calo and Constantinus de Tauromonte, *magistri duane*, requiring them to instruct the *baiulus* of Cosenza to pay the tithes due to the archbishop of Cosenza from royal renders and revenues, as set out in the *quaterniones* of the *curia*. The greater competence of the office by the 1190s is also indicated in Henry VI's charter for the monks of San Leo on Mount Etna, when he bought out their rights to an annual payment of 200 *tari*, earmarked for their clothing, made by William I. He added the detail that the payments had been made *a duana regia*, a phrase not found in William's own grant.

One of the most baffling problems concerning the *diwan* is the nature of its competence on the mainland. On the assumption that the *diwan* developed in Sicily only slowly from the 1130s, it is understandable why in its early years it was unable to extend its scope to the mainland. The only register of information about the mainland is the *Catalogus Baronum*. This was not obviously compiled by officials of the *diwan*; it was not a Sicilian-type register of land-boundaries; its information was of direct concern to the master-captain, not to any fiscal office. However, there are aspects of its compilation that can be linked to developing administration in Sicily. Sometime between the original survey of military obligation (*c.* 1150?) and its revision (1168?), registers had been compiled, to which reference is made in the text. The interest of this evidence for administrative records is increased by the fact that the *Catalogus* claims in passing that the *quaterniones* provided better information than the *defetarii* about the *feuda* held of the *curia* (and called for that reason *feuda quaternata*). Since *daftar* is only Arabic for 'register', it is not immediately obvious how daftars differed from quaternions, but the importance of the reference is that it proves there were already bureaucratic terms in use and how naturally an Arabic word had been taken up on the mainland itself. The use of Arabic jargon surely points to some influence from the island administration in the novel process of compiling registers of fees on the mainland. There can have been no reason to employ Arabic-speaking officials for registering information about military fees, but Greeks, who happened to be familiar with Sicilian routine, could have been useful. It is at least a coincidence that in mid-century there were, briefly, master-chamberlains mentioned in the documents of the mainland with Greek names. If Greeks had taken such Arabic words into their own administrative vocabulary, it is likely that the *diwan* office in Palermo employed many Saracens.

Conclusive proof of the *diwan*'s part in mainland administration is lacking until 1174 when documents show that an office called *duana baronum* had duties there. Eugenius *magister duane baronum* was sent by the king to Salerno in September to check the bailiffs' accounts *pro exigendis rationibus a baiulis partium istorum*. Though it is unfortunately not clear that this was an annual routine, it is significant that the *duana baronum* delegated one of its masters to check accounts in the localities, instead of summoning subordinate officials to the king. While he was in Salerno, Eugenius incidentally authorised the sale of some property, in order that the *stratigotus* of Salerno should be able to repay part of a loan he had been granted by the *dohana baronum*. This extends our perception of the office's function, revealing that it advanced money to one of its local officials. Though Eugenius crops up on the mainland from time to time throughout William II's reign, his only recorded administrative responsibility was the reception in April 1187 of a royal *signaculum* from Palermo, by which William II abolished all tolls at bridges, rivers and on roads throughout the royal domain. Eugenius received orders to secure its publication and did so by sending instructions to the royal *camerarii*.

In the absence of records about the routine tasks performed by Eugenius as *magister regie dohane baronum*, it is worth noting what other duties he discharged. At Benevento (1175), he made a formal record of the boundaries of an estate for Santa Sofia described by the justiciar, judges and good men whom he sent out for this purpose, when royal orders were received. This interest in estate boundaries on the mainland seems to be a natural extension of the *diwan*'s responsibility in Sicily. A more interesting problem was discussed at Nocera in 1178, when Eugenius, now styled *magister regie dohane baronum et de secretis*, gathered a court which actually included most of the judges who had sat in Salerno four years earlier. This time the cities of Amalfi and Ravello themselves were in dispute over jurisdiction. Eugenius acted on a mandate received from Walter de Moac, *admiratus*, also here called *magister regie duane baronum et de secretis*. In a court at Minori, Walter had recently awarded possession of *Furcella* to Amalfi, but reserved the question of right. At Ravello, the question of property was actually less important than the defence of its privilege to be judged only by its own judges and to secure proper respect for a custom which both kings William had confirmed. Eugenius was not able to get the dispute settled, though he intervened in the proceedings and gave decisions on procedure to get the case moving. The business had to be adjourned until September, and when the court reassembled at Minori, Ravello at last secured a judgement in its favour. It produced a letter from Walter about another case he had heard in Atrani, where Ravello had also invoked its privilege of being judged only by men of its own city. Since the king's privilege was concerned, the admiral ordered the case to be transferred to the *regia curia*, by which is presumably meant the king's council at Palermo. The royal authority (*sacra majestas*) upheld Ravello's rights, and a mandate was accordingly despatched to the admiral. Walter duly pronounced Ravello free from liability to answer the case, and on this basis Ravello claimed its privileges in the court at Minori before Eugenius. Although in this dispute Eugenius appears to act under orders from Walter de Moac, their precise relationship is not stated: they are both *magistri* of the *diwan*. Their department was interested in all matters connected with supervision of the fiscal interests of the monarchy, but in these cases they were brought in to settle disputes by the issue of special instructions – they were not performing routine tasks as part of their ordinary duties. More helpful perhaps in illustrating the nature of his routine administrative duties is the notice Eugenius sent back to Palermo of all the places granted by the king to the Cistercian monastery of Santa Maria de Ferraria, so that they could be written into the privilege granted in October 1189. For this purpose, he must have consulted a register of grants on the mainland, of which there was obviously no copy in Palermo itself. From such scraps of information must impressions of bureaucratic competence be derived.

Eugenius is not the only official of the *duana baronum* known before 1189. Gaitus Mataracius occurs in 1174 as both *camerarius* and 'head' of the *duana baronum* (*cui praeest*) when he authorised, probably from Palermo, the loan to the *stratigotus* of Salerno. The next year, as both *camerarius* and *magister dohane baronum*, he paid the count of Marsico, on behalf of the fisc, eight thousand *tari* for the purchase of all the count's houses in Palermo. Mataracius, of Muslim origin, had a Christian successor, Geoffrey de Moac. He is described in a Greco-Latin document of 1180 as *palatinus camerarius et magister regie duane de secretis et duane baronum*. He instructed all the *baiuli* and *portulani* of Sicily, Calabria and Salerno to allow the ships of the bishop of Cefalù their royal privileges of free entry and exit from the ports.

How officials in Palermo with general oversight of the *duana baronum* shared their responsibilities with officials on the mainland cannot be shown. They did not give all the orders, for both Magister Eugenius and others received direct instructions from Walter de Moac. Walter was already prominent in 1168; in 1171 he is called *magister comestabularius*, and his importance can be measured from the fact that, as *amiratus*, he was the first secular witness to Queen Joanna's dowry deed in 1177. In 1178 he was at Salerno, and sent mandates not only to Eugenius, but to a provincial royal *camerarius* in Calabria and to the *baiulus* of Sarno. He had very general responsibilities throughout the mainland provinces, but his exact role in the administration, and his own relations with the office at Palermo, cannot be defined. The very insistence in several instances on the officials' connection with both the *duana de secretis* and the *duana baronum* points to the existence of two distinct offices, which can at some stage have only been amalgamated rather than fused. Can the *duana baronum* on the mainland have developed by absorbing into the royal *camera* the princely *camerae* of the mainland, the last of which would have become superfluous on the death of Henry, prince of Capua, in April 1172? Speculations are rather idle, except for calling attention to real problems that need to be faced. Intriguing and suggestive as our information is, it certainly rules out the existence of a coherent system introduced and developed from the first with clear-cut objectives. Even after fifty years of monarchy, there was still room for improvisation, development and interaction of separate organisations.

THE ADMINISTRATIVE DIVISIONS OF THE KINGDOM

Roger II and his ministers had no Domesday Book to help them manage the kingdom, and we know of no organisational resources at their disposal which could have enabled them to compile a comparable record. The nearest we get in writing to Roger's way of perceiving his kingdom is the *Book of Roger*, compiled by a Muslim savant, Edrisi. Although precisely dated, 14–15 January 1154, just a few days before Roger's death, the book had been in preparation for fifteen years, so the king had had previous access to its information. It was, however, not just a description of the kingdom, but a geographical survey of the known world, illustrated by seventy maps, now known only from late copies. Like many earlier Muslim geographers, Edrisi was more of a compiler than an observer or even a thinker. It is unlikely that he had travelled much himself, and the sources he used were presumably those available, rather than the best. For want of a scholarly edition of his and other related Arabic works, it is as yet impossible to show just what he lifted from other writers and what errors he was responsible for himself.

Following earlier writers, Edrisi divided the inhabited quarter of the globe by latitudes into seven 'climates', each further divided into ten sections, proceeding from west to east. As a result of this method, Roger's own dominions were not described by Edrisi as forming a single unit at all; the record of Calabria is separated from neighbouring Apulia, not only by the voluminous information about lands from Greece to China which comprises the bulk of climate 4, but also by the preliminary sections of climate 5 that stretch between Brittany and Tuscany. Neither Edrisi nor Roger thought it so desirable to bring together the description of all the lands of the monarchy as to introduce any modifications to the intellectual divisions of the geographers, though those who made the maps may have drawn Roger's dominions on a more generous scale. However, geography tended to reinforce the idea that Calabria and Sicily together belonged in a different band from the rest of the kingdom.

The most suggestive feature of Edrisi's compilation for advancing modern understanding of royal government is its habit of listing places along established routes (and where possible along the coasts), which must reflect contemporary ways of travel and have helped, for example, in estimating the number of days' journey required by official messengers. There are only occasional touches of economic interest, such as the notes about Amalfitani keeping their sheep on Capri, or references to the local produce of Sicily and the mainland. Given that the record was compiled over fifteen years and enriched with the help of travellers, merchants and officials, it is rather disappointing. The account of Sicily is better than the rest, but this is undoubtedly due to Edrisi's ability to draw upon earlier Muslim geographical compilations that had dwelt lovingly for three centuries on the resources of this fertile island. This only serves to reinforce the impression that contemporary research played little part in his enterprise.

The *Book of Roger* takes minimal interest in the administrative geography of the kingdom, and in this respect it is at the other extreme from Domesday Book. Edrisi only comments on one frontier – that which divided the Franks from the Lombards, or Calabria from Taranto. He makes no mention of the former division of the island in the Muslim periods into three – Val Demenna, Val di Noto and Val di Mazara. According to him, Sicily was divided administratively into as many as 130 districts, though he does not actually describe quite so many. Each district treated as distinct varies enormously in size, density of population and character. If each was considered a comparable unit of administration and long established, Edrisi gives no relevant information about what this involved. He makes no allusion to such obvious administrative boundaries as those of the dioceses. Even though some of these had been defined in Roger I's time, he probably made some use of older district boundaries. He had obtained the mastery of the island, but it should not be assumed that he could then redraw the administrative map of Sicily at will. Roger I ruled in Calabria before the conquest of Sicily was completed, and his chief residence remained at Mileto until his death. He was not, however, complete master of Calabria, since the dukes of Apulia retained powers there until the 1120s. In the thirteenth century, the Val di Crati, Guiscard's original Italian base, was still administratively distinct, like the *Terra Jordanis*, the name of which may point to an enduring link with Roger I's warrior son, Jordan, who died in 1092. Roger I clearly lived with local variations in Calabria, and could have tolerated an equally haphazard pattern in Sicily. Here his administration was complicated by the necessity of providing for the government of Muslims and Greeks, as well as Latin immigrants from various places and of different social status.

Sicily in the thirteenth century was divided for administrative purposes along the Salso river. This line may even have had some importance in the Muslim period, since it is known to have formed part of the boundary which separated the diocese of Agrigento from the district of Castrogiovanni in 1092. In the mid-thirteenth century, Frederick II remonstrated with his Sicilian officials because they still thought of the Salso river as a real frontier between two distinct regions. Its significance under the Norman monarchy cannot therefore be doubted. Much of western Sicily, predominantly Muslim, must still have been ruled in the early twelfth century by Muslim leaders loyal to Roger II within the traditional boundaries of the districts named by Edrisi. Greeks in the Val Demenna may also have accepted local government from head-men in the villages. In the absence of any established Greek notabilities, the Norman rulers presumably had more opportunity than in Muslim districts to select officials for themselves. Some of these are styled in the sources *stratigotus*, meaning governor or military commander, and could have had responsibility for the local militia, whatever it was. These officials occur in such prominent places as Agrigento, Catania, Lipari and Noto. Others of Edrisi's districts would have been effectively subjected to the new Latin authorities introduced by the Normans – the counts and ecclesiastical 'barons' with jurisdiction. All this reduced Roger II's direct responsibilities for government in the island.

In the northern part of the kingdom, the distinctive history of each region is known, and its divisions are not mere historical surmise. Moreover, they are still recognisable in Frederick II's time. His justiciars ruled over provinces which had once been independent. The Principate and *Terra Beneventana* comprised the lands of the princes of Salerno and Benevento more or less as Guiscard and his son, Duke Roger, had ruled them. Capitanata was the Byzantine new province, occupied after 1042 by various Norman adventurers; Basilicata was the region where other Norman countships had been established in former Byzantine territory, and where Bohemond had held his 'principality' of Taranto; *Terra di Bari* was the land of Prince Grimoald after 1118; and the *Terra d'Otranto* the mainly Greek-speaking lands in the far south-east. The political geography of the region was not frozen as it had been before 1130, but changes under the monarchy had to fit into the realities of settlement and association. Thus the Abruzzi had come into being after the death of Roger II's heir, Duke Roger, in 1149, when the count of Manoppello assumed special responsibility there for defending the newly conquered region against the German emperor.

For reconstructing the administrative geography of the northern half of the kingdom, it is necessary to take into account the enquiry into military obligation traditionally known as *Catalogus Baronum*. At first it seemed similar in kind to the great enquiries of Henry II into feudal service in England (1166) and Normandy (1172), and since it was first printed in 1653, it has received extensive comment. Only very recently (1972), however, has a critical edition by the remarkable Miss Jamison and the detailed commentary by Professor Cuozzo (1984) been published. The surviving manuscript of it, destroyed in 1944, was itself no pristine public monument of much administrative importance under the monarchy, but an early fourteenth-century copy in a royal register of a document compiled in about 1258. This document brought together for the first time three separate lists, of which the first related to an enquiry about defence levies in the duchy of Apulia and the principality of Capua initiated late in Roger's reign, that is, about the time Roger's only surviving son, William, took over the government of the duchy. Such an enquiry would have made good sense as part of William's regime. There is no reason to think that it was part of a general survey of military responsibilities in the kingdom as a whole. It is quite possible that there were no comparable military duties expected of the inhabitants of Calabria or Sicily which could have been recorded. The list of Apulian–Capuan defence levies is believed to have been revised early in the reign of William II, presumably as part of the effort to re-establish royal administration after the disturbances of the previous years. The complicated textual history helps explain why it has taken so long for its real sense to emerge. Now that this record is set out in the thousand pages of the modern edition, it is even more necessary to remember how casually it was looked after, how spasmodically and inadequately up-dated, and how intermittently useful it apparently was to governments of the kingdom over a century and a half. This text has, however, been pressed into historical service, and Miss Jamison argued that it showed how Roger II created a new and comprehensive system of local government, with districts called *comestabulia* where a constable discharged both military and judicial responsibilities. In her edition of the text, she provided a map to indicate their boundaries.

The term *comestabulia* is actually used only ten times in the whole *Catalogus*. The survey of military obligations certainly proceeds methodically from one region to another, according to administrative divisions mostly much older than the monarchy. Beginning in the south-east, it takes in the lands of the former Greek province of *Longobardia*; the ecclesiastical province of Benevento as it had been in the early eleventh century; the principality of Salerno as it was when taken by Guiscard in 1076; the lands of the new county of Molise which actually straddled the duchy of Apulia and the principality of Capua; the rump of the Capuan principality; and the lands to the north, where Count Bohemond of

Manoppello dominated the whole region, later called the Abruzzi. The marks left by earlier administrative geography on the record are therefore unmistakable. The North, which had most recently been drawn into the kingdom, seems to be the least constrained by older boundaries, but even here, as in the treatment of the Molise, the claims of old jurisdictions like Apulia and Capua had not been effaced. As prince of Capua, Anfusus had only recently attempted to reimpose his authority to the north, so there was no question in the 1140s of forgetting claims going well back into the eleventh century.

Count Bohemond of Manoppello's area of jurisdiction in this record of military obligation is referred to both as *comestabulia* and as *justitia*. Three other *comestabulia* are noted in *Longobardia*. Count Roger of Tricarico is the only count (of the many) in the record whose own county is also styled *comestabulia*, though the reasons for this are not apparent. His two neighbour constables had authority in the district of Bari, where Prince Grimoald had ruled in the 1120s; and over the military tenants of Corato, Barletta and Canne, probably because their traditional commander, Count Robert of Loritello, had led the revolt of 1155–6 and was in exile. Unlike the Abruzzi, these *comestabulia* were fairly small territories, and the constables were in effect acting as deputies for the normal, but absent, commanders. In other parts of *Longobardia*, the counts of Gravina, Andria, Montescaglioso and Lecce would have commanded their own soldiers, even though they were not called constables. As counts they enjoyed a greater, not a lesser, dignity.

The other references to *comestabulia* are much more obscure. Where they seem to occur with regularity (as in the sections for Benevento and Salerno), it is not easy to discern the bounds of the districts. In one case, the authority assigned to William Scalfo (who succeeded Roger Bursell) also seems that of the commander of the count-less tenants of the Loritello fees. In another case, that of Guimund de Montellari, he is known from other information to have been a royal justiciar, so his *comestabulia* may imply a military responsibility in the same district. The other references to *comestabulia* (in entries about the principality of Salerno) concern Lampus de Fasanella and Gilbert de Balvano. Lampus, of good Lombard family, had been a faithful vassal of the Norman counts of the Principality: though he served as Roger II's justiciar in Salerno, he joined the rebellion of Count William III of the Principality in 1155, and subsequently lost all his lands and offices. What the *Catalogus* calls his *comestabulia* also appears in fact to be geographically identical to the justiciarate he had exercised in the king's name over the former principality of Salerno. Well after Lampus had left office, the county of the Principality (which was suppressed 1162–8) became a separate *comestabulia* under Robert de Quaglietta. While Lampus was justiciar he very likely commanded the royal forces of Salerno as well as those of the count whose vassal he was. After his fall, the two units of command (the old principality of Salerno and the county of the Principate) would have been divided.

The reference to Gilbert de Balvano in the *Catalogus* is a mere headline. Gilbert had commanded Roger II's army against the emperor Lothar in 1137, and was perhaps (still) in commission at the end of 1154 when he is referred to as *magister comestabulus* of Apulia. He was apparently replaced by the seneschal Simon (brother-in-law of Maio of Bari), who was called in the *Liber de Regno* master-captain of Apulia and Terra di Lavoro from early in 1155. Three years later, a mandate was issued by Maio's own brother, Stephen *amiratus*, then acting as master-captain in Apulia, possibly as Simon's successor. If there was already some continuity of function between Gilbert and Simon and Stephen, the government would have regularly kept an official with quasi-viceregal duties on the mainland, particularly for military purposes.

From these ten references in the *Catalogus*, it is difficult to accept Miss Jamison's arguments about *comestabulia* as convincing. The explanations for the use of the term 'constable' in individual cases point to a variety of reasons for using a military commander where the king, duke or count could not act in person. Some constables with military commands might well have exercised judicial functions too, rather like English sheriffs of the same period. The problem merits further detailed investigation. Professor Cuozzo has recently suggested that the *comestabulia* grouped several dioceses together, mostly *in toto*, which makes them seem less arbitrary units of command. However, since Professor Filangieri has also recently shown how limited was the establishment of military fees and how variable their density from one region to another, this would diminish the potential of military constables for attending to other aspects of local government.

Comestabulia have no existence outside the pages of the *Catalogus*, and they left no mark on the later administrative geography of the kingdom. In Frederick II's reign, the kingdom, even for military purposes, was divided into justiciarates which in extent and by name still reflected pre-monarchical conditions. The Norman kings could not therefore have re-drawn local boundaries in the meantime. It is indeed inherently improbable that kings ever contemplated new schemes for local govern-ment: they worked within the boundaries established under previous regimes. In the long run, any new royal officials would inevitably have ceased to react quite like the local leaders they replaced, but it would have taken a long time to obliterate older divisions. Contemporaries had longer memories of recent times in their own regions than historians allow for. In 1194, a new archbishop of Bari was trying to enforce the provisions of a bequest going back to the days of Prince Grimoald. In this he was opposed by the good men of the city, but both for their different purposes stressed the customs of their own city, rather than those of the whole kingdom, even after sixty years of monarchy. It is sometimes easy to forget that twelfth-century government was most effective at its most local level because it is there that the historian usually has only imperfect, and often only casual, information.

REVENUES

The kings had no established royal fisc for the support of their state. Still less was there any tradition of national taxation, like the geld in England. Roger II's endowment of the monarchy depended on the accumulation of the various lordships comprising the counties of Sicily and Calabria, the duchies of Apulia, Amalfi and Naples, the principalities of Capua, Taranto and Bari. His predecessors in these offices had estates and rights comparable to his own in Sicily before 1127, and all together they constituted an effective base for his monarchy. This should not obscure the extent to which Roger and his successors continued to amass their revenues in traditional ways, without needing to devise new ones or establish new machinery for managing them. The very complications and variety of the rights and renders involved considerable diversity in local estate management, and the use of tax-farmers or officials to collect dues in markets, harbours, pastures and elsewhere.

As an example of the diversity of his resources before becoming king, consider the charter issued by Roger II for the Greek monastery of Agrò in 1115. To relieve its poverty he made a gift of money from his treasure, authorised an official declaration of the lawful bounds of the property, made concessions over rights to pasture, fields both ploughed and unploughed, fruit-bearing trees and others, flowing water for building mills and industrial machinery, and over the services and payments of the men on the monastery's vill (including tithes of their goats and pigs), conceding exemptions for these men from the duty of carrying wood for building walls and fortresses. He gave eight barrels of tunny fish a year from the Oliveri fishery, one boat free from all dues in all Sicilian ports and from tolls in Messina, free pasture for animals in the territories of Taormina and Troina, pannage for 100 pigs in a specified region and a site for building a mill. Such rights, unless granted away, yielded revenues for the count himself. In addition to agrarian renders, Roger obtained revenues from towns. The larger the town, the more it needed and attracted goods for sale, particularly for consumption. Roger normally collected tolls on a variety of transactions. In Palermo, dues were levied on corn, barley, wine, oil, grapes, meat and other foodstuffs, as well as on firewood, timber and clothing. A great many towns were on the coasts, and taxes on entry to and departures from the ports constituted another source of revenue. At times, Roger certainly obtained some renders in kind, as with tunny, rather than in cash.

On the mainland, the position was not different. Counts, dukes and princes all benefited from a comparable variety of resources. After 1127, Roger II added to his own revenues the dues formerly paid to the previous rulers. Roger confirmed to the church of Troia the tithe of his revenues there in the same terms as his uncle Guiscard had given them nearly fifty years earlier in 1081, specifying the nature of his receipts. The dukes of Apulia obtained corn, barley and wine from their cultivated lands; livestock – mares, cows, pigs, sheep, lambs – and animal by-products such as wool and cheese; renders from mills (as dues or as flour); and finally, dues (*datum* and *terraticum*) paid by the men of the city in taxation (*publica redicione*). When the city of Troia was granted exemption by royal charter from *angaria*, *collectae* and other *publicae rationes* in 1156, the king compensated the cathedral for what it lost in tithes thereby with the grant of a whole estate (*casale*).

In 1130, Roger II was the greatest single landowner in the kingdom. A century later, by confiscation and escheat, the king's stake in the kingdom was greater still. The king quite naturally viewed the management of his 'estate' from the standpoint of lordship, concerned to exact his rights and do his duty by his various tenants, servants and petitioners. He did not think immediately of imposing new 'monarchical' obligations, and he did nothing to acquire a monopoly of the right to tax his subjects, the majority of whom continued to pay traditional dues to their immediate lords. Since royal taxation was itself by origin seigneurial, it is difficult to separate the dues rendered to him as landlord from those owed to him as 'sovereign'.

In the thirteenth century, the dues collected by the government before 1189 were believed to comprise: tenths (*decimae*); curial dues (*dohane*); payments in harbours (*anchoragium*), and in ports of call (*scalaticum*); pannage (*glandaticum*); a burial tax (*jus tumuli*), gabelle of gates (*portus*); fish levies (*piscaria*); the right to take men into dependence (*jus affidaturae*); payments for grass (*herbagium*), pasture (*pascua*) and slaughter-houses (*beccaria*); and tolls on crossing rivers or into Sicily (*passagium vetus*), with renders in some parts of the kingdom, but not everywhere, on cheese and oil. This miscellaneous list itself suggests how little sense there was even then of any general category of public taxation. Nor had the king become the only lord to collect such dues. Frederick II himself recognised that all the king's counts and barons still exacted and received from their holdings a variety of dues that the king collected from those living and sojourning on his domain lands, namely, *fidagium, herbagium, plateaticum, aquaticum, ripaticum, portulaticum, glandaticum,* and others.

Frederick himself claimed the right to grant exemptions for individuals from the demands of counts, barons and other faithful men to 'public' dues such as *dazii, collectae, adjutoria, bannae publicae et privatae,* and *defensiones.* Earlier rulers had also sometimes exercised the right to limit seigneurial exactions, though this cannot seriously have eroded the lords' rights. Clergy had, for example, obtained royal privileges conferring on them exemptions from pasture dues or tolls even on the lands of royal vassals. Not surprisingly, William II forbade anyone to charge his monks of Monreale pasture dues. Yet when he abolished tolls on the royal domain throughout the kingdom, he did not presume to touch the tolls due to others. The most important precedent for Frederick's claims to interfere with the taxation due to his barons was the law of William I, which defined the occasions on which lords might impose *adjutoria* on their tenants. Occasional taxes seem to have been resented in the twelfth century, perhaps because they were then still novel, or merely because they could not be planned for. Honorius II, coaxing Troia into acceptance of his lordship in 1127, promised not to impose *datae* or *adjutoria,* as though they lay entirely within his discretion. Shortly before this, Duke William, when granting property to Cassino, had reserved his right to demand an *adjutorium,* when need arose, which at least indicates that contemporaries expected some justification to be offered for such a tax. The nature of the 'aid' (*adjutorium*) as an offering from 'vassal' to lord did not preclude the vassal from seeking assistance from his own dependants when presented by his lord with requests for aid. According to an agreement reached in 1163 between the bishop of Marsico and the collegiate church of Saponara, the clergy were expected to make a contribution when the pope or king asked for *adjutorium* from the archbishop of Salerno who, for this reason, or for urgent needs of his own, would customarily ask help from the bishop, *ut juris et moris est.* Apart from sharing in this way the costs of a levy which had passed down the seigneurial ladder, the clergy were also expected to pay the bishop *adjutorium* every year at the rate of one *tari* for each priest. For this, they were to be exempt from any other requests for help. Even in this instance, the bishop obviously had to negotiate separately with the different churches of his diocese, and was in no position to promulgate any general rules. The details of taxation as it impinged directly on the local populations are mostly lost, but it is important to recognise that what is known implies considerable diversity and no general conception of taxes for the kingdom as a whole.

The confusion of terminology reveals the complexity of the taxation pattern in the kingdom and the enormous scope this gave for local variations and indeed bargaining. At Bari in 1132, Roger negotiated for the surrender of the city by promising immunity from *data, angaria* and the *adjutorium* which [*quod*] our people usually call *collecta*, here therefore used as a local variant of 'aid'. *Collecta* became the name of the main tax imposed annually from 1235 by Frederick II, but was in the 1130s not an exclusively royal tax. The count of Monte Scaglioso gave the bishop of Tricarico a privilege exempting him from various dues – *elactione, tallia vel collecta, fodro exeratu seu cavalcata,* where *collecta* looks like the equivalent of tallage. It was not, however, imposed on the servile population alone. William II, when preparing an expedition in 1185, imposed a *collecta* on the whole kingdom to pay for it. Although it is not known for certain that *collecta* already denoted taxes raised for specifically military purposes, claims for exemption were put in and sustained by reference to certain registers (*quaternia in quibus universa servitia comitatus* – in this case of the Molise), so recurrent and not isolated exactions were involved. This *collecta* of 1185 was called *adjutorium domini regis* at Santa Sofia, Benevento, and the monks produced before royal justiciars, in proof of their exemption, a privilege given by the lord of Campolieto before 1124. Even if the kings had introduced 'new' taxes, therefore, they were rooted in existing obligations, and the new records (*quaternia*) of services can at best have only redefined old terms. Privileges over *collecta* were not, however, only exemptions from payments. At Cassino, the abbot claimed the privilege of personally collecting what was needed to provide for the soldiers he owed to the king, and thus did not allow other officials to encroach on his land, rights and vassals.

Given the nature of royal occasional taxation in the twelfth century, it is less surprising that supervision of collection was left to local men: judges, notaries and constables or others. When William II issued an exemption from payment of *collecta* for the church of Troina in 1169, it was addressed generally to all men responsible for collecting it, not to any particular royal tax officials. Until 1231, the great regional overseer, the master–justiciar, was the only major official with responsibility for taxation. Apart from the detailed instructions for the levy of the *collecta* published by Frederick II in 1238, the earliest source of more specific information about tax gathering seems to be an inquest at Brindisi in 1261. Evidence was given by collectors from the several districts of the city, and by the local constable (*comestabilis*), whose duty it was to

summon the citizens and get their consent when the galley-subsidies
were due. The king's tax-men acted essentially to organise the efforts of
the many local tax-gatherers in the field.

The delegation of some of the responsibility for tax-collecting will no
doubt have reinforced an established tradition of negotiation between
lord and taxpayer. In 1254, a new count of Molise confirmed for his city
of Isernia the ancient privileges granted by his twelfth-century predecessors, including the provision that if he wanted an *adjutorium vel
collectam seu subventionem*, he would seek the prior consent of the *populus*,
but never for more than forty *romanati*. The townsmen probably took
advantage of this opportunity to put limits on other legal and financial
implications of lordship. Some of these were designed to obtain
guarantees as to their lives, limbs and property, the rights of heirs, and
judgement before local judges, not strangers, and according to Lombard
law and custom. But they went on to list ways in which the count might
abuse his rights of lordship for financial profit: demanding aids and
angaria; taking money for the appointment of judges and notaries;
demanding services from widows and minors with military tenures;
abuse of rights over weights and measures, fairs and markets and over
licences to admit newcomers to the town or embellish houses on the city
wall; claims to interfere with customary rights to water, pasture and
military obligation; or to exact *pedagium* and *plateatica* in his domain
lands from the town's men. It was foreseen that the lord might abuse his
right to issue general letters from the court as a kind of 'stamp' duty, the
presumed ancestor of the present-day Italian *carta bollata*. There were
obviously many ways in which twelfth-century lords, kings included,
must have been able to raise money and use their rights to press for
uncustomary increases.

No doubt stiff resistance was also offered, and lords must have
frequently bargained for the best terms, since it would have been
extremely difficult to enforce unacceptable burdens. The bishop of
Ravello asked his clergy to contribute to expenses incurred at the Fourth
Lateran Council as a legitimate seigneurial aid. He claimed that his
predecessor had been entitled to a quarter of the tithes on wine,
chestnuts, oil and vegetables; a quarter of chapel burial fees (if the bells
were not tolled); a quarter of the oblations of the dying, with specified
variations of tariff for guildsmen or for the cities of Scala and Minori;
and finally, eighteen pieces of pork a year (shoulder or loin). In return,
the bishop would throw two banquets a year for the clergy, on Maundy
Thursday and on the Feast of the Assumption. Such taxation on regular
dues and renders, with its sweetener, helps to establish a context for the
management of the monarchy's own finances in the twelfth century.

It is obviously impossible to quantify these dues, and not until the mid-thirteenth century do records shed light on their relative importance. The only official register of Frederick's reign now surviving relates to escheats in Capitanata, and records the payment of money dues for justice, markets, pasture and slaughter-houses. In each place the dues were of relatively different proportions. The most important single source of revenue and renders is everywhere likely to have been grain, since most ploughed land was liable for *terraticum*, paid in kind. The amount was fixed by weight, though what proportion it might be of the yield is now unknown. Where there was no other immediate lord to collect, it would have been claimed by the king. In this way, the monarchy was endowed with the traditional renders of all the king's subjects who were not in lordship.

The rights of some lords extended beyond the bounds of their seigneurial estates over public interests such as water, pasture and woodland. The exercise of such rights did not depend on specific grants of privilege from sovereigns, nor on local usurpations, but on the survival of very ancient practice and the continuing regard for the *respublica*, not only in the lands of the Greek empire, but also in the Lombard principalities. In some places, even building-stone was considered a public asset and its use controlled, but stone was not so obviously in need of protection as woodland, which was depleted daily for ordinary domestic purposes. Since monks might find their concessions defined as one cart- or donkey-load of wood, woodland must have been regularly patrolled to deter and punish encroachments. 'Foresters' seem to have been given a general commission to check on all land-use and to protect pasture and water-supplies, all of which may have been already in limited supply and in need of protection. Grants of pasture rights were also regularly made to clergy by counts. The physical limits of their pastures were never defined in geographical terms, and it is only a guess that the counts' jurisdictions were defined by the territory of their counties rather than, say, by those of the diocese or former *contado*. 'Royal' rights would have been established by consolidating the rights of former counts, dukes and princes, whose place the king had taken.

There is no indication of the relative value of these rights over public spaces, as compared with the value of cultivated land. Dues were certainly rendered in kind rather than in cash: a complaint made against officials at Castellaneta in 1176 asserted that as payment of the *herbaticum*, they took the best sheep, instead of taking the twentieth one, as it came. It is possible that the authorities who collected the dues were expected in return to guarantee certain facilities – such as drinking-troughs or supplies of water for grazing herds. Likewise, ferry- and bridge-tolls,

harbour-dues and mooring-rights may all have been considered payments for services rather than arbitrary exactions. The public authorities
had at least to provide bye-laws and policing of quaysides or markets.
The public authorisation of mill-building is certainly connected with the
need to prevent diversion of water-supplies from existing installations.
General supervision of the waters as public reserves may also explain
how rulers came to take such interest in fishing rights. There are even
already signs in the twelfth century of royal interest in salt-making.
From all these sources, rulers obtained supplies of flour, fish and salt,
either for local consumption or for sale.

There remains for consideration one more important source of
revenue: the issue of a gold and silver coinage. Before the monarchy
there was a long-established tradition of minting gold coins in the South,
designed to be acceptable on the gold markets of North Africa and
Constantinople. The rulers of Muslim Sicily, unlike those of North
Africa, had issued coins not of a *dinar*, but only of a quarter *dinar* (called
rubā'ī in Arabic), suggesting that Muslim Sicily was relatively backward.
On the mainland, however, these Sicilian coins were popular and
known as *tari*, a term probably derived from the Arabic meaning 'freshly
minted'. From the mid-tenth century, the princes of Salerno also struck
coins called *tari*, imitating the Sicilian ones; similar coins were issued at
Amalfi, probably before the end of the tenth century. When the
Normans conquered Palermo and Salerno, they continued to strike
coins of these types, retaining their Cufic inscriptions to satisfy the
requirements of trade. Roger II's unification of the southern lordships in
effect gave him the *de facto* monopoly of striking the principal coins in
the kingdom. He was the only Christian ruler of the west who minted
gold coins at all. His *tari* was struck at sixteen and a third carat gold, with
some alloy of silver and copper, and the monarchy maintained a high
standard of issue and vouched for it by the royal stamp. Coins were
struck at Palermo until 1194, and a new mint on the island at Messina
remained in use until the death of Manfred. On the mainland, the
principal mint remained at Salerno until it was transferred to Brindisi at
the end of the twelfth century.

Gold coins did not constitute the only specie in circulation in southern
Italy and Sicily. Most common were copper coins, originally of Greek
type called *follis* or *follari*, which from the mid-eleventh century were
also struck at Salerno by the Lombard princes and by the Norman rulers
of Capua and Mileto. Roger I in addition struck silver coins at Mileto,
though other silver *denarii* from Lucca and Pavia circulated in the South.
Roger II's chief monetary innovation concerned the copper and silver
issues. In 1140, he scrapped the existing copper coinage and replaced it

with small copper *follari*, such that sixty *follari* were worth one *tari*. A new silver coin, the ducat, was of rather low purity; two and a half ducats were equal to one gold *tari*. Silver coins of the twelfth-century kingdom are now comparatively rare, but it seems they were not of notably poorer quality than other silver coins of the time, though the value of the ducat fell slightly in Roger's own reign and again under William II, whose ducat was called *apuliensis*. The only chronicle reference to any of Roger's changes was made by Falco of Benevento, who was hysterically critical and probably voiced widespread outrage when the traditional coins disappeared. Roger's intentions could have been as much political as economic. There is no way of guessing how much financial profit kings drew from their minting rights. It is also worth noting that the king's subjects did not always calculate prices exclusively in terms of the king's coins. Some of the words in use were originally derived from the name of Greek coins but, even before the death of William I, there are also references to the use of the money of Provins (*provesini*) where actual coins from northern Europe are implied. The South was part of the western economy and must have welcomed many northerners with their coins, so that the southern economy was not anchored to the royal money supply.

The Norman kings can seem to have disposed of wealth like the monarchs of fairy-tales: inexhaustible treasure, accumulated without visible effort and garnered with magic efficiency. This impression is not derived from patient analysis of mountains of record, for only scraps of information are available. There is really no way of estimating royal revenues or expenditure in the twelfth or thirteenth century, though there are pointers to the kind of sums involved. Thus Constance allotted Innocent III 30,000 *tari* a year (at today's prices of 392 dollars to the ounce of gold, this translates as £200,000) for running the kingdom *in absentia*, with promises to repay extra expenses incurred for military purposes. In quite different circumstances, Frederick II aimed to raise from his kingdom by taxation as much as £12 million in 1241, and twice that in 1248. Only in his reign is there enough evidence to justify describing any 'system' of royal finances, yet even Frederick, who had not inherited a centralised financial system, did not create one. The Normans cannot be seen as having at their disposal a system comparable to Frederick's, for Roger II and his sons simply took over the existing complement of officials of earlier rulers on the mainland. Individuals might be changed, but this did not itself entail overhaul of the general structure.

LOCAL GOVERNMENT

Defective though the information about sources of revenue may be, the lists of dues granted away seem to be exhaustive, in contrast to available evidence about the many officials presumably involved in managing interests and collecting dues for the government. Because of the earlier history of the different Norman territories, officials bore an astonishing variety of names derived from different regimes. Duke Roger Borsa, for example, when giving Bishop Gerard of Troia an estate in 1092, had to warn his *stratigoti, turmachae, vicecomites, forestarii* and *terraticari* to respect his gift. This implies that the Apulian countryside was already crawling with ducal officers. Unfortunately, charters which reveal the existence of these men provide little information about them or the nature of the offices they served. However, it is certain that until all the responsibilities of the mainland princes were vested in the king (as was effectively the case only after the accession of William I), there can have been no single direction of all local officials, who continued therefore to work within the circumscriptions of the old principalities, duchy and counties. After the creation of the monarchy, there were still many counts, and their officials would have changed nothing of their traditional management.

How Roger II's government itself dealt with the local authorities before 1127 can be illustrated by a paper mandate, a fragment of which survived into modern times, though it is now lost. Written in both Greek and Arabic and provided with a wax seal, it was sent by Roger II's mother, Countess Adelaide, as regent, in 1109 to various officials of Castrogiovanni (Enna). She ordered them to protect the monks of San Filippo di Fragalà in the Valle San Marco, and to make them a due allowance of salt each year. Such routine instructions would normally have vanished without trace, and the substance of this one is only known because the abbot produced a copy of it from his own archives in 1145 and had it confirmed along with twelve other documents (mostly granted thirty or fifty years before) as proof of his rights. Knowledge of local officials rests on a depressingly small number of such documents, often in unreliable Latin translations, which rules out the possibility of reconstructing the nature of early administration as a whole.

Each of the princely governments in the early twelfth century had its own administration, both for drafting documents and collecting revenues. Several princely cameral offices survived at least until the end of Roger II's reign, since his sons needed to maintain some organisations of their own for looking after their interests. This necessarily deferred the creation of any central cameral organisation on the mainland. The king even seems to have been content to take advantage of existing arrangements. Robert fitz Malfridus, *camerarius* of the count of Lesina, for example, issued a summons *ex parte regis et domini nostri comitis Goffredi* in 1156 for the session of a court held to settle a dispute over mill-sluices between two monasteries. The nature of the business before the court appears to be of a kind that frequently involved *camerarii*: disputes over natural reserves. The king's own *camerarii* were regularly involved in disputes about public property, as at Capua in 1161 when a *camerarius* judged a case involving the erection of buildings on allegedly public ground near the city walls and bridge. A more unusual document of 1178 records an accusation made by the king's *camerarius* in the local court at Sarno that an individual was trying to cheat the *curia* of its rights to his services (*debet facere parti rei publice angarias*). The charge was denied on the grounds that God did not wish it (*nolit deus quod angarias facere debeat*), and a settlement was reached by agreement. *Camerarii* kept a close watch on the minutiae of local life, but accusations were still heard and rebutted in local courts. *Camerarii* also provided courts for the settlement of disputes between private individuals over property.

From the reign of William II, more central supervision of *camerarii* may have left them with less initiative, at least in some respects. The procedures can be demonstrated from the muniments of Corazzo. Abbot Joachim obtained a grant of lands in Calabria from William II, who sent orders to Walter de Moac (admiral and *magister regie duane de secretis et duane baronum*) to have the boundaries marked out by the local *camerarii*. The abbot was not satisfied with the way this was done and applied to the king for a document (*privilegium*) giving the bounds. This was refused because the royal *curia* did not know for certain how the boundaries had been made. The admiral was authorised to issue such a privilege himself. His document was accordingly prepared in the light of information provided by the letters of the *camerarii*, the testimony of the *boni homines* and the inquest (*inquisitio*) made on the admiral's orders. More precise information about the role of the *camerarius* in such transactions is given in a later document from the same house. In this case, the *curia* sent a royal order (*praeceptum regium*) directly to the *camerarius* of the Val di Crati ordering him to see that Abbot Joachim got land enough for six teams of oxen (*paricla*). This could only be done by assigning him parcels of land in several places. After further dispute, another assignment was made, under the eye of a new *camerarius*, by sixteen *probi homines* and the ploughman (*fidelis agricola*) who confirmed on oath that he had sown the seed. The *camerarius* himself drew a line round the property, *linea circumcingere feci*. The *camerarius* had clear responsibilities for subordinate officials within his district, and was himself subject, not so much to any one particular central office, as to the highest officials of the government itself. Yet at the same time his effectiveness still depended on local co-operation. He was himself in no position to lord it over the king's subjects in the king's name.

One of the routine tasks of royal *camerarii* everywhere was to find suitable resident 'officials' for local districts: the *baiuli*. These men had considerable scope for arbitrary actions, both in the courts and by their own executive powers, for they everywhere bore the day-to-day burden of local management. Judging from lordly concessions, communities tried to protect their members by securing exemptions from the lord's right to pluck out at will men to act as his *baiuli*. This may have been done to spare individuals the thankless task of having to try and satisfy lords. On the other hand, communities themselves may have had an interest in being spared administration by one of their own neighbours, well able to use his local knowledge to his own advantage. Nevertheless, if *baiuli* had enjoyed no opportunities to profit from their office, the system would never have worked at all. Although hundreds of bailiffs must have been in office at any one time in the kingdom, there are very few details about this level of local administration. Queen Margaret sent instructions to *baiuli* in 1171 about the collection for *angaria*, *lignamina* (timber dues) and *adjutorium*, where money payments are implied. Nevertheless, since in general most 'officials' probably farmed their offices, the crown would rarely have taken much interest in the specific collection of the various individual taxes unless sufficiently forceful complaints were received about the violation of particular privileges. According to an enquiry held at Taranto much later, successive *baiuli* in William II's time held office for two, three, six, even ten years at a stretch, collecting various royal revenues from sea and land, rivers, lawcourts as well as slaughter-houses. The rights to collect the dues and exercise the office were sold at variable sums, presumably at the highest rate the government could get at any given time. Since the sums quoted range from forty down to fifteen gold ounces, variations may be explained as lump sums offered for different numbers of years. The *baiuli* did not collect only money, since some dues were rendered in kind. One witness in 1249 claimed to have seen payments made in William's reign (sixty years before) from the tithe of the *baiulatio* to the canons of Taranto in bread, cheese and wine. At Bisignano much later still, a witness affirmed that the *baiuli* of the city (the catapan and two other named persons *et alii qui pro tempore fuerunt baiuli*) collected the rights, rents and produce (*iura, redditus et proventus*) due to the fisc from the bench, slaughter-house, market and other dues (*altra iura*). Nor were the *baiuli* simply managers: they are recorded as taking the local public notary with them to the *casale* when they held court there (*regebant curiam*). They were in charge of their districts.

They were not however entirely immune from scrutiny. Over-zealous *baiuli* who tried to exact dues of corn, barley and wine contrary to custom or privilege were summoned to court in the presence of local judges sitting under the *camerarius* of the district, as at Sora (1173) or Teano (1174). At Aversa in 1158, a *baiulus* was convicted of constructing two mills without authority, this time not by the *camerarius*, but by justiciars, since it had not proved easy to discipline him. His excesses had been first challenged in court before Nicola, *magister camerarius*, and heard there by local judges and bailiffs, who settled rights over one of the mills. Only the persistence of the bishop of Aversa brought the matter of the second mill to a higher court, where it was the archbishop of Capua himself who pronounced the final verdict.

Baiuli had powers to hold courts of their own, but complaints about their proceedings *sine judicio* show they did not always bother with formalities. The most detailed charges against them are recorded at Castellaneta in 1176. The *baiuli* here were accused, not only of carrying away private property without judgement and holding men like robbers in small pits (*foveas*) unless they could find warrantors, but also of maintaining men of ill-repute, who tore their own faces with chains and made false accusations against the inhabitants in order to claim compensation at thirty ducats for each wound. They also improperly seized local horses and rode them at their pleasure; as payment of *herbaticum*, they took the best sheep instead of taking the twentieth one as it came; they abused their control of markets by demanding dues on individual pigs when slaughtered if any was sold by the owners. The opportunities for abuse of power were certainly extensive. The competence of the courts of the *baiuli* was formally reduced by a royal ordinance denying them jurisdiction over criminal business and over feudal property, but they still enjoyed ample opportunities to abuse their authority. By law, they had to make preliminary hearings of misdemeanours (*minimis offensis*), arrest thieves, sequestrate their goods, and hand them over to the justiciars and collect judicial fines. In practice, their powers over the countryside remained comprehensive.

The legal traditions of the kingdom did not however tolerate local tyranny. Formal documents show local courts functioning regularly under local law-worthy persons, fully familiar with the routine of legal proceedings. Humdrum everyday legal business is naturally inadequately reported. Local judges appear most often in legal documents, such as sales or bequests declared in public and committed to writing by notaries. These judges are sometimes called royal judges, perhaps when appointed on crown lands; but others, appointed by counts and bishops, exercised comparable powers. In 1158, after a dispute heard before royal justiciars, a local catapan was authorised to take any further action he wished in the royal court of the *castellum* of Modugno. The judge of this court then took the initiative, questioned the catapan, and required several men of the district to give evidence on oath by their fealty to the king. On their evidence, the judge took the advice of the court and ordered one of the parties to swear on the Gospels with twelve *juratores*, one by one, as to the truth of the plea. The judgement was put into writing by a notary, and the judge himself was the first of its several witnesses. The justiciars had left the catapan free to take the matter, if he so wished, to the local court, so there was some connection between the local arrangements and the king's justiciars – but the local judge was hardly dependent on the justiciars' direction. He was at no loss as to how to proceed in his own court where the legal procedures were thoroughly traditional, requiring no monarchical innovations. Although the extent to which the doing of justice remained a local matter in the twelfth century cannot be demonstrated in detail, it ought to be assumed in general.

The punishment of serious crime in the region did not begin with the creation of the monarchy. Before 1127, crimes were punished by many different authorities. Counts normally seem to have reserved for their own courts the exercise of the 'sovereign' right to inflict capital punishment for the most serious offences. This itself was probably not a Norman innovation, though the Normans do seem to have been thought responsible for introducing trial by battle as a novel procedure for dealing with serious crimes punishable by death or mutilation. Only in very exceptional circumstances did Norman rulers allow privileged groups exemption from it and give permission for them to wage their own customary law. The proclamation of Roger II's decree on peace-keeping at Melfi in 1129 did not itself introduce any new laws in this respect, nor did it limit established rights to criminal jurisdiction. These remained well entrenched in the twelfth century, judging from the precious little information available about how crime was punished and the peace enforced. The counts of Loreto made arrangements in 1114, and more specifically again in 1172, with the abbots of Santa Maria di Picciano for the punishment of violence amongst the monastery's men. On their *casale* of Picciano, the abbots were granted complete jurisdiction (*libertas et franchitia*). The count also conceded that the monastery should hold *in baroniam* such of its men as were in the count's *comitatus*, and over these the abbot was allowed to do justice except in cases of homicide, arson or the like, where the penalty was death. In those cases, offenders should be handed over to the count, though the abbot got all their forfeited property, *stabilia et mobilia*. It is probable that serious crimes were still normally reserved for comital justice throughout the kingdom. Where there were no counts, the royal justiciars of the district enforced the law. The case of Picciano shows, however, that where the local lord was granted a *casale*, he could have full jurisdiction and enjoy a 'liberty' to execute felons.

Further light is shed on traditional enforcement of the criminal law by the difficulties experienced by reforming clergy who tried to secure changes in those rules which concerned them in particular. When, for example, they tried to obtain jurisdiction of sexual offences for clerical courts, the king insisted that though the spiritual offence might be judged there, any violence involved remained a matter for secular courts (and not specifically royal ones). William II, who wrote on behalf of the bishop of Minori on this matter, gave instructions to counts, *camerarii*, justiciars, barons and *baiuli* – all of whom might in some way be involved with the punishment of such offences as adultery. That secular lords continued to take their own rights for granted is borne out by a dispute between the bishop of Troia and the lord of Biccari, who claimed if not jurisdiction, at least the fines from convicted adulterers. The pious William II himself made no concessions to the clergy in such serious crimes as treachery, homicide or other wrongdoing touching royal majesty (*maleficium quod spectet contra majestatem nostram*), claiming them for his own courts.

The king did not, however, attempt to assert exclusive jurisdiction over all serious crimes. When Roger II reserved at Cefalù in 1145 royal pleas (*regalia*) and felonies (*fellonia*) defined as *traditio* and *homicidio*, this meant that the canons did not obtain jurisdiction over these cases because it was not considered fitting for clergy to be involved with offences punished by the shedding of blood. Such crimes throughout the kingdom were not generally regarded as 'royal pleas'. One of Roger's barons, Girald de Fray, and presumably other barons too, had the right to deal with homicide as well as other crimes (arson, theft, rape, brigandage and fruit-tree felling). According to the 1190 confirmation of local customs at Montecalvo in Roger's time, even homicide and treachery as well as other major crimes (adultery and arson) had all been judged by the men of Montecalvo itself, and not by any royal judge acting under royal rules. Montecalvo is not likely to have been the only community with traditional rights of this kind. There is no positive evidence that kings in any way attempted to curtail the exercise of 'private' criminal justice; rather the contrary. William I himself extended to the bishop and chapter of Troia, acting jointly, the power to act as the 'justiciar', not of the whole diocese, but of their own men. The only cases he reserved there were of *lèse-majesté*, presumably judged by justiciars of the region.

Nevertheless, it is significant that serious crimes did begin to be described in the sources as royal pleas (*justitia domini regis*) once the king became recognised as the supreme judicial authority in the kingdom. In a charter of 1153, issued by the count of Molise, a list of royal cases was given: homicide, arson, rape, violent house-breaking, assault and robbery on the highway, theft of working animals (*latrocinia*), theft of goods worth more than one gold ounce (*furtum*, grand larceny), and the cutting-down of fruit trees and vines. But all these were apparently judged by the count in his own court. Although nothing is said about *lèse-majesté*, for most purposes, if not all, the counts acted as the king's 'justiciars' in their circumscriptions. Only where there were no counts to enforce justice had the king to appoint special officials to deputise for him. Counts themselves were apparently judged by their peers in the king's own court in Sicily, if the one detailed report of a trial given in the *Liber de Regno* can be regarded as typical.

Although there is no specific reference to the *justiciar* of a particular region until 1175 (Terra di Bari), it seems probable that from the first, justiciars operated within established bounds. Such early justiciars as can be identified from other sources were well connected and might serve for long periods of time. Florius de Camerota was a nephew of Archbishop Alfano of Capua. He acted as justiciar in the principality of Salerno for Roger II, and after a brief exile (1165–8) resumed judicial duties at least until 1189. His colleagues were also well born. They may have been recruited from families particularly devoted to the monarchy, but it is just as likely that kings would have wanted to make the most of well-disposed local families to harness their strength for the monarchy.

The most obvious explanation for the appearance of justiciars by that name is the appointment by Roger II of such officials to carry out judicial functions on his behalf for those lands he became directly responsible for on the mainland after 1127 and could not deal with in person. The use of the term 'justiciar' links it firmly to the tradition of the Anglo-Norman realm where justiciars, acting on behalf of Henry I, also appear for the first time in the early twelfth century. Their representative function is brought out by the explicit statement of the bishop of Aversa in 1158, that the justiciars in court represented the king: *justiciariis vice domini regis fungentibus*. In one text, they were specifically assigned responsibility for dealing with the crimes of theft, house-breaking, offences on the highway, violence to women, homicide, the ordeals (*leges parabiles*), false accusation (*calumpniae criminum*), arson, crimes punished by confiscation of goods (*forisfacturae omnes*), and generally with all other offences for which men were liable with life and limb. Although this text makes no mention of *lèse-majesté*, a charter of 1200 for Gallipoli specifically reserves judgement of both homicide and *lèse-majesté* to the justiciar, so that his competence to settle all kinds of criminal cases must have been complete. Evidence as to how justiciars carried out their duties is slight. Their activities can, in fact, only be casually illustrated from the disparate records that survive. There is no reference to the keeping of any official records of their judicial business, and no indication that they were expected to report regularly to any high court, or to the king in person. When they can be identified, they appear to be of local origin and not, as itinerant justices in England, sent out from the king's court to different districts as required. The records that survive about justiciars do not often seem to have been composed by their own staff, and most were preserved because they constituted evidence of title to property after successful litigation. The nature of the justiciar's powers over matters of civil law are nowhere specified, and it is possible that any private suits adjudicated before them were only incidental to their main business, since some of the records state that plaintiffs put in pleas for justice when justiciars happened to be present on the king's business. Unfortunately, what royal business brought the justiciars into the neighbourhood, on occasion, or regularly, the sources do not say. It can only be surmised that they made their rounds mainly to enforce the peace.

From the records it seems that, in court, justiciars usually sat in pairs together with a considerable company of other persons: local judges and 'suitors', barons, knights and other *probi homines* (though never counts), who gave judgement when called on to do so by the justiciars. There was certainly therefore some regularity of procedure. In those cases where justiciars held court in several different places within their circumscriptions, there must have been local anticipation of when they would be due in the neighbourhood. Judgement depended on the availability in court of informed local witnesses and judges. What justiciars brought to the proceedings must have been the authority to investigate and decide; they may have had special power as royal representatives to order local inquests, as in England.

Whatever the merits of the system for the private litigant, it could not guarantee to satisfy them all. Thus the Carpineto chronicle gives a very jaundiced view of the local operations of royal justice, in this case by the justiciar, Count Peter of Manoppello. The author of the chronicle, Alexander the monk, himself travelled to the king's court, at least as far as Salerno, for one hard-contested suit, and was obviously deeply involved in managing the complicated legal business of his house which he summarised in his text. The abbot had actually secured some hearing of his grievances at the king's court itself, though where this met is not stated. The defendant, Richard de Padula, had thus been obliged to appear to answer the abbot's plea (*appellatio*). This was not, however, the end of the affair, for the count of Manoppello was several times required to supply crucial evidence in writing about earlier hearings from which the abbot had appealed *ab iniquibus judicibus*. However, the king's court only sent back the case to Manoppello with instructions to settle it so that there should be no further complaints about want of justice. But at Manoppello, Richard (*dilationis amator*) prevaricated, and saucily claimed that since the king had given him the *castellum* in question, he would call the king as his witness. This case was not resolved by the time of William II's death, though it had originally begun some ten years earlier. Despite his pleas for royal intervention, the abbot was regularly out-manœuvred by powerful men in his region. While the count was justiciar, the king's mandates were not disregarded; but the plaintiff was not satisfied. This may explain why, when the monastery complained to the king about the destruction of some of its churches by Marsilio and Rao de Puliano, a mandate was sent to both the count of Teramo, Rainald, and the justiciar, Bartholomew, so that by their joint efforts justice should be done and no further complaints about the defect of justice be voiced.

Even if they could not satisfy everyone, justiciars exercised real powers in unexceptional circumstances. They punished false accusations by the confiscation of all movables to the king. Lands in dispute were formally taken into the possession of the court; when a decision was reached, the justiciars invested the successful party with the *proprietate et possessione*. In 1148, two royal justiciars holding court in the bishop's palace at Aquino received a complaint from the local abbot against Pandulf, lord of Aquino; they promptly ordered the abbot's advocate to produce written proof of his claim, and when they were satisfied, confirmed his rights. In this case, the local judge was left with nothing more to do than draw up the record. On other occasions, justiciars required local judges to settle legal disputes and might even delegate decisions to a special panel. In the suit between Monte Cassino and the bishop of Teramo about the bishop's jurisdiction over one of Cassino's dependent monasteries, three bishops, a bishop–elect, the count of Chieti, and many others, clerk and lay, were given such authority (April 1148). Similarly, a dispute between the canons of San Leonardo and the bishop of Dragonara was settled by two judges from Dragonara and Fiorentino, in the presence, and by the command, of the two royal justiciars holding court in Dragonara (October 1148). The justiciars did not pass judgement, but their authority persuaded the bishop to submit to the court's jurisdiction. The justiciars might also take the initiative in bringing the parties to a concord. On occasion they could even order them to compromise in this way. In either event, the court's witness to such agreements provided binding legal authority. Often the records of such proceedings were made by the local judge or his notaries. Only occasionally did the king ask to be informed in writing of their decisions so that he might also add his confirmation. More common was the procedure whereby the plaintiff secured a royal writ requiring a settlement to be reached in the justiciars' court, so that there should be no further pleas to the crown for justice.

The evidence for the local justiciar in Sicily is not so interesting. There may have been rather less scope for such justice on the island. The Muslims would have been generally judged by Islamic law, certainly in the west, and the Greeks likewise would have been subject to their own (written) law and professional judges, though in practice the local official, called the *stratigotus*, must surely have acted in effect as the local justiciar. Justiciars are not named in the island before 1145, and almost invariably appear thereafter in connection with the definition of estate-boundaries which, as a new concern of government, called for new representatives of royal authority. The justiciars (or judges, *krites* in Greek) of Castrogiovanni and Val Demenna in 1154, for example, collected evidence about properties belonging to the church in Messina. Val di Noto also had its own justiciar under Roger II, and again in 1172, when Geoffrey de Moac (*magister justiciarius*) received instructions from the king and the magnates of the *curia* (Archbishop Walter, Matthew the vice-chancellor and Henry, count of Noto) to settle bounds, and travelled from Syracuse to Noto to do this. The procedure had been regular from the start. In October 1145, for example, William Avalerius, Avenel de Petralia and William de Pozzuoli on royal orders settled bounds for estates in the northern part of the island in dispute between Cefalù and Gratteri, holding an inquest and perambulating the bounds before reporting back to Roger II. Only then did they draw up a formal record. A more contentious problem was judged by Avalerius and Avenel in 1150. Although they passed judgement for the bishop of Cefalù against Aychardus, who was fined and forfeited his property in Cefalù, the justiciars begged the bishop to restore Aychardus' property to him and pardon him the penalty of thirty-six *solidi* due to the bishop's *curia*. The justiciars were instruments for seeing that justice was done, and their effectiveness was rooted in the co-operation they received from the countryside, particularly in defining land boundaries. It is worth noting that the collaboration of the countryside might not always have been spontaneous. In 1182, witnesses who claimed they had not formally been summoned to swear as to the truth of the bounds, were fined for their truculence in dealing with royal authority.

The evidence for twelfth-century justiciars as a whole is rather disappointing and needs fuller investigation. Justiciars even with royal backing were certainly not always able to impose binding judgements. Although William I's justiciars in Calabria induced the abbot of Sant'Eufemia to abandon his claims on the canons of Bagnara for pasture and cultivation rights, the abbot was bold enough to reopen the issue in 1168, when a special tribunal was set up specifically to deal with it since the quarrel threatened the king's peace. There was no established appeal procedure. On this occasion the archbishop of Reggio (who had been present in the previous justiciars' court) presided in a court at Messina with the bishops of Malta and Mazara.

The justiciars must also be recognised as working in a long-established tradition which aimed to resolve quarrels by arbitration. This continued to have its attractions. In 1174, for example, a *curia* was held at San Salvatore del Goleto when, without the presence of any justiciar, the dispute between the bishop-elect of Sant'Angelo dei Lombardi and the abbess over a church in his diocese was resolved by a panel of two bishops (Bisaccia and Monte Marano), the count of Balvano, various barons and some canons of Conza. Although ecclesiastical law was involved, it was not judged exclusively by clergy, and the court was not set up by the church. This way of settling legal problems through the good offices of persons of local consequence without resorting to formal proceedings in law is still found to be of value at the very end of William II's reign. According to the agreement reached in 1187 between the abbey of La Cava and William, lord of San Severino (himself at the time a royal justiciar and constable), William was induced to make concessions over various monastic *casalia* within the limits of his barony of Cilento by the offer of 100 *unciae* in Sicilian *tari*. The agreement and the definition of the boundaries was secured by judges specially designated by the king for this particular suit. There was a problem of rival lordships. If any of William's vassals had fiefs on monastic land, they had to swear fealty to the abbot (*salva fidelitate . . . regis*). William and the abbot agreed not to take oaths of vassalage from one another's vassals, or to let them live on their lands, except as *affidati* (*nisi per modum affidacionis*). In spite of the care taken by the king's judges with the terms, it was feared that disputes might recur between the vassals or between their lords. In such cases, both parties agreed not to take them to the king again, but instead to nominate an arbiter. What is striking about the 1187 case is the willingness of both parties to consider dispensing with the king's legal authority and seek a local settlement. Some limitations on the monarchy's powers to give effective and decisive rulings are openly admitted. After nearly sixty years, the monarchy was still operating in a very traditional society.

9

THE KINGDOM'S DEFENCES AND ITS ENEMIES

Warfare was endemic in most medieval western European states, for various good reasons. Their rulers were invariably soldiers themselves, and the notables of their dominions, clergy unashamedly included, retained military men. The states had no stable frontiers and though defence might be focused on border castles, even within the territory there were important fortifications in towns and commanding positions which could become centres of military operations. Nor did rulers confine their military objectives to defence. They might effectively deter enemy attacks not only by threats, but also by unprovoked raids, and might trumpet plausible grounds for annexing neighbouring states. Even when rulers had no serious anxieties about their neighbours, they could engage in warfare in order to keep their barons happy by successful campaigning, or to keep them from fighting on their own account. Barons not led to battle by victorious lords were not disposed to meek subservience; only martial distinction commanded uncritical admiration and earned rulers respect. Although successful wars paid for themselves in booty and conquests, great enterprises needed to be launched on an impressively large scale. This was costly, and only rulers with considerable resources and sound credit could compete. Rulers showed resource in efficiently squeezing more out of their ordinary revenues, and ingenuity in devising new reasons for making their subjects pay taxes. Military affairs played an important part in the calculations of the great men, but elude our deeper understanding. Apart from being out of sympathy with their predominantly bellicose inclinations, we are also too dependent for information either on clerical writers who had little appreciation of warfare, or on poets who dwelt on its heroic and romantic aspects, rather than its realities.

MILITARY RESOURCES

In several ways the military problems of the southern kingdom were unlike those of other western European states. In particular, the kingdom was unusual in having a clearly defined territory by 1156, and was not therefore committed to territorial expansion or attempts to overawe insubordinate neighbours. Moreover, its frontier across Italy was extremely short – only about half the length of the whole frontier of ducal Normandy. Since it ran across difficult country, it was also easily defended by the local inhabitants against invaders unfamiliar with the mountainous terrain. The main problem for the government was not so much military as political: to keep the local lords loyal. Across the frontier, the potential enemies were either the papacy or the western emperor. After 1156, the papacy was in no position to maintain its earlier hostility and itself became fearful of Frederick Barbarossa. For his part, Barbarossa had no hope of reaching the kingdom until the papacy had been dealt with. An invading force would have to rumble south either down the Adriatic coast road or through the papal state. It was impossible for the kingdom to be surprised by its enemies. Their purposes would anyway be to overthrow the monarchy rather than nibble at the territory, and this committed them to marching deep into the kingdom, where they became much more vulnerable. The kingdom was therefore remarkably defensible. As for his acts of aggression, the king was mainly interested in naval engagements against the Greeks or Muslims, so he had to be more interested in humouring his mariners than in deferring to his baronage. Unlike the other new kingdom of the twelfth century, in the Holy Land, the Sicilian kingdom did not have to live with a perennial military problem, and this affected its political outlook. William I, who had a justifiable reputation as a soldier, gave up campaigning; William II, though he launched successful naval expeditions, engaged himself in no wars. He did not even have palace regiments to keep employed.

Soldiers

Before the monarchy, fighting had obviously been organised by local commanders such as the counts or the duke of Apulia. Nothing is known about how such armies were composed, led or maintained. The count of Sicily certainly made use of Saracen troops, even on the mainland, but they could have been recruited by local levies, or supplied by Muslim 'vassals', or possibly constituted a personal comital bodyguard. Before the Norman settlement, the Lombard princes had various contingents of soldiers at their disposal; so too had the Greek imperial government in southern Italy. Norman auxiliary contingents had been useful when they first arrived in Italy to all the princes of the South. It was through infiltration of those forces that the Normans first gained mastery of the region. In every district, settlements were also traditionally defended by the local inhabitants. In 1111, Duke William ordered that in time of war, all men living within the bounds of La Cava's estates, even if they did not belong to the monastery, should help defend the monks' *castellum* of Sant'Adiutorio; if they failed to do so, they would be guilty of defying the duke's order. The monarchy changed little. In 1190, the abbot of Sant'Elena, near Larino, confirmed for the men of Montecalvo the customs of King Roger's time, including those of the knights and those who lived under military discipline (*qui militari lege vivunt*). Any man of the *castrum* who wanted to become a knight needed only the monastery's permission to do so. He might serve with a war-horse (*destrenus*) or with a *ronzinus* (which was only half as valuable). The war-horse could not be used for ploughing or milling, and had to be fed with barley and used in the monastery's service (so obviously not only in war). These knights needed arms and were liable for some royal service. They had certain financial advantages, and sons were not liable for service during their father's lifetime. Men of rural condition, who ploughed or milled, could clearly serve on occasion as royal knights, and the monarchy did not establish a military elite or tenures for mounted soldiers which would have clearly distinguished the king's knights socially from the others. All available knights could serve together when summoned. As late as 1243, Frederick II must have obtained just such an army when he mustered the forces of his prelates, barons and other powers, with their weapons, horses and archers, throughout the maritime province; they were commanded by his captain-general of the district, Count Simon of Chieti.

Such armies also included *servientes*. These are mentioned in the *Catalogus Baronum* as totalling over eleven thousand (as against its 8,620, mainly enfeoffed, knights). They were not enfeoffed with estates, but served as required with their lords. Though numerous, they are not given much attention by our sources. Some of them were certainly cultivators and only part-time soldiers. Others were perhaps professional military men, acting as attendants on knights and ready to serve with them. *Servientes* were still of service to Frederick II, often constituting the majority of his castle garrisons, though the king considered rustics (*pagenses*) serving as *servientes* less useful than the others. The great numbers of *servientes* makes it absurd to think that *milites* were the only soldiers of consequence in the kingdom: moreover, account must be taken of the fact that the 'military' contingents were not drawn from only one social and economic category.

The monarchy does not appear from thirteenth-century evidence to have modified the traditional obligations of service. The comital charter of 1254 for Isernia, which aimed to restore the good old customs of the past, still envisaged the faithful city militia as operating within the limits of one day's journey from the city, or up to three days' at the count's expense. The kingdom's military resources were by origin neither royal nor Norman. Some new military tenures had certainly been established on estates in land of variable size, with the services defined exactly, without regard to any special military requirements of the moment, but the ancient obligations of service in the kingdom, understood to be necessary for the self-defence of every settled community, had not been changed. Some churches succeeded as a matter of privilege in getting remission or reduction of the services due from their estates; clergy did not as such enjoy immunity from military obligations for their properties.

Castles

Whereas in England, the Norman conquest is usually regarded as an important break in English military arrangements, for southern Italy there is no single 'event' of Norman conquest which can be made to serve the same historical purpose. What precise military innovations the Normans introduced is not certain, but castle-building as such was certainly not one of them. Defensive structures had been built in the South before the Normans arrived, and labour-services had already been established to secure their construction. The Greek government had raised imposing fortresses in Sicily even before the Muslim invasions, and was still building them on the mainland in the early eleventh century as defences for the Lombard frontier, as at Troia, Lucera, Fiorentino, Civitate and Dragonara. In the 'free' Lombard regions, inhabited settlements were frequently protected by walls and towers, called *castella*, as defences in chronically unsettled times. The fragmentation of princely authority had also encouraged local rulers, counts and *gastaldi* to build their own fortresses called *rocche*. The abbots of Monte Cassino themselves built 'castles' to defend their lands against the early Normans and other unreliable neighbours. The Normans may have shown more ingenuity in knowing how to build castles for short-term objectives. For example, they may have consolidated their conquests in Sicily by constructing temporary wooden ones, which were abandoned once the frontier-zone was pushed forward. To what extent local lords built small castles for themselves has not yet been estimated. There were certainly some Norman small fortresses with quadrangular towers and 'donjons', significantly making use of the French word, as though there was no established local term for such buildings. Larger castles above the principal cities were, however, already familiar in the South. As the Normans assumed local political responsibilities, they obtained these fortresses and enlarged or rebuilt them as necessary. They played an important role in dominating the cities beneath, and were resented by some citizens who destroyed them if they got the chance to do so. Under the monarchy, kings did not normally allow cities to retain fortresses in their own hands.

Before the monarchy, castle-building appears to have been already controlled by counts or other rulers exercising 'sovereign' powers, who authorised their vassals to build them, as at Gioia where Richard the Seneschal duly obtained his lord's permission to erect a *castellum* in 1111. Similarly, Duke William of Apulia allowed the monks of La Cava in 1123 to build a *castellum* at Castelabate with all necessary fittings for defence (*girones* and *turres et omnia alia edificia que pro suprascripti construendi castelli tutela atque defensione necessaria sunt aut fuerint ubicunque vobis oportunum visum fuerit*). For this construction, the monks would have to find suitable workmen, but once built, the monks obtained full authority over the *censiles* and *homines* brought to live in what would become a fortified village. When Roger II became king, therefore, he had useful precedents for supervision of castle building. He certainly appreciated fully the arguments for keeping certain strongholds in his own hands and the cities under surveillance, but it is not known how difficult he found it to control castle building by individual Norman lords in isolated but naturally defensible sites. Certainly after 1189, in the disturbed conditions prevailing over the next thirty years, many castles were put up for purposes of immediate defence. Frederick II set out to have these destroyed as illicit after his return to the kingdom in 1220.

Only with Frederick can the monarchy be seen for the first time to have pursued a systematic policy of castle building and control. A list of *c.* 1250 shows that by then there were about 240 separate sites distributed throughout the seven major districts of the mainland. Each castle was at the centre of a zone, from which it could count on the men of the principal settlements to undertake castle repairs. Lists of the twenty to twenty-five settlements traditionally liable (*ex antiquo*) for the repair of the fortress of Sant'Agata di Puglia, survive from this period. It seems likely that all castles had depended on such assistance from quite remote times. Castles known to have had only a few, distant settlements to call on for this purpose, like Sant'Agata dei Goti, appear to be exceptional foundations which probably date from the Norman period itself, since they were not, like most others, centres of jurisdiction under the Lombard princes. This system of castle support had presumably originated therefore in the pre-Norman period. Although most parts of the kingdom must have been liable for services at castles in the twelfth century, the monarchy appears to have called upon them only intermittently until Frederick's reign. Frederick was still prepared to allow leading vassals to hold castles. Their obligations were quite specific. The archbishop of Salerno, for example, was responsible at Olevano for providing the castellan, *servientes* and watchmen (*vigiles*) with supplies of corn and wages; but he also paid for their wine and *companage*, a woman domestic for preparing corn (*ad purgandum frumentum*), a chaplain, horses, pack animals, oats, horseshoes and coats (*tobaliis*). Frederick II's officials noted every small detail.

After 1230, Frederick set up new overseers for his castles, but apart from his instructions to them, there is little evidence of how effective these administrative reforms proved to be in practice. A brief episode recorded after Frederick's death shows, however, that orders from on high were not necessarily obeyed. When Conrad IV's officials tried to get local communities to contribute to the repairs required at Boiano, the *universitas* of *castrum Pinearum* steadfastly denied that it owed any service. The commissioner there was powerless to enforce obedience, and was reduced to asking the local judge to make a formal record of the protest in order to exculpate himself. The peasantry cocked their snook at officialdom.

The fortifications of the kingdom depended on the talents of engineers no less than on the availability of labour, but the sources are uninformative about the kings' military experts. In Roger II's time, many sieges are mentioned by the chroniclers and the king deployed impressive machinery, not always successfully. The fortifications clearly served their purpose and some cities, such as Naples, could endure siege or blockade for a long time. Nor, until Frederick II's time, do the sources allude to the problems of procuring weapons and armour. It is not therefore known to what extent the Norman kingdom was self-sufficient in military equipment or in technical talent, though Edrisi helpfully reports that the kingdom produced so much pitch that some could be exported: at least for ship building, all the necessary raw materials were available locally.

Naval strength

Working on castles was not the only military burden resting on the districts. The *Catalogus* mentions responsibilities for coastal watch (*ad custodiam maritime*). Even apart from the dangers presented by pirates or enemies like the Pisans, some kind of watch on shore was maintained, if only to enforce seigneurial rights such as wreck. Most people in the kingdom would have been aware of the problems inherent in having a long coastline, and would have accepted the need to provide for defence from the sea. Yet once again, there are no details until the reign of Frederick II. His mandates take twelfth-century precedents for granted. He ordered the *turres . . . in maritima* to be brought back into a sound state of repair, according to the *statutum* of his Norman predecessors, especially to meet the danger from piratical attack. There ought to be men constantly on watch (*die noctuque*). The responsibility for repairs and providing coastguards had been, at least in some cases, specially assigned, so that each tower was held by a prominent royal vassal, secular or ecclesiastical, presumably on such terms as were negotiated with the archbishop of Salerno at Olevano.

As a maritime state, the kingdom made claims on its subjects not merely for defence, but also in connection with its own belligerence at sea. The foundation of naval strength was the services of the Greek subjects, initially from Calabria, later from the Apulian ports, but also firmly established in Sicily, where Messina became the chief royal dockyard. Sicily provides tantalising evidence about other obligations for naval service. At least some of the free Lombards paid a tax (*marinaria*) through the *baiuli*. Personal service in the fleet was performed by those without privileges. When the men of Caltagirone bought two estates from the king for forty thousand *tari*, they became liable for a payment of five thousand *tari* a year as rent, and had to be ready to send 250 sailors (*marinarios*) for the fleet wherever the king wanted them. Before 1189, the men of Nicosia owed 296 sailors to the king; until 1177, the bishop of Patti owed 20. The naval burden certainly seems heavy. In the early thirteenth century, some obligations were notably reduced, and even payments of *marinaria* in cash remitted, probably because a weaker government found it difficult to deny some petitioners. The burden on the island was not however limited to service at sea and taxes. Count Roger granted, and Queen Margaret confirmed, an exemption for the monks of San Filippo di Fragalà at San Marco of various *angaria*, including coastguard duty and supply of wood for building, ships included. Well before the creation of the kingdom, the Muslims too had been felling trees for shipbuilding. The Normans may well have inherited traditional impositions on the countryside, and not needed to introduce new ones. The government's insistence on its rights to dues for the navy (*statutum navale tributum*) is well illustrated by a case involving a poor man in the reign of William II, who tried to get out of his obligation to pay a tax of a mere three *tari* a year guaranteed by his small vineyard *pro bellico apparatu*. Because of his desperate financial circumstances, he sought the consent of the *comes* of the Messina galleys (who consulted his five subordinate officers) to the sale of his vineyard, so that he could pay his debts; they agreed, but only on condition that he bought another property with the residue, which would give him an adequate revenue for meeting his continuing tax liability. The burden of the fleet was therefore heavy and not easily shifted.

No naval officers are mentioned as such in the sources until 1154, but since Roger II's privilege for the new archimandrite of San Salvatore in Lingua Maris included rights over forty sailors when the fleet was enrolled, without hindrance from other officials, it looks as though the monastery had to find a captain for its own sailors. This could hardly have been difficult, considering their Greek credentials in Messina. *Comites galearum*, officers in command of a group or squadron of fighting ships, are the only early commanders mentioned before the term 'admiral of the fleet' appears for the first time in 1177. *Comites* are mentioned in the island, at Palermo in 1168 and at Messina in 1176, and they occur at Monopoli in Apulia in 1154 and at Mileto in Calabria in 1165. The kings could also call on the services of sailors in the great ports of the mainland: Bari, Naples, Salerno and Gaeta, and could usually count on the willingness of the ports and their inhabitants to engage in lucrative or necessary expeditions. Such communities had a long history of comparable enterprises on their own account. The main change for them was the size and ambition of the royal expeditions.

The great fleets sent overseas were commanded by the *admiratus*. George of Antioch, the first admiral known, was also closely identified with the royal administration, like his successor Walter de Moac. From Admiral Margaritone onwards, this office was exercised by a professional sailor, and often held in conjunction with the county of Malta, which furnished valuable resources and played some part in the preparation, harbouring and manning of royal ships. The population of Malta remained preponderantly Muslim, even under Frederick II. Later admirals were appointed from outside the kingdom. The earliest surviving instructions setting down their duties are those issued by Frederick to his Genoese admiral, Nicola Spinola, in 1239. Naval operations then still involved the direct use of pirates or freelance auxiliaries. The commander had to be both a practised diplomat and an effective disciplinarian if the forces available to him were to be manipulated successfully for Frederick's purposes. Earlier admirals almost certainly had a freer hand, but all were expected to keep themselves in business by seizing enough prizes and booty. Even ship building is unlikely to have been directly commissioned by the monarchy. The conduct of naval operations did not wait upon royal initiatives. Royal expeditions against the Greeks or Muslims were only conceivable because the sailors of the kingdom were already engaged in enterprises of their own requiring skill, audacity and an eye to the main chance. To this extent, the king's most important and elaborate military adventures did not have so much to be paid in full by taxation, as launched with public enthusiasm in the expectation of considerable profit. Royal summons to battle under William II may therefore have been greeted enthusiastically by his subjects, not resisted as unwelcome duty.

THE KINGDOM'S ENEMIES

Chroniclers of contemporary events rarely attempted to conceal their feeling about their rulers and the effects of the government on their subjects; however partial or casual these comments, historians cannot avoid taking them into account. Foreign, as distinct from domestic, affairs rarely had comparable interest for chroniclers, few of whom had any real conception of the nature of conflicts between peoples or kingdoms. Serious study of foreign affairs had not yet been devised, and it must be doubtful whether even rulers themselves had much grasp of what might be called the underlying issues in their confrontations with each other. The crusades, which were themselves a new attempt to unite Christian people against the Muslims, had only a limited success in doing so; no comparable effort was put into the task of promoting national solidarities. Churchmen naturally put ecclesiastical interests before those of the kingdom; secular magnates lived by a code which stressed a primary loyalty to kin and connections, rather than blind duty to the kings. They certainly believed that as great men in their own right they were entitled to interpret their obligations to kings and lords for themselves, and were not bound to defer to kings and puppet advisers. Great men were then entrusted with power and exercised it; they were far from being mere ornamental dignitaries. Such men, if they fell out with their sovereign lords and had to go into exile, frequently sought to recover their positions by securing help from neighbouring rulers. Though they might be denounced for treasonable activities by their former lords, the latter were themselves engaged in the same business of harbouring exiles and fomenting such intrigues as would at least embarrass their rivals, if not secure them some advantage. Such affairs necessarily exploit opportunities as they occur. They are extensions of domestic broils, quite independent of the substantial factors of foreign policy, such as resources in men and money or strategic geography.

Apart from the issues of personal diplomacy, deeper problems were perceived by contemporaries far more dimly, if at all. They could not therefore be resolved by statesmanship and long-term strategy. Historically speaking, however, the long-term future of the kingdom can be seen to have depended on the interaction of four main protagonists: the two empires, east and west, the papacy and the kingdom. There were theoretically five possibilities: that the kingdom would be absorbed into one or other of the empires; that it would survive independently; that it would enlarge its dominion over all or much more of Italy; or that it would become a mere client-state of the papacy. In the mid-twelfth century, the southern Italian kingdom was a newcomer in western Europe. It proved in 1156 that it would not quickly fade away, but what its future would be remained doubtful. The papacy's long-term plans to suppress the kingdom had necessarily to be suspended after the failure of Adrian IV's assault in 1156; the schism in the church, created in 1159 when Adrian died, unduly prolonged this period of papal passivity to the point where the papal alliance could be taken for granted and fear of its former antagonism forgotten. Imperial hostility was in no way diminished, and Frederick Barbarossa's support of Victor IV against Alexander III indicates how confidently he reckoned to act in Italy by that time. Even so, his more immediate objectives meant that he did not threaten the kingdom directly. In the long run, Barbarossa may have been content to contain the kingdom by his own more effective government elsewhere in the peninsula. At the end of his life, he had become interested in taking the kingdom into close alliance, rather than working for its total destruction. As early as 1162, Barbarossa may have already begun to rethink his strategy following the failure of the purposeful attempts to destroy Roger's monarchy after his death. The eastern empire caused the kings more anxiety.

The Greek empire

Any threat to the kingdom presented by the eastern empire may historically seem illusory by 1159, but contemporaries cannot be expected to have realised that the empire had already reached its final stages. The brilliant Comnenus dynasty that had saved the empire after 1080, somehow failed to resolve all its major problems. After Manuel's death in 1180, this was quite plain because uncertainty in the succession and public violence proclaimed the empire's weakness. These opened the way to the occupation and partition effected by Latin armies in 1204, which destroyed its real substance for ever. Since the Normans and the Sicilian king in particular had played a part in weakening the empire, the kingdom would in other circumstances have surely profited from the later assault and partition of 1204 to acquire lands in the Balkans, as Robert Guiscard had done when the Macedonian dynasty had similarly broken down in the eleventh century. Quite fortuitously, the Sicilian kingdom in 1204 was in no position to take advantage for itself of Greek weakness. This proved to be very unfortunate; for better or worse, the fate of the eastern empire had implications for the kingdom. The elimination of the Greek empire as a contestant for power in Italy also created an entirely different situation in the peninsula, and almost immediately the western empire and the papacy found themselves able to confront one another without fearing complications from the Greeks. Events in the east, for which the west itself had little direct responsibility, played their part in transforming western affairs. No Sicilian calculation of reasonable self-interest in the twelfth century would have underrated the empire's importance.

Whatever its latent defects, the eastern empire continued to display plenty of spirit in the mid-twelfth century. Although after Manuel's defeat in Italy he concentrated instead on Balkan and Anatolian affairs, this prompted relief in the west, rather than any expectation that advantage could already be taken of his weakness. Manuel was himself in some ways sympathetic to western ideals, which both impressed fellow rulers in the west, and profoundly disturbed many of his subjects. It was the anti-western reaction in the empire after his death that gave the excuse and opportunity for western intervention. This anti-western reaction itself indicates how deeply rooted the empire still was in its own traditions. Manuel's admiring biographer, Kinnamos, who found some of Manuel's personal enthusiasms embarrassing, more confidently stressed his very traditional role as intellectual defender of orthodoxy. Kinnamos took for granted Manuel's awareness of the historical role of the emperor in Italy, which educated Greeks derived from their reading of Procopius. This sense of history gave Greeks an understanding of the relations between the powers, and a sense of historical geography that was unmatched in the west.

Greek officials had operated in Apulia and Calabria as recently as the second half of the eleventh century, and some Norman counts had formally recognised Alexius Comnenus as emperor; some of their heirs naturally took refuge from Roger II at the imperial court from the 1130s. There were many Greeks in southern Italy who maintained close ties with the empire. Kinnamos had grounds enough for assuming that the universal emperor would recover his rights there some day. What frustrated such hopes was the development of a quite new practice of government, that found the formal submissions required by Manuel far too artificial to serve their former purpose. Kinnamos could not see that in practical terms the new kingdom provided a different kind of public authority from Manuel's, and that even Greeks, let alone Lombards, were beginning to derive advantages from an effective government at Palermo that they would not willingly forego. The only places in the kingdom which accepted Manuel's intervention in 1155 had, like the dissident nobles, particular reasons of their own to rebel; any general restoration of Manuel's power had little appeal for the kingdom's subjects. Their indifference to the empire would have baffled educated Greeks like Kinnamos, who was not concerned with understanding the factors involved or assessing Manuel's chances of reimposing Greek authority; he had no conception of any possible alternative order of government. From his point of view, southern Italy outside the empire enjoyed no better government than any of the other barbarian peoples – Hungarians, Serbs or Bulgars.

Kinnamos did have his own views of the purpose of the empire; how emperors could be expected to hold their own and impress their neighbours as serious statesmen. He had some historical idea of what territories had formerly been subject to Rome, which marked out for Manuel his proper theatre of action. The Comneni had mainly to impress the restless peoples of Asia Minor and the Balkans with their credibility. This required regular displays of military skill and the diplomatic handling of local feuds and rivalries, matters of which the government had long experience. It enjoyed such traditional respect that dissident princes and generals regularly fled to Constantinople in search of armed assistance. The Roman role required emperors to intervene whenever their prestige was at stake. Though they could suffer reverses, they believed in their own civilised superiority over disorganised barbarians to such an extent that they did not seriously live in dread of being overwhelmed. It was next to inconceivable that God would desert the empire. In fact the peoples they opposed, however violent, did not have the qualities of organisation required to supplant the empire. By marching in and out of the lands of these barbarians, as far as Antioch or Belgrade, Manuel kept reminding them of what the Roman empire could do. Beyond these frontiers, the western barbarians and the crusading estates that depended directly on them, also required Manuel's attentions. Manuel had real hopes of success in Italy where, by the beginning of his reign (1143), the new king of Sicily had forcibly obtained papal recognition of his conquests. Manuel was no more prepared than the western emperor Lothar to countenance Roger's pretensions. The kings of Sicily steadily considered the rulers at Constantinople their major enemies, and proposals to mend relations by marriage alliance regularly foundered.

The first hostilities occurred in the autumn of 1147. A Norman fleet left Otranto and first seized Corfu, where it placed a determined garrison of soldiers, before sailing round the Greek coasts as far as Euboea. It took possession of some other key ports, and raided the important cities of Thebes and Corinth before returning to Sicily laden with booty. At the time, Manuel was himself braced to meet the western leaders arriving in Constantinople for the crusade, and quite unprepared to deal with Roger. However, in March 1148 he made a treaty with Venice, which secured for him additional ships and collaboration until September for a great campaign designed to punish Roger's audacity and restore imperial authority in Italy. Unfortunately, his fleet was not in place to begin the siege of Corfu until the autumn of 1148, by which time Manuel was distracted by a Balkan invasion. He could not personally assume command of the blockade until the spring of 1149. The long siege of the Norman garrison severely strained relations between the Venetians and Greeks. Since the Greeks could not do without Venetian ships, the quarrel had to be patched up. In the early summer, Roger II despatched another fleet from Sicily to ravage the Greek coasts and tempt the besieging vessels into pursuit. A detachment of the Greek fleet did fight the Sicilians off Cape Malea (south-east Peloponnese), and according to Kinnamos, defeated most of it, but no less than forty Sicilian ships escaped. They sailed on to Constantinople, where they set fire to wharves across the Bosphorus, so the imperial forces can hardly be said to have achieved their main object. Moreover, the Norman fleet, before returning to Sicily, intercepted ships carrying the government's revenues from Crete. It also rescued Louis VII, and eventually his queen too, from Greek ships that had detained them on their way home after the crusade. Roger's cocky sailors ran rings round Manuel's forces, though the garrison at Corfu was starved into surrender and the military bases on the mainland lost. Encouraged by his re-capture of Corfu, Manuel was still bent on pushing ahead with the project of invading Italy when news of further unrest amongst the Serbs obliged him to return inland. Worse still, the fleet which he ordered to go to Ancona never crossed the Adriatic, and many of the ships were destroyed in the equinoctial storms.

These two years of conflict between Roger and the Greek empire coincided precisely with the operation of the second crusade, and need to be understood in a broad context of affairs. The chronicle of Romuald of Salerno, which gives a summary account of the expeditions, explains them instead as Roger's revenge against Manuel for spurning proposals for a marriage alliance. Kinnamos confirms the story, adding that such proposals had been initiated even before Manuel's accession in 1143. Roger, who had optimistically expected to be treated by Manuel as an equal, became angry with Manuel's scornful attitude towards him, constructed his fleet and waited for the right moment to use it. Romuald knew nothing of Roger's unsuccessful attempts to take part in Louis VII's crusade, and therefore missed Roger's motives for choosing to attack the Greeks just when the kings of Germany and France were approaching Constantinople. Roger's attacks on the Greeks were probably designed to show the western kings how strong he was at sea, and were not due to his part in any French conspiracy to seize Constantinople from the treacherous Greeks. Roger's attacks nevertheless made Manuel more determined to obtain Conrad's alliance for joint intervention in Italy whilst Conrad was still in the east and susceptible to Manuel's charm and persuasion. If Roger hoped his raids would exacerbate tension between the crusaders and the Greeks, he acted with heedless perversity. The main value of the raids to Roger lay in the booty he collected and the experience he gained; the smack in the face to Manuel was an ill-judged insult which can have given Roger only short-term satisfaction. Roger's concentration on seizing Corfu shows how much he intended to exploit his naval strength. Unlike Guiscard, Roger II made no attempt to seize a foothold across the Adriatic in the Balkans.

In order to counter-attack, Manuel needed both the naval co-operation of the Venetians (who feared Roger's domination of the lower Adriatic) and other allies in Italy itself. He kept Norman exiles at court, and no doubt found their intelligence reports and family connections useful. Above all, he deemed co-operation with the western emperor indispensable. Conrad, who had proposed to deal with Roger on his own account before crusading intervened, welcomed the prospect of such concerted action when he got back. Even so, he cannot seriously have intended to leave Manuel in possession of southern Italy, so negotiations between the two emperors necessarily involved much subterfuge since both expected to obtain the conquest by out-manoeuvring a less-adroit ally. After Conrad's death in 1152, his successor, his nephew Frederick, sent an embassy to re-examine the possibility of a joint attack in the South. From this time, Manuel gave much thought to Italian affairs. They seemed to offer him great opportunities to exercise the traditional Greek skills of intrigue and diplomacy. Given the tensions between pope and emperor, between the Lombard towns and Barbar-

ossa, quite apart from his belief that Roger's subjects would welcome
him as a deliverer, Manuel thought he had a good chance of being
recognised again in Italy as emperor. The emperor had much money to
spend, troops of his own, and would have been satisfied with formal
deference and payment of tribute.

On his accession in 1154, William I had apparently more reason to
fear the imminent arrival of the German king than of the Greek
emperor. He made a major diplomatic effort to detach both the papacy
and the eastern emperor from Frederick, and, if possible, to make an ally
of the king of Hungary. Kinnamos claimed that William offered to
return to the Greeks the booty taken in 1147. Whatever exactly was
proposed, Manuel rejected negotiations out of hand and prepared a fleet
and army for an Italian invasion. William's position seemed very shaky,
and Manuel could not sit by and watch Barbarossa invade Italy. He sent
off his uncle, Constantine Angelus, and part of the force with orders to
await the rest in southern Greece. Constantine, however, alerted to the
presence of another Sicilian fleet returning with booty from Egypt,
decided to intercept the enemy. The audacity was ill judged. The Greeks
were dispersed and Constantine captured. Manuel's opportunity to
punish the insolent king of Sicily did not therefore come until the
following year.

Manuel needed to find a bridge-head for his operations in Italy. By
1150, the representatives sent to work on his alliance with the western
emperor had persuaded the people of the region of Ancona to assist his
design. When the great revolt against William I broke out in the
kingdom in the spring of 1155, one of the principal barons, the count of
Loritello, was promised Greek assistance in the rebellion. One of the
emperor's agents, Alexander of Gravina, had been exiled twenty years
before, after his own rebellion against Roger. The other Byzantine
ambassadors, Michael Paleologus and John Ducas, themselves promptly
became combatants and deployed the men they had hired in Ancona by
moving into Apulia.

Vieste was taken without trouble; when Trani showed no willingness
to accept Manuel's forces, they moved on to Bari, where within a week
gold had overcome resistance not merely in the town but in the citadel.
The fall of Bari duly persuaded Trani, Giovinazzo and Ruvo to
surrender. Only the royal chancellor, confined to Barletta, and Richard,
count of Andria, continued to resist. After Richard was killed in a battle
with Ducas, Andria too submitted. A large royal force, sent against the
invaders as they besieged the neighbouring castle of Bosco, failed to carry
the day. Though Monopoli secured a month's respite by armistice, other
places (Montepeloso, Gravina and upwards of fifty villages) submitted to

Manuel's forces. His commanders then began negotiations with the pope, and told Loritello bluntly that they had come not to fight for him but to take possession for Manuel. When Paleologus, the commander, fell ill and died at Bari, Ducas extended the campaign to the South, taking Mottola, Massafra and Monopoli. Royal forces under Roger Fleming, despite being more numerous, took refuge in Taranto rather than risk open battle. But Ducas remained apprehensive, and wrote to the emperor asking for reinforcements in soldiers and ships, anticipating that the king would lead a great force against him. Nevertheless he moved on to Brindisi and took the town, though he failed after several attempts to take the citadel. When the reinforcements Ducas had asked for did not arrive in requisite numbers, Loritello found excuses to withdraw his support; the hired knights from Ancona also departed when their request for double wages was refused. Moreover, on the arrival of William's great force, some of the Norman troops hired by the emperor defected to him. When battle was joined (28 May 1156), the imperial forces were overwhelmed. Ducas and the emperor's cousin, Alexius, were captured. Manuel's audacious reassertion of his claims and his run of luck in preserving them collapsed totally.

Manuel's failure to dislodge William on this occasion relieved fears of what the Greeks might do: in effect when peace was made with Manuel in 1158, the emperor assessed the situation rationally. In return for the release of his captured soldiers he accepted William, says Kinnamos, as his ally in the west. (And so it proved: when William's death in 1166 gave him another opportunity to intrigue again, he declined to get involved.) Romuald claims that this time the emperor only came to terms after William had sent another large fleet in June 1157 to raid Euboea. Nicetas Choniates adds that this fleet pressed as far as Constantinople, where the sailors proclaimed to the startled inhabitants the name and dignities of King William, as though the object of their journey was to reiterate this political point. Manuel had, however, already understood only too well. In the same year, he sent Alexius Axouchos to Ancona with a double mission, as Nicetas Choniates explains. He was to prepare another great expedition to 'Calabria' in order to create the impression that he was still seriously committed to conquest, yet at the same time he was to negotiate with William in Palermo, for the best terms he could get. The captive Greek generals were used in the negotiations, and took the opportunity to secure their own release as quickly as possible. As a result, they could conveniently be blamed for the ignominy of the terms of the peace treaty. Kinnamos provides another crafty cover for the blatant failure of Manuel's plans. He attributes to the Sicilian negotiators an ingenious plea to Manuel's better nature. They pretended that Manuel's campaign was no more than a merited revenge for the Sicilian raid on Euboea in 1147, besought him to make peace now his honour had been vindicated, and not to insist on an excessive punishment for the offence. In this way, Kinnamos scaled down the real nature of Manuel's intervention and presented it as a success, to have plundered and frightened the king.

Manuel did not make the mistake of thinking he could intervene to his own advantage in the kingdom's affairs again, but it was not because he had lost interest in Italy all together. By 1158, when the treaty was agreed, Manuel could see that the papacy itself had endorsed William's kingship, and Adrian IV urged Manuel to make peace. Moreover, papal recognition of the kingdom had seriously offended Frederick, who found his own projects for the kingdom frustrated. Although Manuel had hoped to forestall Frederick's intervention in the South by seizing it himself, he had at least the satisfaction of knowing that Frederick too had been kept out of it, quite apart from the fact that Frederick had difficulties simply holding his own in northern Italy too. Manuel's projects for exercising influence in Italy were not therefore necessarily compromised by his new understanding with William. If his representatives had been tempted momentarily to think that disaffection against William could be exploited to restore Manuel's direct rule, Manuel had to accept that William's victories no longer gave him the internal collaborators indispensable for the vindication of his claims. William's willingness to secure peace and recognition at Constantinople adequately satisfied Manuel's sense of his own superiority.

Chroniclers looking back, like Kinnamos and Romuald, found nothing more of moment to report regarding the eased relations between the kingdom and empire. Manuel focused his Italian plans on subsidising the Lombard cities against Frederick, and on intrigues with Alexander III, who was at odds with the western emperor and his anti-popes. Manuel gave no support to the rebellions against William I's authority in 1160–2; the rebels then expected help only from Frederick. The pope continued to regard Manuel's Italian concerns as potentially useful in his own struggles with Frederick, and therefore tried to maintain amicable relations between Manuel and the kingdom. However, there was no real hope of overcoming the genuine reluctance in the kingdom to countenance any revival of Manuel's real power in Italy. Manuel was reduced to invoking the help of Louis VII of France when he tried to improve his relations with the kingdom. However, early in 1166, Manuel sent Jordan, son of Prince Robert of Capua, to the pope with further proposals for a reunion of the Greek and Latin churches, and for a coronation ceremony for himself at the pope's hands. Perhaps in connection with this project, he offered to marry his daughter and heiress, Maria, to the new king, William II, on his accession in May 1166. Many embassies passed to and fro, but the project fell through, *propter multa capitula* as Romuald somewhat vaguely explains. At the most, the peace treaty with William I was renewed, and Manuel resumed his dealings with the northern Italian cities. The situation was tense when Frederick himself returned to Italy at the end of 1166 and laid siege to Manuel's base at Ancona in the spring of 1167. William II's government decided to mass its own troops defensively on the north-east frontier and there were skirmishes, but Frederick had to abandon his threatened invasion. The queen regent then adopted a policy of allowing exiled rebels to return, and of releasing political prisoners, which succeeded in uniting the kingdom against the western emperor. This made Manuel's alliance seem less valuable.

As Manuel's projects in the Balkans matured, his plans for the recovery of Dalmatia compromised his friendship with the Venetians who enjoyed lavish trading concessions in the empire. When Manuel ordered all Venetians in his lands to be detained on 12 March 1171, he provoked a violent reaction in Venice itself, where a fleet was prepared to ravage his coasts. At this juncture, Manuel again sought a more binding relationship with the king of Sicily. Maria, though no longer his direct heir, remained unmarried, and this time William II, now of age, agreed to the match. William left Sicily to meet his bride at Taranto in April 1172. When she failed to arrive, his indignation knew no bounds. From this time, the idea of an *entente* with Constantinople was definitely abandoned. William made a treaty with Genoa in 1174, and in 1175 reached an alliance with Venice for twenty years, directed against Manuel. Alexander III himself may still have counted Manuel amongst his allies until the autumn of 1176, but after the arrival of the news of Manuel's defeat at Myriokephalon by the Turks in August 1176, Manuel's reputation plummeted. Romuald of Salerno considered it justifiable retribution on the emperor who had treated his own king, William, so ignominiously in 1172. He contrasted the hopes he ascribes to William II of being able to prosecute holy wars against the Muslims with those of rulers who made pacts with them, a dig at Manuel. Detestation and scorn of the Greeks had replaced the alarm and respect shown to Manuel in his earliest years. The peace negotiated at Venice in the summer of 1177, which opened a new phase in Italian politics, ignored Manuel altogether, even though the Greeks still clung to Ancona as a token of their commitment to Italy. Yet within a few years, the uncertainties of Constantinople, which followed the succession of Manuel's eleven-year-old son, Alexius II, in 1180, gave William II the opportunity of interfering in the empire, receiving Greek exiles at court and sending his own soldiers and ships to Greece. The roles had been reversed. It was the Sicilians' turn to exploit the internal difficulties of the empire.

The western empire

Frederick I's plans to restore imperial authority in Italy had to take account of the kingdom in the South, which by defying him could damage his standing throughout the peninsula. Yet despite his six journeys to Italy, Frederick himself never ventured further south than Rome. Even if in retrospect his belligerent talk can be seen to have induced nothing worse than rare frontier skirmishes, his own contemporaries remained fearful. At the beginning of his reign he had made an alliance with Eugenius III against the kingdom, and even Adrian IV had welcomed the renewal of the policy that had so nearly destroyed Roger II in 1137. William I had forced the pope willy-nilly to change this policy, and the papacy eventually began to appreciate its alliance with its vassal-kingdom, as Frederick himself became more frightening and his position in northern Italy more oppressive. When Cardinal Roland, who had negotiated at Benevento in 1156 and confronted Frederick at Roncaglia in 1158, was elected pope on Adrian's death in 1159, Frederick's decision to support a rival candidate elected by a few cardinals is understandable, though it proved to be a major mistake. Instead of coaxing Alexander into a close imperial embrace, Frederick forced him into the arms of the king of Sicily and into an international network of relationships from which Frederick was totally excluded. Alexander's frantic activity in assembling the coalition while in France from 1162 deterred Barbarossa during his short third visit to Italy in 1163–4, though there was some renewed trouble on the frontier in the regions of Frosinone and Alatri. Much more serious plans were laid for his fourth journey after the death of William I. When the queen regent offered a generous amnesty to the rebels, Frederick could no longer count on their co-operation, though Andrew of Rupecanina and Richard of Fondi renewed their raids in the north-west. To distract Manuel from Italy, Frederick persuaded the Hungarians to keep him occupied in the Balkans. Frederick's army under Christian, archbishop of Mainz, accordingly set about the siege of Manuel's base at Ancona in the spring of 1167 with some confidence; both Rupecanina and Loritello were present there. William II's army gathered apprehensively across the Tronto to meet any full-scale invasion. There were skirmishes, but the armies did not meet in open battle. In a few weeks the emperor was in full retreat from Rome, beaten not in battle, but by sickness. His triumph had nevertheless been sufficiently dramatic and frightening while it lasted to unite his enemies. Manuel began to negotiate with Venice, and spent money encouraging the Lombard towns to form a league.

Frederick did not reappear in Italy until 1174. In his absence, the management of the kingdom's affairs had been assumed by William II. The young king was not implacably opposed to Frederick, and after the humiliating collapse of his plans for a Greek marriage was eager to recover his prestige with distinguished rulers of the north. The astute Frederick quickly made overtures to the king for a marriage alliance that would draw his kingdom into the imperial orbit. The pope, alarmed by the good prospects for sealing an agreement, acted to secure for William an alternative match with Joanna, daughter of King Henry II of England, urging the undesirability of the German alliance. William allowed himself to be persuaded. When Frederick resumed his military operations in 1176, royal forces under Tancred actually saw action against the Germans (and were defeated). Only Frederick's spectacular defeat by the Milanese at Legnano, 29 May 1176, brought all parties to agree to the negotiation of a general settlement.

The fullest account of the protracted diplomacy conducted at Venice in the summer of 1177 comes from Romuald, archbishop of Salerno, sent by the king as one of his representatives to the conference. This detailed report, originally drafted for the king's information, not surprisingly seeks to stress the Sicilian role at Venice, and no doubt exaggerates it. Nevertheless, in itself, it indicates that the kingdom had at last openly assumed a role commensurate with its real powers. Since Frederick and the king had not been open enemies, the main problems of the conference were to resolve tension between Frederick and the Lombard towns. Frederick's chief purpose was, however, to undermine the coalition between the towns and their backers, the pope and the king, which had successfully induced him to negotiate. Released from the diplomatic cul-de-sac created by his support for schism in the church, he could resume his plans for the revival of the empire in Italy on a more promising foundation. He had no plans to do more for Alexander than he had to. He was interested in taking the opportunity to exercise his exceptional talents on the impressionable Sicilian envoys. If he could tempt them into a more friendly relationship, he hoped to weaken the bond which had so improbably brought the papacy and kingdom together. Created by the common fear of Frederick, it could as quickly be dissolved when Frederick changed course. The stuffy and unctuous Romuald, who spoke for the Sicilian delegation (at least according to his own report), cannot fail to have been impressed by the emperor's fair words and accommodating demeanour. Frederick tolerated his anxiety to have the king treated as a ruler of equal rank to himself; he flattered Romuald's status by allowing him to address the emperor seated. Romuald in his oration derided the notion that the two rulers had been, or would be, enemies. He publicised William's total indifference to Italian affairs, and his zeal to renew the wars against the infidel. By this he presumably intended to win admiration for the king's piety, without realising what conclusions Frederick might draw from it about the negligible opposition Sicily would put up to his own Italian plans.

Frederick may not have believed that the archbishop represented the most shrewd political judgement available in the southern kingdom, but in his answering oration he encouraged Romuald and William to believe that a very amicable settlement could be worked out in the fifteen years of truce agreed on at Venice. Romuald promptly secured the swearing of oaths from the German princes to confirm the treaty, and appears to have become correspondingly anxious that the German delegation took so long to reach Sicily for the reciprocal ceremony required there. At last this too was done, but when the German party withdrew, the government was highly embarrassed by an 'incident' in which the delegates were set upon by 'peasant' bandits at Lagonegro and robbed. Since they even took the copy of the treaty, this must raise suspicions about their real status. The government offered profuse apologies to the Germans, and handed out savage punishments on the criminals, whose dismembered bodies were sent to the chief cities of the kingdom to be displayed as warning – another hint that it was not just banditry. Frederick discovered, therefore, that Romuald's eagerness to secure his friendship was certainly shared in high places. If he had any doubts about the 'incident', or interpreted it as a sign of German unpopularity amongst the people of the kingdom, he did not allow this to deter him. Relations between the empire and the kingdom had taken a new turn; after years of apprehension, the kingdom no longer had to fear the emperor's vengeance.

By the time Frederick returned to Italy for his sixth and last visit in October 1184, peace had been settled with the Lombard towns at Constance (1183), and his imperial authority in Italy was reaffirmed. His friendly relations with the southern kingdom were sealed by the betrothal of his son, Henry, to William's aunt, Constance. William's willingness to leave Frederick unchallenged in northern Italy could have been inferred from his clear commitment to high-level piracy in the Mediterranean. There is no strictly contemporary evidence of any anxiety about the future of the kingdom. William's wife Joanna, daughter of King Henry II of England, was reported in Normandy in about 1181 to have given birth to a son, baptised Boamund, who was invested by his father as duke of Apulia. Nothing more is known about him or about any other children of the marriage. Although Richard of San Germano believed, in the early thirteenth century, that William II had been childless and had dedicated the church at Monreale to the Virgin in the hope of obtaining an heir of his own body, his evidence is not reliable. It is therefore quite possible that when the marriage of Henry and Constance was agreed, William still had sons living and did not regard Constance as his heir presumptive.

Constance was already thirty, and why William had not previously been concerned enough to find a husband for her remains obscure: the initiative for a proposal to marry her to Henry, twelve years younger, certainly came from the emperor. William considered it a dazzling proposal, and only later evidence survives of possible differences of opinion about the wisdom of the arrangement. If Pope Lucius III, who succeeded Alexander III in 1181 after years as one of his key lieutenants, had any misgiving about the royal alliance, he could not afford to protest because the chances of his return to Rome from enforced exile in northern Italy would be improved by this agreement between the two major Italian powers. William II himself may not have been particularly anxious about the effects of the alliance either for the papacy or for his kingdom, since there is no reason we know of for him to have anticipated his own death within four years. He gathered an appropriately regal dowry for Constance – in gold, silver, costly fabrics and furs – and sent her out of the kingdom on 28 August 1185 with a cavalcade of 150 pack-horses. According to later reports, he had required his vassals to swear fealty to Constance as his legitimate heir, if he died childless, but too much weight should not be attached to this testimony.

THE ENTERPRISES OF WILLIAM II

William's insouciance about the possible consequences of this marriage for his kingdom has, not surprisingly, been much criticised. Even if he himself expected to have a direct heir as his successor, there cannot be any serious doubt that Frederick negotiated the marriage with a particular end in view, though at the time it might have seemed improbable in the kingdom that Constance would herself bear a child. If Frederick I did entertain such hopes, they were not realised until after his death when Constance was in her fortieth year; her child, Frederick II, was no weakling but the wonder of his age. William's continuing confidence in his own future is conveyed by his decision to resume the aggressive policy of Roger II at sea. His understanding of the possibilities of Sicily's role in Mediterranean affairs suggests that in this respect he was actually the forerunner of Frederick II. William pursued the proper interests of the kingdom as he saw them, and this involved rejecting plans focused narrowly on weakening Barbarossa's power in Italy. In the light of previous experience, William II might have concluded that the Germans would always face too many difficulties in northern Italy to become really dangerous to the kingdom in the South. He obviously no longer feared that disaffected nobles would prefer the Germans to the native monarchy, and this was in general soundly calculated. Above all, he had no fear of papal hostility to the kingdom, for Barbarossa's power in Italy had obliged the papacy to tread warily.

In the very same month that Constance left the kingdom, William's forces, in a more ambitious campaign than usual, succeeded in forcing their way by land and sea into Salonika. The capture of the city provoked great alarm in Constantinople, particularly when the Sicilian fleet arrived in its vicinity and awaited the arrival of the army, intending to take the capital itself. Though this disaster did not occur, the empire had been so seriously shaken that on 11 September, the last of the Comnenus emperors, Andronicus, was overthrown and replaced by Isaac Angelus. This was the first tangible indication of how western intervention in the empire could precipitate political action at Constantinople. It was a foretaste of what would happen in 1204. William II's projects were not fanciful; they were premature.

Information about this and other flamboyant assaults on strong and rich Mediterranean cities derives, however, from non-Sicilian historians, whose views of the kingdom picked out rather different elements from those of concern to ecclesiastical chroniclers. William II's promotion of raids in Egypt, Greece, Spain and North Africa have earned him little admiration in modern times. There is no proof from these hostile sources that such raids were actually profitable in booty, though this must be presumed. Nor do there seem to be any long-term prospects of the ability to hold on to any of the places seized. Yet Romuald's exposition of William's policies hints at no dissatisfaction. On the contrary, there was some measure of popular approval for attacks on public enemies such as the Greeks and Muslims. William II, when he came of age, almost without needing to think about it, relaunched expeditions of the kind Roger II had thought worthwhile. When William I abandoned this policy under Maio, this was not attributed to his good sense, but ridiculed. The *Liber* claims that propaganda by Maio about the burden of the African outposts being greater than the honour was worth, served only to create an impression of how mad he was: it did not make any sense to contemporary opinion. Guiscard and Roger II provided admirable precedents for attacks on Greeks, even if they were fellow Christians. After the *entente* established with Constantinople in 1158 broke down in 1172, William II had no scruples left. The initiative in securing William's interventions was even taken by Greeks at odds with their own government, so it is a tribute to William's standing that his court should attract foreign dissidents and exiles, much as Guiscard's had done a century earlier. William's support for dissidents was not only proof of his 'great-power' status; it neatly paid back the Greeks in kind for their own comparable activity. To censure William's behaviour is to misunderstand (twelfth-century) politics. William's attack on the empire in 1185 was moreover only one of many reactions to the usurpation of Andronicus Comnenus in September 1183, which had provoked revolts and secessions in the empire as well as other foreign interventions, such as those by Bela III, king of Hungary, or Sultan Kilidj Arslan II from Iconium (Konya). It would have seemed foolish and cowardly of William to stand back at this juncture.

In 1184, two Greeks reached the kingdom urging William to back their claims to be regarded as lawful rulers at Constantinople: one, a boy of twelve alleged to be Alexius II, whom Andronicus had deposed and murdered; the second, another Alexius, a member of the imperial family. William chose to recognise the boy's rights, but it was the other Alexius who accompanied the expedition when it set out in June 1185. It sailed with good prospects that its arrival would coincide with a revolt of magnates against the tyrannical Andronicus. William's forces had been secretly assembled from motley sources over many months. The fleet was commanded by the king's cousin, Tancred, count of Lecce, whose brother-in-law, Count Richard of Acerra, shared command of the army with a Count Alduin (probably the royal seneschal). The forces landed first at Durazzo, which fell on 24 June, and the army advanced unopposed to Salonika just over a third of the way to Constantinople, while the fleet sailed round the Peloponnese. The army arrived at Salonika on 6 August, the fleet on the 15th. The city fell on the 24th. In his account of the siege, Eustathius, the archbishop who experienced it, accused David Comnenus, the garrison commander, of cowardice and treachery. The garrison and the inhabitants did vigorously defend themselves from the enemy, but certain individuals – two Illyrians, half a dozen Germans and even a Greek guide – were implicated in treasonable contacts. Though Andronicus sent reinforcements, they were ineffective because the only generals he could trust were incompetent.

The whole siege of Salonika lasted only eighteen days, so Andronicus' direct responsibility for failing to prevent its fall cannot be sustained. It suited later writers to pile up the case against his tyrannies and the terror he inspired in his subordinates. Andronicus remained confident that the enemy, advancing deeper into the empire, would become more vulnerable to indiscipline, disaffection and shortage of supplies. Since Andronicus expected to play a waiting game, he put the defences of the capital into good shape, and himself withdrew to a villa outside the city where, only eighteen days after the fall of Salonika, he was unexpectedly toppled from power. The new emperor, Isaac Angelus, sent out an army under Alexius Branas, which adopted Andronicus' own tactic of mopping up contingents of the enemy as they ranged about in search of booty. Demoralised by this harassment, the invaders withdrew to Mosynopolis. Here, Branas frightened them into a retreat towards the river Strymon, where part of their force had been left to keep an eye on Philippopolis. After the failure of attempts to secure a truce, the Greeks fell on the enemy on 7 November at Demetiza, dispersed the army after fierce fighting, and captured both their generals and Alexius Comnenus, the ostensible pretender. Those who escaped fled back to Salonika, where the garrison hastily decided to embark for home. Others continued along the road to Durazzo, which held out against the Greeks until the following year. Meanwhile the Sicilian fleet, which had been vainly awaiting the arrival of the army in the sea of Marmara off Constantinople, advanced on its own account towards Nicomedia. No naval engagement was fought, attempts at landing were repulsed, and eventually Tancred abandoned his vengeful tactics and returned to Sicily.

William II lost many soldiers in battle, and captives died in such numbers that the king appealed to the emperor to show the rest some compassion. Not until 1187 were the survivors released, only to be enrolled as imperial infantry. They then found themselves led by their general, Branas, against Constantinople in an unsuccessful attempt to supplant Isaac Angelus. William's generals may not have been released until a peace treaty was agreed, probably late in 1187, after the capture of Jerusalem by Saladin gave William II a new cause to fight for. His enthusiasm for warfare in the empire was not, however, dampened by the failure of 1185. The ruler of Cyprus, Isaac Comnenus, who faced an imperial force sent to recover the island in the spring of 1187, received naval support from Sicily under Admiral Margaritone. When the imperial generals were captured there, they were sent to Sicily for imprisonment. Margaritone also seized the Ionian islands, Cephalonia, Zante and Ithaca. The Sicilian fleet at least had profited from the disorder in the empire to demonstrate its own supremacy. When William decided to play a leading part in western plans to punish

Saladin, it was natural for the leaders of the third crusade to count on naval support from Sicily and co-operation from the Cypriots.

William's credentials as an enemy of Islam were also impeccable, as Arabic sources explain. In 1173, Amalric, king of Jerusalem, sent to the west for help in a plan to collaborate with Fatimid groups in Egypt to overthrow Saladin's military government. Though Saladin got wind of the plot and executed the leaders (6 April 1174), this remained unknown to both Amalric and the king of Sicily, who had been drawn into the scheme. However, when the great Sicilian fleet and its thousands of men, numerous horses, siege engines and supplies reached Alexandria (28 July 1174), the force from Jerusalem had not arrived: King Amalric had died on 11 July. The Alexandrian campaign thus became an entirely Sicilian enterprise. The troops disembarked unopposed and set about the siege of the city. Even before Saladin was able to arrive, however, the local forces succeeded in burning the Sicilian siege engines and forced the army back into its boats by a night attack on 1 August. Muslim sources claim that they left behind an enormous booty and three hundred knights.

William II did not conclude that such adventures were ill advised. Twice within the next four years the Sicilian fleet attacked the town of Tinnis in the Nile delta. On the second occasion, the town was occupied for four days before the fleet departed with prisoners and plunder. In 1177, when Romuald expounded William's policy to Barbarossa, he claimed that the king prepared his *biremes* every year, sparing no expense to pursue the enemies of the cross by land and sea with bitter hatred (*crudeli odio*), and to clear the way for pilgrims to the Holy Sepulchre. The details of such apparently successful plundering are not available. The other naval expeditions known about involve the Balearic islands, where the Sicilians are alleged to have been drawn into the conflicts between the rulers of Majorca and the Almohades in North Africa. Information about Sicilian relations with North Africa is confusing. Some kind of agreement seems to have been reached with the Almohad ruler, Abu Yusuf Yakub, involving payment of tribute to Sicily, possibly as the price of trading in the island without fear of Sicilian corsairs. William's relations with the Muslim rulers of North Africa must have been influenced by his rule over his own many Muslim subjects, which is not a matter ever considered in Romuald's chronicle.

Whatever William's private feelings about Muslims at home, there is no reason to doubt his genuine desire to punish Saladin after 1187, nor the ability of the kingdom to contribute ships, money, provisions and equipment as well as experience to the enterprise. His contingents, as in 1185, could have been composed of individuals from many lands, and not necessarily a body of men trained only in the kingdom. Would

William himself have departed on crusade? As a ruler he was lavish in his
expenditure on warfare, but he had no experience of fighting and never
acquired a reputation as a sporting warrior. No other ruler of the day,
not even Louis VII of France, still less the great rulers of civilised
Constantinople, had so slight a military reputation as to defy contemporary expectations of kingship. Whereas other rulers, however martial,
needed time to muster their force for the crusade, William was,
however, already prepared by the spring of 1188 to send another fleet
under Margaritone to the Holy Land. The admiral had himself formerly
been a pirate, and his colourful exploits caught the imaginations of the
Christian world in Constantinople and in northern Europe. Arab
historians played down his success while acknowledging his importance.
He stood in a long tradition of Sicilian audacity and ingenuity, and the
acquisition of the Ionian islands, which he held of the king as a personal
fief, recalls the exploits of those Norman conquistadores a century
earlier, on whose achievements the monarchy had been raised.

In his last years, William II confidently acted out the role he thought
appropriate to his status. He was actively engaged in intervention in the
Greek empire; the German emperor was his ally; the papacy, overawed
by Barbarossa in Italy, cultivated his friendship, without hoping to drag
him into alliance against the Germans. William's confidence in dealing
with the papacy has to be contrasted with the position of both his
predecessors who had good reason to be wary of papal dislike. William
II could take papal backing for granted, and this may also have given the
kingdom a sense of being fully accepted and, in effect, capable of
standing on its own feet. Professor Ménager commented on William II's
extravagant claim to Henry II's ambassadors, not altogether truthfully,
that he was not in the habit of swearing oaths, since they imposed
limitations on his independence. But this may explain the strange fact
that, despite his good relations with the popes, he is never recorded as
having met one personally, and was therefore not able to perform
homage in person as his father had positively insisted on doing. It would
have been perfectly understandable if William II had himself gone to
Venice with Alexander III, but he stayed in Sicily. Could it be that
William II sedulously avoided all personal meeting with the pope in
order to evade the ceremony of homage which was bound to be asked
for? By not doing homage in person, did William II intend to spare
himself the semblance of humbling his royal dignity? The fact that he
could get away with it indicates, however, that the kingdom had
travelled far, even under such a seemingly mild ruler. There was no
discussion of the nature of his ties with the papacy until 1188 when,
early in his pontificate, Clement III made a number of important

concessions to William, either as a token of favour, or with the deliberate intention of winning him over to the papacy. Clement III relaxed his right to take William's homage, and even opened up the possibility that such a favour might also be accorded to William's heirs, provided that fealty itself would be sworn at least once by kings in their lifetimes to the papacy. This important concession, coming at the end of William's reign, opened up the prospect of a different kind of relationship between king and pope for the future. Within ten years, events had taken quite a different turn again.

By 1188, the fall of Jerusalem to Saladin made the organisation of a powerful force, led by western kings, the papacy's most urgent task. Sicilian participation was taken for granted, and William II's monarchy did not itself seem to be in any immediate danger. His death in November 1189 immediately changed everything. The eastern empire itself could take no advantage of it, but for everyone else, William's death had profound implications. The claims of the still childless Constance to the throne were asserted by her husband. The papacy acquired a new significance as nominal overlord of the Norman kingdom. The peoples of the kingdom itself were left with political responsibilities they little knew how to exercise. Remarkably in the circumstances, the kingdom did not collapse. There was less evidence than in 1155 of any eagerness on the part of the nobles to seize the opportunity for purely local advantages: instead, there were only rival bids for the whole monarchy. The monarchy obviously faltered when there were rival candidates for the kingship, but the Norman dynasty was not immediately destroyed by the Germans. Eventually in 1194, when Henry VI did obtain the kingdom, the papacy was powerless to make any use of the sovereign rights forced on it by the Norman kings. The southern monarchy had established itself as a viable political entity but, like England in 1066, it could therefore be taken over in one piece. For better or worse it was thereafter firmly anchored to the rest of the European mainland, and the future prepared for it by William II as the base for a predatory central-Mediterranean enterprise was abruptly cut off.

PART IV

THE NORMAN LEGACY

IO

THE KINGDOM IN DISARRAY

·

The death of William II without direct heirs on 17 November 1189 opened a long period of difficulties for the kingdom. Its immediate effect on the government of the country can be directly illustrated from the Carpineto chronicle's account of the monastery's protracted lawsuit with Richard de Padula. On Christmas Eve, he simply occupied the lands of his great-grandfather, which he had been trying to recover by law, and sealed his victory by sending Abbot Bohemond back to his home monastery of Casauria as an alleged simoniac. Since Richard had the backing of Roger, count of Teramo, who had sworn allegiance to the emperor, the monks of Carpineto sent a representative to Lombardy to get the imperial marshal, Henry Testa de Bappenheim, to put pressure on the count. For practical purposes, the authority of the Sicilian monarchy counted for nothing on its northern borders. The eagerness of certain groups to take advantage of the hiatus in government was shown also at Naples, where the citizens seized properties taken from them by the men of Aversa. In both Naples and Amalfi, the citizens established communes for self-government. Although this time the whole kingdom was not ready to break up into fragments, there is no doubt about the eagerness of some groups to take advantage of the opportunity to get their own way. How all the different parts of the kingdom fared remains obscure, for the sources of information available are themselves scanty and discontinuous, but over the next generation, recurrent uncertainty about the future encouraged much dissent and unrest. As a result, William II's reign came to seem an ideal period of peace and justice, and this nostalgia goes to show that the kingdom did not wish to disintegrate altogether. In fact, since the monarchy created by Roger II proved capable of surviving without continuous masterful kingship, by 1189 it must have been broadly acceptable to most of the influential people of southern Italy and Sicily. If the will to preserve the kingdom had come by then to depend on rather more than the monarch himself, it is nonetheless difficult to grasp exactly whence the young kingdom drew its essential strength in this period: it can be sensed rather than demonstrated.

William's only surviving legitimate relation was his aunt Constance, married to the German king, Henry, in 1186. William is reported to have made his subjects swear loyalty to her as his presumptive heir, but only by sources written after his death, and in 1189, few great men in the kingdom accepted her claims as binding. Constance had little to commend her. At the time in her mid-thirties, she still had no child of her own, and her German husband represented the long-resisted pretensions of the western empire to the southern kingdom. Under them, the independence of the kingdom would have been compromised, and even if Constance had died childless, Henry would undoubtedly have tried to keep the kingdom in his empire. Constance's claims in 1189 could only have been imposed by force, and since the German emperor himself had left on crusade in May 1189, there was a reasonable chance that the Germans would be too distracted to undertake campaigns on Constance's behalf. The kingdom anyway had had much previous success in wearing down German attacks. Only on the northern border closest to the German bases in central Italy can there have been any calculation in favour of the Germans. The attraction of the German claim there stemmed from the consolidation of imperial authority in central Italy in the previous ten years. This had anyway made it imperative for the kingdom to come to terms with the realities of this new Italy, and there was some danger that the kingdom would actually be pulled apart if government in Palermo failed to assert itself on the mainland and repel any rival imperial attraction.

KING TANCRED

If Constance was considered unacceptable, who could be made king? Tancred, count of Lecce and *magister justiciarius*, was the chief official of the mainland, pre-eminent both as soldier and administrator. His father had been Roger II's oldest son; his only certain blemish was his illegitimacy. His brother-in-law, Richard, count of Acerra, was an energetic and able lieutenant. The head of the civil administration, Matthew of Salerno, is said to have favoured Tancred's candidature.

Pope Clement III was also consulted. Tancred's coronation was performed by Archbishop Walter of Palermo in January 1190. Against Tancred was set Roger, count of Andria, Tancred's fellow *magister justiciarius*, who had enjoyed prominence as military commander and governor on the mainland. Roger was so strongly opposed to Tancred that he called on the Germans already in Italy for help. Support for this cause was limited to some of the counts and a few of the bishops of the northern mainland, so that the count of Acerra was rapidly able to impose Tancred's authority in Apulia, obtain possession of Roger of Andria at Ascoli (and murder him), and then advance into Campania. A German force which invaded the kingdom from Rieti in May accomplished little against Tancred's forces. By June 1190, the commune of Naples was already willing to recognise Tancred's kingship. Other comparable groups may also have realised that it was preferable to rally to the monarchy than persist in separatist courses, which would play into the Germans' hands. In September, the German forces withdrew, covering their retreat by sending optimistic reports about Henry's prospects to encourage him to leave Germany. By the autumn of 1190, therefore, when the kings of France and England arrived in Tancred's dominions on their way to the Holy Land, Tancred looked reasonably secure. Even Duke Leopold of Austria, who travelled with a crusading contingent of Rhinelanders, gave no trouble as he passed peacefully through Apulia on his way to Brindisi.

When the crusade had originally been planned, William II had himself expected to play a prominent part in it. For this reason Tancred found himself obliged to receive Philip II and Richard I. Richard was characteristically belligerent about the rights of his widowed sister, Joanna, and his own claims on bequests made by William II in ships, provisions and money for the crusade. His six months in Sicily were not the easiest for Tancred. But Tancred kept his patience, and even successfully negotiated an alliance with Richard to deal with Henry should he invade while Richard was still in the kingdom.

Although Henry himself reached Italy before the crusaders were ready to leave Sicily, Richard did not wait for Henry to arrive in the kingdom. Henry entered Rome to find Clement III dead. His successor Celestine III, eighty-five-years-old, appears to have deliberately taken his time in getting himself consecrated, which delayed Henry's imperial coronation (15 April 1191). Otherwise, Celestine had only verbal weapons to stem Henry's plans for an invasion of Tancred's kingdom, and before the end of April, Henry had crossed the border. In May he began to besiege Naples, where the count of Acerra led the resistance: the Neapolitans stood by Tancred, whose concessions in June 1190 proved sufficient to secure their loyalty. On the other side, Henry's pact with Pisa proved inadequate for his purposes, so he had to negotiate with Genoa as well for the extra assistance needed by sea. Unfortunately for him this did not bear fruit until mid-August, which was too late, though it had probably prompted Tancred to make generous concessions in July to the men of Gaeta, to be sure of getting their maritime help. Henry saw that he had to abandon the siege of Naples, and Richard of Acerra promptly recovered the places taken in Campania. Constance, however, who had accompanied her husband and taken up residence in Salerno, was detained there by the citizens, and sent by them to Palermo to assuage Tancred's wrath with the disloyal city. Although Henry's retreating forces held on to some frontier posts of the kingdom to cover their possible return, Tancred had good reason to rate his own prospects for survival as high. Pope Celestine III, satisfied that Henry had been repulsed, sent proposals to the king in Germany for concluding a truce. Henry furiously rejected any such notions, in spite of the fact that his wife remained in Tancred's custody. His German captains in Italy, therefore, kept up the sniping in both Apulia and Campania. There was, however, no sign that Tancred's regime was unpopular, so that disaffection could not be used by the Germans against him. Tancred had his son, Roger, crowned king in anticipation of his succession, and arranged a prestigious marriage for him with Irene, daughter of the Greek emperor Isaac Angelus, in the summer of 1192. Celestine III was in no position himself to put pressure on the king; nevertheless he induced Tancred to allow the release of Constance without conditions. This must reinforce the impression that Constance's cause was not popular enough in the kingdom to excite Tancred's uneasiness. The pope's own willingness to endorse Tancred's kingship proves that by the summer of 1192, Tancred looked likely to prevail.

At William's death in 1189, Clement III did not hesitate to recognise Tancred's succession, since it offered the chance to break up the kingdom's alliance with the Germans. The pope was prepared to face Henry VI's fury, and trusted that it might somehow be deflected. Celestine III recognised the sense of Clement III's policy, and in order to preserve the *entente* with the kingdom, did not even press for serious modifications of its special ecclesiastical privileges when Celestine's envoys met Tancred at Gravina in the early summer of 1192. The terms agreed at Benevento between Adrian IV and William I in 1156 formed the basis of the discussions. Tancred accepted that legates might after all be sent to Sicily every five years or so, or even more frequently if the king asked for them; the king accepted some diminution of his rights to object to candidates elected to ecclesiastical office: if the king considered

any of them to be an enemy, he was to inform the *curia*, so that the
Roman church itself should condemn them (*reprobabit*) on the king's
evidence. For the rest, the clauses of 1156 were incorporated so carelessly
into Tancred's privilege that even the reference to the king having done
homage to the pope was repeated. In fact, homage was not done.
Tancred admittedly promised the pope's envoys that he would do
homage when the pope came into the kingdom. For this purpose he
actually moved in June to Albe, near the northern border of the
kingdom, to await Celestine's arrival. In the event it proved impossible
for the pope to leave Rome, so Tancred simply took the traditional oath
of loyalty to the pope's representative. Tancred had not been obliged to
make very substantial concessions to secure papal recognition, and they
did not anyway have any long-term significance. When Henry VI made
good his own claims on the kingdom in 1194, he did not consider himself
bound by any of Tancred's acts, and insisted on the same privileges as
those enjoyed by Roger II, his wife's father.

Tancred reappeared in the northern provinces after Henry VI's
departure in 1191, but it cannot be shown for certain to what extent his
authority was re-established there. He forced the bishop of Troia,
Walter of Palearia, a supporter of Henry VI, to return with Henry to
Germany, but according to the Carpineto chronicler, in slightly garbled
words from the prophet Isaiah (II, 4), it was only under Henry VI that
peace was restored to this part of the kingdom ('swords were beaten into
scythes and lances into plough-shares'). Local strife may therefore have
persisted under Tancred in some parts of Apulia. On the island too, the
disruptions caused by the Saracens were not all dealt with. Otherwise,
royal government seems to have continued as before 1189: Tancred had
already acquired considerable experience of both political and administrative affairs before he became king. The disparaging remarks made
about him by Henry VI's eulogist, Peter of Eboli, are no more than
caricature. Of his diplomas, only thirty-five survive. There are seven
more for the five months' reign of his successor, William III, and even
these include grants for mainland clergy at Casamari, Sambucina and
Taranto. Tancred's government therefore proved to be sufficiently stable
and widely recognised to create some prejudice in favour of the
continuation of his regime. The royal administration under Matthew of
Salerno, whom Tancred at last promoted chancellor, remained intact.
Tancred also had a *palatinus camerarius* who was *magister doane baronum*
with authority at Salerno (1190) and at Brindisi (1191). He continued to
draw his supplies of salt from Naples. He made grants at Trani and
Giovinazzo in Apulia and to Count Anfusus of Squillace. The abbot of
Venosa complained to him about land taken by his late rival, Roger of

Andria, and the king ordered the captains and *magistri justiciarii* of Apulia and Terra di Lavoro (Count Berard Gentilis of Lesina and Count Hugh Lupinus of Conversano) to make due enquiries. Although there are no royal documents dated later than July 1193, there is no other reason to believe that Tancred's government lost its grip in its last few months. The general recognition accorded to his son and successor, William III, in the brief period before Henry VI staged his successful second bid for the throne, would be inexplicable if Tancred's authority had been seriously undermined within the kingdom already.

However, the chances of survival for the dynasty were drastically reduced by the death of Tancred's heir, Roger, only a short time before that of his father on 20 February 1194, since Tancred's only surviving son, William, was a mere child. When the news of Tancred's death reached the mainland, a prominent official was on the point of writing an elaborate letter to a friend in Palermo. The news caused him to abandon his plans for celebrating the seasonal return of springtime, and to try something in a more elegiac mood. He already feared the worst, though on the surprising, but significant, grounds that the Christians and Saracens would probably not be able to agree on the choice of a valiant successor. He anticipated, correctly, that this time Apulia would fall speedily to the terrible Germans, but rather unconvincingly hoped that at least the cities of Sicily would be spared German conquest. In fact, they turned out to be quite unprepared to put up any resistance. In these circumstances it was unrealistic to advance the nomination of Tancred's son William as king, even if Celestine III did give his approval. By June, William had been crowned and his mother, Sibylla of Acerra, accepted responsibility for a regency. Henry VI, who had been preparing to relaunch his bid for the kingdom even before Tancred's death, had renewed his alliances at Genoa by June and at Pisa by July to make sure that this time his fleet auxiliaries would be ready promptly. These allies were so eager to avail themselves of Henry's patronage to establish themselves in Sicily that they arrived before him, entering the Straits of Messina on 1 September. Naples (and possibly Messina) had by then already made overtures to Henry, and his maritime allies were so confident of their triumph over the forces of the kingdom that they set about fighting one another at Messina for the spoils. When the Pisans proved stronger, the Genoese moved on to Catania and Syracuse, with the result that the eastern part of the island was mostly subdued and Palermo outflanked well before Henry himself arrived. This time Henry came, not only forewarned and calculating; he came rich with the money paid from England to ransom Richard I, who had been released in February before Henry left Germany. When Henry arrived in the kingdom, he probably bypassed the main royal army in order to reach Sicily more quickly. He pushed ahead without Constance, who was pregnant. When he crossed the Straits of Messina, Sibylla sent her son to safety and negotiated for him the grant of his father's county of Lecce and the principality of Taranto. The city of Palermo admitted Henry VI on 20 November, and he was crowned there on 25 December.

HENRY VI AS KING OF SICILY

A few days after his coronation, Henry VI abruptly arrested many prominent persons in the kingdom allegedly involved in a plot against him. There are some grounds for suspecting Henry's good faith. His prisoners, including Tancred's family, were bundled back to Germany out of harm's way. His heir, Frederick, born far away in Iesi (Ancona) a few days later, strengthened Henry's prospects of holding on to his acquisition. He did not lack support in the kingdom. His chancellor, Walter of Palearia, bishop of Troia and of the noble family of Manoppello, eventually proved to be a man of great weight in government, without becoming subservient to German interests. There were certainly others prominent in the nobility and the church who rallied to Henry and Constance, and perhaps still more to the prospects for the infant Frederick, however many others feared and resented the new regime.

Henry could now rule as he pleased, without restraining his natural imperiousness. Unfortunately the full extent of his changes cannot be measured. That he never intended to be a resident ruler he is said to have admitted to the Genoese when promising that his conquest would save his honour but serve their advantage. After a few weeks in Sicily, he crossed to the mainland, and by late April 1195 he had travelled north through Apulia and out of the kingdom, sending Constance back to Sicily to represent him. Conrad of Urslingen, duke of Spoleto, was for a time in 1195 called royal vicar (*vicarius totius regni Sicilie*) and given instructions, but little is known of his effectiveness.

The death of Henry's father, Barbarossa, on the way to the crusade in June 1190, and the activities in the Holy Land of the kings of England and France, would anyway have spurred Henry on to use his new Sicilian riches to advance the cause of the crusade. In the course of 1195, the situation opened up at Constantinople by the *coup d'état* of Alexius Angelus strengthened Henry's resolve to accumulate fresh glory. Some of the great riches he had obtained in Sicily were to be expended on a force of three thousand men, mainly recruited in Germany, to be kept in the Holy Land for a year. With this in mind, Henry returned north, not only to urge forward the crusade, but also to arrange for the succession of the infant Frederick to the empire. Though Henry's hopes of obtaining a formal law of hereditary succession were thwarted, Frederick was nevertheless elected king of the Romans in December 1196. By that time, Henry had already returned to Italy, where for several months he concentrated on trying to get papal agreement to an elaborate project for ending tension between papacy and empire.

Celestine's strained relations with both Henry and Constance can be sensed from the strong protest made by Constance on 3 October 1195 about what she regarded as unprecedented papal infringement of her ancestral rights. Unfortunately, the three incidents she complained of are not known in detail, but they were all connected with the traditional privileges of the monarch over legates, elections and consecrations. Constance claimed that Celestine had acted in a novel way by denying her the rights which her father and his legitimate successors had enjoyed. According to Constance, the papacy had in the past sent legates into the kingdom only to the king in person, or on their way to Greece, when they were graciously allowed transit. By appointing Cardinal Peter with a general commission on the mainland, Celestine was responsible for an intolerable innovation. Next, Constance denounced Celestine's letter to the monks of San Giovanni degli Eremiti in Palermo for instructing them not to abandon their support for the abbot-elect, whom she called a blasphemer and a traitor to the king, probably because he had been chosen before Henry VI's conquest. Constance, however, was particularly incensed because this monastery had been founded by her father next door to the royal palace, and she resented papal interference since it curtailed her ordinary rights of patronage. This, of course, was only to be expected, she says, of a pope who by his earlier support of Tancred had attempted to cheat her out of her paternal inheritance. Lastly, she denounced the pope for consecrating Master Hugh as archbishop of Siponto. Here her scorn and anger knew no bounds, for Hugh, she said, had consistently worked at the *curia* itself to undermine all her projects. Her husband also remonstrated with Celestine about this consecration. When the pope tried to explain how he had only acted at the behest of Henry's representatives, the bishops of Padua and Worms, the emperor flatly disowned the bishops. Hugh's consecration had thus been carried out contrary to the customs of Henry's predecessors. Henry was particularly offended because this indifference to the law of the kingdom diminished his own honour; instead of being treated as greater than previous kings, as was proper considering his greater (imperial) dignity, he was being put down. Both Henry and Constance were clearly very sensitive to any shift, and suspected Celestine at every turn. Their statements about what they took to be the royal rights are both helpful and likely to be true. It is difficult to believe, however, that Celestine thought he was acting in any unusual way, and his explanations over the case of Master Hugh betray a characteristic wish to placate Henry rather than to defend his exercise of papal prerogatives. Nothing in the terms of the Beneventan pact precluded the appointment of a legate on the mainland with general powers, and the pope had not relied on the new terms agreed with Tancred to extend the legate's jurisdiction to the island. At San Giovanni degli Eremiti, Celestine's letter may have been intended to do no more than deny the monks the freedom to change their mind once an election had been made.

It is possible that Celestine's opposition to Henry encouraged Henry's enemies in the kingdom to turn to the pope for help. What may be an example of this occurred in 1195, when the abbess of the short-lived church of St Thomas at Barletta rather surprisingly took to Rome, rather than to the new government of Henry VI, her complaint about the criminal activities of some local clergy. The prior of Montepeloso and the vicar of Barletta had broken into her church at night with an armed force, and had in the process tried to strangle her with a rope. Her church was shortly afterwards acquired by the new hospital of the Teutonic Order, which Henry founded, and the assault on the abbess may well have had a political dimension. In 1195, the kingdom was certainly restless. It was believed in Germany that Constance had political differences of her own with her absent husband. These encouraged plots, of which even the pope was informed. The reason Henry's negotiations with the papacy in 1196–7 were so protracted may be connected with Celestine's expectation, or hope, that Henry's regime would soon be toppled. Alternatively, he expected his own death might spare him the embarrassment of a permanent settlement of the imperial–papal quarrel.

Henry did not re-enter the kingdom until November 1196, and did not reach Sicily itself until March. Here he escaped a conspiracy against his life (in May), which was believed in Germany to have been savagely repressed. The details are not clear, but there was certainly a rebellion, culminating in a siege of Castrogiovanni which took Henry some weeks to deal with. One way or another it created in Italy an ineradicable impression of German cruelty. Yet Henry did not live long enough to savour his revenge. Taken ill hunting in eastern Sicily early in August, he died of dysentery on 28 September 1197.

EMPRESS CONSTANCE

Henry and Constance were reported in Germany to have fallen out over the way the kingdom was governed, and the empress was so much suspected of involvement in the conspiracy on his life, that she was obliged to be present at the horrible execution of its leader. During Henry's absence, however, Constance had presided vigorously over the government of Sicily for about two years, and this new experience for her and the kingdom may have encouraged hopes that the Germans could be dispensed with after his death. Henry's suspicions of his wife's loyalty may have had no more substance than his own resentment of her independence.

The unpopularity of the Germans in power was made inevitable by their new prominence throughout the kingdom. When Henry himself was removed by death, his Germans remained. Constance's own impregnable position as queen of Sicily now made her indispensable to the pro-German party itself. The German presence was more deeply entrenched on the mainland than in the island, but it is nowhere easy to substantiate in detail. For some reason, Henry issued a general mandate at the end of 1196 requiring all his own privileges to be handed back for renewal, and few documents survive for his last months. Henry certainly made grants of confiscated lands and titles to his countrymen, and had consistently refused to accept any of Tancred's privileges. Henry, like William II, had never sought papal investiture with the kingdom, but he also behaved as though the kingdom was not a papal fief but part of his empire. Constance herself, however, in her concessions stressed continuity with her own father's regime.

Henry VI's brutal seizure of the kingdom provided it with ruthless government for less than three years, and his sudden death threatened to usher in another period of political uncertainty. His only son Frederick, not yet three-years-old, had unchallengeable rights to the succession, but his role was complicated by the fact that he had already, in his absence, been elected king of the Romans. Henry VI's German supporters naturally thought first of the considerable problems involved in making good Frederick's claims in the empire. Henry's brother, Philip, immediately returned from Italy to Germany to rally supporters. They, not surprisingly, insisted on more purposeful leadership than a regency could provide. It was probably after Constance heard that Philip himself had been formally elected king in Germany (8 March 1198) that Frederick was summoned from Apulia and crowned king of Sicily (17 May 1198). Thereafter all reference to him as king of the Romans was dropped.

Unlike Margaret of Navarra in similar circumstances in 1166, Constance, as Roger II's own child, could reasonably count on the loyal support of her subjects, and she immediately enhanced her standing by driving her husband's henchman, Markwald of Anweiler, out of the kingdom. He withdrew to the March of Ancona where he continued to exercise responsibilities for the empire. By the death of Henry VI, Constance had at last come fully into her own inheritance. Though the great men of the kingdom had not been prepared for this solution in 1189, they were now happy to accept her and not allow the excesses of Henry's Germans to prejudice them against her. Constance had, however, no motive for reverting to the defiant stance of Tancred's monarchy, and naturally did not intend to secure the release of Tancred's supporters from Germany or to welcome other exiles who had earlier been opposed to her rights. She herself was not nearly as dependent, as Henry had been, on German support for her rule. She could now count on an influential native nobility who had thrown in their lot with her cause and who would work with her for Frederick's eventual succession. Nevertheless, she remained the head of a party and sensed an undercurrent of unrest. The fragility of her position tempted the Genoese to think they could take the law into their own hands with impunity. William Grassus, who had been Henry VI's Genoese admiral and count of Malta, was evicted from Malta and Gozo by the local inhabitants, and the grateful Constance rewarded them by taking the islands permanently into the royal domain. The Genoese were even impudent enough to challenge the government's authority in Palermo itself. When they encountered in the harbour ships belonging to a certain Recupero, whom they considered an enemy pirate, they seized the ships. However, they were obliged to change their tune when the resolute Constance showed her mettle by rounding up Genoese merchants in the city and keeping them in prison until the Genoese galley commanders agreed to negotiate. Yet it was a nasty sign of things to come. If Constance died, what then?

Had she lived longer, she might have succeeded in raising her son to be the natural successor to her own father, which could have severed his German links, or at least fatally weakened their claims on him. In the few months remaining to her between Frederick's coronation and her own death (28 November 1198), it was not so much her own capacity as the situation facing her that threatened to frustrate any such hopes. Philip, as king in Germany, however preoccupied, had no intention of forgetting his nephew, nor the incorporation of the kingdom into the western empire. The many Germans in Italy left leaderless by Henry's death naturally looked to Philip as their lord. Could Constance keep them out of the kingdom if they ventured to assert Philip's rights?

As against the claims of the empire, Constance not surprisingly turned to the papacy, by whose interventions she had herself been released from Salerno in 1192. The ancient Celestine III had died in January 1198 and been replaced the same day by the energetic Lothar de Segni, fifty years his junior. He was consecrated as Pope Innocent III six weeks later. Negotiations had by then already been opened between him and Constance over the church of St Anastasius at Capua, of Greek rite but in Rome's protection, and it is likely that she was represented at his consecration ceremony. Days after it, Innocent wrote imperiously to Germany demanding the release of the archbishop of Salerno, the unhappy Queen Sibylla, her son and daughter, and others of the kingdom, who were still languishing in prison. The queen and her family did manage to escape to France; the archbishop was duly released, but Constance still would not admit him to the kingdom. Innocent's intervention certainly signalled the arrival of an energetic new papal policy with regard to the kingdom, but the pope pursued his own objectives, not Constance's. On the other hand, when Innocent a few days later absolved all Christians in Le Marche from the oaths they had sworn to Markwald, Constance would have seen in the pope an ally of potential value, for a pope prepared to take on the Germans so confidently offered her some real protection. So, as against the claims of imperial overlordship, she preferred those of the papacy itself. The formal submission of the king to the pope had been insisted on from her father's time; since 1156, friendship between the kingdom and the papacy had become not only traditional, but a guarantee that imperial power in Italy could be checked. Once Constance had decided to look after Frederick's interests in the kingdom without German help, a new understanding with the pope was probably inevitable.

Constance sent Berard, the Benedictine archbishop of Messina, in May to Rome on business of such urgent importance that he was allowed to be absent from Frederick's coronation. No details of any negotiations are known before the autumn, however, when fresh discussions about royal rights over the church finally resulted in a formula acceptable to Innocent. By that time, Markwald of Anweiler had recognised Philip's authority and threatened to invade the kingdom on the grounds that the testament of Henry VI awarded him the custody (*balium*) of the king and kingdom. This may have cut short further haggling by Constance. The chancellor, Bishop Walter, and his brother, the count of Manoppello, are said in the *Gesta Innocentii* to have been suspected by Constance of favouring Markwald's claims. If true, it shows they already recognised that he had the force and the will to intervene, whereas Innocent did not obviously have comparable military strength on which the kingdom could call. His emotional language about German atrocities in the past could have seemed to them impolitic and provocative rather than reassuring. When the pope's terms for settling ecclesiastical disputes became known, there may have been further dissatisfaction that Constance was buying papal support too dear. Before the final terms reached Palermo, however, she had died, naming the pope as the regent of the kingdom and guardian of her son. Papal intervention in the kingdom's affairs became, for better or worse, unavoidable.

Constance's death must have come as a surprise to the pope, who only a week before (19 November 1198) had published his grant of the kingdom to Constance and Frederick. This concluded the formalities of recognition which had involved sending (20 October) the senior cardinal, Octavian, bishop of Ostia, to take Constance's oath of fealty, recorded in two schedules, each sealed by the other party, with the promise to do liege homage whenever the pope was able to enter the kingdom to receive it. In a separate document, the pope prescribed the future mode of proceeding with the selection of prelates in the kingdom.

Innocent himself later claimed to be content with these ecclesiastical arrangements negotiated with Constance (although she had not lived to ratify them). Innocent refused to confirm Clement III's privilege as to the 'four points', but professed to have granted one of Constance's requests, as far as respect for justice and the canonical liberty of the churches allowed: a formula for elections of bishops and abbots throughout the kingdom. The new formula required the chapter to inform the monarch of the vacancy. Then, once the chapter had elected a canonically suitable person, royal assent was required. The election was, however, to be published before the royal assent was given, though until this arrived, the elect was not to be formally installed; nor was the elect to take on his administrative duties until his election was confirmed by the pope. None of this precluded informal pressure or consultation, and according to the pope's rebuke to Frederick written ten years later, Constance had in return abandoned her efforts to get papal approval of the traditional royal rights over councils, legations and appeals. If Constance yielded, it was because she had gained her main point: Innocent was fully committed to recognising Frederick's rights in the kingdom. In return, she undertook to pay the usual census: 600 *schifati* for Apulia and Calabria, and another 400 *schifati* for Marsia. When she died, leaving Innocent the *balium* as chief lord of the kingdom, he was entitled as well to 30,000 *tari* per annum from public revenues.

INNOCENT III AS SICILIAN OVERLORD

No previous pope had been given such an opportunity to act out the role of feudal lord of the kingdom thrust upon the papacy since 1130, and no previous pope would anyway have enjoyed the responsibility half as much as Innocent. It cannot be expected, however, that Innocent III could even understand, still less discharge for another, the duties of kingship. Constance, granted that she had no option and must have died fearful of the consequences, was in the main vindicated: the Germans were kept out and her son's inheritance salvaged, and Innocent did labour to see that the kingdom's independence survived. At the beginning he ordered all the great men (*nobiles*) of the kingdom to take oaths of loyalty to himself and the king. His main consideration was, however, not the well-being of the kingdom, but the defeat of German designs for the restoration of the empire of Henry VI. In the meantime, Innocent proposed to use the occasion to deprive the monarchy of its peculiar ecclesiastical customs and to establish valuable precedents as to the implications of his role as feudal lord.

What had been a legal fiction designed to suit the monarchy from 1130 now became a weapon in papal hands. The pope was immensely pleased with the role so gratifyingly bestowed on him by the dying Constance, and rarely refrained from alluding to the powers conferred on him. At the same time, however, Innocent III behaved as though he owed his role less to Constance's trust in him as pope, than to his rights as feudal sovereign of the kingdom. The kingdom was not the only one ever held in papal sovereignty, but Denmark, England, Hungary and Aragon were far away and could not be really governed by the pope. Distance made them neither so potentially dangerous, nor so useful to the papacy. This vassal-kingdom bordered on the papal state itself. In the hands of Henry VI for nearly three years, it had given the German emperor an unprecedented power to overawe the papacy. Innocent III not surprisingly considered that recognition of the papal overlordship in 1198 gave him a providentially contrived opportunity to put the papacy on a new course. The kingdom would be treated as little more than an extension of the papal state. By reputation it was both fabulously wealthy and meekly obedient to its rulers. It was a most valuable acquisition.

The pope could not, however, rule directly in a kingdom which had become habituated to effective kingship. It was no longer that ramshackle collection of lordships which had individually accepted Paschal II's suzerainty. The kingdom needed a real ruler. Quite apart from the fact that Innocent was temperamentally incapable of trusting anyone to carry out the task for him, there was no obvious person whose rights to act for Frederick the pope could endorse. The king's surviving relations were in Germany, and Innocent intended above all to thwart any efforts made from that quarter to intervene: it seemed obvious that this opportunity had to be seized to sever the tie between the kingdom and the empire. Since Innocent did not intend at first to impugn Frederick's rights in the kingdom, he concentrated on trying to weaken the Staufen family in Germany, where the election of Frederick's uncle, Philip, as king threatened to prolong the Staufen hegemony. Innocent had also conceived a detestation of the German captains introduced into Italy by Henry VI because they naturally continued to look to Germany for approval and support. Innocent tried to galvanise Italian xenophobia against them. He did not give adequate attention to the problem of recruiting comparable military strength to oppose them with. Nor did he consider trying to woo the Germans to a new Sicilian loyalty, for he was too anti-German to think coolly about how their real power could be rendered harmless. As was his wont, he seems to have thought that by appointing papal legates, presenting his legal credentials, and indulging his rhetorical skills he would get what he wanted.

Innocent was no politician. Although he has a reputation as a jurist, he was a theologian, and as a clerk by profession, his political ideas had no secular dimensions, except those he brought from his family of minor nobility in the Campagna. As his dealings in Germany and England confirm, Innocent conceived his role as that of the judge before whom everyone else, kings included, would stand as mere defendants at the bar. Understanding how people might be governed, or governments sustained, were not things that he thought about. He appears to have supposed that whipping up anti-German feeling in Italy and keeping Germany itself in ferment would make the imperial menace fade away. In the South he intended to use his authority to suit the interests of the papacy. Granted his priorities, it is not difficult to see why he did this, but since his concerns were with the papacy, not the kingdom, it is not surprising that the leading men in Sicily distrusted his ambitions. It is also clear why Frederick, after he came of age, was determined to prevent the papacy from ever again finding an opportunity to abuse its sovereignty and interfere in the kingdom's affairs.

Without Constance, Innocent III would never have been given any chance to interfere in the kingdom. The chief men in the royal government at Palermo, even the clergy, showed their distrust of the pope from the first. How Innocent expected the legates he sent to the kingdom to fulfil their task remains a mystery. Early in 1199, Innocent sent Cardinal Gregory, 'a true and old friend of Sicily', to act for him in Palermo, but after taking oaths due to the pope, Gregory returned within a few months, frustrated by the unwillingness of the *familiares* to work with him. Markwald did not immediately threaten Sicily itself, and the *familiares* did not react as incisively as the pope expected when the Germans invaded the northern part of the kingdom and laid siege to the abbey of Monte Cassino. The pope became irritated when Palermo did not hand over the money needed for troops to deal with the emergency on the mainland. Nor could the pope understand why, by February 1199, he had still not received a copy of Constance's testament. In due course, the pope's defensive account of why his own men had allowed San Germano to fall to Markwald, and taken refuge at Cassino, coupled with his rhetorical denunciation of Markwald, alerted the cautious *familiares* to the pope's actual shortcomings in dealing with Markwald – that the necessary army had yet to be assembled. He had, however, deployed no less than three cardinal legations on the mainland: Jordan to the counts of Celano and Chieti; John and Gerard to the count of Fondi; and the trusted archbishop of Taranto in Calabria and Apulia.

Despite all his indignant reminders of Markwald's enormities in the kingdom, Innocent's campaigning came to nothing. Then, out of the blue, Innocent happily announced in August that Markwald had repented of his offences and, being reconciled to the church, had been absolved from excommunication. Special pleading for him and with him in early summer from Germany helped to bring about his volte-face; even then, Markwald was far from abandoning all his claims to be procurator of the kingdom and steward of the empire (*imperii senescalcus*). And within a month the pact was all over anyway. Innocent was made to look ridiculous and, angrier than ever at being fooled, tried to explain himself to the sardonic Sicilians by resuming his complaints about the seneschal's perfidy.

The seneschal now left the mainland and arrived at Trapani in October 1199. He found willing allies in the dissident Saracen population concentrated in western Sicily, whose leaders' advice was to follow Markwald. Together their forces proved sufficient to enable Markwald to hold his own in Sicily for about three years, despite being twice seriously defeated in battle. The pope did not repeat his earlier mistake of negotiating. He kept up an unremitting hostility to Markwald, offering the same indulgences for fighting him as were offered for fighting in the Holy Land (24 November 1199), on the grounds that Markwald was impeding the success of the pope's new crusading venture and himself had Saracen allies: he was manifestly an enemy of Christians. Innocent's desperation concerning Markwald showed as early as spring 1200, when he entered into a discreditable alliance with ex-Queen Sibylla's son-in-law, Walter of Brienne, who eventually turned up in southern Italy and ruled there with Innocent's blessing (1201–5). But despite the pope's frantic exhortations, he would never actually confront Markwald in Sicily, and Innocent's principal objective was therefore not attained. Moreover, by encouraging Brienne's intervention, the pope also roused considerable disquiet in Sicily over his genuine concern for Frederick's interests. While it is understandable that Innocent felt so hostile towards the perfidious Markwald as to reject any compromise proposed, it is no less clear that the *familiares* in Sicily recognised, even if Innocent did not, that they needed, in the interests of the whole kingdom, to secure an understanding with the German leaders. Contrary to the slanders circulated by the pope, Markwald never made any attempt to do away with Frederick and make himself ruler. Markwald's intentions probably were, as he claimed, to exercise the custody of the kingdom in the Hohenstaufen interest until Frederick should come of age. He succeeded in extending his base in Sicily, gained possession of Frederick himself in November 1201, and was on the point of taking Messina when he died as a result of abdominal surgery (September 1202), not from any military encounter. After his death, Philip nominated a successor, thus adding credence to Markwald's claim to have acted on his authority. Those who had reconciled themselves to Henry VI's rule after 1194 presumably favoured Markwald because he promised to perpetuate that settlement; these men had ample reason to doubt whether the pope could guarantee comparable order.

Understanding the course of events is inevitably hampered by the lack of material evidence from all the main participants except the pope himself. Local factors were clearly crucial. The principal native politician of the kingdom remained Walter of Palearia, royal chancellor, who proved remarkably agile in holding on to office. Appointed bishop of Troia in 1189, he owed his political rise in the first place to Henry VI and inclined generally to the Staufen. He could also count on his family, which was from the northern part of the kingdom. Walter first received news of the pope's credulous faith in Brienne at Messina in May 1200, only a few weeks before Markwald laid siege to Palermo. A serious defeat was inflicted on Markwald between Palermo and Monreale, and it is therefore significant that, instead of following up this victory as Innocent's partisans expected, the chancellor decided to negotiate. As a result, Markwald was left with the government of most of the island, though the chancellor's brother Gentilis retained the custody of Frederick for a time in Palermo itself. A consequence of this diplomacy was that the chancellor fell out with the pope, ceased altogether to call himself bishop (Innocent III deposed him from his see at Troia where he was replaced by 1201), and withdrew to the mainland where, in

September 1201, he campaigned with other Germans against Innocent's
protégé Brienne. When he tried to raise money for the king's cause by
alienation of royal domain rights on the mainland, he was successful
enough to provoke the pope into giving counter orders to the *magistri
camerarii* of Apulia, Terra di Lavoro and Amalfi. However, a year later,
Walter resumed negotiations with the pope and offered security for his
future trustworthiness. The pope continued to refer to him as chancellor, though he does not reappear in royal documents as such until 1207.
Back in the king's service, he was elected to the island see of Catania in
the summer of 1208; two years later he was again out of favour with
Frederick himself, and it was the pope's turn to remind the king of his
many services: to no avail. The strength of his personality eludes analysis,
but his value to those he served is not in doubt. For a time he had aspired
to the archbishopric of Palermo itself, which was effectively without a
consecrated incumbent from 1201 to 1214. Walter's political strength lay
most obviously in his secular family and his own political instincts for
survival. His willingness to recover the pope's favour in 1202 must be
seen as proof that by then he considered the pope's policy to be working.

Markwald's death in 1202 had given Innocent new hopes for Sicily.
He released the archbishop of Messina from excommunication and
added him to the small number of loyal Sicilian prelates. Caro,
archbishop of Monreale, however, was in trouble, not only with the
Saracens, but also with the monks of his own church, and he could not
hold the king's government together. For some unknown reason,
elections at Palermo were not brought to fruition. According to the
Gesta Innocentii, it was because Palermo fell under the influence of
William of Capparone after Markwald's death that Walter returned to
the pope's side. Capparone is a much more obscure figure than
Markwald. Nevertheless, by obtaining possession of the young king at
the end of 1202, he became the key politician of the kingdom for four
whole years. During this period, documents issued in Frederick's name
were dated by the use of Pisa, so some of Capparone's officials were
certainly from Pisa. Capparone did not enjoy the backing of the Staufen
party. He played his own game and the *familiares* would never really
trust him as a legitimate ally. However, Philip's troubles in Germany
diminished their expectations of his return to Italy, so they looked for
other allies to support the young king. Innocent devised a plan to marry
Frederick to a sister of the king of Aragon, which would have offered
some tangible prospect of military help (to be paid for by the kingdom)
without entailing such objections as made Brienne on the mainland so
unacceptable to the *familiares*. The better relations between the pope and
the *familiares* were reinforced by the appointment of Cardinal Gerard as

resident legate in the spring of 1204, assigned to negotiate a settlement with Capparone so that peace and order could be restored to the king and kingdom.

The cardinal's negotiations with Capparone appeared to result in his acceptance of the papal *balium* and the promise to obey the cardinal as the pope's representative, so the cardinal himself travelled to Palermo to try and make peace there between Capparone and the chancellor. Although he boasted that the young king had enjoyed his company, he otherwise failed. Capparone always promised more than he delivered. It was another two years before Frederick was eventually freed from Capparone's control and brought into the hands of the chancellor and legate. This time it was thanks to the cajolery of Dipold, another German captain on the mainland.

The death of Brienne and the changing situation in Germany had encouraged Dipold himself to seek reconciliation with the pope; to seal the new arrangements for the kingdom, Dipold wanted the agreement of Capparone and the king. Despite the important service he rendered, Dipold was rumoured to be still plotting treachery and was seized by the chancellor. Rather characteristically, he escaped, and returned to Salerno to renew hostilities. By this time, the chancellor had re-established his political authority on the island, even though he could not dislodge Capparone from the royal palace itself. How muted the papal role remained may be measured from the fact that the chancellor's brother-in-law, Peter, count of Celano, *magister justiciarius* in Apulia and Terra di Lavoro, received an admonition from the pope because he was not respectful enough of papal authority. The following summer, the pope received further complaints from the bishop of Mileto, a former papal chaplain, about the depredations of Count Anfusus and his brother in Calabria. This provoked another exasperated outburst of papal wrath against the nobility of the kingdom. But Innocent could not do much more than rail.

The disarray of government in the island during these years was accentuated by the persistent war between the Pisans and the Genoese. Both these had reckoned to gain advantage for their commerce from their alliance with Henry VI in 1194. In fact, Henry had disappointed them, so that after his death they were not only more eager than ever to seize their rewards; they put aside all scruples, since they felt themselves aggrieved. Given a chance, they would have cheerfully reduced Sicily to the same state of dependence on themselves as both Corsica and Sardinia. After 1198, there was little that government in Palermo could do to stop them. The Genoese deliberately set about their task, posing as allies of the pope and the infant king. Already before September 1202,

Markwald had quarrelled with and imprisoned the Genoese admiral, William Grassus, whom the Genoese government vainly attempted to rescue. Markwald's death naturally gave the Genoese more hope, but it was the Pisans who were able to profit when Capparone took command in Palermo. The principal Genoese leader at this point became Grassus' son-in-law, Henry, who somehow recovered the title, count of Malta. Henry, like Grassus, was an enterprising pirate in the manner of the earlier Count Margaritone, and his authority had to be accepted by Frederick II when he came of age. The Genoese also drove the Pisans out of Syracuse and installed their own count, Alamannus, who ruled there until Frederick II removed him in 1221. Not content with securing bases of their own, the rivals carried on their blood-letting in the major ports of both Messina and Palermo. The Pisans besieged Syracuse for nearly four months at the end of 1205, before the Genoese, who had found other allies such as Count Anfusus, overwhelmed their land forces. All this goes to prove how helpless the nominal government actually was, even in the island. Nor must it be forgotten that the Saracens had broken all ties with the Christians, and rejected obedience to the king. They withdrew to the mountains but descended to ravage properties belonging to Monreale, such as Corleone. They had become an autonomous power in the island. By October 1207, it is not surprising that the pope issued (for the first time) an appeal to the counts and barons to provide for the king's needs in food, arms, ships and men. Ten years after Constance's death, the pope had little enough to boast about.

The state of the mainland in the same period is more difficult to describe. Documents were certainly dated by Frederick's regnal years in several different parts of the kingdom, and some counts were perhaps as loyal as they had sworn to be. But if they chose to be independent there was no way to bring them to heel. The careers of both Brienne and Dipold show what was possible. According to an enquiry made in Capitanata about 1277, while Frederick was a child there had been major warfare (*maxima guerra*) in that district, and Count Matthew of Lesina had usurped authority there. This Count Matthew was, however, in September 1208 captain and master-justiciar, and early the following year went to Aragon to fetch Frederick's bride; the government in effect had to endorse local men of consquence if it could not replace them. For the same reason, Count Peter of Celano and Count Richard of Fondi held comparable posts. There are only occasional glimpses of local troubles. In August 1201, the abbot of Cuti near Bari promised not to take action against those who had threatened his monastery when attacking the king's enemies there, out of recognition of their loyalty to the king. Two canons of Bari on their way to Rome the year before had been taken prisoner by

Germans and had to pay ransoms. In 1205, the archpriest of Corato compensated his church for two silver chalices which he had lost during the devastation of the city. The church of Santa Maria de Mari was so devastated in the wars that it was granted, as a ruin, to the Hospitallers of Barletta in 1224. The bishop of Teano wrote in July 1206 of trouble caused by Germans during the grape-picking. Yet Frederick's government also issued diplomas for Capua in the spring of 1206, and sent instructions to the justiciars, Henry of Apulia and Leo of Andria, in a matrimonial dispute at Capua in the summer of 1207, as though such a personal matter could not be settled without appeal to the highest authorities in the kingdom. It is possible that royal officials everywhere attempted to remain loyal to the king, but how the government could supervise and appoint them in troubled times is obscure. Shortly after the death of Constance, a dispute between the abbeys of San Giovanni in Fiore and Tres Pueri in Calabria was still being referred to and from Palermo, where Archbishop Bartholomew was then the chief minister of government. He issued instructions to the provincial justiciars and the master-justiciar as though the ordinary machinery of justice remained in working order. Yet a few months later at Brindisi, in September 1199, mere local officials drew up terms of a settlement with the captains of the Venetian fleet who had arrived in port to punish Pisan corsairs and others. What Constance had done at Palermo in 1197, the men of Brindisi had to do for themselves in 1199. However difficult the circumstances, local government, which had never been emasculated by the monarchy, was quite equal to the tasks that fell upon it.

Innocent himself belatedly entered the kingdom in June 1208. He held court at San Germano and issued various instructions for the well-being of the kingdom. Peter, count of Celano, was still master-justiciar in Apulia and Terra di Lavoro; the count of Fondi had a special role in Naples. Both were appointed master-captains for the military situation, to preserve peace and get 200 *milites* to the king by September for one year's service. The pope issued exhortatory letters to go with his orders, but pleaded the summer heat as his own excuse for not venturing deeper into the kingdom. Instead he sent Cardinal Gregory as legate, with an acolyte. The two counts soon turned to matters of greater concern to themselves: fighting one another for control of Capua.

Innocent's last effort on behalf of Frederick before he came of age had been to arrange his marriage. When he first proposed an alliance with Aragon in 1202, Innocent had envisaged the dowager queen accompanying the bride and acting as foster mother to Frederick, then still very young. Frederick instead spent the next four years in the care of soldiers, so that the Aragonese were not eager to conclude the match. When King

Peter of Aragon made a ceremonial visit to his feudal overlord the pope, at Rome in November 1204, in order to receive his military belt and royal diadem, Innocent pressed him on Frederick's behalf, but in late February 1208, the pope was still wondering at the delay in completing the arrangements they had discussed. He wrote exalting Frederick's birth and virtues, as well as the wealth and nobility of the Sicilian kingdom, which he called, with a somewhat misty-eyed enthusiasm, *umbilicus et portus aliorum regnorum.* By 1208, Frederick's intended bride was Constance, another of Peter's sisters and widow of the king of Hungary. She was some ten years older than Frederick. They were eventually married in August 1209.

KING FREDERICK

When Frederick came of age, at fourteen in December 1208, the effectiveness of Innocent III's sovereignty was put to the test. The adolescent king promptly showed that he intended to resume the practices of his predecessors in the matter of episcopal elections. The evidence all relates to instances where the papacy complained of improper royal interference. These cases indicate that Frederick either interpreted the rules differently from the pope or thought that he could disregard them; they certainly do not imply that there were other occasions when the king observed them. Papal protests were probably only made when disgruntled clergy insisted on trying to get papal backing for their cases against the king. Innocent's formula, as agreed with Constance in 1198, in itself was obviously not expected to shut out royal influence over elections altogether; there remained plenty of room in it for the king to inform the chapters whom they should elect. Frederick seemed barely of an age to have a mind of his own when he began to assert himself. Palermo being without an archbishop, the cathedral chapter made supplications to the king for the mere permission to elect a new one. When at last this was allowed, it was required by the king to invoke the Holy Spirit and agree on a suitable candidate. At this point, the cantor and two others not only resisted the king's orders, but forbade the chapter to proceed to a nomination while they appealed to Innocent. Frederick was furious, and promptly sent them into exile. This provoked a predictably sanctimonious lecture from the pope, who naturally appealed to the legal terms he had agreed with Constance. Nothing more was heard of the affair, but Frederick made friends with the chapter by making benefactions, and in due course dodged another confrontation with it by persuading Innocent himself to translate

Berard, archbishop of Bari, to Palermo, where he remained for thirty-five years, totally loyal to his king.

The king's role in elections was also acknowledged at Policastro in 1210. The canons actually went to Sicily to get Frederick's approval of their choice. This is itself notable. In the eleventh century, the arch-bishop of Salerno had received papal authority to make elections and consecrations of the bishops in his province. He had lost all his powers over the election by 1210, but he still retained the right to consecrate, which he would not exercise until he had obtained Innocent's opinion about the appointment of Frederick's physician, James. Archbishop Nicholas, son of Matthew of Salerno and erstwhile exile in Germany, had motives of his own for complicating the issue. There is only Innocent's word that the canons had elected James unwillingly and to please the king: even the papal legate wrote a letter on James' behalf. The matter dragged on. James got himself consecrated elsewhere – which certainly did not help his cause, and the canons refused to receive him. Papal judges-delegate could not proceed because the archbishop of Salerno diplomatically pleaded that the disturbances caused by Otto IV deterred him from travelling. The outcome is not known – but the protracted discussions themselves show how little power anyone had to thwart the king.

Very little impression of what was happening can be drawn from the chronicles. The *Gesta Innocentii*, in large measure dependent on the pope's own letters, focuses its attention outside the kingdom, and anyway gives no information about events after 1208. The first version of the chronicle of Richard of San Germano, written by a local notary for Abbot Stephen of Montecassino (1215–27), begins in the year 1208, when Innocent III visited San Germano and discussed with magnates of the kingdom how the king could be helped, but the chronicler's interest in the affairs of the kingdom remained very local to San Germano until the return of Frederick from Germany at the end of 1220. He did not neglect to notice great events as they occurred, particularly military confrontation with Muslims, recorded in some detail both for Las Navas de Tolosa (1212) and for the campaign against Damietta (1219). He demonstrated his concern for the east by verbatim quotation from papal letters; he gave a detailed account of the Fourth Lateran Council which he attended with Abbot Stephen. As a notary he may even have had responsibility for keeping copies of official letters, many of which he incorporated into this version of his chronicle. The only letter of importance for secular affairs that he gives for these years indicates how remote Frederick in Sicily seemed to be at Cassino. The abbot had intended to send a monk to represent him at Frederick's marriage, but

decided against doing so when he heard that Frederick had arrested
Count Anfusus on his way to the wedding. Allegedly, this rumour
similarly deterred the counts of Celano and Fondi. Frederick wrote to
the abbot with some irritation about misrepresentations of his efforts to
stamp out disorder and treachery. This was not the first letter in which
he had tried to explain himself to the abbot. He denounced the counts
Paul and Roger of Gerace because they had renewed their conspiracies
against him after military support brought from Aragon by his wife had
been depleted by disease and death. He castigated the insolence and
insubordination of Count Anfusus in Calabria because he set himself up
as the king's equal there, destroyed churches and kept castles at his
pleasure. Frederick wrote that his aim was to recover his own domain
property. He claimed that, thanks to God, by January 1210 he had
already recovered the greater and better part of his property in both
Sicily and Calabria, and intended to inform other faithful subjects of the
kingdom of this. Frederick makes no allusions to his rights in Apulia. By
1211, Otto IV was recognised there, and support for him was briefly
extended as far as the Calabrian border, but who might previously have
held them for Frederick must remain unknown.

By the time he came of age, Frederick was not only king of Sicily, but
also head of the Staufen family, and within a year some persons from the
family duchy of Swabia were already encouraging him to think about
his other responsibilities outside the kingdom. His troubled childhood
and the irksome restraints of his situation may have made his father's
homeland seem attractive to him. He spent only three and a quarter
years becoming acquainted with his kingdom, between coming of age
and leaving for Germany in March 1212. During that time he had to
watch with increasing apprehension the activities of the Welf emperor,
Otto IV. This enemy of his had been encouraged by Frederick's
guardian, Innocent III, as king in Germany, and was crowned emperor in
Rome on 4 October 1209. Innocent had his own reasons for warning
Otto to keep out of Frederick's kingdom, but Frederick is not likely to
have felt particularly grateful to the pope for this. He is more likely to
have remembered how the pope had also manœuvred with Otto to keep
Frederick out of his *paternal* inheritance. Moreover, Frederick may well
have understood better than the pope why Otto could not resist
invading the kingdom of Sicily, which he considered part of the empire.

After Otto's coronation in Rome, he withdrew to Tuscany, reaching
Pisa by 20 November where, however, he was tempted back to
intervene in the affairs of the kingdom, probably at the instigation of the
counts Peter of Celano and Dipold of Acerra, both ill-disposed towards
the young Frederick. These proposals would certainly have been

welcomed by the Pisans themselves. Over the next few months, Otto had to work at reconciling Genoese and Pisan interests. Although in the end the Genoese still would not openly support him, the Pisans, who were eager to do so, at least became less apprehensive of Genoese treachery. In the meantime, Otto hurried south to meet the conspirators from the kingdom, probably when he was at Terni in December. The pope had already been alerted to Otto's new plans before the end of 1209, when he warned Frederick; early in the new year he began to try and create embarrassments for Otto in Germany, and here too Frederick began to cultivate his own contacts in Swabia.

Otto's invasion of the kingdom did not actually take place until November 1210, though he appears to have dated his regnal years in the kingdom from early in 1210. In the west, Capua and Naples fell to him, though Aquino, Amalfi and Ravello remained loyal to Frederick. In Apulia he was recognised in Terlizzi as early as May 1211, but not at Bari until November–December 1212. Otto had, however, been obliged to leave the kingdom for Germany late in 1211, and who sustained his cause in this part of the kingdom is not known. Not until March 1214 does Frederick's name reappear for certain in the dating of documents there; Naples held out for Otto until 1215.

Frederick's decision to go to Germany himself was already taken in 1211, while Otto was still on the mainland of the kingdom. Frederick saw this as the best way to deal with the problem. The birth of Frederick's son, Henry, in 1211 liberated Frederick to accept nomination in Germany as king in place of Otto (October 1211), on conditions defined by Innocent III: his Sicilian kingdom was to be surrendered to the infant Henry, who was left in the charge of Queen Constance as regent. It is unlikely that Frederick left Sicily with reluctance. Recent events had proved there could be no security for the kingdom without a settlement of the German problem. The prospects for the infant Henry's government were not as doubtful as his own had been in 1197: Queen Constance appears to have been an effective regent, and there may have been some hope that this time Innocent would leave the queen's *familiares* to manage the government on their own. The pope's main concern for the kingdom remained the defence of ecclesiastical rights, and these Frederick formally confirmed at Messina in March 1212. He promised that elections should be canonically free, provided that this concession should not detract from the royal dignity. (This last phrase was not just a face-saving formula. The king later claimed that he was entitled to make grants of property belonging to churches because of the *antiqua dignitas* he had *in ecclesiis vacantibus*.) According to the terms agreed in March 1212, the king was to be notified immediately a see fell vacant. When the chapter had elected a suitable person, the king had to give his approval before the bishop could be enthroned. The pope also had to authorise the bishop to exercise his episcopal office. Within this formula for canonical elections, there was still scope for the king to secure the promotion of candidates of his own.

The negotiations at Messina did not involve any attempts to redefine the nature of the papacy's formal claims over the kingdom. When Innocent III visited the kingdom in 1208, Frederick had not done homage to him. Only in February 1212 did Frederick swear the traditional oath of fealty to the pope at his meeting with the papal legate, Cardinal Gregory. He also then promised to do homage to Innocent III in person when required to do so, and in the kingdom, at some place where it would be safe for him to travel. Although these conditions reflect the fact that parts of the kingdom at the time recognised the authority of Otto IV, the nature of the terms shows the same basic assumption as those sworn by Tancred in 1192, when Celestine III had been unable to travel to the kingdom to receive the king's homage in person. When, only a few weeks later in April 1212, Frederick did actually meet the pope in Rome, would he then have done liege homage to Innocent, as was claimed by the papal party in 1245? This is not very convincing. The oath of February 1212 stated explicitly that homage would be done in the kingdom itself, and there was no precedent for doing it at Rome. Homage done by Frederick to Innocent III at that time would, moreover, have compromised the position of Frederick's son, Henry, who was, significantly, crowned as king of Sicily at Messina in March 1212. This was the guarantee the pope needed, and Innocent III could therefore be satisfied with Frederick's oath. Homage had not in fact been done to the pope by any king since 1156, and it was not therefore considered indispensable by either side, once the papacy had abandoned its overt hostility to the kingdom as such.

For the next four years some official documents for the kingdom were issued in Henry's name, coupled with that of his mother Constance. Nearly a dozen of their diplomas are known, which show them moving around the island, at Messina, Palermo, Catania and Caltagirone. But those who obtained documents from them also included prelates from Campania, such as the abbot of Casamari and the archbishop of Salerno, as well as the Calabrian monks of San Giovanni in Fiore and the bishop of Martirano closer to Sicily. Their administrative acts involved the assignation of revenues from the *doana* in Palermo and the defence of royal clerks from the jurisdiction of the archbishop of Messina. Though no references to any authority in Apulia survive, someone in the service of the monarchy was responsible in this period for eliminating pockets of

Ottonian obedience. By April 1215, Liupold, bishop of Worms, ruled as Frederick II's legate for the kingdom of Sicily, apparently with complete viceregal authority, though he is only known to have acted in Apulia and at Aversa (when he was in camp near Cicala in July 1215).

By then, Frederick was well established in Germany. He had rapidly won support in southern Germany as his father's heir and papal protégé, but his crowning as king of the Romans in December 1212 had had to be held at Mainz, since Aachen, the normal place for German coronations, was still held for Otto IV until Otto's defeat by the French at Bouvines in July 1214 destroyed his credibility. In July 1215, Frederick at last entered Aachen for his official coronation, and from this time he formally reckoned his reign to have begun. His first act was to vow to go on the new crusade being planned by Innocent III. Frederick cannot, however, have really envisaged leaving Germany in the near future. The prospect of the crusade nevertheless provided him with a further objective, and one which already signalled his intention of not spending the rest of his life in Germany. In effect, his pious undertaking, however sincere, liberated him politically from the northern exile which Innocent III had attempted to impose as a permanent obligation.

In his early years in Germany, Frederick is found occasionally issuing documents himself for the southern kingdom, and his promise to Innocent III to renounce Sicily to Henry when he became emperor, indicates that from the first he did not propose to relinquish it before reaching Rome for his imperial coronation. Just before Innocent's death, Frederick renewed his pledge to assign the southern kingdom fully to Henry when he became of age, which would not have been sooner than 1225. Immediately after Innocent died, however, in the autumn of 1216, Frederick summoned both Henry and Constance to Germany. It seems possible that Frederick was already contemplating the transfer of his royal powers in Germany to Henry as soon as he could get away himself on crusade. The formalities were not in fact settled until three and a half years later, mainly because Frederick's own position in Germany did not become entirely secure until the death of Otto IV (19 May 1218) and the submission of his brother Henry (July 1219). Only then was the way open for Frederick's departure the following year, first for his imperial coronation in Rome, and second for the crusade itself.

The crusade was both an imperial duty and a practical way of furthering the work of reconciliation in Germany. Frederick could hardly have evaded the crusade, even had he wanted to, given the pressures on all contemporary princes, the traditions of his own family, and the fact that the crusade was one of the papacy's most cherished projects. When the crusading project was announced at the Fourth

Lateran Council in 1215, it was proposed that the crusaders should assemble at Brindisi and Messina in June 1217. Frederick's southern kingdom was deeply involved, and Frederick could hardly stand aside. With Apulia back in his own hands, he was from 1215 making benefactions in the ports of Barletta and Brindisi to the religious orders, particularly to the order of Teutonic knights which he did so much to promote, and by these means helped to prepare a secure base for the coming campaign. Nevertheless, it has been doubted whether the crusade was Frederick's main motive for leaving Germany: historians have attributed to him a strong emotional preference for returning to the South and a dislike of Germany itself. But Frederick showed no indecent haste to leave Germany, and he carefully prepared for its government in his absence. Henry was elected king of the Romans in April 1220, and a council of regency was appointed. After Frederick left Germany, he retained the goodwill of the princes. When he had to return in 1235, it was to deal with the troubles caused by his son's rule, not because of any need to reimpose himself over rebellious subjects. His own emotions did not swamp his political judgement: this was one of the reasons why he became such a formidable ruler.

If, for whatever reason, Frederick was already planning his own return to the South from the summer of 1216, he probably gave the situation there some thought, but unfortunately, the history of the kingdom in those four years is very obscure. It is not even certain that anyone was appointed to take the place of the queen once she reached Germany. One document which seems to assign the role of vicar to Rainald, archbishop of Capua, may possibly relate only to the Terra di Lavoro. Frederick's most loyal churchman, Berard Castanea, archbishop first of Bari, then of Palermo, who represented the king at the Lateran council, escorted the young Henry to Modena on his way to Germany in 1216, and may have returned to Sicily with quasi-regal powers. There are occasional glimpses of administrative officials. In 1219, Frederick wrote to the justiciar, judges and *secretus* in Palermo about the excessively zealous behaviour of *doanerii* and *cabelloti*, as though the gamut of administration was functioning normally. At Salerno, in July 1220, the archbishop was allowed to act as justiciar of all his lands and men, which would only have been a valued privilege if the other justiciars were in place. Also at Salerno, the *stratigotus* collected royal market and dyeing dues. In March 1218, Count Henry of Malta made a trip to Germany (possibly in connection with Frederick's proposed departure on crusade), and while there obtained Frederick's confirmation of Genoese rights in Sicily, presumably to impress any royal officials who had been challenging Genoese 'usurpations'.

From 1219 particularly, a number of petitioners from the kingdom came to Germany to obtain privileges from the king. Frederick had reserved real powers in the kingdom for himself, and the kingdom was sufficiently docile to be managed effectively by remote control. Shortly after his arrival in Germany, Frederick had shortened his formal style for the kingdom to *Rex Sicilie*, and he must have maintained a small but separate Sicilian establishment in Germany for the seven and a half years he spent there. After the arrival of the young Henry in 1216, there are more signs in Frederick's documents of southern influences, best explained on the assumption that Henry had brought competent officials with him to strengthen Frederick's administrative establishment. Nearly seventy privileges for the southern kingdom were issued by Frederick while in Germany, mostly written by notaries from the South, using different styles of composition from those of the German kingdom. Eight distinct notaries have been identified, though it has not been possible to regard them as forming a distinct 'Sicilian' chancery. A very high proportion of Frederick's documents in these years, even for Germany itself, were anyway written by persons not formally trained in chancery usage. A few names of officials are known. Frederick's *familiaris*, Richard, *privatus camerarius*, a southerner, who remained active in southern administration after 1220, was consistently with Frederick in Germany from 1214. One of his southern notaries, James of Caltagirone, received a prebend in the Capella Palatina for his services, and he made one of his chaplains bishop of Syracuse in 1215. The petty details of appointments show that little can have been delegated to any viceroy in the kingdom. The canons of Cefalù were paid, at last, for the sarcophagi removed by King William II; Frederick assigned revenues from the customs (*doana*) at Bari in 1215. How much Frederick needed to do to keep the administration moving properly in the kingdom, the sources do not say. The chancellor, Walter of Palearia, gave orders in November 1217 concerning a court case over a vineyard brought before Berard de Caczano at Salpi on the mainland. If only in connection with preparations for the crusade, Frederick would have been obliged to get the southern administration into some kind of working order until such time as he should return and introduce any radical changes. For this reason, when he did arrive, his administration was obviously already in place. It might have needed an overhaul by 1220, but it had survived some bad patches and proved its ability to tick over, even when the king was far away.

After Frederick's return to the kingdom in 1220, Richard's chronicle leaves no doubt about the galvanising effect of the king's presence, his activity, his projects of reform and renewal. Frederick's crusading vows committed his kingdom to heavy expenditure, effort and sacrifices, which could only reinforce the chronicler's evident concern for the east. The new note is sounded from the moment of Frederick's arrival at Rome, where the magnates of the kingdom attended his imperial coronation and made their peace with him on his own terms. In a few weeks he was in the kingdom itself, making new appointments, recovering royal domain, and publishing at Capua a famous set of *assizes* in which the key phrase is the confirmation of the good uses and customs observed *tempore regis Guillelmi*. The emperor's plan to restore the good old days of his cousin who had died more than thirty years before may have inspired a whole generation. When Richard revised his chronicle, he pushed back the starting-point of the new version to 1189 giving a summary of the reign of William II, described as prince of princes without earthly equal, with whose death, heirless, the blessed time of peace for the kingdom had come to an end. This view of William's reign may have been common in the kingdom before Frederick's return. If so, his insistence on the desirability of restoring the good old customs expressed not only his own determination to accept no precedent from the times of troubles, but would also have satisfied his subjects that there should be no compromise with those who had taken advantage for themselves of the kingdom's misfortunes. Richard's chronicle suggests that Frederick could count on many able and willing servants of administration. The speed with which the new policies were implemented shows that the machinery had not rusted in the meantime. Despite the shortage of information about it, the administration of the kingdom had somehow continued during the years of troubles, even without close supervision from above. It may not indeed be possible to imagine clearly how it could have held together without continuous authoritative government. Perhaps the very number of local authorities, adventurers, nationalities and officials involved helped to hold the centrifugal forces in equilibrium. The thirty-three years of monarchy after 1156 had at all events proved sufficient to see the kingdom through the next thirty-one years of disarray. By 1220, the kingdom had weathered the storm, and was eagerly anticipating the young king's return and the promise of renewed vitality.

11

THE KINGDOM REVITALISED

•

After his return to Italy in 1220, Frederick spent most of the rest of his life there, with only two long spells away: one year on crusade (1228–9), and much of the years 1235–7 in Germany. No other ruler of Italy until modern times devoted himself to the affairs and problems of the whole peninsula with comparable zeal and intelligence. In the South, Frederick had little difficulty in restoring vigour to the monarchy, and his problems elsewhere did not noticeably weaken his regime in the kingdom. It remained loyal and was effectively managed by devoted public officials, promptly carrying out his instructions and constantly under scrutiny. But the kingdom could not preserve a splendid isolation from events elsewhere in the peninsula. Its regular government, its prosperity and its example made it the greatest 'power' in Italy, and it could not avoid the consequences. If it did not take the lead in the peninsula's affairs, it would be at risk from others.

Though Frederick could govern the kingdom *in absentia*, he may well have preferred to be there when he could, and only urgent business drew him away. In his favourite region of sojourn, Capitanata, it was easy to gather intelligence from Sicily on the one hand, and along the Adriatic coast into Lombardy and Germany on the other. Here, as early as 1223, he ordered a palace to be built at Foggia, and there he several times mustered impressive assemblies to discuss great matters of state. He spent nearly twice as much of his time in the kingdom as in other parts of Italy. In the first part of the reign, before the long break in Germany, he spent three quarters of his time there. During this period, he had to renew the effectiveness of the monarchy, assemble his crusade, deal on his return

315

from it with the consequences of papal invasion of the kingdom during
his absence, and restore his authority. He was hardly able to enjoy a long
rest there after years of exile. But his kingdom was where he felt most
appreciated and could best develop his interests in building, learning and
sport. There is no need to doubt his expressions of pride in being
Apulian. Frederick was actually born at Iesi, just outside the kingdom,
and spent his youth in Sicily; he had not actually seen much of the rest of
his kingdom before he went to Germany in 1212. It cannot have been
nostalgia for his Sicilian youth that brought Frederick south again, for he
had no political reason to reflect happily on the difficult years he had
spent there as a child. From the first he realised that, with his other
responsibilities, he could not make Palermo his residential capital in the
manner of his Norman forebears. For his kingdom, Frederick's itinerant
style of government was a departure from Norman precedent.

THE RESTORATION OF ROYAL GOVERNMENT

On the mainland, where the kings of Sicily had not previously taken up
residence, Frederick was not surrounded by Muslims or Greeks, and his
intellectual inspiration was certainly Roman. Frederick had probably
received a good bookish education for his day, and since he had not had
the opportunity to learn about rulership and war by youthful experience
under his father, his reading became correspondingly more important in
shaping his understanding and kindling his ambition. In Germany, he
was exposed to the vigorous Staufen traditions of the empire. The past
mattered in fact more to Frederick's concepts of government than they
had done to either of his distinguished grandfathers. This intellectual bias
in his rulership attracted to his service educated and cultivated men in
every branch of learning and from many lands. There were some
Sicilians, but also others from the mainland, such as his most famous
minister, Peter de Vinea, from Capua. The help, loyalty and enthusiasm
of such men for serving him, encouraged Frederick to cultivate the
abilities of his subjects for reordering royal administration after its
comparative neglect during the previous generation. From the beginning,
he found he could rely on the competence of his officials and the
willingness of enough of his subjects to take part in the process of
restoration.

Before leaving Rome for the kingdom, Frederick gave the pope a
specific undertaking not to rule the empire jointly with Sicily. He also
acknowledged, as his mother's family had traditionally done, that the
kingdom was not part of the empire, but a vassal state of the papacy,
though there is no record of his taking the customary oath or doing

homage to Honorius III. Almost immediately, however, he gave practical expression to the kingdom's separateness by preparing a different seal for use in the kingdom. It is attested from 1221, though only one late example of the gold-bull type survives. On the reverse it gives a curious map of the kingdom centred on Messina, where the matrix was very likely made. His administration was likewise entrusted to officials from the kingdom, not to Germans. Frederick continued to have about him a considerable number of German nobles and officials, but there was no German infiltration or take-over of the kingdom itself, as had happened in 1194.

The amount of reorganisation Frederick needed to undertake after 1220 would be easier to estimate if more information had survived about how royal administration had functioned in his absence. The writing office was in good enough shape to produce royal documents in the manner of his Norman predecessors, though documents for the empire continued to be written according to imperial conventions. The continuity in the traditions of the writing office can be confidently attributed to the long chancellorship of Walter of Palearia. On the other hand, there is little sign of how the financial offices of the crown survived in Palermo, and the alienation of the Saracen population must have had serious implications for the management of the royal estates in the island. Frederick's decision not to maintain a fixed capital in Palermo anyway meant that he needed to develop a quite different style of financial management. There were, however, no signs that Frederick would find it difficult to rule effectively from the first moments of his return. Pope Honorius III himself used his influence with the clergy in Frederick's favour, being eager to smoothe the way for Frederick's prompt departure on crusade. The great men of the kingdom actually came flocking to Rome itself at his coronation to pay their respects and establish their claims on his favour. Even Thomas, count of Molise, one of the least deferential nobles, who would not come himself, had prudently sent his son with peace overtures. Frederick was confident enough to reject the proffered submission, presumably because the terms were unsatisfactory, and no settlement was actually reached with Thomas until 1223. His defiance did not, however, have the effect of encouraging others.

Frederick arrived in the kingdom as a giver of laws. He had promulgated some laws (*constitutiones*) in Rome at his coronation, and thought sufficiently well of them to have copies sent to the *studium* of law at Bologna, expecting them to be incorporated into the Roman laws of his imperial predecessors. These constitutions affirmed ecclesiastical liberties and denounced heresy. Three final clauses extended royal protection to survivors from shipwreck, to travellers, and over oxen and

implements of the country working population, against any kind of
expropriation. He was still in the lawgiving frame of mind when he
reached his kingdom. He held a great court at Capua where he published
decrees, which were in fact instructions to his officials. They were told
for many purposes to disregard the precedents and privileges of the years
since 1189. The good old customs of William II, rather than of his father
Henry VI, were to be enforced: specifically, the old practices with regard
to the payments of tithes, the rights of the royal domain, the recovery of
rights alienated since 1189, the holding of fairs and markets. Other
decrees affected public order and the king's authority over the forces of
the military. No castles were allowed outside the royal domain other
than those already put up by 1189; the carrying of arms and the wearing
of armour was forbidden in and out of cities; royal approval was
required for the marriages of counts and barons; all baronies were to be
held from the crown and not sub-infeudated; services between lords and
vassals were to be as in 1189. All dues imposed since the death of his
parents for markets, tolls, ports, customs and anchorage (*plateaticum,
passagium novum, portum novum, duanam* and *plantaticum*) were invali-
dated. All his father's and mother's privileges were also to be submitted
for confirmation, on the grounds that their seals had been improperly
acquired by Markwald (Frederick's one-time kidnapper); such documents were illegal and consequently invalid. The remaining clauses
provide for the exclusive royal appointments of justiciars; for the
justiciars to take oaths to do justice quickly and honestly; for the
settlement of all grievances in their courts, and not by private and violent
self-help; for justice to be done on thieves and robbers caught at their
misdeeds; and lastly, for confining the activities of castellans and their
sergeants to their castles. The powers of the king's government (*curia*)
were affirmed by endorsing all the privileges it issued and its sole right to
appoint the king's official (*bailivus*) in the cities. Counts and barons had
no authority to make grants of baronies without special royal licence.
None of this was designed to be new: it was intended to re-establish an
order that had wilted for lack of royal attention. It could even have been
consciously modelled on the bishop's right in canon law to recover
property of the church alienated by improvident predecessors. No
protests were heard that the order of events since 1189 had installed a
preferable system to earlier royal tyranny, and Frederick did not expect
opposition. A few weeks later at Messina, he added a few more decrees
inspired by the Fourth Lateran Council, affecting Jews, blasphemers and
gamblers.

The most convincing evidence of his real authority is the speed with
which holders of privileges issued since 1189 hastened to get them

confirmed as soon as they realised that Frederick's officials were poised to enforce the new decrees. What cannot be known is the number of cases where confirmations were refused: unconfirmed grants having no legal force after 1221 did not need to be well looked after. The difficulties of knowing what had happened in those intervening thirty years are multiplied by Frederick's reform. Those who grumbled later give some idea of what happened. The orders of the Hospital and Temple, for example, claimed that much property granted to them in the cities by Tancred had been lost by Frederick's decree. The Genoese were also affronted because they stood to lose advantages gained since the triumph of Henry VI. Count Henry of Malta had indeed lost his lands before the end of 1221. But Frederick did not have to confront much opposition, and there must have been general acceptance that he was entitled to re-establish his effective authority. The existing machinery of administration soon demonstrated its capacity to deal with the imme-diate duty of scrutinising all recent charters, on the mainland within four months, and on the island by Whitsun, though in fact this must have placed some strain on both the royal writing office and on local government. Frederick himself did not anticipate having time to attend personally to the management of the kingdom: early in 1221 he was committed to going on crusade before the end of the year.

Since Frederick did not leave for the kingdom of Jerusalem until June 1228 (and had first taken crusading vows at his coronation at Aachen in 1215), it is often taken as self-evident that Frederick was a reluctant crusader and that papal impatience with him was natural. Such a conclusion would be less than just to Frederick. Though his inner disposition to the crusade must remain unknown, it was actually in character for him to prepare the way thoroughly, to prefer diplomacy to warfare, and to take his time in bringing projects to fruition. This was admittedly not the traditional way, which relied on enthusiasm to assemble crusading forces. Frederick's concern to achieve results, as in 1228–9, also contrasts strongly with that of the papacy, which stressed the importance of crusading with the right spiritual disposition. In 1221, Frederick's sincerity was not in question. He still enjoyed a good understanding with Honorius III, and had been making sacrifices of men and money since 1215. Though he had not himself been able to leave with the (fifth) crusaders in 1217, he remained in touch with the forces that reached the Holy Land in the summer of 1218 and gave instructions as though he were their commander. At his imperial coronation in Rome, he had also renewed his vows to go east to Cardinal Ugolino (later his enemy Pope Gregory IX). Within a few months of his reaching the kingdom he sent out forty galleys in response to the pope's urgent appeal to provide the crusaders, by then at Damietta, with support (June 1221). This was financed by a general levy on all produce in the kingdom, belonging to both clergy and laymen, with only victuals and working animals exempt from liability. When the galleys arrived, they found that the crusading force, disobeying its orders, had ventured up the Nile where it had been captured: the men were only released in return for the surrender of Damietta. This deprived Frederick of his expected base and set back the whole crusading project. Frederick had good reason to reproach the commanders, for all the previous efforts had been expended in vain. A new strategy would have to be devised.

Over the next few years, all Frederick's decisions were reached after full consultation with the pope. Early in 1222, he talked over the problem with Honorius and they agreed jointly to summon an assembly to Verona in 1223 in order to launch another crusade. In the meantime, Frederick was obliged to return to Sicily to deal with his own rebellious Muslim subjects. It was there in June 1222 that his first wife, Constance, died. When Frederick returned to the mainland, he was therefore free to marry Isabella of Brienne, heiress to the kingdom of Jerusalem. Frederick met her father, King John, with the pope in March 1223. A new scheme was now worked out. Frederick gave an undertaking to depart for the Holy Land within two years. The following spring (1224), a hundred galleys and fifty cavalry-transport ships (*usseria*) were ready for the expedition. Frederick found, however, that this time he could chivvy the pope because the preaching of the crusade had not been impressive enough to produce an adequate force of crusaders. Frederick was anyway already fighting Muslims who were no less persistent and difficult enemies in Sicily than in the Near East. When, at the end of July 1225, Frederick and Honorius finally agreed on a new departure date for the crusade, Frederick swore, under sanction of excommunication, that he would leave by August 1227. His precise obligations in men and money, and for how long, were precisely itemised. To clinch matters, Frederick married Isabella of Brienne at Brindisi in November 1225. He immediately required her father to hand over the kingdom. Frederick was certainly entitled to do this, but John was affronted and became an enemy.

Although the crusade was delayed therefore, it remained in practice a constant preoccupation. For the kingdom, it also represented a steady financial burden: according to the agreement of 1225, 100,000 gold *unciae* for the soldiers and the cost of the galleys in construction, and manning them. In answer to later papal accusations, Frederick listed what he had done for the crusade. He cited the provision of 700 knights from north of the Alps, 400 men from Lombardy, 250 knights from the kingdom, and another 100 knights from his own household and others. Even in manpower, the kingdom was heavily committed. Some men actually left in 1226, even if Frederick himself did not. The kingdom was making sacrifices for the crusade throughout the 1220s. It also had problems of its own.

On Frederick's arrival in the kingdom, there were two particular issues – what should be done first about the defiant count of Molise to the north, and second about the turbulent Saracens in Sicily. Following the decrees at Capua, Frederick wanted to take possession of the useful strongholds of the realm and destroy the rest. He left the count of Acerra, who had been appointed captain and master-justiciar of Apulia and Terra di Lavoro, to take charge of operations against Molise, in effect reviving the old system of a regency on the mainland, which enabled him to go himself to Sicily. Many of Molise's barons and towns submitted, but the count was still secure enough to raid at will from Celano until he was besieged in the town by the master-justiciar. In 1223, by the mediation of the papal *curia* and the master of the Teutonic order, the count was induced to surrender his fortresses and allowed to keep his county, provided he kept out of the kingdom for two years, either in the Holy Land on the projected crusade, or elsewhere. Soon after, however, he was found guilty of not observing the terms of the treaty and lost the county for contumacy. Celano itself was destroyed. Its population was at first dispersed, but much of it was later rounded up again and sent to prison in Sicily in 1224 and only released in 1227. No other feudatory tried to emulate Molise, whose bid to preserve a position of independence was no longer justifiable. Frederick's authority in the rest of Italy diminished the significance of what had formerly been important military districts on the kingdom's northern frontier.

The difficulties in Sicily were much less simple to resolve. Saracen relations with the Christian population had probably deteriorated inexorably, though gradually, during the twelfth century, as the Muslims felt themselves increasingly pushed to the fringes of island society. The subjection of the remaining 'homeland' to the royal monastery of Monreale in 1182 must have been the last straw, to judge from the fact that when William II died, Monreale immediately became the object of attack. Though details are lacking, at some point the Saracens advanced to the very walls of the church and drove all the Christian people out of the region. Intermittent government after 1189 allowed the Saracens to organise themselves. When Tancred died, the importance of getting their consent to the succession was already appreciated; six years later, Markwald recognised their real power and must have made an alliance with them to have been able to enter the island at Trapani.

The most specific evidence about them in this period depends on an enquiry made in 1260 for the diocese of Agrigento. Only by then did conditions seem sufficiently stable to make possible an enquiry into the history of the previous seventy years. Some witnesses, who must have been very old, said that its bishop, Urso, had been expelled from the diocese three times: first, by Henry VI for being the son of King Tancred; second, by Capparone for refusing to take the oath of fealty; and third, when the Saracens had kept him in prison for fourteen months at Guastanella, while they despoiled the church and occupied both the cathedral *campanile* and houses of the church. The Saracens had obviously been able to take advantage of the disruption attendant on the circumstances of succession to the kingdom. One witness reported that incessant warfare had prevented episcopal visits to the church at Rifes after 1189: no Christians had been able to reach it even for baptisms. Warfare between Christians and Muslims in the Val di Mazara had frightened men so much that they had not ventured away from their settlements, even to cultivate the vines. Though the proctor of the diocese had found farmers for certain tenements, witnesses claimed that they had not dared to travel about in the diocese. Other witnesses saw the church pillaged of its fittings by the wife of Count Bernardino, who, with Saracen help, had actually taken and sacked the city of Agrigento itself. This puts a different complexion on Saracen disaffection. Some bishops had on occasion brought their attendants to round up their flocks of animals, or for recreation and the hunting of wild boars. Once, witnesses said, the *secretus* Raymond (in the 1220s) had sent an army to crush the countess' forces. The Saracens were not, therefore, the only problem facing local authorities, but in western Sicily much depended upon their attitude. Frederick believed that his first urgent task as ruler was to confront them in Sicily.

The district of Mazara was subjected to the authority of the emir, Ibn 'Abbad, who held many fortified points in the mountains of central Sicily, and exercised a paramountcy over other Saracen leaders (*reguli*). Frederick found that pacification of the island required a prolonged period of attention; at least seven months in 1221, and five more in 1222. Only then were the emir and his sons captured, after the siege of *Giato*, near Trapani, and hanged in Palermo. Many other Saracens were forced out of their mountain retreats. Muslim sources claim Frederick deployed 2,000 horse and 60,000 infantry soldiers. Frederick had German vassals with him in 1222 and called on the services of his own counts, but the details of what he did on the island did not reach, or did not much interest, the chronicler, Richard of San Germano. At the end of 1223, tremendous efforts were still required to restore tranquillity. Frederick imposed arbitrary levies on the mainland to provide him with funds; nine months later he demanded as much again. What he did in the island during these two years is not recorded, but even after he left Sicily (spring 1225), his barons and infeudated knights were summoned to force more Muslims out of their mountain hide-outs, so after four years, the problem had still not been solved. A great proportion of the Saracen prisoners were sent to the mainland (where a colony was created for them at Lucera), but there were still rebels in the mountains in 1230. Further details are wanting, but the nature of the problem should not be underestimated.

Protracted spells in Sicily removed Frederick from direct influence over the recovery of royal authority on the mainland. From his correspondence, it seems that he had to restrain his officials' zeal, rather than urge them to greater efforts on his behalf. While in Sicily, Frederick took the important decision to set up a *studium generale* at Naples, the principal function of which was to train men of law for his service in the kingdom (summer 1224). This would reduce the cost of study to individuals who would otherwise have travelled to Bologna, and Frederick's decision certainly had something to do with the difficulties of his own relationship with the restless city of Bologna. More specifically, it also indicates that after three years back in the kingdom, Frederick perceived that he needed better-trained officials. Native wit was itself not sufficient for his purposes, and since the individual enterprise of teachers could not be relied on to provide these studies, Frederick deliberately founded a university. It was the first European university to be formally instituted. Frederick took no chances: his subjects were forbidden to leave the kingdom to study elsewhere. To promote the new establishment, he offered professors favourable contracts to come to Naples, *mater antiqua studii*, with its natural advantages, its site, prosperity and fecundity. Little is known of its activities at the time, but an indication of the way it could have repercussions in the kingdom is provided by a contract of 1224, whereby a professional scribe in Bari agreed to write out a copy of a collection of *Decretales* and the gloss of Master Ugolino for a client in Salerno. If the kingdom did not already have many professors of its own, there were certainly copyists who could profit from the new patronage.

While Frederick characteristically thought in the long term, some of his subjects wanted immediate results, and in various ways showed their impatience. The presentation of old charters to be confirmed turned out to be only one of the consequences of the king's wishes to restore the good old customs of the past. His officials began to reassert royal rights in such a way as to provoke a general demand by churchmen for exemptions from taxation and secular judgement, whether the particular house had received special rights or not. The renewed vigour of secular lawcourts also encouraged those with grievances to hope for a favourable hearing. If rights of any kind were not now certainly established, they would be lost for ever. The king was naturally concerned to recover all his own domain *villani* if they had been acquired improperly by others in his absence, but he also needed to reassure his barons that their legitimate rights would not suffer. The monks of Monreale, who had hoped to recover their Saracen work-force, had obtained charters from Frederick for this before he left Germany. Other monasteries did the same. But even some *villani* expected to get royal protection for their own rights.

As the royal progress moved south on the way to Sicily in 1221, it was already intercepted by a delegation from the *villani* of four properties belonging to the Cistercian monks of Santo Stefano del Bosco. They complained of the monks burdening them with unlawful services and molestation. The petition was passed on to the court of the *camerarius*, who immediately warned the abbot to stop his unjustified oppression (*indebita molestatione*). The abbot's proctor, suitably alarmed, presented himself to the justiciar of Calabria when he was in court at Nicastro in March; he protested that the monastery had been grievously misrepresented, and requested the justiciar to summon the *villani* to his own court and make them prove their allegations. When they came, they said they were ready to perform the services due and did not want litigation. Then, a little later, they took advantage of the abbot's visit to Rome to refuse the due and customary services. They reapplied to Frederick, by then at Messina, for another order to the abbot not to impose more dues and burdens than were authorised by charter. This time the abbot took the matter to the archbishop of Reggio, whom the king had made judge of all the monastery's affairs. The archbishop, acting with the justiciar in court at Syracuse (where they were both on royal business), imposed a fine of five thousand *tari* on the *villani* for their refusal to come to court and explain their defiance of the abbot. This induced the *villani*, through their proctor, to put their case in more detail before the archbishop at Gerace on the mainland in August. At issue was whether they were still bound by the terms of Count Roger I's grant to St Bruno, which had imposed perpetual servitude on the men assigned to the monastery as punishment for their treachery to the count. Abbot William had more recently issued a charter defining their obligations. These dues were formally set out and the court required the *villani* to accept them or have their goods confiscated. Even so, they did not give up. A mere two months later, the abbot's proctor was back in the justiciar's court at

Tropea complaining that the *villani* were still refusing to do what had been stipulated. In court again, the indomitable *villani* brought more letters from Frederick, issued this time at Trapani, on behalf of his *fideles* (the abbot's *villani*), accusing the abbot of disregarding earlier royal letters and continuing to demand uncustomary services. The abbot had to defend himself from this slur on his fealty, and denounced the *villani* for lying to Frederick. The justiciar listened to both sides and adjourned the matter for two weeks, giving his definitive sentence at Nicotera. He confirmed the fine of five thousand *tari* for defying the Gerace judgement and for lying to the king. This may seem to have been the end of the matter, though a charter of 1224 claims that Frederick, incensed at having been tricked, reduced all the *villani* again to the state of utter servitude to which their ancestors had been sentenced by Count Roger I.

That this dispute was not so exceptional is shown by a similar set of lawsuits begun the following summer between the *villani* of Sorrento and various churches, monasteries and knights of the city. The *villani* complained to the king of the injuries (*gravamina*) and insults (*contumeliae*) to which they had been subjected and asked to be taken into the royal domain. This was agreed to. The knights objected that the story was a fabrication; the *villani* belonged in fact to the lords of Sorrento. Only then did Frederick instruct the master-justiciar, Henry de Morra, to conduct an enquiry and send in a report. In the end, though the *villani* were returned to the old lordship, their future dues and service were exactly specified. This was of clear advantage to them; by drawing the government into their affairs, they may have achieved their main purpose.

These cases are valuable on a number of counts. They show how Frederick was prepared to throw his weight behind the *villani*, his *fideles*, in their struggle against old lordships, and the importance of securing the formal authority of royal courts for defining labour services. Above all, it shows a system of royal justice in working order from the first days of the king returning to the kingdom, with its own routines and procedures for dealing with business in regular sessions and not by improvisation. Both the *villani* and the greatest lords of the kingdom sought justice in the public courts of the justiciars as they moved from one city to another within their jurisdiction. The novelty was that Frederick was now himself in the kingdom, assisting the enforcement of custom as it had been before 1189 by the regular use of writs to the courts. No objection in principle was voiced. If he thought this was to the general advantage of the crown, others were not slow to see that it might be made to serve their interests too, and the crown was not therefore the only one to profit from it. At Santa Maria de Luco in 1224, a formal enquiry into the position under William II revealed that the provost had indeed exercised his responsibilities as he claimed, so the *curia* itself failed in its attempt to recover alleged rights. The general enquiries throughout the kingdom were not, therefore, a mere device for reimposing royal powers. They served to reaffirm the validity of custom, even against the crown itself.

These activities of the administration raise two points of more general interest: first, about the officials themselves, and second, about the reaction of 'public opinion'. In the early years, Frederick notably made use of several prelates in judicial business, alongside laymen with experience. On Frederick's accession, the chief royal minister had been the chancellor. In 1220, as in 1195, this was Walter of Palearia. In the summer of 1221 he was sent with the count of Malta and a lot of money to succour the beleaguered garrison in Damietta, where he was compromised by his failure to prevent the surrender of the city. He never returned to the kingdom, but went to Venice, and then to Rome, and lived on to a great age in ever-greater poverty until he died *c.* 1232. Frederick never appointed another chancellor. Already, by 1223, Henry de Morra, master-justiciar of the great court, had become his principal minister. Though frequently at Frederick's side, he also acted on occasion as the king's deputy, serving faithfully for twenty years until his death in 1242.

Frederick's relations with his ministers are not easily studied. Royal privileges were written by several different notaries, but unlike those for the empire, did not require to be witnessed, so that it is not possible to learn from them who was in regular attendance on him. Frederick paid great attention to the formalities of government administration. As early as 1220, he insisted on a reform in the handwriting of documents in the cities of Naples, Sorrento and Amalfi in order to make their documents more easily decipherable. The reform would not have been effective at all had there not been enough suitably trained young men in the kingdom to take on the task. Some of them were taken into the king's own service. It was about this time that he engaged Peter de Vinea, by then in his thirties, recommended to him by Archbishop Berard of Palermo and probably by Peter's fellow-countryman, James of Capua, bishop of Patti.

The officials who provoked most criticism were those connected with fiscal administration, but official records of this have been lost. The best evidence for their activities comes in fact either from the chronicler, Richard of San Germano, or from clergy with grievances. Richard may be an intermittent chronicler of Frederick's own deeds, but he is punctilious in his account of how the government affected his locality. He notes changes of the coinage (1221, 1222, 1225, 1228), the details of the subsidy for the Holy Land (1221), the arrangements for securing fixed prices for all goods in each place by six good men when there was much uncertainty about the quality of the currency, and the ban on the export of precious metal (1222). The effectiveness of these regulations seems to have turned on the diligence of the six men appointed in each place to make constant enquiries. As an incentive, they were offered a quarter of the fines exacted from offenders: the *camerarius* took the rest for the king. Merchants who contravened the regulations had their goods confiscated by the local government officer, the catapan. The next year, everyone was required to declare on oath how much had been paid, and to whom, for various impositions, tithes, corrodies and military operations in the Molise. Later, when lump sums in taxation were imposed for the Sicilian campaigns, the whole district had to send two persons from every place to collect the proportion of the tax assigned to it. In May 1224, inquisitions at San Germano concerned not only the taxes and dues (*collecta* and *dazia*), but also the enforcement of the decrees of 1220 and 1221 regarding the carrying of weapons and gambling. The people of the kingdom thus became quite familiar with royal orders enquiring into infringements of regulations, including those by royal officials.

Frederick set out to bring abuses to light. At Catania, in January 1224, he ordered the justiciars to enquire into the substance of countless clerical complaints that their exemptions (from *dazii*, tallages, *collecta* and other public services) were being disregarded, despite their willingness to be of service to the crown and provide special subventions. Frederick insisted that the clergy and their men were only liable for such tallages and *collecta* as had been paid under William II. The king was determined not to lose his rights to knight-service and the repair of castles, so that churches which had acquired since 1189 properties liable for such dues, would have to meet them. It was feared that blanket clerical exemptions would tempt men to flee into dependence on the churches in order to escape tax liabilities. Those with the privilege of receiving freemen as *affidati* were recommended to exercise it with moderation, or risk having it revoked altogether. The king's anxieties about clerical privilege are made plain. The public was invited to recognise that clerical privilege could rebound to general disadvantage.

When Frederick returned to the mainland, still expecting to leave for the Holy Land in the summer of 1225, he summoned a solemn assembly to meet him at Foggia in June in order to make arrangements for the peace of the kingdom in his absence. He proposed to answer all the complaints of the clergy against his officials, which had been accumulating since his return to the kingdom. Complaints were to be put in writing so that they could be looked into. After the heavy financial commitment for the crusade accepted by Frederick in July, however, there can have been no expectation in the kingdom that the fiscal pressure would be relaxed. A heavy *collecta* in the place of a loan was imposed throughout the kingdom in August. On the lands of Cassino, this involved more inquisitions: who should pay up? how much? who was excused? who knew about evasions? Although royal initiative was required to prompt these inquests, they were not against local interests. At Cassino, doubts about exactly what *jura* and *rationes* had applied in the time of William II were resolved by inquest. To meet the expenses of royal visits to the monastery, the abbot was authorised to make a levy (*collecta*). If a criminal was condemned by the justiciars, the abbey was entitled to keep his land and his goods. Since, in Henry VI's time, the abbot had been allowed to retain for himself what was collected from his estates when the *redemptio* was levied throughout the kingdom, this too had become a right. The king was entitled to impose *servitia* on the monastery: if he sent a fleet to the Greek empire, the abbot had to send ten knights on the expedition, but was allowed himself to collect their stipends from his estates. The monastery's men owed labour services at Gaeta castle. Frederick's exactions may seem burdensome, but his care to keep a check on custom and call his officials regularly to account represents an aspect of his government that is far from arbitrary and tyrannical. This kind of pressure was sustained until he actually sailed to the Holy Land in June 1228.

As distinct from grumbles, it is difficult to assess the extent of disquiet caused by Frederick in the kingdom, though there was certainly some. Two letters written to Frederick by Thomas of Gaeta in this period (1223–5) beg him to reduce the *collecta* and exactions damaging the kingdom and oppressing the people, especially because of the building of so many castles. Thomas had conducted the diplomatic business of the monarchy with the papacy for over twenty years. Although he gave the burden on the people as justification for his intervention, his candid advice that Frederick should invest in buying the friendship of one or two cardinals in Rome reveals his deeper worry. He understood how the papacy must react to a royal vassal building fortresses as close to the patrimony as Gaeta, and shrewdly sensed that Frederick risked making enemies his castles could offer him no protection against. Frederick had set about restoring and rebuilding fortifications on a grand scale, but Thomas' protests are the only evidence of public reaction to them, and his comments are more subtle than they seem. The reactions of the clergy and papacy were strong, but muted. How the secular nobility felt about the assertion of Frederick's power is in some ways more important, but impenetrable. In 1223, Frederick summoned several barons from the mainland to Sicily, ostensibly to help him fight the Saracens, but while there he seized and imprisoned the counts of Fondi, Caserta, Avellino and Tricarico for reasons unknown. Released through the intervention of the pope, they were nevertheless exiled from the kingdom and had to give hostages as a guarantee of good behaviour. Their example must have been sufficient to impress others of the inadvisability of disaffection, for Frederick did not have to take comparable action later on. Yet his style of rule did not in fact tolerate the kind of role played, notably in justice, by counts under the Norman kings. By insisting that justiciars were all appointed by him and by denying counts the right to appoint justiciars even in their own lands, Frederick in effect provided for a new kind of judicial administration throughout the kingdom. When that system becomes historically visible, the nobility seems to play only a minimal role in it. In some cases, the county unit might be retained, but the office was left vacant. Molise, for example, became a normal adjunct to the province of Terra di Lavoro as managed by Frederick's justiciars. How exactly Frederick succeeded in making himself so masterful and why the comital families submitted so meekly to his rule, the available sources do not explain. Did his status as emperor, or as crusader, impress them? Or were they, for the most part recently ennobled, less conscious of the older justifications of comital power which had sustained the ambitions of their predecessors?

In the absence of powerful checks at home, the most considerable of his critics became Honorius III. After only a year in the kingdom, Frederick had to bear papal remonstrations about the way ecclesiastical privileges were being brushed aside. Even more promptly, in March 1221, the pope had expressed uneasiness about the Capuan decrees in case they should be interpreted to include concessions made to the Roman church since 1189. Though he was reassured on this point, he remained troubled on account of churches in the kingdom to which the king was less beholden. After his meeting with the pope at Veroli in April 1222, Frederick still insisted that his officials should respect only privileges enjoyed by the clergy in 1189, and to disregard later accretions. The clergy were, however, inclined to take the view that they had exemptions by virtue of their calling, and not by special privilege. Nor were they much interested in when exactly they had obtained privileges over *collecta, exactiones, angaria, parangia, exercitus* and *procurationes*, or exemptions from the jurisdiction of secular tribunals for civil and criminal offences. Frederick was adamant that clergy as such did not enjoy tax-exemptions on their temporalities, and that they were as subject to secular justice as they had been in 1189. Frederick would not concede that the decrees of the Fourth Lateran Council on this point should prevail. Disputes with the papacy about such matters were not confined to this kingdom in the thirteenth century, but the papacy was obviously unwilling to make concessions in a papal vassal-state, so close to itself and vulnerable, as it hoped, to pressure, particularly when recent precedents gave it grounds for protest. But the churchmen of the kingdom were not united behind the papacy. Frederick found that important prelates, even abbots, like those of Cassino and La Cava, could be very co-operative and provide him with resources when in need. Frederick could also be conciliatory. There were therefore no concerted protests about royal exactions, only complaints about particularly high-handed actions. Frederick attempted to parry criticism by ordering careful investigations of grievances. The kingdom was not disposed to quarrel with the king it had recovered, and not even the papacy found a way to weaken Frederick's grip in the South.

The breach with Rome was occasioned by events elsewhere. Frederick's other Italian subjects, who saw less of him, were not so easily bidden as those in the South. When he ordered the men of the duchy of Spoleto to accompany him to Cremona, where the crusade was to be discussed with his German and Lombard vassals, they refused, on the grounds that the pope had forbidden them to do the emperor any service because they held directly of the Roman church itself. The king was furious, but his anger provoked a no less violent attack on him by the exasperated Honorius, whose pent-up frustrations boiled over. This serves to show how deeply the papacy resented the recovery of royal powers. The first sign of really strained relations came in September 1225, when Honorius filled the long-vacant sees of Capua, Salerno, Brindisi, Conza and Aversa. Frederick considered this an infringement of his rights, but Honorius would not apologise. His new boldness may be connected with the fact that since July, Frederick was bound by oath to go on crusade within two years, and was therefore now at the church's mercy. Honorius made a long and rhetorical outburst, charging Frederick with attempting to appropriate papal lands. He threatened him with excommunication if he did not respect papal rights. His sanctimonious interpretation of the deaths of Frederick's grandfather, father and uncle must have been calculated to wound and offend. Frederick's reply has not survived, but it was sufficiently galling to stimulate the pope to a second rebuke. Its reading of the past, with its legalistic appeal to the documents of the papal archive, was tendentious, and points the way to later papal polemic. Honorius went over the whole history of papal relations with Frederick. Not without malice, the pope threw back at the king his own earlier and tactful words of

gratitude for the papacy's care of him in his youth. Frederick's dissem-
bling of his bitterness in the past for the sake of peace became itself another
motive for papal criticism. Honorius scoffed at Frederick's defence of the
so-called kingdom's law (*jus regni*) concerning episcopal elections as
against the papal *constitutiones*; he marvelled at the sudden and total fall
from Frederick's favour of the archbishop of Taranto, and at Frederick's
complaints about the bishops of Catania (Walter of Palearia) and Cefalù
(Aldoin). Apart from the individuals, the pope had more general
complaints about the king's claim to jurisdiction over criminal charges
against clergy; he argued that Frederick used the excuse of recovering
royal rights lost during his absence as a means to encroach on the property
of others, particularly because churches were alleged to have received
suspected runaways; he also reproved his treatment of the count of Molise
and his fellows for whom the papacy had secured favourable terms that
Frederick had not honoured, and of other counts – Conversano and
Fondi – the details of whose cases are not known.

Nevertheless, the quarrel with the papacy was not pushed to
extremes. The emperor's return to Lombardy had excited enough fear
there to cause some of the cities to renew their league, as though they
intended to revive the cause of the communes against imperial authority.
But Honorius would not allow himself to be drawn into any confrontation with Frederick that might sabotage the crusade. Both pope and
emperor settled for a compromise. Nevertheless, honeyed harmony
with the papacy was over.

It is not possible to judge between Frederick and the popes. The
sincerity of the parties is not at issue and not relevant. Both sides stood
for incompatible principles. Frederick may not have realised at first how
difficult the papacy could make it for him to achieve his objectives. He
obviously expected early on to get his own way by patience and
diplomacy. The papacy, which at first regarded Frederick as a willing
vassal, was both surprised and horrified when the poor orphan turned
out to be a remarkable ruler with views of his own. Honorius III
expected to be able to deal with the problem simply by putting his own
foot down; Gregory IX discovered that he needed to make use of
Frederick's enemies; Gregory's successors had to call on all the spiritual
and material resources of western Christendom to secure the annihilation of Frederick's family. In the longer term, however, Frederick's
cause has worn historically better than the papacy's, since his apparently
represents the attempt, reactionary, premature or anachronistic, to
provide for effective civil government at a time when outside his
kingdom, men of education and idealism only put their faith in the order
of spirituality within the church. In these circumstances, however, it

must seem unrealistic for Frederick to have persisted in defiance of the papacy. Yet at the same time, contemporaries clearly never anticipated the lengths to which both parties would be prepared to go to pursue their quarrel. Frederick's appeal to traditional custom seemed no more outrageous or unrealistic in his kingdom than Henry II's had been against Becket in England. The papacy itself was far from confident that Frederick would fail.

Probably without much premeditation, Frederick had learned how to get round Honorius III by telling him what he wanted to believe about the crusade. Only as the pope got older and weaker did he certainly begin to lose both patience and hope. During the 1220s, Frederick himself also began to realise that he had more to do than act as the pope's military commander overseas; he suspected, rightly or wrongly, that the pope was probably counting on the likelihood that his absence from Italy would weaken imperial authority there. The pretensions of the papacy to interfere in both the kingdom and empire since 1198 had certainly rankled with Frederick, but for nearly twenty years he tactfully swallowed his resentment at the papal treatment of himself, his empire and his kingdom. Thanks to this 'subterfuge', he had been able to return to the South and put the kingdom into good working order. As much as anything, his effectiveness there alerted the placid Honorius to the dangers. Already in his last months, he bluntly denounced Frederick's intolerable behaviour. This makes it less surprising that Gregory IX wasted no time on being patient with Frederick when he succeeded Honorius in March 1227.

Gregory IX's hostility to Frederick cannot be explained as the result of personal antipathy. Nevertheless, it is impossible to discount the importance of the personal animus Gregory brought to the same problems as had in fact confronted Honorius III. Gregory was twice as old as Frederick in 1227, but it is somewhat unsatisfactory to see the pope as trying to put him down by insisting on his own role as Frederick's spiritual father. The very extravagance of his words and actions appears to have sprung from a profound fear of what the younger man would do if he were not summarily jerked back to heel on the papal leash. In its own way, it is a tribute to the impression Frederick had made on the kingdom after six years. The troubles and confusions there since 1189 had certainly encouraged, at the papal *curia* from Innocent III's time, the idea that the kingdom was a docile vassal-state incapable of giving trouble once its legal status had been clearly defined. Gregory IX, as Innocent III's nephew, was personally affronted to find that Innocent's protégé was behaving like an emperor; moreover, Gregory, as pope and a canon-lawyer, perceived the implications of Frederick's ability to draw upon a rich tradition of non-ecclesiastical learning and ideals for the management of his realm. Gregory may even have feared that Frederick voiced the aspirations of a whole generation that would, if unchecked, overthrow the achievements of Innocent III. Had Frederick been a solitary dreamer, like Otto III, he would not have been so frightening. When Gregory took on Frederick he discovered that he was indeed every bit as dangerous, clever and irrepressible as any pope could imagine.

The occasion of the first break with Gregory IX was Frederick's return to Apulia shortly after departing on crusade in August 1227. For this he automatically rendered himself liable to excommunication. Frederick was certainly unwell, but probably not so sick as to be unable to continue on his journey or recuperate somewhere *en route*. Frederick appears to have taken it for granted that he would somehow escape Gregory's censure. This fecklessness was matched by the truculence of the pope who seized the chance to cut Frederick back to size: not for nothing had Gregory taken the papal name most identified with hostility to secular pretensions. As cardinal, he had watched his uncle's policy languish in the hands of the feeble Honorius; he was eager to show that there was to be no more shilly-shallying. Like his namesake, Gregory had no doubts about his own rectitude. He did not stop to calculate his chances of success, since he was confident God would never abandon his church.

Frederick never understood Gregory and did not know how to deal with him, except by parrying the blows. Frederick was a pragmatist. His expedition to the east depended, in his view, on a number of factors – his own health, and that of his force; his confidence that his lands were secure during his absence, to mention only the Italian ones. Frederick assumed that the pope would appreciate these points. By the time Frederick was reassured and ready to leave for the Holy Land in June 1228, Gregory had not softened. He still maintained his sentence of excommunication, and vindictively encouraged the clergy in the Holy Land to thwart Frederick there. This proves how little Gregory really cared about the practical considerations of crusading warfare. This was not the worst. While Frederick was away, Gregory allowed Frederick's kingdom to be invaded in January 1229, certainly hoping to shatter Frederick's authority in Italy by attack where he was strongest. Whatever excuse Gregory IX thought he could offer to justify this invasion, and whatever approval might be given it by papal friends and Frederick's enemies, Gregory cannot have been under any illusions about Frederick's likely reaction.

Richard of San Germano presented the papal invasion of the kingdom as designed to draw Rainald, duke of Spoleto, out of Le Marche which

Rainald claimed to have invaded only in pursuit of some rebellious lords from the kingdom. Gregory retorted this was just an excuse for occupying Le Marche as far as Macerata on Frederick's behalf. It is, however, beyond belief that Frederick could have authorised any such move while he was away. Moreover, to check Rainald, there were certainly less provocative reactions than invading the kingdom. While a large papal army of knights and infantry under John of Brienne and Cardinal John of Colonna was deployed to defend Le Marche, Gregory sent into the kingdom another army, commanded by the papal chaplain, Pandulf of Anagni, as legate, under the captaincy of two exiles, counts Thomas of Celano (Molise) and Roger of Aquila (Fondi), 18 January 1229. This forced its way across the bridge at Ceprano but, confronted by troops under the command of Henry de Morra, proved unwilling to venture far from its base until mid-March when, as a result of a skirmish near Monte Cassino, Morra abandoned the monastery to the legate and withdrew to Capua. Towards the end of March, the papal army resumed its advance. Gaeta was cowed into submission and its castle destroyed. At this point the Beneventans joined the assault on the kingdom by undertaking a cattle-raid into Apulia, which provoked reprisals from Morra. The legate decided to continue his advance towards Capua. Since it was too strongly defended, the army moved on to take smaller places like Alife and Telese, eventually joining its allies in Benevento. It took a number of other outlying districts before reports of Frederick's return stopped it in its tracks. Meanwhile, the other papal army had driven Rainald out of Le Marche. While this army was besieging him in Sulmona, Pandulf called on it for help, because his own frightened army was beginning to break up. Although all Marsia had been occupied in the name of the pope, the two papal armies now went on the defensive. Frederick sent ahead reinforcements to encourage the Capuans in their resistance until he could come himself. He had at his disposal not only the military force of Apulia, but also some German crusaders returning after him. He also tried diplomacy. Although Gregory would not listen, his legate found an excuse to slip away from the army as Frederick advanced on the Terra di Lavoro. The siege of Capua had therefore been abandoned before Frederick arrived in September. The papal commander was desperate to find money for his troops, and the army took to its heels and fled back into Campagna. Frederick recovered most of the cities captured some weeks earlier, though at Cassino, the papal commander continued the fight and both Sora and Gaeta declined to submit. In a letter to the northern Italians, Frederick reported the rapid recovery of his dominions, but still asked them to send reinforcements with horses and arms to conclude the war.

Sora was captured and plundered on 24 October, though the *rocca* held out. By now anyway, the king expected to resolve the issues by diplomacy. The arrival of Cardinal Thomas of Capua on 4 November signalled Gregory's recognition of the need to negotiate. Although the papal forces in Cassino were allowed to depart in safety, diplomatic moves to end hostilities went on for months, as different embassies passed to and fro. Not until the end of May 1230 did cardinals come to absolve the emperor from excommunication. Even then the matter was not concluded because Frederick would not accept the pope's stubborn insistence on keeping the enclaves of Sant'Agata and Gaeta. A formula was not found until 9 July: the future of both places was to be resolved by discussion and, if necessary, by arbitration within twelve months. For the rest, Frederick pardoned all those who had joined the papacy against him, reinstated disloyal bishops, promised not to encroach on papal rights in the duchy of Spoleto or in Le Marche, and confirmed the ecclesiastical privileges of the kingdom. Frederick was not absolved himself until 28 August. He met the pope at Anagni on 1 September, where Gregory pardoned the prelates of the kingdom who had remained loyal to the king.

Gregory insisted on a *mise-en-scène* which secured Frederick's formal submission as errant son to benign father. Frederick appears to have dissembled his feelings and intentions for the sake of peace, but the few weeks of hostilities brought the formerly latent tension between Frederick and the papacy into the open. Whatever may have been the case in the past, fair words for the future could no longer be taken at face value, and both sides remained wary of each other. Within six weeks of their convivial encounter at Anagni, Gregory was already warning Frederick that his unforgiving treatment of the rebellious towns of Capitanata would cause the breakdown of their agreement. For the time being, however, Gregory preferred not to force any disagreements to the point of rupture.

THE REORDERING OF THE KINGDOM

The king did not allow criticisms to deflect him from the purpose of reordering the kingdom. Frederick's concern for the government of the kingdom after the settlement with Gregory should not be considered out of its proper political context. The special pressure applied to the kingdom was not derived from any political ideology but from a response to circumstances. Had Frederick not become justifiably suspicious of papal intentions, or determined to reimpose his imperial authority when it was challenged by the Lombard League and in

Germany, it is possible that he would not have been driven to develop his royal powers in the loyal kingdom. Its potential had in fact been revealed by its capacity to meet the economic burden of crusading: from the experience of his Sicilian youth, Frederick can hardly have anticipated milking its resources to such a degree. After 1230, the pressure on him never slackened, and correspondingly he did not relax his demands on his subjects, but he had no time to devise new methods and worked within the existing framework. Modern historians tend to see him as the originator of the modern state; Frederick saw himself as the renovator of the Norman kingdom and the Roman imperial ideal. Nor can his contemporaries in the kingdom have found his political notions so novel. Rightly or wrongly, he had claimed since 1220 only to be restoring the good customs of William II, after years of turmoil. What we know points to general acquiescence in his management. Experience of disorder had made it clear to his subjects that any alternative to him would only serve special interests. Even many clergy saw no sense in weakening his authority, however much they continued to hope desperately for better relations with Rome. Despite the determined and rhetorical reports of Frederick's tyrannies, put about by the papacy and its allies at the time and thereafter, our perception of his government makes it certain that no other ruler would have done more for his subjects. The kingdom had no reason to think that other princes of the time had more intelligence or scruple in discharging royal obligations. The surviving administrative records are patchy, but they adequately demonstrate that the king was conscientious and his officials dutiful. Many of his subjects can be seen from them to have trusted the king to be merciful and do justice, according to the expectations of the age.

The only contemporary chronicler in the kingdom to deal with Frederick's reign, Richard of San Germano, prepared the second version of his work after Frederick's return from the Holy Land, adding to it regularly, perhaps even monthly, until his own death late in 1243. As with the first version, he is most painstaking in the record of what concerned his home-ground – the monastery and town of Monte Cassino. Frederick is without question the principal protagonist. The chronicler makes little comment on the events recorded, but Frederick's actions are never presented unfavourably. From other sources, Richard is known to have been sufficiently trusted on occasion with the carrying of royal treasure through the kingdom. Despite his commitment to the abbey of Cassino, Richard shows no signs of being sympathetic to the papal cause. His occasional references to disaffection and treachery in the kingdom present them as always promptly smothered, and do not read like uneasy attempts to pass quickly over disagreeable events; he does conscientiously notice isolated cases of disloyalty. Richard's chronicle is the only record available which could conceivably be regarded as the voice of public opinion in the kingdom. As such, it records a kingdom loyal to the king, supplying him dutifully with the men, money and resources he so regularly demanded for dealing with his problems elsewhere. There is a matter-of-fact monotony about the records of the years, the imposition of taxes (*collecta*), the routine changes of provincial officials, the publication of royal ordinances plainly intended to serve the public good rather than the emperor's greed. There is no special pleading to prove Frederick's concern for his kingdom or any hint that Richard was aware of criticisms that needed to be answered. Richard's loyalty to Frederick is never in doubt, and Frederick's confidence in his kingdom seems equally serene.

As in all thirteenth-century kingdoms, Frederick's government depended for its functioning on the extensive use of written documents. Few officials or magnates in the kingdom enjoyed sufficient authority to act without constant reference to him or to the records of their predecessors in office; they were also obliged to compile reports and memoranda intended to justify their conduct or control the actions of others. Local officials were assumed in 1240 to be capable of giving accounts about their administrations going back to 1220; some evidence survives of registers kept by central government from 1230. The accumulation of records in Frederick's reign must have been prodigious, and care was taken to keep them in safe custody. Many registers were prepared in triplicate, so that the king and the 'head office' responsible, as well as the official on the spot, could each have a copy. Justiciars had in their provinces separate registers of crown lands, military tenancies, inquisitions *post-mortem*, declarations of outlawry, and other judicial *acta*, records of priests' sons authorised to hold lands by inheritance in return for annual rents to the crown, and lists of all other tax-payers of *collecta*, some apparently going back to 1220. In Sicily, the justiciar made a record of Saracens forcibly removed from Centuripe and Capizzi to Palermo. Sicilian registers were kept at Messina and Palermo and were not copied for the king's benefit, probably because of the need to use them in conjunction with older records already deposited there. Some earlier record-keeping could be taken for granted throughout the kingdom, but from 1230, a new drive for making registers and keeping them up-to-date was launched. Payments of a twelfth of all domain produce, voted in 1231, were noted locally and made up into *quaterniones* for the king; registers of all artificers were compiled to make it easier to check on fraud and negligence; inspectors of castles made inventories of all weapons, animals and victuals in each stronghold. When regional escheators were appointed in 1240, they made registers in duplicate of all domain lands, death-duties (*morticiniis*), escheats, rents, and all other curial rights in every city, castle and place in their areas. Financial officials and accountants obviously kept registers from which it was possible to control claims for official expenses. Record-keeping was clearly intended to provide for a close scrutiny of the whole machinery of royal administration and not designed solely for financial purposes.

There is no record of all this material ever being deliberately destroyed. Early Angevin rulers still had access to it. As time passed there must have seemed ever-less reason to treasure the routine documents of an earlier administration, so that by the sixteenth century, most of it had been lost. The registers were made of paper, not parchment, and may have been considered expendable. Contemporaries considered paper too fragile for records of lasting value. By 1782, when the only surviving register of Frederick's official correspondence (for the year 1239–40) was published, no more than a substantial fragment of it remained. It was thereafter painstakingly studied as a text and manuscript until it was blown up, along with the rest of the Neapolitan archive, by German soldiers in 1944. Other documents issued by the government are of course known; some may still be found in the archives of the great churches of the kingdom, but the government's own archive has been eliminated. Whatever it once was, it now bears no comparison to what survives, even for the France of Louis IX, let alone for England or the papacy.

The best official information now available about the kingdom for the years immediately after Frederick's return from the crusade comes from a 'register' still preserved in Marseilles, in which Andrew of Isernia, an Angevin government official of the early fourteenth century, copied extracts of financial and economic interest from Frederican records compiled between 1230 and 1248. These extracts have been used to work up accounts of Frederick's notions of political economy, though it may be doubted whether he had thought through any long-term plan of reform. Changes in taxation, for example, can be regarded as mere expedients, and on his death-bed he could order the level of taxation to be restored to what it had been in 1189 without any sense of repudiating calculated improvements. The sequence of ordinances issued between the spring and autumn of 1231 were parts of a plan only in the sense that they were designed to foster the recovery of the kingdom after recent hostilities. In April, he introduced a state monopoly of commerce in salt; in May, a review of the management of property escheating to the crown; in June, new regulations for the siting of slaughter-houses, a state monopoly of trading in silk and iron, as well as the negotiation in a representative assembly of a grant of a twelfth of all domain produce; in August, tariffs of harbour dues and regulations for the registration of all trades (specifically pharmacists, metal-workers, makers of arms and harness, butchers, fishmongers and candlemakers); in September, a reform of the coinage to complement the earlier economic and fiscal measures.

Whatever Frederick's short-term intentions, his innovations with regard to raising money were, of course, not forgotten or repudiated: as *statuta nova* they became an integral part of the kingdom's medieval taxation system. When introduced, however, they were not only intended as ways of finding cash promptly to repair the damage caused by the recent war, but by their very character released Frederick from dependence on papal authority to impose general taxation. This had been possible in the 1220s because of the crusade, which remained for the papacy itself such an unimpeachable excuse for raising taxation that crusades came to be preached against papal enemies of all kinds. Frederick needed some alternative justification for his taxes. The Norman monarchy itself had exercised important powers with regard to its properties, its supervision of rare resources, including manpower, and its rights to collect dues in markets and ports. Frederick only extended the scope of these existing rights.

In the thirteenth century, the dues collected by the government before 1189 were believed to comprise a great number of different taxes. Frederick's innovations were by comparison few. The *major jus* was on iron, salt, pitch and steel. In Apulia, salt was produced locally, but the government (*curia*) itself had to import salt from Sardinia to supply the needs of the Terra di Lavoro. On the Adriatic coast between Siponto and Taranto, the many salt-works and salt-trading may have been supervised by the king even in the twelfth century, and in Sicily, William II allegedly granted privileges over it to Santa Maria Latina at Jerusalem. Frederick saw his way to making a substantial profit from creating a state monopoly of supply. He was not able to nationalise an existing cartel. The various producers of salt were required to sell all their salt to the *curia* at one gold ounce to the measure. Wholesalers then acquired their supplies from the government's salesmen at four times the price; retailers paid six times, perhaps a device to limit wholesalers' profits. The salesmen got a fixed percentage (eight and a third per cent) as their cut. The profit on iron supplies was less great, since the stock was bought at two gold ounces and sold at three, but the main purpose of this monopoly was probably to control 'strategic' materials, rather than obtain much financial advantage. Royal supervision of iron production was not new. Two Calabrian monasteries, Sambucina (1208) and San

Giovanni in Fiore (1210), had needed royal permission to extract iron on their own lands, and royal rights to regulate this must have been recognised before 1189. Special officials to handle the royal interests in salt and iron were appointed in June 1231 when the king held an assembly of prelates, counts, magnates and cities at Melfi. It was this assembly which approved an annual grant to the fisc of one twelfth of all domain produce in foodstuffs, linen and hemp, in remission of all earlier impositions, so here too adaptation of earlier payments was involved. The producers had to transport the twelfth of domain produce to new royal warehouses, and were free to dispose of the rest of their goods as they chose. Royal warehouses were set up on the island, at Palermo, Messina, *Mortemari* (near Augusta?), Syracuse, Licata, Sciacca and Trapani; on the mainland, at Naples, Siponto and elsewhere. These warehouses collected a due of fifteen grains to the ounce on goods deposited there (about four per cent), but not on animals, cloth or meat. Precious goods and delicate fabrics (*merces subtiles*) were not thought to be safe in the warehouses. The warehouses were supplied with scales for assessing dues according to weight. Merchants were supplied in return by the wardens of the adjacent hostel with beds, lighting, straw and firewood (*lignis*). In June 1231, when the *curia* created a monopoly for the acquisition of silk throughout the kingdom, this was farmed to a firm of Jewish partners at Trani; in the autumn, Frederick added control of the dyeworks in the kingdom, appointing two Jews at Capua to draw up regulations for the industry. Steps were taken to diminish any popular hostility to these changes. New officials, for example, were ordered to discuss with the local inhabitants of Apulia where to establish new slaughter-houses with retail counters. Variations in conditions in the kingdom were taken into account when fixing port dues and duties imposed on wood and timber. Even changes in the dyeing industry may have been less radical than they seem. The Jewish involvement in it was already noted by Benjamin of Tudela, and the Jews of Rossano were clearly regarded as part of the dyeing industry there, when it was granted by Constance to the cathedral church. The royal dye-works at Patti had only been granted away as recently as 1207. Frederick's improvements grew out of firmly established economic traditions. These continued to develop. By 1239, Jews from Djerba had been tempted to settle in Palermo and offered to grow henna, indigo and other seeds (*semina*) from their native island not yet established in Sicily, no doubt for their potential use in the dyeing industry.

Regulation of trading conditions was closely connected with Frederick's diplomacy. His earliest economic reforms exactly coincided with a new trade treaty with the ruler of Tunis, Abu Zacaria, which also agreed to a mutual exchange of prisoners (or those who had remained faithful to Christianity or Islam). This allowed freedom of trade and navigation between the Africans and Christians, promising restitution of all the booty previously taken by Christian pirates subject to Frederick's jurisdiction. Frederick had a Muslim governor for the Muslim population of Pantelleria, and he agreed to share the tribute due with Abu Zacaria. The treaty was initially negotiated to last ten years. The tariffs set out for Naples and Siponto harbours (August 1231) show that although Saracens and Christians paid the same rates for the export of cheese, nuts, tunny, spices, cotton and linen, Saracen traders were made to pay import dues of ten per cent as against a rate for Christians of only three per cent. The *curia* published a comprehensive tariff of dues in October 1232. It was because citizens of their own cities paid only customary dues on imports and exports that some merchants from outside the kingdom attempted to pass themselves off as denizens in order to evade duties. On the other hand, Frederick had also, in the autumn of 1231, tried to attract immigrants (probably as cultivators in particular) by offering them a ten-year immunity from public taxation. The conflict between the short-term interests of the treasury and the long-term prosperity of the kingdom could not be plainer. A year later, when Frederick was in Venice, he granted Venetians the privilege of travelling and trading in his kingdom at fixed rates of one and a half per cent, payable in goods at the choice of the royal officials. The king renounced any claims on the property of Venetians who died in the kingdom or whose ships suffered wreck. His own merchants were allowed to carry to Venice goods they had bought in the kingdom, though nothing was said about any dues payable there. Frederick's concessions were certainly designed to discourage Venice from joining the Lombard League. Six months later, when the Genoese appointed a Milanese supporter of the League as their *podestà*, Frederick seized all Genoese merchants trading in the kingdom and their merchandise. Frederick's economic grip on the kingdom cannot be separated from other aspects of policy. Northern Italians wanted to benefit by trading in the South, and Frederick saw no reason why they should be free to benefit and use their strength to defy him. The Pisans saw the point and got permission to travel and trade in all his kingdoms, but especially at Messina and Palermo (April 1234).

The scope of Frederick's concern for the economic interests of the kingdom has a surprisingly modern aspect, but makes good sense in the context of Frederick's own position. Behind Frederick lay a tradition in the kingdom of seigneurial rights and dues that had already been exploited by the Norman kings. In a broader sense too, Frederick faced economic conditions without parallel in other contemporary European kingdoms. The continuing problem of Saracen unrest in Sicily was partly resolved by massive deportations of the peasantry, which in turn made it necessary to consider how the de-populated lands might be cultivated or made profitable. Frederick's concern for the position in Sicily was accentuated by his commitments as king of Jerusalem, and his continuing plans there for his son, Conrad. Though it seems unlikely that he seriously contemplated returning to the east himself, he still supplied money and men, as well as nursing his political relations in the region. For Frederick, the well-being of his dominions was not a narrowly economic preoccupation. It would have been very uncharacteristic of him to shut his eyes to the real importance of maintaining prosperity for the success of his whole state.

The most famous record of Frederick's government in this period is not, however, related to his financial problems but to law, by tradition the king's prime concern. The codification of the kingdom's laws, usually called the *Liber Augustalis*, was published at Melfi in August 1231. There is no reference to this project until 1230, when the pope wrote in some agitation to Archbishop James of Capua and forbade him to assist in an enterprise the pope thought likely to threaten the special status of the clergy. Canonists like Gregory had made extensive use of old imperial law, but they were far from welcoming a modern secular lawmaker: this would detract from the pope's special role as sovereign. Given Gregory's reaction, it is not fanciful to suppose that Frederick himself recognised the prestigious character of lawgiving. From his decrees of 1220–1 at Rome, Capua and Messina, it is known that Frederick took pains with legislative enactments. In 1230–1 he went further, and imitated Justinian in gathering together all earlier royal edicts into one collection – those attributed to his Norman forebears accounting for about one third of the whole.

Part of the process of codification is known: every justiciar was required to choose four of the older men in each part of his jurisdiction and send them to the king so that he could be informed orally about the assizes of King Roger and the uses and customs of the times of Roger and William II. (These were obviously not already available to him in official written form.) The bulk of the code comprised texts issued by Frederick himself, though he had drawn on traditional sources of learned or customary law for his inspiration. Some of his laws were published formally in 1220–1, but most of Frederick's 'legislation' was not apparently issued in this way, but rather in connection with particular lawsuits, or in response to problems raised in the *magna curia*. Frederick gave as his reasons for codifying the laws the dislocation of the kingdom's legal system, caused by his own youthful inexperience and the recent invasion. It was not particularly remarkable to have completed the work of codification in a comparatively short time, given the dedicated way in which Frederick expected his officials to work for him. Many of his own decrees incorporated in the text must have been issued before he went on crusade, in the years when his subjects were looking to him for decisions and clarifications in the law. His judges would themselves have been expected to keep records of such decisions. It was standard scholastic practice to amend the law-books with *novellae*, and his own new law school at Naples would have put them in some order as they were published.

Secular legislation had itself been naturally prompted by reforms of church law, not only in Frederick's kingdom, but also in England and France, though in different ways. The decree of the Fourth Lateran Council, which forbade the clergy to participate in the procedure of the ordeals, had obvious effects in southern Italy as elsewhere, and Frederick II advocated a more reasonable way of finding the truth by enquiry and examination of witnesses. He was reluctant even to allow the use of trial by battle between champions as a way of settling lawsuits, though it remained popular, and Frederick is found condoning its use on occasions. Frederick also needed to specify the processes required for getting disputes into court and managing the business there, matters not regulated by earlier rulers. The new instructions inevitably, and unremarkably, drew upon Roman law. One of the most extensive and early demonstrations of its importance for legal technicalities is the voluminous record of the long-drawn-out case against Aldoin, bishop of Cefalù, Frederick's former notary, who was accused in the royal court by his chapter in 1222 of wasting the cathedral's property. In the early years after Frederick's return, when extensive use was made of prelates in judicial business, the adoption of formal rules from written law would have passed without comment, and would certainly have carried no specifically secular connotations. Some ideas of this kind could affect even such secular rules as inheritance of feudal tenures. Frederick insisted on changing the French custom of denying daughters the right to inherit property in default of sons, pleading for the equal rights of women.

Much of Frederick's legislation, however, seeks not so much to reform as to clarify and systematise. Some of it expresses Frederick's personal reverence for law, like his insistence on respectful behaviour in court, with no ranting and shouting, for all ranks from counts downwards. The rules reflect not only the emperor's own intelligence and authority, but also the intellectual character of his officials and advisers, including many clergy, of that generation. Its most important innovation for Sicilian law is the arrangement of appeal from lower courts up to the crown itself, certainly adapted from the church's own hierarchical system. Frederick himself was fully aware of his responsibilities, both as lawgiver and as fount of justice.

Order mattered more than innovation. The practice of instigating enquiries amongst local jurors for the resolution of administrative and judicial problems was well established, and Richard of San Germano reports the holding of several general inquests or enquiries. In May 1231, the archbishop of Reggio conducted an enquiry at San Germano itself into those considered 'notorious' and 'suspect'. Two months later, the master-justiciar delegated to Robert de Busso another inquest into gangs (*compagniis*), falsifiers, dicethrowers, taverners, homicides, 'luxury' living, the carrying of weapons and violation of women. When the master-justiciar himself arrived the following January, he provoked much ill-feeling by publishing the results of the enquiry, with the names of the informers and the catalogue of offenders. A little later, in March 1232, the archbishops, to satisfy a papal instruction, ordered the bishops to conduct an enquiry into the sexual conduct of the clergy. The next summer, Frederick ordered his justiciars to examine the grievances of the prelates, and the bishop of Caserta to enquire into the activities of Patarene heretics. At a local level, the king ordered two judges to enquire into the revenues of San Germano in 1234, and early in 1235, renewed investigations throughout the kingdom as to the whereabouts of men belonging to the royal domain. After Frederick's departure for Germany, further enquiries could still be initiated. When a new abbot was to be elected at Cassino in 1237, a judge from the *magna curia* made a thorough investigation into the suitability of the abbot-elect, questioning men from every one of the monastery's settlements (*castella*). The same autumn, the master-justiciar came to San Germano asking about men who had been taken away from the work of strengthening local fortresses, and imposed fines for this offence.

These recurrent official enquiries forced the local population to participate in the work of government, as Frederick himself worked on improvements in his administration. Though certainly burdensome, they helped, as in contemporary England, to create a sense of public involvement in administration, to give locals opportunities to make their views known and to look to the king for action. Even after the second papal excommunication of March 1239, the king did not cease to count on his subjects, as he might well have done had he been doubtful of their future loyalty. In 1240, when inspectors for the royal castles were appointed, some of the king's faithful subjects were delegated, amongst other things, to make weekly visits to the castles to see that they were properly manned and that what was lacking was made good. A general inquest was also instigated into the way taxes had been collected the previous year, as a check on the honesty of the collectors, and to give loyal taxpayers some satisfaction. When the Venetians raided the coastal regions of the Lower Adriatic towards the end of the year, the king had no fears about ordering local defence forces in cavalry and infantry to defend the coasts throughout the kingdom. At San Germano, as no doubt elsewhere, the temporary custody of goods seized from the churches for the war effort was entrusted to the twelve men of most consequence in the district. The king did not expect them to have more sympathy with the church than himself. Since Frederick's government is often described as operating exclusively through officials, it is worth stressing how much even their activities depended on the co-operation of the local communities. Not only was local self-government still part of the kingdom's own traditions; Frederick also had no way of suddenly acquiring a force of officials adequate to enforce his bidding in the modern bureaucratic manner.

Frederick's concern to secure 'popular' approval and consultation in his government is also shown by the summoning of consultative assemblies like the one that had met at Foggia in 1225. Frederick stressed that the grant of a twelfth of domain produce had been made with the advice of prelates, counts, nobles and many citizens at Melfi in June 1231. Frederick's 'parliaments' are rather mysterious, and their importance has been disputed in the absence of detailed information. Richard of San Germano, for example, states only that when Frederick summoned two of the best men from every city and *castrum* of the kingdom to meet him at Foggia in September 1232 for the general advantage of the kingdom (*pro utilitate regni et commodo generali*), San Germano was represented by the *miles*, Roffrid de Monte. From the royal register it is known that Frederick similarly summoned representatives of the cities to meet him at Foggia on Palm Sunday 1240, when he returned to the kingdom after five years' absence: eleven cities from Sicily and thirty-four on the mainland were concerned. It would certainly be very odd if parliaments had immediately exercised institutional functions, but this did not mean that they were a sham or useless, and their consultative value cannot be doubted.

An edict issued at Messina in January 1234 also required solemn provincial assemblies to meet twice a year in May and November in convenient centres: Piazza for Sicily, Cosenza for Calabria, Gravina for Apulia, Salerno for Campania and Sulmona for Abruzzi. Four representatives from each of the major cities of the region and two from the smaller ones and the *castella* would meet, together with the prelates, counts and barons for a week, or two if necessary, putting forward complaints about the conduct of officials and compiling reports for the king. There is no other information about such provincial assemblies apart from later evidence that takes their existence for granted. Given Frederick's reputation for autocracy, they are surprising proof of how little his government has been understood. The idea may have grown out of Frederick's recent experience in putting down disaffection in Sicily, but his departure for Germany in 1235 probably weakened its prospects. Officials left behind to manage the kingdom would not have been very convincing instruments of such a policy. In the king's absence they themselves had to be trusted and treated tactfully rather than harried. Despite these practical considerations, the king's willingness in principle to consult local opinion is noteworthy.

The extraordinary range of the king's projects to regulate the affairs of the kingdom across the whole social order cannot be paralleled in earlier reigns, but the main innovation was the energetic drive to supervise, launched with such vigour in 1231–2. Less is known about how the officials performed than about what the king expected them to do, and how the king's subjects reacted to it all must remain in doubt. Messina became the scene of a dramatic confrontation with the king's justiciar in August 1232, and the insurrection obliged Frederick to go in person to the island with a great force to deal with it. Though he spent eight months or more there, what exactly he did is not known. He seems to have hunted down opposition mercilessly, and used the excuse of eradicating heresy to commit great numbers of men to the flames. This was a recently discovered obligation. Gregory IX had urged him early in 1231 to deal with the heretics of Naples and Aversa, and the king may at that point have discovered the convenience of using the cover of heresy for dealing with dissent. His methods in Sicily nevertheless stirred up such protests that the pope himself counselled moderation. In Germany, where similar methods were applied at the same time to deal with disaffection, it is known to have been whipped up by Frederick's political enemies, and it is possible that the troubles in Sicily were also artificially fostered, but proof of this is lacking. Richard of San Germano barely refers to events in Sicily, where pockets of defiant Saracens apparently remained beyond the king's reach. On the mainland, however, there are no comparable signs of public disorder.

The elaboration of Frederick's organised bureaucracy from the machinery existing on his return in 1220 depended on the quickening pace of administration rather than on any one particular creative act. Similarly, in the five years before his visit to Germany in 1235, when Frederick gave very close attention to the state of his government, changes were not introduced as part of a preconceived system. The arrangements were constantly being revised, not only in response to later events, such as Frederick's own absences or papal hostility, but no doubt also with regard to the availability of suitable officials. Frederick's administration remained experimental, tentative and flexible, and was made to serve his immediate purposes. He did not aim precociously to impose an autocratic order. The attraction of Frederick as a prototype for Fascist Caesarism in inter-war Italy and Germany need not be enlarged on, but it has had the effect of misleading historians. The cause of understanding has, as usual, not been served by the cloak of relevance flung round his shoulders.

Frederick was able to give his personal attention to the kingdom for the best part of six years. He consolidated his hold on the kingdom, and so strengthened his position there that his enemies never ventured to attack the kingdom again while Frederick was alive. The stability of his government was demonstrated by his long absence of five years, between the spring of 1235 and March 1240, during which his trusted *familiares* (Morra, Count Thomas of Acerra, the archbishops of Palermo and Capua, with the bishop of Ravello) had no difficulty in keeping the administration in good order. It was while Frederick was committed in Germany and northern Italy, that Gregory IX decided to excommunicate him for a second time (20 March 1239). This quarrel with the papacy was never healed, and it deeply affected the character of Frederick's final years. Most, though not all, of the reasons given by the pope for his decision to renew the sentence of excommunication relate in point of fact to conditions in the kingdom. Some of the pope's more general complaints were repeated almost word for word from the earlier sentence of 1227. Frederick had undertaken in 1230 to mend his ways, for example, by allowing clergy exemptions from taxation and from secular judgements. In practice, however, Frederick did not allow any general clerical claims of exemption to prevail against the customs of the kingdom. When general *collecta* were imposed from 1235, the clergy had to pay, like barons and knights, on their patrimonial estates. Frederick's implementation of his promises had been closely monitored by the pope from October 1230. Although he delivered several rebukes and reminders, Gregory had not pressed Frederick too hard. The time had not come for that. In March 1235, Frederick provided forces to help Gregory deal with disaffection in Rome, and Gregory arranged and smoothed the way for the emperor's third marriage to Isabella of England. Frederick dutifully paid the *census* owing to the pope from the kingdom until 1237. Gregory's register shows that the pope had frequent opportunities to be drawn into the affairs of the southern churches since

Frederick did not attempt to bar papal action of this kind. How the king tried, if at all, to influence the choice of new prelates is not explicitly mentioned by the pope, and elections deemed unsatisfactory by the pope were tactfully blamed on the cathedral chapters concerned. Prolonged vacancies could only be regarded as Frederick's fault though, in some cases at least, other factors are known to have been involved. Disorders in the southern church were not, however, notably greater than in other parts of Christendom.

Early in 1236, Gregory began to formulate his complaints with greater determination. In the summer he adduced some dozen instances of abuses concerning individual prelates and churches, quite apart from his less specific charges. Frederick had prepared his own counter-list of complaints. Over the next three years there were probably several exchanges between pope and emperor on these and other points. Given the scrappy and partial nature of the evidence, it is impossible to be sure of the rights and wrongs of the particular cases and still less of the more sweeping allegations, though in some instances these seem to rest on very slender foundations. Frederick's willingness to explain his side of the story in the detailed instances discussed with papal representatives in October 1238 shows that he was then still unabashed, and not anxious lest these problems provoke Gregory to a second showdown. Since the same complaints reappeared a few months later in the bull of excommunication, the pope had either been unimpressed by Frederick's explanations, or had simply closed his ears. During the years in which these arguments rumbled on, the management of the kingdom owed much to the unimpeachable archbishops of Palermo and Capua, and it is difficult to believe that the conditions of the kingdom's churches can have so seriously deteriorated. Gregory, however, chose to believe that it was all Frederick's fault: no one could move hand or foot in the kingdom, he wrote, without Frederick's command. This does not mean that Gregory had no case, but only that what he complained of in 1239 was nothing particularly new. The main reason for piling up the grievances was to try and make a better case for the excommunication, given the impossibility of avowing his real motive for breaking with the emperor in the winter of 1238–9. Once he recognised that he could no longer hope to work effectively with the emperor, he decided to support the Lombard League as the only practical way to weaken Frederick's real political domination of Italy. From that position, the papacy never looked back, though Frederick himself never gave up hoping that a change of pope would open the way to reconciliation.

Frederick's excommunication made no immediate difference to the kingdom itself. It remained so tranquil that it may not at first have appreciated what Frederick's problems were elsewhere. Richard of San Germano, who appears to have had little interest in or understanding of issues outside the kingdom, may reflect the general attitude of his countrymen to Frederick's other lands. Frederick's quarrels with the pope did not upset religion in the kingdom or diminish loyalty to the king. Since the kingdom was fundamentally loyal, it had little need of Frederick's personal attention. His officials faithfully acted for him. During his lifetime, the papacy sensed no groundswell of discontent on which to wreck his government. To destroy him, as the papacy eventually set out to do, he had to be attacked as emperor, not as king, and to do so the papacy found it needed all the resources of Christendom. The conduct of the papacy is the best proof of Frederick's strength in the kingdom.

Frederick's government of the kingdom at this period can be studied in greater detail than for any other part of the reign from the one register of his administration to survive until modern times. Though only a fragment remained for the months October 1239–June 1240 (the official year began on 1 September), it contained copies of about 600 letters sent out by the king's central writing office to various officials of the southern kingdom. Since this register was compiled for reference, it was presumably intended as a comprehensive record of curial business. It is assumed to have been one of a series of such registers, and a comparable series is believed to have been kept at the same time, containing copies of letters issued for private individuals seeking royal mandates. Most of the letters copied into the surviving fragment were written while Frederick himself was still in northern Italy and they show, therefore, how his government, with its core of advisers and notaries, kept in touch with the southern provinces, giving instructions, answering queries and commenting on the zeal and effectiveness of the many different officials working in the kingdom. The copies were entered day by day in the same register by several different notaries working under leading figures in the administration, such as Peter de Vinea or Taddeus de Sessa. Although some of the business was of particular concern to such ministers as the royal *camerarius* or the marshal, they clearly had no separate secretariat of their own, nor did specialised departments develop within the writing office. While this remained, in general terms, the office for all royal correspondence, the absence of material relating to the high court of law (*magna curia*) gives grounds for supposing that this court at least must have kept its own records.

The more routine letters could have been prepared in the office by the most senior officials, but many letters in the register cannot have been drafted without direct reference to Frederick himself. Despite being preoccupied with problems on the spot, Frederick kept a close eye on southern affairs, giving careful, detailed answers to the many questions referred to him for decisions. Frederick's concern for his kingdom can be presented as a very material anxiety for the protection of his major source of revenue. He made no attempt to conceal his constant need of ready cash from the kingdom, but had Frederick's interest in it been simply financial, it would hardly have been necessary for him to probe so deeply into its affairs. He could have unleashed tax-farmers to do what they liked to get the money needed. Instead, considerable care was taken with the way royal officials collected direct taxes. The justiciars responsible were all summoned together at Foggia to be instructed about the process of assessment and collection; each in turn was then expected to engage in extensive consultation in every city with persons of standing in the neighbourhoods, and to check procedures with previous tax-collectors and through the *quaterniones* of earlier levies. The king was determined to get the money he needed, but never doubted that this would be possible merely by strict enforcement of traditional practices. Local communities likewise expected that taxation would be paid, not by arbitrary impositions but in ways settled by local custom. Frederick set up no new central tax-office for these exactions. Somehow his officials were able to estimate what gross sums would be needed and how the burden should be distributed amongst the provinces. Within the provinces, however, local arrangements and precedents were used to conciliate public opinion.

Frederick's letters make constant reference to economic and financial affairs, but since all his financial records have been lost, it is not known how the government was able at any one time to take stock of its overall financial position. The official with general financial responsibilities was the *camerarius*. By 1239, this was John Morus, a black slave promoted for his ability and later a figure of influence in the Saracen community at Lucera when the royal treasure was deposited there. It seems probable that the *camerarius* already held that commanding position in all matters financial first described in a document for the Angevin *camerarius* in 1295. He controlled the expenses of the royal household and that of the master-justiciar; he had custody of the royal jewels and treasure; he was responsible for the condition and state of all the rights of the fisc; he received all the day-books recording receipt and expenditure from whatever office; it was in his office that the curial auditors carried out their duties of checking the accounts and appointing new officials. Fifty years earlier, Frederick's *camerarius* may not have had his functions so precisely laid down, but the general nature of his duties must have been similar. The development of the office is difficult to trace, but in 1239 it was probably still in its early stages. There is no reference to any central depository for the royal money until 1239, when it is first recorded at the royal castle of Naples. In 1240, the royal treasure was transported to Antrodoco castle in the north of the kingdom. Even so, some treasure was still deposited in regional centres: at Naples for Terra di Lavoro, Molise, the Principate and Terra Beneventana; at Bitonto, for Abruzzi; at Melfi, for Capitanata, Basilicata, Bari, Otranto and Malta; at Nicastro, for Calabria and eastern Sicily; at Palermo, for western Sicily. The dispersal of his treasure must have made it difficult for Frederick and his *camerarius* to be sure of their current balances. The decision to create a central treasury, taken rather late in the reign, is paralleled by an attempt in 1240 to provide for a single audit office set up at Melfi, in premises hastily provided by the bishop. All officials were required to submit for scrutiny the records of their administrations since Frederick's coronation in 1220. Although this must indicate that no accounts can have been centrally rendered for twenty years, it is no less certain that officials were assumed to have records available, perhaps for provincial accounting, of which there is some notice earlier. The attempt to make a central audit office at Melfi may have been intended as a reform of the system of auditing at Frederick's own itinerant court, which was anyway inconvenient and presumably came near to breaking down altogether while Frederick was out of the kingdom. But the office did not last long at Melfi; it had already been transferred to Barletta by 1247–8, when a new arrangement was devised to give four regional offices, one for Sicily, probably with Calabria, and the others on the mainland: at Monopoli (for Bari and Otranto); Melfi (Capitanata and Basilicata); and Caiazzo (the rest). Frederick hoped that his accountants would continue to consult together as to his best interests, but the division of the office indicates how incapable it had been of coping with general responsibilities. On a financial level, the kingdom was still fundamentally divided into two halves: Roger II's patrimony, and his acquisitions. Frederick had not inherited a working financial office for the whole kingdom, and he did not succeed in creating one. His *camerarius* had oversight but no government department as such to help him.

Given Frederick's attitude to financial matters, it does not seem reasonable to conclude that his main interest in the kingdom was profit. His willingness to consider capital investments for the longer term and other ways of improving his domain lands and stock prove that his urgent needs did not blind him to the future. He was notably a builder, not only of castles which had an immediate military purpose, but of palaces and country retreats. Frederick's most famous building still standing, the Castel del Monte, shows how much care and money he was prepared to lavish on a small residence for his moments of relaxation when he went hawking. Approving the proposal to sell surplus corn in North Africa, where a good price could be got, he asked his agents to use the profit not only to buy good horses, but also leopards, either for his menagerie, or for hunting. Nor were all his purchases mere self-indulgence. He also authorised an order of fresh tunics, shirts and skirts for his Saracen boys and girls at Lucera. Scrupulous attention to every detail of administration was expected by Frederick of all his officials. They in turn had to keep themselves informed, and dutifully consult the records of their predecessors in office. The king's care for the integrity of public administration was not only self-serving, and was presumably perceived at the time to be for the public good and appreciated as such in the kingdom.

Because Frederick himself directed his government, no officers of state emerged with departments of their own in his reign. He had no chancellor, despite the importance of his writing office. From time to time, he appointed a master-justiciar with military responsibilities; in 1239–41 there were two, one for each part of the kingdom north and south of the Porta Roseto. For nearly twenty years, the most eminent of his officials was Henry de Morra, master-justiciar of the great court, who also frequently acted as the king's lieutenant when he was absent from the kingdom. In all that time Morra did not obviously acquire any separate administrative department of his own, and after his death, it was four years before his place in the great court was taken by Richard de Montenero. Reorganisation of legal business in 1246 kept Montenero busy with judicial duties, and he never enjoyed the same kind of general authority in the kingdom as Morra. Unfortunately, little is known about the great court itself. On occasion, its judges settled cases out of the kingdom in northern Italy, so its functions were derived from Frederick's personal authority to give justice rather than from any institution of the kingdom.

Frederick's most important advisers, such as the archbishops of Palermo and Capua, who helped govern the kingdom in his absence, did not hold public offices in his government, but were honoured with the style *familiaris*, as William II's advisers had been. While Frederick was in Germany, such men were left to govern for him, but little is known about how they did this. A writ sent by two of them (the archbishop of Palermo and the bishop of Ravello) on behalf of the abbot of La Cava was issued at Melfi, where there may have been some provisional government headquarters. *Familiares* as such were no part of any government department; their normal place was at court as trusted advisers.

The uneven quantity of evidence for different points in Frederick's reign adds to the difficulty of perceiving how his style of government may have changed over the years. Some historians have been struck by what seem to be contrasts between the arrangements assumed in the *Liber Augustalis* and those revealed by the register fragment, and have been tempted to argue that in practice his government was, or became, much less highly principled. For this, the conflict with the papacy may be seen as either cause or consequence. Difficult relations with the papacy had to have serious implications for Frederick's rule, but the records of his last years cannot be seriously interpreted as evidence for increasing arbitrariness. Frederick was constantly making changes in his administration, and any differences between the blueprint of 1231 and the execution of 1239–40 cannot be explained mainly by reference to changes in his standing with Gregory IX. Nor is it acceptable to regard the *Liber Augustalis* as some kind of written constitution, set down once and for all like a tablet of stone. Frederick continued to issue new laws and amendments as seemed necessary, notably at Foggia in 1240 on his return to the kingdom. Most thirteenth-century copies of the *Liber Augustalis* incorporated the revisions into the text without apparently noticing any discrepancies. For contemporaries there was no perceptible difference between the basic laws and the amendments, and the text therefore carried ambiguous or contradictory readings. And while the law of the kingdom continued to grow under the king's hand, Frederick himself continued to insist on the traditional character of his rights, as though William II's reign remained his model. From the disparate evidence we have, it seems very unsound to argue that Frederick's government shifted its basis in his last years. Since he had begun to rule early in 1209, he may actually have found it rather difficult after thirty years to change his habitual style. Personally, he may have felt more vulnerable, particularly after the papal bull of deposition in 1245, but this in itself would not have been sufficient to require institutional changes. When, for example, his difficulties with the church did in time mean that so many bishoprics were vacant, by the death or defection of prelates, that it became necessary to appoint special overseers for church lands, Frederick still insisted on respect for the norms of royal custody, as traditionally claimed by the monarchy in vacancies. He gave way to no temptation to pillage church property in vindictive retribution. Frederick retained a high sense of his commitments as Roman emperor.

Autocratic tendencies in Frederick's government were, however, curbed by more than his own political good sense. His government could only be as effective as the officials at his disposal. At the centre, these were exposed to his direct scrutiny and chosen for their loyalty and proven worth. In the provinces, Frederick needed trustworthy men, competent and willing to serve him, whose confidence in him as legitimate ruler he had to retain even against papal anathemas, but it was much more difficult to control all these appointments himself. Most offices responsible for the collection of money and the oversight of legal processes were in practice entrusted to men who put themselves forward for the royal service, especially by paying lump sums to the government for the right to hold office year by year and collect the government's dues. Some provincial offices were assumed in this way by partnerships and there may even already have been enterprising businessmen investing in government posts, as was certainly the case later. The alternative to farming the offices was appointing agents to account for all the individual sums due. Some offices were farmed one year and given to agents the next. The processes of appointment are not visible in detail, but in many cases the outcome probably depended on the best deal that could be arranged at any one time. There was no real alternative available since the state had no thought of paying for a professional civil service. Between the men who made the system work and the king there was a comparatively small number of provincial 'managers', whose efforts on his behalf Frederick directed, but even some of these farmed their offices from the crown. Frederick could replace them if they proved unsatisfactory, but to some extent he could not avoid being dependent on men with reasons of their own for serving his administration. This curious organisation, despite its limitations, held together during Frederick's lifetime and may be judged, in general, sound.

In Frederick's youth, the kingdom had been ruled by powerful men, often counts, with scant regard for central direction. Frederick had only himself to thank if, by 1239, he could take obedience to his direction for granted throughout the kingdom. His counts no longer played any part in provincial administration; they had lost their right to make justiciars in their own lands, and the enforcement of the criminal law had become the exclusive responsibility of the king's provincial justiciars, with the exception of a few privileged cities. There were no marcher lordships and no privileged enclaves where the king's writ did not run. There were rebels (in Sicily) and outlaws, but the government of the kingdom lay in the king's hands alone. Frederick's programme of royal supervision was openly proclaimed at Capua in 1220, when it was nevertheless presented not as innovation, but as a return to the good usages of King William II's time. Frederick's eleven justiciarates (also called provinces and regions) were in large measure determined geographically by the political divisions of the kingdom before the creation of the monarchy, like the continuing importance of the distiction drawn between the kingdom north of Porta Roseto and south of it, that is, Calabria and Sicily, the original dominions of Roger II. These provinces had, in the Norman period, been regularly visited by pairs of justiciars travelling to do justice in the king's name, but it is less certain whether they constantly referred back to Palermo for instructions on all manner of business in the way that Frederick took for granted. What Frederick had made of any Norman legacy was therefore as important as the tradition itself. Unfortunately, it is not possible to show whether Frederick had to coax the justiciars into a new role. Apparently, the formal order of administration was already complete by 1231 and can be seen working smoothly, even by remote control, in the register fragment. Despite the appearance of uniformity, however, differences in the provinces remained, and Frederick was prepared to tolerate them. He listened patiently when his officials reported how attached his subjects were to their own local ways. Though the provincial structure was useful, Frederick was prepared to override it on occasion, as when provinces were grouped together in various ways for parliamentary assemblies or for audit purposes. Frederick's administration constantly adapted to changing demands and pressures. The system, which is suddenly exposed to view in the register fragment, was composed of many different services, operating in the same area but belonging to overlapping organisations. Royal administration continued to change after 1240. It is certainly wrong, therefore, to think that Frederick had conceived his administration as a whole at any one time.

Once Frederick had eliminated the local authority of the counts, his major problem was to provide an effective management of the provinces. He did not opt for a system of shrieval direction, but preserved the older arrangement of the twelfth century which entrusted the jurisdiction over crime to the justiciars, but left the *camerarii* to look after the royal estates and see to the enforcement of the civil law. By 1231, some of the powers of these two chief officials had already been defined, and subsequent amendments and refinements show that Frederick's ideas developed, no doubt in response to his growing experience of what could be done and what should be prevented. Quite early in the reign, there often seems already to have been only one justiciar, instead of two as in the past, for each province, though this did not become a formal requirement until 1246. At the same time, Frederick likewise decreed that each province should have only one master *camerarius*. No justiciar might be appointed to office in his own province, and Frederick issued several edicts designed to eliminate bribery and favouritism likely to prejudice honest administration of the law. By 1246 he had established a system of annual appointments, making justiciars remain another fifty days to ease their successors into office and keep them available to answer complaints about their own administrations. From 1231 there is evidence that Frederick was prepared to offer justiciars an emolument, and they were probably appointed as in the past from men of distinguished family. *Camerarii* who were not part of the justiciar's staff may have been men of different stamp, continuing for a time to farm their offices and obliged by their duties to seek out and negotiate with men prepared to manage royal estates or farm the various royal dues. Whereas the justiciar's functions therefore came to be more closely defined, those of the *camerarii* remained extremely varied.

South of Porta Roseto, the duties of the *camerarius* were discharged by an official, usually called *secretus*, who belonged therefore to a tradition of service in the *sekreton* which was in various ways different from the corresponding office of the mainland. These differences are puzzling, and must have as much to do with the social and political order created by Roger I as with any peculiarities of the *sekreton* itself in the twelfth century. What exactly happened to this office under Frederick II is far from clear. As late as 1229, a citizen of Catania who obtained royal confirmation of his uncle's grant to him of an estate *nomine pheudi*, applied for a copy of the statement of its bounds from the *magister questorum* because he still kept the *quaterni de secretis* in which were written the boundaries of all the cities, castles, villas and estates (*casalia*) of Sicily. Later, cameral officials of both Palermo and Messina are referred to in some documents as *magistri questorum*, and one of them, Obert Fallamonaca, possibly of Saracen origin, even wrote his name on one document in Arabic. Under Frederick II there is, however, not much evidence of Saracens in his administration. An office slave, Abdullah, who was taught to read and write Arabic, had to be sent away to learn it from master Joachim, so there cannot have been any substantial Arabic schooling available. The old term 'duana' itself became more narrowly applied to indicate the payments of excise duties, as on salt, exports and port taxes, as laid down by the *duana*: *secundum usum et consuetudinem doane*, where Sicily is invariably in question.

Whatever established routines the *secretus* could draw upon, the register fragment proves his need to consult Frederick on many points. A new *secretus* at Messina was concerned not only to perform his own duties punctiliously, but also to hold his own against the governor (*stratigotus*) of Messina and the king's admiral. He had no rule-book to refer to, apart from his predecessor's own records, and though he could solve some problems by relying on local precedents or by conducting local enquiries, he called on Frederick to give rulings for the settlement of many problems. Frederick did not reprimand his *secretus* for ignoring instructions or disregarding basic principles, accepting that it was proper for officials to bring him all their difficulties. A few principles were taken for granted. All moneys due to the government (*curia*) from whatever source, including the *collecta* and port dues within the jurisdiction of the *camerarius*, should be paid in to his office; likewise, all officials of the district could claim their expenses from him. At Messina, the *secretus* had to select not only the many familiar agents of the crown, castellans, farmers of royal estates, *baiuli* and *granitterii* (to gather the corn into barns), but also notaries in the royal mint. His duties included the sending of corn to the Holy Land, supplying the fleet with money, iron, pitch and ramming instruments (*tuppos?*), as well as hauberk-makers with iron and steel for their craft; the royal stables, stud-farms and herds were under officials who received their salaries and expenses from him; he licensed hunting in the royal forests, and supplied fresh pork from them to feed the king's guests; when there was a dearth of natural feed for the pigs, he saw to a general cull and had the meat turned into bacon. Although there was a major-domo to look after the queen's household and the *camerarius* had only to pay his expenses, the care of empty palaces and hunting seats was a direct responsibility: he provided for structural repairs and found jobs for the idle household staff; he looked after the lands of churches taken into the king's hands during vacancies, and had to provide for the clergy and see that they received the tithes they had been entitled to in the time of William II; he farmed out the royal monopoly of silk, dealt with the sale of salt on the mainland and kept an eye on the king's rights in shipwrecks; he had to try and limit the trickery practised by money-changers, repay royal debtors and negotiate with a consortium of Romans for the striking of a new issue of coins. The *secretus* of Messina had a greater range of duties than some of his counterparts elsewhere in the kingdom, but his case serves to illustrate the extent to which royal administration could impinge on the kingdom.

Communicating regularly with his provincial officials not only kept Frederick himself fully informed of what was happening, but encouraged each of his correspondents to expect Frederick's personal support for their commissions. It is not possible to know whether they cultivated the friendship of men at court, thought to have particular influence, in order to secure Frederick's favour as against rival officials, but the very directness of their approach to the centre and the absence of 'usual' channels of communication makes this probable. The flow of correspondence in the register fragment seems to show no serious delays: officials are rarely reprimanded for being slow. The system of course had its weaknesses. The *secretus* of Palermo had to write to Frederick at Sarzana for authority to get copies of his own predecessor's registers out of the royal palace in Palermo, because the castellan would not surrender them without it. But when an enterprising new governor of the port of Augusta needed the co-operation of the *secretus* of Messina and the admiral, the most effective way to obtain it was by writing to Frederick at Pisa and getting his approval. Not many examples of the exchange of missives can be so precisely dated as to make it certain how long it normally took for Frederick to be informed of the execution of his instructions, but it took two months on one occasion to get a report back from the archbishop of Capua, who even on his sick-bed did his best to comply with orders. The notaries of the royal writing office were expected to get their letters dispatched within two or three days of composition, and delays in dealing with correspondence at court were due to the time required for consultation with Frederick not to any bureaucratic inertia. Their business may be demonstrated by the fact that on Christmas Day 1239, as many as four royal notaries were kept busy enough to write fourteen pages of the register. Frederick drove his men hard, but the administration did not succumb either to structural faults or to human weakness.

It has become something of a modern obsession that both the Normans and Frederick operated a rational, systematic type of administration, whereas what we see in the records is something still much more pragmatic. The king resisted any tendency to routine, changing officials often and shifting some of them from post to post, which may have encouraged them to think of themselves as belonging to a cadre of state servants. Any improvement in the 'professionalism' of officials presumably owed something to royal patronage of the University of Naples, though its early years are badly documented. The more experienced justiciars and *camerarii* cannot have been students there, and only guesses can be made about the way they entered Frederick's service. Had they perhaps come forward while serving with him on the crusade? Some of them, like Henry de Morra and Peter de Vinea, who joined him shortly after his return to the kingdom, cannot have been trained in any conscious way for a life of public service, yet Frederick clearly knew how to attract many men of considerable talents and loyalty. Given time, his administration could have settled into an orderly system. Under Frederick, however, it seems safer to recognise that his adminis- tration continued to respond directly to him, and this may help explain why, after his death, it could not on its own keep the kingdom together. Only Frederick could do this.

Frederick's commitments in Germany, the warfare in northern Italy and the open breach with Gregory in 1239 complicated his government of the kingdom, but even if Frederick had not found himself at odds with the papacy, he would have continued to develop his government, for methodical and persistent scrutiny came naturally to him. But in his own time, some of his innovations would certainly have been regarded as necessarily temporary. It was, for example, quite impossible for him to think of permanently isolating the kingdom and its clergy from the papacy. Close royal supervision of the churches was only bearable as long as the clergy could at least hope for a change of pope, ruler or heart, which would eventually restore 'normal' relations between church and state. In itself, this would inevitably have brought clergy back into his own administration. For this reason the papacy held a trump card: the king could not permanently exclude his kingdom from the papacy's care. Frederick, however powerful in this world, was only a transient figure who would eventually be replaced. The popes who waited and prayed for this were uncharitable, but they were not stupid. However anxious they became, they also had good grounds for confidence, quite apart from their faith in God's providence.

After his second excommunication (March 1239), Frederick did not return to the kingdom until the following March, and he remained for three and a half years. It was the last time he was able to spend such a long period there in one stretch. Nevertheless, he spent some part of every year thereafter in the kingdom, except in 1248, when the problems of Parma prevented his return for over two years. Unfortunately, the evidence for his government of the kingdom in his last decade is not adequate to the task of assessing in detail the effects there of his final quarrel with the papacy. The death of the chronicler Richard of San Germano in 1243 and the dearth of surviving royal documents mean that the bulk of the evidence is provided by papal polemic. From this it might be easy to conclude that the eventual triumph of Frederick's enemies was taken for granted everywhere and undermined his conduct of affairs. But the force of the propaganda itself suggests that the papacy was not so confident as it seemed.

Although the main lines of the dramatic confrontation with the papacy are known, it remains difficult to describe how the kingdom

itself fared in the last few years. The chance survival of an official register
of escheats for 1249 at Monte Cassino hints at considerable confiscations
of lands for treason, but refers only to the situation in Capitanata.
Conclusions drawn from it cannot be supported by much evidence
elsewhere, though later Angevin records add some names of great men
who had forfeited their lands under Frederick II, without indicating how
they had offended, or how relatively important they were. The real
impact of papal censure came not immediately after the excommunication of 1239, but only when Innocent IV formally deposed Frederick at
the Council of Lyons (17 July 1245). Several influential figures in
Frederick's government did then succumb to papal pressures.

The worst conspiracy was instigated by some Lombards, including the
Parmigiano, Bernard Roland Rubeus, the pope's own brother-in-law.
He suborned Tebald Franciscus while serving as *podestà* at Parma, with
the promise that the pope would give him the kingdom of Sicily if he
managed to kill Frederick and his son, King Enzo. Somehow Frederick's
son-in-law, Richard, count of Caserta, found out about this plot to
secure Frederick's political assassination. One of the conspirators, Pandulf of Fasanella, the imperial vicar of Tuscany, fled to Rome; another,
James de Morra, son of the former master-justiciar, Henry, fled back to
the kingdom. The other principals, Tebald and William de San Severino, when they heard that the plot was known, also fled to the kingdom.
The conspirators barricaded themselves into the royal castles of Scala
and Capaccio with the connivance, or the complicity, of Andrew de
Cicala, *capitaneus* of Frederick's mainland army. Any plan the conspirators may have had to raise the kingdom against Frederick was, however,
thwarted by the prompt reaction of loyal local forces which besieged the
castles, so that the stronger one, Scala, was quickly recaptured. Frederick
hurried back to the kingdom and set about investing the castle of
Capaccio. In spite of his optimism, it took three months to obtain
possession of it (21 July 1246), and it was only the shortage of water in
the summer months that forced the surrender. Both those who had
escaped from the kingdom and those besieged in the castles received the
badge of crusaders from some Franciscans on papal authority. Frederick's letter of 25 April does not otherwise refer to any popular support in
the kingdom for this conspiracy of great men, but rather the contrary.
When Innocent heard about the conspiracy, he wrote urging the people
of the kingdom to overcome their fear of this new Nero and throw off
their allegiance, but Frederick's letters only ever complain of the friars as
papal agents, trying to stir up trouble in the kingdom. Nevertheless, 150
men were taken at Capaccio and a number of noble wives with them.

Their fates in Frederick's prisons fuelled stories of Frederick's demented cruelties. Bernard Roland Rubeus, the head and tail of the conspiracy, had himself nothing to do with the kingdom. He was not captured until March 1248.

Nor were all Frederick's problems in the kingdom due to the pope or conspiracy. Saracen rebels, for example, were still troublesome as late as April 1248, and may indeed have taken advantage of the king's embarrassments for their own purposes. Sicily was said to be still turbulent in March 1249 when a new captain was appointed for the island. Frederick's representative, Peter Rufus, later threw in his lot with Innocent IV, but it is very unlikely that he dared court papal representatives openly while Frederick was still alive. The most famous of the 'betrayals' was that of Peter de Vinea, who had been an outstanding public servant for a quarter of a century. He was still being promoted in 1247, but fell abruptly from power in March 1249 for reasons which are still disputed. He was accused of planning to poison Frederick. Blinded and led away to be paraded as a criminal around the kingdom, he managed to cut short his own ruined life by dashing his brains out against the walls of his prison at San Miniato. Although he was from Capua and his family were obviously suspected of complicity, there is no suggestion that Peter had been involved in any conspiracy of southerners, or even of fellow curials. It remains, indeed, an open question whether he was simply framed by enemies at court, or driven by court intrigues into an impossible position. His fall casts no light on the position of the kingdom as such.

Frederick made no bones about his vengeance on traitors after 1230, and his cruelties not surprisingly figure large in the polemics of his enemies. What was worse, Frederick became suspicious even of those who had served him well, such as Peter de Vinea, proceeding to summary executions on the unsuspecting, and driving others who feared his suspicion to disloyalty. In these circumstances it became difficult to establish who was actually guilty of what. For this atmosphere of hatred, the papacy was responsible. In the terrible years that followed Innocent IV's decision to refuse any peace with Frederick, it became impossible for anyone to be sure of habitual loyalties. The papacy openly encouraged rebellion and deceit. Frederick was not surprisingly anxious, and his distrust alienated some of his most loyal servants and gave unscrupulous advisers some hold over him. Frederick's violence and anguish belong together, but they cannot be explained simply as the reactions of a guilt-ridden tyrant. The kingdom itself does not seem to have seethed with discontent. Some of the clergy still appealed to the king for justice in the ordinary courts. Where there is evidence, it shows the administration in order and royal mandates passing down from the provincial commands to the local officials.

From these depressing years of Frederick's rule, there is also one monument of another kind. It was then that Frederick completed his book, *The Art of Hunting with Falcons*, probably in Apulia, where he had practised the art since the 1220s and where he maintained an establishment of birds and falconers. If he had begun to fly falcons as a youth or in Germany, it may not have been until his return south that he took up the sport in earnest. His sojourn in the Holy Land certainly stimulated his appreciation of the finer points of the sport. Opportunities to study birds occurred while he was in the kingdom, and his book indicates that Frederick not only recorded his personal observations and drew conclusions from them, but that he also carefully read such books as dealt with the subject. In this way he showed himself to be the true heir of the tradition of courtly learning, cultivated in his kingdom since the time of Roger II. The oldest known text of Frederick's book survives in an edition prepared for his son, Manfred (1258–66), and Frederick therefore knew how to transmit his enthusiasm to the next generation. This manuscript has famous illustrations for the first two of its six books. Frederick's own copy was lost after the battle of Vittoria in 1248. It is appropriate that Frederick's greatest legacy to later generations was a scientific work embodying his own personal observations and enthusiasms. It sets him firmly in a context of southern learning, and shows how wide of the mark it is to present Frederick as an isolated genius. Frederick was prepared to learn from the best teachers of the day, and in turn to contribute to the store of human learning.

12

THE KINGDOM BETRAYED

•

The contemporary chronicler Jamsilla claimed that the death of Frederick II did not immediately provoke the disturbances usual on the death
of princes. But within a short time, a covert conspiracy spread from the
Apulian towns to Capua and Naples, followed by open rebellion with
the formation of a league of certain magnates hostile to Berthold of
Hohenburg, the principal German leader serving Frederick in Italy.
Frederick had left both the empire and the kingdom to his oldest
surviving son, Conrad, then still in Germany, so provision was made for
the government of the kingdom to be carried on until Conrad should
return by his younger brother, Manfred, whose mother's family of
Lancia were prominent in Italy and able to help the eighteen-year-old
prince. Though well educated and admired, Manfred had no military
experience and did not at first inspire confidence or respect. He acquired
these by prompt and audacious confrontation with the dissident towns
of Andria, Foggia and Barletta, while Hohenburg dealt with Avellino.
Manfred then made a brave but unsuccessful attempt to take Naples and
Capua. The disaffection of the kingdom was not merely a spontaneous
reaction against Frederick's system of government. Innocent IV had
already attempted to infiltrate the kingdom with his agents to recover
what he claimed were the lawful rights of the papacy. In 1247, he made
paper grants in the kingdom as direct feudal overlord 'because there was
no king'; in 1248, he had a crusade preached in Rome for the recovery of
Sicily which was threatened with interdict if it did not submit; in 1249, he
appointed a cardinal legate to collect an army and free the kingdom from
Frederick II. Nothing was accomplished before Frederick's death really

gave the papal party the chance it had been waiting for. Innocent IV, on
hearing of the death, prepared to return from exile. Though it took him
nearly three years to reach the Lateran, which he entered only in
October 1253, he had in the meantime urged his representatives in the
kingdom to take over papal properties there, dispose of rebels' lands,
make common cause with all who repudiated their Staufen allegiances,
and allow his fellow countrymen, the Genoese, and other allies the
privileges he had granted them. The real effectiveness of Cardinal Peter
as legate in 1251 may be judged from the willingness of both Manfred
and Hohenburg to accept investiture at his hands (of the principality of
Taranto and of the county of Andria respectively). Nevertheless, their
own successes in Apulia had also impressed the legate sufficiently to
secure for them papal endorsement. It was short lived. Before Christmas
1251, the pope had already decided to break with Manfred; he
applauded the resistance put up by the Neapolitans against him, and
thankfully approved their commune. This was the confusing situation
faced by Conrad IV when, at last feeling able to leave Germany, he
reached the kingdom in December 1251; he ruled there for about two
and a half years.

Conrad's position was a very uneasy one. He did not want to neglect
his interests in Germany for long, yet he had no one he trusted to rule the
kingdom of Sicily for him. He was suspicious of Manfred's good
intentions, particularly after Manfred's reputation had been made by
prompt action on Conrad's behalf. Ostentatiously friendly relations
between the brothers soon broke down. Conrad reduced Manfred's
honours and forced his mother's family into exile. Conrad imposed
respect in other ways. He successfully reasserted his authority against the
remaining rebellious towns – Aquino, Sessa, San Germano and Capua;
Naples itself fell to him on 10 October 1253. A German captain was
appointed as justiciar from the Capua river to the frontier: the old order
was to be re-established. To stabilise the situation, however, Conrad
needed papal recognition. Although Innocent agreed to a truce with
Conrad in the autumn of 1252, tactical concessions did not deflect
Innocent from his main purpose of making certain that no Staufen was
ever recognised as king or emperor again. When Conrad left for Italy,
the party opposed to him in Germany agreed to deprive him of the
duchy of Swabia, a decision endorsed by the pope. A few days after this,
the pope decided to follow it up by starting intrigues to get either the
king of England or the king of France to send his brother (Richard, earl
of Cornwall, or Charles of Anjou, count of Provence) to take the *regnum
Sicilie*. These startling proposals took a long time to affect the situation in
the kingdom. Conrad probably did not consider them likely to produce

an immediate challenge, and Innocent himself certainly never intended to allow any foreign prince to cheat the papacy of its own rights in the kingdom. He was frightened into such negotiations when it looked as though Conrad would not be overthrown unless a papal champion appeared in Italy. Negotiations between the pope and Conrad were to this degree artificial, since Innocent was not interested in getting an agreement, and Conrad could not do without one. The pope's desperation is shown by his need to drag out the discussions by instigating a bogus examination into the orthodoxy of Conrad's beliefs (February 1254). It was probably the death in December 1253 of Conrad's young half-brother Henry, nephew of Henry III of England, which removed any of that king's remaining scruples about accepting the kingdom for his own younger son, Edmund, and this was presumably already clear to Innocent when he decided to excommunicate Conrad on 9 April 1254. Edmund was recognised as king by the pope on 14 May; a week later, Conrad himself was dead.

Conrad's death opened another period of uncertainty which lasted about four years. Conrad left his own two-year-old son, Conrad(in), as a papal ward. If Conrad thought that this new responsibility would induce the same sentiments roused in Innocent III when the young Frederick was in his charge, he was grievously mistaken. No pope showed any concern for Conradin's rights. For that matter, Innocent no longer had much interest in working for Edmund, whom he had nominated to replace the Staufen. Conrad's death in effect opened up the exciting possibility for Innocent of ruling the kingdom directly. By September 1254, Innocent was prepared to move there in person. He ordered an assembly to meet him at Capua in November, where he would make arrangements for the government. Innocent's confidence in dealing with the situation rested on his calculation that now that there was no legitimate heir of Frederick II to take Conrad IV's place, Manfred, along with others such as his brother, Frederick of Antioch and Hohenburg, could be persuaded to take posts within a papal organisation that would satisfy their ambitions without compromising papal interests. Since this papal regime did not in fact last very long, it is difficult to assess what the pope seriously envisaged as its long-term prospects. It was not so obviously outrageous as to provoke immediate rebellion. By patronage of the influential magnates, Innocent expected to secure their acceptance of his decision to enlarge the papal patrimony at the kingdom's expense: Calabria and Sicily and other places, such as Amalfi, Atrani and Melfi, were simply annexed to the papal domain. The kingdom itself was to be subjected to papal lordship, and money raised there for papal purposes. King Edmund remained absent and though

Innocent threatened to give the kingdom to another if Henry III did not act promptly and send Edmund south, Innocent did not really now need a king there. Any king would have found himself in the pope's way and been expected by his subjects to defend them from the arrogance of the clergy.

Had he been born legitimate, Manfred might reasonably have expected to be offered the leadership of the whole Staufen cause in Italy immediately after Conrad's death. As it was, Manfred at first felt sufficiently unsure of his position to be obliged to acknowledge the better rights of his nephew Conradin. Not only had Conradin been formally provided with the pope as his guardian; the protection of his interests, along with the royal treasure and the German troops, had also been entrusted by his father to Hohenburg, not Manfred. Not until Hohenburg realised that he could not unaided hold off the papal army preparing to occupy the kingdom in the autumn of 1254, was Manfred even pressed by the Staufen party to take the lead. By that time it was too late to keep Innocent out. With Hohenburg disgruntled and Manfred distrustful, the pope's agents infiltrated Calabria and Sicily, then ruled by the quasi-independent *baiulus* Peter Rufus.

In these circumstances, Manfred himself agreed to compromise with Innocent. He accepted papal lordship of his principality of Taranto and the county of Gravina, and allowed the pope to enter the kingdom, saving the rights of Conradin and himself. Manfred duly acted as Innocent's groom (*strator*), leading his horse when he crossed the bridge into the kingdom at Ceprano on 11 October 1254. The papal court reached Naples on 27 October where it settled down for several months. (Though Innocent died there in December, his successor, Alexander IV, did not depart until the end of May 1255.) Whatever Manfred may have hoped or wished for, he cannot have been prepared for this direct and continuous papal presence. It became personally humiliating and did not disguise its aim of annihilating the Staufen interest altogether. When Manfred's enemy, Borello, lord of Anglona, was murdered, Innocent fastened on what seemed the perfect justification to destroy Manfred. He was not interested in hearing excuses. Manfred understood only too well that his moment had come. In an extraordinary adventure described by Jamsilla in exciting detail, Manfred slipped away from Teano and crossed the mountains by arduous paths to reach Lucera early in November. Here he succeeded in winning entry to the town, getting his hands on the Staufen treasure, and winning the allegiance of the Saracen troops. This quickly persuaded the leading figures of Apulia to treat Manfred with more respect, and the legate's army of Germans at Troia either withdrew or deserted to Manfred's cause. By the time Innocent died (7 December) the papal presence in Apulia had so faded away, except in the Terra di Bari, that individual cities and captains felt free to make their own terms with the triumphant prince. When pressed to pay his respects to Alexander IV, the new pope, Manfred was still prepared to make peace, on condition that the kingdom should remain in the lordship of Conradin and under his own tutelage (*baliatus*), though he offered in addition to pay more for the census due to the Roman church. Instead of negotiating, Alexander IV pressed the charge of Manfred's part in Borello's murder, and when Manfred declined to present himself for judgement, excommunicated him on 25 March 1255. By forcing Manfred into a position of fighting for himself, the papacy pushed him into the role of saviour of the kingdom from papal despoliation.

Alexander IV was by then disposed to leave Naples. He appointed a new legate, Cardinal Octavian, to raise a new army. While Manfred was dealing with the situation in the Salentino, he learnt that Rufus had been chased out of Messina and taken refuge in Calabria. This gave Manfred an unexpected opportunity to interfere directly in the affairs, first of Calabria, and then of Sicily. Forced out of Calabria, Rufus joined the papal *curia* before it left Naples, where he prepared a two-pronged attack on Calabria by land and sea. The army destined for Calabria had, however, to be diverted to help Octavian's army in Apulia, and the force which Rufus successfully brought by sea failed on its own to consolidate its hold. As a result of this, the reputation of Manfred's party improved so much in the South and in Apulia, that the very large papal army refused to risk a battle. Manfred still felt unable to count on the cities of the region to support him, but relied on his German and Saracen troops to keep up the pressure on the timid legate. During a truce, arranged so that discussions with representatives of Conradin's maternal uncle could take place, the papal army allegedly took unfair advantage but, in retaliation, Hohenburg's army, which was co-operating with the legate, was badly mauled by Manfred as it tried to rejoin the papal force at Foggia. The cautious legate therefore agreed to negotiate. Manfred offered to cede the Terra di Lavoro to the papacy, provided he was allowed to hold the rest of the kingdom in his own name and for King Conradin; should the pope not confirm the treaty, Manfred would take the Terra di Lavoro back into the kingdom. Manfred also agreed not only to pardon nobles exiled by his father and restore their lands, but also to pardon Hohenburg for his disloyalty to himself. The nature of Manfred's concessions is interesting, but since Alexander refused to endorse the peace terms, they have only diplomatic importance.

Released from all commitment to the papacy, Manfred was free to put the kingdom in order. He held a *curia generalis* at Barletta in February 1256. While Calabria was almost entirely submissive to Manfred and his uncle Frederick, count of Squillace, as vicar-general, Sicily, for the most part, still obeyed the papal vicar, a Franciscan, Fr Rosino. However, when the pope's men were arrested in Palermo by supporters of Manfred, many other cities changed allegiance, until only Lentini and Messina still held out against Manfred. Messina had set up a commune, as found in Lombardy and Tuscany, with a Roman citizen as its *podestà*, and it raised a respectable army which regarded Calabria as its proper playground. However, the growth of Manfred's party in Sicily provided for the creation of a sufficiently impressive army to overawe the Messinesi, so the count of Squillace was able to enter the city. The news of this success reached Manfred just as he was preparing to descend on the Terra di Lavoro; both Naples and Capua concluded it was prudent to surrender without putting up a fight. Disputes between the two factions at Aversa were eventually resolved in Manfred's favour, and all the places across the Volturno submitted to him, except for Sora and Rocca d'Arce which, under German captains appointed by Hohenburg, continued to defy him. However, the few places in the kingdom which still held out eventually decided that submission was the better course. Brindisi, Oria and Otranto fell to him when the leader of the local resistance, Thomas of Oria, was betrayed; Ariano was taken by stratagem.

These dramatic successes on the west coast of the Adriatic had immediate repercussions on the other side of the sea. In the spring of the following year, several cities in the Epirus already acknowledged Manfred's lordship. Michael Angelus, despot of the Epirus, recognising his power, opened negotiations. As a result of these, Manfred eventually obtained Michael's daughter, Helena, as his second wife, and her dowry brought Manfred some ports and islands of the Epirus as well as Corfu. Like his great predecessor Guiscard, Manfred had no need of a royal title to become a major influence in the affairs of the eastern empire at a critical stage of its history. In these years, the Greek princes were already preoccupied with the problem of who among them would recover Constantinople from the Latin emperors (which Michael VIII of Nicaea did in 1261); to them, Manfred already seemed a Latin prince considerable enough to be treated carefully.

Manfred's triumph could not be complete until Sicily too was his. His supporters took Piazza by assault and Castrogiovanni, worn down by a long siege. Manfred himself proceeded to Sicily in the summer of 1258. Rumours of Conradin's death in Germany were now circulating, possibly by design, and Manfred decided to assume the kingship without more delay. With a creditable array of secular and ecclesiastical barons to make his coronation convincing, he was duly anointed and crowned in Palermo on 11 August 1258. He and his supporters had reassembled the Norman kingdom piece by piece, and Pope Alexander had not known how to prevent it. Manfred appeared to be irresistible, and those who had remained rebellious bowed to the obvious. The kingdom did not resist reintegration: in its own way it showed its own will to survive dismemberment at the hands of the papacy. The chronicle of Jamsilla ends on this positive note.

By his coronation, Manfred obviously alienated the supporters of Conradin, whose pretensions, had he lived long enough, Manfred would no doubt have had to face in due time, but in 1258 Conradin no longer had any Sicilian champions. For the four years since Conrad's death, Manfred had himself consistently defended the rights of Conradin in the kingdom, but even without the rumours of Conradin's death, the logic of events by the summer of 1258 probably forced Manfred to assume the crown of the kingdom he had had to reconquer. Though as early as September 1257, Manfred recovered from Venice the royal *iocalia* (crown jewels) which Hohenburg had placed there for Conradin as security for a loan, he may have only gradually come to recognise the need to take personal responsibility for the government of the kingdom. The first step in brushing Conradin aside as irrelevant in the South had been taken by the papacy. For the papacy itself to denounce Manfred as a usurper was mere propaganda. Manfred alone had the chance to rally sentiment on behalf of the Staufen. If his father's kingdom was to be ruled at all, Manfred had to do it.

Manfred ruled for less than eight years. During his lifetime he was vilified by the papacy, from whose records much of the history of the reign has to be written. After his death, Charles of Anjou refused to ratify his enactments, and comparatively few documents of his government have survived. Yet after the battle of Benevento, Charles acquired a functioning kingdom, managed in the manner of Frederick II, so there can be no doubt that Manfred had effectively reconstituted the kingdom. Manfred's success can be measured by the eagerness of other princes to obtain his friendship, and by the rapid recovery of the Ghibelline cause in the rest of Italy. Though neither legitimate nor emperor, Manfred made a creditable show of recovering his father's authority in Italy. Until his death, the papacy feared and loathed him. This appears to have unfairly damaged his historical reputation.

The main commentary on Manfred's reign is the chronicle of Saba Malaspina, written after the death of Charles of Anjou (1285). Despite his conclusion that it was Manfred's own pride and perversity that brought about his merited downfall, Malaspina also firmly recorded Manfred's outstanding qualities in a patriotic way. He claims that Manfred kept the kingdom in peace after 1258, though he gives little detailed account of his domestic government. The chronicler's information about Manfred's involvement in affairs outside the kingdom remains generalised, in the manner of someone writing nearly thirty years after the event. He presents Manfred as ready to negotiate with Urban IV by the end of 1262, and offers rather a hollow explanation of why the pope rejected the opportunity and would not go back on his commitment to Charles. He shows that the murder near Trapani of Frederick Maletta, Manfred's lieutenant in Sicily, was quickly punished. He does not interpret the incident as representing any general dissatisfaction with Manfred's government. Even the unrest provoked in the island by John of Cocleria, a beggar who, by virtue of his alleged likeness to Frederick II, allowed himself to be taken for the emperor, was easily put down by the governor Richard, count of Marsico. Malaspina says that though Manfred thought the fraud should be punished only by public derision, others thought it fitting to execute the imposter and his eleven principal followers. The episode hardly bears out the view that the island submitted unwillingly to Manfred, or that the Guelf party had much hope of playing on popular sympathies for the papacy: it was Frederick II who had left a popular impression.

The stiff resistance which different towns all over the kingdom had put up against Manfred's claims proves, however, that the new ruler could not simply take their loyalty for granted. Many of the clergy also put their allegiance to the church first. Had the papacy been able to supply the military force and leadership required to defeat Manfred, there might still have been some popular sentiment in favour of a papal regime. But papal interests and outlook necessarily disapproved of strong government, and this only encouraged local patriotism to emerge. The death of Frederick II, which gave northern Italian cities the chance to develop individually, in a similar way permitted the kingdom to fragment institutionally under direct papal lordship. Jamsilla's account of Manfred's campaigns highlights the particularities of each stronghold, and what induced their leaders to make decisions for their own localities. The southern towns had not, however, known the anti-imperial leagues, nor had they been given the opportunities of local self-government which had fostered Lombard and Tuscan cities. In some respects they certainly drew upon smouldering traditions of autonomy, memories of fierce resistance to royal governments, and on a strong sense of local self-sufficiency in economic, legal and social terms. But every place was riven with factions; every town stood on its own, not only against any royal oppressor, but also against its hostile neighbours. Had the kingdom fallen apart into its constituent elements it would not have promoted a golden age of free communities, but would have generated incessant local conflicts which could only encourage new despotic regimes. The southern kingdom had very recent experience under Frederick II to confirm its nostalgic memories of the monarchy of William II, which had preserved peace and justice. Jamsilla, in his account of Rufus' assault in Calabria, explains that when his messenger called on the *universitas* of Cosenza to submit to the papacy, those left in the town were uncertain how to reply. Their best men (*meliores homines*) had left with Manfred's captain for military duties in Val di Crati; this meant that only *populares*, some nobles, or those without military ability were left to face Rufus: inexperienced and indeed ignorant of warfare, because of the long period of quiet and peace which they had known under Frederick II. The same conditions everywhere meant that the *universitates* were generally unprepared to deal with the breakdown of public authority themselves, and too frightened to trust others. They blindly put their trust only in their own efforts, and in the remarkable defensive sites of their towns. A city like Messina, which could have created a successful city-state by spilling over into Calabria, brutally exposed the dangers that it would represent for others, and this in turn stimulated a fresh awareness of the advantages brought by princely rule. The potential ambitions of the greatest cities, such as Bari, Brindisi or Naples, were choked by the too great proximity of frightened rivals. The defence of local autonomies inevitably gave real power and responsibility to the military rather than to the civil leadership. It is not surprising if the pacification of the kingdom was achieved by Manfred's forces, since they proved more resilient and determined than those of his opponents.

The main question posed by Manfred's kingship for modern historians has been the difficulty of measuring its acceptability in the kingdom. Manfred may seem to have been betrayed at the end because the nobility lost confidence in him, and this would have to be attributed at least in part to certain weaknesses in his own character. Up to a point, his shortcomings may be used to excuse papal opposition to him and make Charles of Anjou's vengeance look like just retribution. Manfred's problem as king was that he could not rule indefinitely without papal recognition, not because of the kingdom's vassal status, but because the loyalty of the clergy could not be guaranteed until the papacy endorsed his kingship. But Manfred should not be made to bear all the blame. His eventual failure was really due to the papacy's refusal to recognise his position. In other hands than those of the two French popes, Urban IV and Clement IV, the papacy might have eventually negotiated. Louis IX of France urged this policy, and tried himself to work for a settlement. The popes themselves would not give way. By refusing to contemplate any recognition of Manfred's real power, they were convinced they could bring him down somehow in the end. This actually required of them efforts on an unprecedented scale, and Manfred cannot be blamed for not anticipating that they would be successful. Papal hostility also affected the manner of his government, for he had to devise a system which would be effective, and yet unable to take the tacit moral support of the clergy for granted. Some of the more powerful clergy did support him, but only by incurring papal displeasure. Unlike Frederick II, Manfred had no time to secure ecclesiastical preferment for men of proven loyalty to himself. Nor could he fall back on loyal secular vassals. When he began his battle for the kingdom, effective power lay not with the old nobility, but with the soldiers, particularly with the Germans and Saracens. After his personal breach with the papacy, Manfred had to rely mainly on his relations, especially, though not exclusively, on those of his Lombard mother. This is not surprising and hardly in itself blameworthy, though the rewards given to the Lombard supporters of his family unfortunately provoked discontent in Sicily and elsewhere. Manfred had no choice. The only persons of consequence left to him after years of conflict with the papacy were local notables with local aspirations. Some of those who had thrown in their lot with the Staufen cause felt uncomfortable about abandoning Conradin. Manfred's position in this respect was not exceptional. Both Innocent IV and Alexander IV, when they had tried to rule the kingdom, had been unable to trust the kingdom's own nobiilty and had nominated their own men to positions of importance. Manfred obviously could not place any hope in those nobles whom his father had sent into exile, for they continued to put the papacy first.

Manfred's style of government was naturally modelled on that of his father. Those who, because of such procedures, had had to flee the kingdom under Frederick II, might appear capable of offering an alternative style and one more acceptable to contemporary opinion, had they been able to return from exile. After 1258, however, these allies of the papacy were no longer in a position to work for an alternative regime in the kingdom. They had either to accept Manfred or to support a foreign prince strong enough to overthrow him. The kind of kingship Frederick had created was restored, and the kingdom was reconstituted. It would remain. Later, Charles of Anjou himself could do no better than maintain the old regime. The papacy was no longer in a position to work for a real change of government when it opposed Manfred. It aimed only to change the monarch.

The inadequacy of the papal programme for the kingdom adumbrated in 1254–5 followed from the fact that the papacy could only have held on to political power by exercising the political and military responsibilities concomitant with it. Churchmen not surprisingly proved to be less competent at this than laymen. Even the layman who was prepared to collaborate with the church, Charles of Anjou, soon provoked the anger of the clergy who found him insubordinate. The clerical *curia* was too blinkered by its education and its prejudices to appreciate that kingdoms could not in fact be run by clergy. Innocent IV's determination to protect the church by destroying the kingdom began to turn the church itself into a political, rather than a spiritual, force in European affairs. A certain sophistry that argued that the church by definition could have only spiritual interests was not deployed cynically, but grew out of intellectual confusion and the Roman clergy's real ignorance of political realities. Rome could not calculate the practical consequences of its policies, not merely for the kingdom or the papacy itself, but for the English, French, Germans and Spaniards who were all eventually drawn into the tangle.

At the beginning of Manfred's reign, the pope was Alexander IV, the indecisive representative of the great house of Segni from which had come Innocent III and Gregory IX. Alexander was obliged to abandon Innocent IV's idea of direct papal rule in the South: the kingdom was too strong for him. He himself left Naples before his army had properly come to grips with Manfred. Thereafter, he and his successors depended for deliverance from Manfred on whatever prince from the North God chose to send them.

At the beginning of Alexander's pontificate, the nominee, King Edmund, still showed no sign of coming to claim his kingdom, though Alexander renewed the grant to Edmund (April 1255), and at last even approved Henry III's long-expressed hopes of discharging his crusading vow by serving in Sicily. There is a certain unreality about the Sicilian question from Henry III's point of view, as well as the papacy's. Nevertheless, Henry personally put great store by the concession of the kingdom: as late as 1263, he was still trying to insist on Edmund's rights. Yet, apart from the money and credit he committed to the cause, which Alexander always found inadequate, Henry did nothing to advance Edmund's chances. Various deadlines for the arrival of king and troops came and went. Alexander saw that his threats of excommunication and interdict for non-compliance had to be postponed until early in 1258, when Henry became so anxious about his impossible commitments that he sought baronial help in dealing with the situation. The political difficulties this created for him thereafter barely left him free to negotiate peace and concord with the king of France. From beginning to end, the English involvement was, in this sense, little more than a papal diplomatic manœuvre. But the papacy itself probably never realised, still less repented, the consequences of trying to set Henry III against the old Staufen enemy of his family in Sicily. And in a sense, Henry had only himself to blame for getting caught in the papal trap. Henry's crisis was Manfred's opportunity, and made Manfred's coronation an urgent political necessity.

The original offer to Edmund had been made at the same time as one to Charles of Anjou, count of Provence. By bad luck, his brother, Louis IX, was on crusade, and Louis seemed to the papacy to be steadily opposed to the project from beginning to end. He had regarded Frederick II as a good ally and had continued to intercede for him after the papal condemnation at Lyons. He may also have had doubts about Charles' own suitability for the role assigned him. He was probably realistic enough to anticipate the real expense and risk. He was shrewd enough to estimate the negligible return for the church or the papacy in the long run, and was characteristically still trying to make peace between Manfred and the pope as late as 1263. His failure to give Charles encouragement is shown by the fact that even as Charles drew near to realising the papacy's objectives, Clement IV was still writing dolefully to Louis about the hazardous outcome and begging him to help Charles, apparently without much hope of success. If Charles was eventually brought to Italy as papal champion against Manfred, it was not therefore due to Louis. The main instigator of the policy was another Frenchman, Urban IV, working particularly through his French legate, Simon de Brie (former canon of Tours and much later Pope Martin IV). The Roman pope, Alexander IV, had no one seriously in mind to take Edmund's place when his English plans fizzled out, despite the obvious fact that Manfred's success made finding a papal champion indispensable if Manfred were not to be recognised. The total disarray of the *curia* at this turn of events was compounded by the fact that Alexander IV had at the time been obliged to leave Rome because of local hostility to him, and it was therefore mainly at Viterbo, Orvieto and Perugia that he and his successors had to prepare their revenge. When Alexander died in 1261, the *curia* was so irresolute that it took three months to find a successor to him, and it saw no one in the vicinity, clerk or layman, able to rescue it from its own follies. It took an outsider like the new pope, Urban IV, to press for a drastic change of course.

By the end of 1261, Manfred looked to everyone else like a very convincing ruler. Manfred's success at home enabled him to secure marriage alliances with other princes. He himself married Helena of

Epirus after his coronation, and was active in Balkan negotiations until his death. Even more important was the link with the king of Aragon, whose heir, Peter, was married to his daughter, Constance, in 1262. Urban IV was furious with the king of Aragon, and the marriage did indeed have profound consequences twenty years later when the Aragonese were able to profit from the Sicilian Vespers which effectively broke Charles of Anjou's domination of Italian affairs. Manfred's Mediterranean alliances indicate the sureness of his hold in the kingdom and the respect this properly inspired abroad. The refusal of Urban IV to come to terms with this phenomenon was not, however, mere wilful obstinacy, though it certainly suggests a frightened inflexibility. Manfred represented the dreaded Staufen charisma not only for the pope, but for all those many elements in Italy that had suffered from Frederick's death and papal triumphalism. Only some of these elements were turbulent and anarchistic. Other Ghibelline supporters of the empire, hostile to the church's temporal pretensions, had perfectly legitimate grounds for finding Guelf dominance in the 1250s, both partial and partisan. When Manfred emerged victorious in the kingdom, he was naturally expected to take an interest in his father's other Italian kingdom. As he began to look more like his father, the Guelf parties also began to fear that with him Frederick's authority would be recovered. In this way Manfred could hardly avoid accepting the role his birth and distinction cast him for. He appointed representatives to lead the pro-Staufen party in Liguria, Tuscany and the March of Ancona. The new confidence of his party was reinforced by the victory of Siena over Florence at Montaperti (4 September 1260). It was this which precipitated Alexander IV's second excommunication of Manfred in November as the soul of the Ghibelline revival. Malaspina blames Manfred's cupidity for taking more than he already possessed, and sees this as the moral fault which caused his downfall. Modern historians dress up the old argument in modern style when they argue that if Manfred had been content to remain king of Sicily and had avoided further antagonism of the papacy, he could have survived.

It was not Manfred's ambition that compromised him, but the situation of the kingdom of Sicily in Christendom. Both the empire and the papacy had for generations refused to allow the Norman kingdom a quiet life. They had dragged it into prominence. Given the chance, they had abused and mutilated it to suit their own requirements. Its very strength made it a power to be reckoned with. It could not be isolated from events elsewhere. It is absurd to think Manfred could cut himself off from well-wishers and supporters in Italy. The papacy had no scruples at all about involving remote rulers in the affair. The fate of the kingdom had become a general problem, and the solution of the papal difficulty had the most profound consequences not only for the kingdom, but for the papacy too. Manfred reckoned that his best chance of securing recognition of his rights in the kingdom was to put pressure on the papacy in central Italy where it was vulnerable. Manfred attempted what his father had tried before him. It was nearly successful. The only escape for the papacy proved to be Charles of Anjou's successful intervention. In the long term, however, this was to put the papacy even more at the mercy of the French than it had ever been at German hands; that the papacy was driven so far by desperation in the early 1260s only emphasises how close to success Manfred had actually come.

Charles very nearly failed to reach Italy at all, and Manfred could not at first have been seriously concerned about him, rather presuming that the pope would see the sense in reaching a settlement of Italian problems with Manfred himself. Manfred's reasonable political calculations for his cause foundered in effect on the papacy's absolute indifference to any political interest or moral consideration other than its merciless defence of the rights of the Roman church. Effective communication between the papacy and the churchmen of the kingdom was suspended after 1255–6. The papacy concentrated instead on proving its ability to dispose of its royal fief at will, whatever the cost. Manfred was not emperor and did not aspire to be: he represented no imperial cause to challenge the papal 'sovereignty' of the west. Yet in a sense he represented a point of view flatly opposed to papal theory: he worked for a pragmatic *modus vivendi*. The papacy would not have it. If the kingdom was the papacy's, it would be given on the papacy's terms and the pope would brook no opposition. Negotiations between parties with such different concepts of power would never bring about a settlement.

Within about six months of becoming pope, Urban IV had his conditions ready for submission to Charles of Anjou, and over the next four years the papacy shut its eyes to any other resolution of the problem. Manfred's offer to negotiate in the autumn of 1261 may have been prompted by knowledge of Urban's discussions with Charles, which Manfred may initially have interpreted as a means to force him to make concessions. However, in fact, Urban IV soon showed that he was not prepared to find any good in Manfred nor in his alliance with James of Aragon, though he was not above pleading with both for the release of his nominee, the bishop-elect of Verona, when he fell into Manfred's hands. Urban IV devoted himself to getting Charles' consent to his enterprise. This was not easy, as may be seen from the fact that negotiations about the terms dragged on for over two years, and the haggling did not stop then. Not until the end of 1263 did Urban prepare to send his legate to work in France; only in March 1264, did Urban impose a tax of tenths for three years from the clergy in several ecclesiastical provinces and sees (Cambrai, Tournai, Lyons, Vienne, Embrun, Tarentaise and Besançon) to provide Charles with credit. The legate was armed with authority to preach the crusade in France against Manfred and his Saracens, and even before he arrived in France, Urban had secured Charles' appointment as senator in Rome for life (summer 1263) where Charles appointed his own vicar to act for him. He still did not come to Italy himself. In the summer of 1264, the anxious pope warned Charles to be on his guard against some (Spanish?) apostate of the order of St James whom Manfred had sent with two donkeys and fifty different poisons under the safe conduct of the duke of Burgundy, and by the time Urban IV died in October 1264, it was still not certain that Charles would leave, despite all the frantic efforts of pope and legate. There was then a further hitch, caused by the delay of several months before a new pope, another Frenchman, Clement IV, was elected (5 February 1265). He immediately hastened matters by annulling any earlier grant to Henry III's son, and conferring the kingdom on Charles (26 February). There followed a flow of papal letters designed to provide Charles with the money required. Even when Charles did reach Rome in May 1265, Clement was still not confident that Charles would eventually triumph. In November 1265, the pope was still pressing for Louis IX to provide fraternal assistance, for the preaching of the crusade to be renewed, and for more money to be found, all the while bewailing Charles' desperate position.

There is no sign of the pope drawing any comfort either from signs of disintegration in Manfred's power, or even from Charles' arrival in Italy. Manfred's dignified protest to Clement that Charles had come to take away his lawful inheritance is not the plea of a king who fears betrayal. Clement's pitiless reply that Charles had come not to rob Manfred, but to defend the church, loftily ignores the actual issue in order to insist once again on the papal rights to the kingdom. But it is a tribute to Manfred's kingdom and its strength that the papacy, to put its champion into the field, had had to drain Christendom of every available penny. This involved such heavy borrowing from banks in Siena, Florence, Orvieto, Perugia and Montpellier that, incredibly enough, England was also considered a possible place to raise loans. The unhelpful attitude of Louis IX and Queen Margaret drove Clement to distraction. Only relentless papal pressure (and Charles' ambition) had brought him to Rome in May 1265, sadly short of men and money. Within a month, the pope was complaining that his champion had allowed his troops to insult the papacy by invading the Lateran palace. Despite the fact that

Charles turned out to be far from ideal, the die was cast. Charles was invested with the southern kingdom on 28 July 1265.

Manfred had expected Charles to be intercepted by Manfred's Lombard allies, but once Charles reached Rome, Manfred had to defend his own kingdom himself. He was at Tagliacozzo in the summer of 1265. He moved against Rome, though without inducing Charles to come out and fight him, and after a skirmish at Tivoli, Manfred withdrew. Manfred probably calculated that should Charles ever venture to attack the kingdom, he would be more vulnerable there. Manfred may even have had an overambitious plan to lure Charles deeper into the kingdom, giving himself more time to assemble all his forces and lengthening Charles' communication with his Roman base.

Charles left Rome on about 20 January; the final battle was fought at Benevento on 26 February, five weeks later. Many precise details of what occurred in this period went unrecorded, and every attempt to understand the sequence of events has to cope with the rumours and recriminations that followed. Charles certainly negotiated with some of the barons in the territory on the border with the papal patrimony, where the papacy had in the past counted many friends. Manfred probably accepted this as inevitable: it was another reason for staging the decisive engagement further to the south. Manfred may not, however, have suspected his brother-in-law, Richard, count of Caserta, the captain of the kingdom, of conspiring with Charles. Richard is said to have suggested to Jordan, count of San Severino, that they should allow some of Charles' men to cross the bridge over the Liri at Ceprano and enter the kingdom so that the force could be more easily defeated when it was divided. When Jordan thought the time to attack had come, Richard advised caution because too many had already crossed (2 February). The fact that Richard's vassal, Gennario Gauniario, who held the castle at Rocca d'Arce for Manfred, surrendered it to Charles, and that Richard himself obtained Charles' favour after the death of Manfred, naturally prompted later suspicions of his loyalty. Yet if it is true that Manfred's strategy did actually require Charles to venture deeper into the kingdom, Richard's 'treachery' at Ceprano may have been misunderstood later, and anyway cannot have been crucial. When a few days later Charles reached the second line of defence at San Germano, Richard fought in this battle with Jordan against Charles, who was victorious. Far from reassured, however, by this success, Charles tried to make for Benevento by advancing through Telese in order to avoid Manfred's main force. It was Manfred, hurrying after him to forestall his arrival at Benevento, who forced him to do battle on

26 February. In a fierce engagement many thousand were slain until Manfred's force was overcome and he himself killed.

The pope was in such anguish about Charles' slim chances of success, that his victory, when it came, seemed like providential intervention, equally unexpected by friend and foe. But if Manfred's fate was decreed by heaven, it was still possible, even necessary, for his supporters to identify the traitors who failed to fight for him in battle. Many of these, as prisoners, had to identify Manfred's corpse and bewail his death. Their treachery has also encouraged the subsequent suspicion that Manfred's cause was not 'popular'. Had his usurpation and tyranny prevented all his nobles from supporting his cause and checking the intruder? Even Malaspina blamed the barons for deserting Manfred. He did not name individuals, but clearly took it for granted that the future of the kingdom would depend, not just on Manfred, but on its great men. In similar circumstances, in 1189 or 1251, the barons had kept the kingdom going; this did not happen in 1266, so the nobles in effect, if not by intention, betrayed the trust placed in them. Yet, Malaspina, though a Guelf, does not pretend that Charles was welcomed in the kingdom as a liberator from Manfred's tyranny. He actually describes in some detail the horrors of the Angevin occupation of Augusta, from which he himself made a lucky escape. The merciless cruelty shown by the Angevin conquerors against all persons – even women and children – identifiable with the Staufen cause, not only in 1266 but into the next century, hardly encourages the idea that the occupation was anything but bloodthirsty and ruthless.

Modern historians have, however, not shown Manfred much sympathy. They have been less concerned with the history of the southern kingdom than with the future of Italy. They see that Manfred's support outside the kingdom began to fall away as soon as Charles appeared in the peninsula. They see Manfred as a ruler in the mould of his father, and have few regrets about the failure of Staufen plans for the whole of Italy, which are presented as though they promised only a repressive dictatorship and the suppression of civic liberties. For such reasons, Manfred's defeat has been considered a personal misfortune rather than an institutional tragedy.

In its own way, however, the battle of Benevento is an event of the same order as the battle of Hastings. Nobody could have imagined at the time what results would flow from a simple change of ruler. Those who equivocated or betrayed Manfred in 1266 had no inkling of what would follow. They thought only of their own interests and convenience without weighing the price that would be paid. The structures of

Frederick's kingdom survived in Angevin hands, and in the 1270s, Charles became the dominant force in the peninsula, but any similarity with Frederick is illusory. The Angevins owed their presence in Italy to papal approval and remained there as champions of the Guelf cause. They had no traditional claims of their own on the loyalty of Italians outside the southern kingdom, such as the Staufen, as emperors, had found. Frederick II had offered the southern kingdom a viable future as the leading power in the peninsula. When the kingdom passed into the hands of the Angevins it was condemned to decay and stagnation. After the partition, achieved in the war of the Sicilian Vespers (1282), the great kingdom of Frederick was divided between two foreign dynasties. It was the first key move in the subjection of the whole of Italy to foreign domination. Historians have been mesmerised by the achievements of northern Italian cities after Manfred's fall, and have overlooked the extent to which the papal defeat of the Norman kingdom was more than a southern misfortune. The papacy itself was so corrupted and weakened that it became politically dependent on French influence, and this had profound effects on its development. Italy and Germany bore the scars of the ruin of the Staufen empire into very recent times. As with Hastings, it is not difficult to find points of continuity before and after when assessing the results of the battle of Benevento. The Angevins were few and could not change everything at once. But the momentum of the monarchy which Roger II had created and which Frederick II had known how to sustain now began to run down. It was not inappropriate that the future of a kingdom won by the sword should be settled on the field of battle. No king since William I at Benevento in 1156 had had to fight personally for survival. No king had ever been killed in battle. It is not just romanticism that has caused Manfred's reckless heroism to be admired. Manfred was prepared to die to save his kingdom, if possible, and to win or lose by his own efforts in the way of his great Norman predecessors. He was a daring young man worthy of his ancestry, and his kingdom never again had rulers worthy of its founders.

FURTHER READING

Primary sources

Narrative

Del Re, G., *Cronisti e scrittori sincroni napoletani editi e inediti*, I, *Normanni*, Naples 1845, II, *Svevi*, Naples 1868.

Delogu, P., *I Normanni in Italia. Cronache della conquista e del regno*, Naples 1984.

Amatus of Montecassino, *Storia dei Normanni*, ed. V. de Bartholomaeis, FSI, 76, Rome 1935.

William of Apulia, *La Geste de Robert Guiscard*, ed. M. Mathieu, Istituto Siciliano di Studi bisantini e neo-ellinici. Testi e monumenti 4, Palermo 1961.

Geoffrey of Malaterra, *De rebus gestis Rogerii Calabriae et Siciliae comitis et Robertis Guiscardi ducis fratris eius*, ed. E. Pontieri, RIS 5 (1), Bologna (1927–8).

Gesta Francorum, the Deeds of the Franks and other Pilgrims to Jerusalem, ed. Rosalind Hill, Edinburgh 1962.

Falco of Benevento, *Chronicon*, in Del Re, *Cronisti*, I, pp. 157–276.

Cassino Chronicle, ed. H. Hoffmann, MGH, ss. 34 (1980).

Alexander, abbot of Telese, *Gesta Rogerii Regis Siciliae*, in Del Re, *Cronisti*, I, pp. 81–156.

Edrisi, *L'Italia descritta nel'Libro del Re Ruggero'*, trans. M. Amari and C. Schiaparelli, Rome 1883.

John of Salisbury, *Historia Pontificalis*, ed. M. Chibnall, London 1956; reprinted with corrections, Oxford 1986.

Liber Pontificalis, ed. L. Duchesne, 2nd ed. Paris 1955.

(Falcandus, Hugo), *La Historia o Liber de Regno Sicilie e la Epistola ad Petrum, Panormitane Ecclesie Thesaurarium*, ed. G. B. Siragusa, FSI, 22, Rome 1897–1904.

Chronicon Ignoti monachis Cistercienis sanctae Mariae de Ferraria, ed. A. Gaudenzi, Naples 1888.

Romuald, archbishop of Salerno, *Chronicon*, ed. C. A. Garufi, *RIS*, 7(1), Città di Castello–Bologna 1914–35.

Kinnamos, John, *Deeds of John and Manuel Comnenus*, trans. C. M. Brand, New York 1976.

Choniates, Niketas, *Annals: 'O City of Byzantium'*, trans. H. J. Magoulies, Detroit 1984.

Jubayr, Ibn, *The travels of Ibn Jubayr*, trans. R. J. C. Broadhurst, London 1952.

Ahimaaz Chronicle, trans. M. Salzman, New York 1924.

Benjamin of Tudela, *The itinerary*, ed. M. N. Adler, London 1907.

Peter of Eboli, *Carmen de rebus Siculis*, ed. G. B. Siragusa, *FSI*, 39–40, Rome 1905–6. Ed. E. Rota, *RIS* 31 (1), Città di Castello 1904.

Richard of San Germano, *Chronicon*, ed. C. A. Garufi, *RIS*, 7(2), Bologna 1937–8.

Gesta Innocentii papae tertii, *PL*, 214, cols xvii–ccxxviii, 1889.

Philip of Novara, *Wars of Frederick II against the Ibelins in Syria*, trans. J. La Monte, New York 1936.

Jamsilla, Niccolo, *De rebus gestis Frederici II imperatoris ejusque filiorum Conradi et Manfredi Apuliae et Siciliae regum*, in Del Re, *Cronisti*, II, pp. 101–200.

Malaspina, Saba, *Rerum Sicularum Historia (1250–1285)*, in Del Re, *Cronisti*, II, pp. 201–408.

Fuiano, M., *Studi di Storiografia Medioevale*, Naples 1960.

Acta Sanctorum, 68 vols., 1643–1940.

Documents

Ughelli, F., *Italia Sacra*, 2nd ed. N. Coleti, Venice 1717–22. Vols. I (Dioceses directly dependent on the papacy), VI (Campania, Aprutium, Hirpinarum), VII (Lucania, Apulia), VIII (Samnium), IX (Terra d'Otranto, Calabria), X (Calabria).

Pirri, R., *Sicilia Sacra*, 2 vols., 3rd ed. A. Mongitore and V. M. Amico, Palermo 1733.

Kehr, P., *Italia Pontificia*, IV, *Umbria, Picenum, Marsia*, Berlin 1909; VIII, *Regnum Normannorum, Campania*, Berlin 1935; IX, *Samnium, Apulia, Lucania*, ed. W. Holtzmann, Berlin 1962; X, *Calabria, Insulae*, ed. D. Girgensohn, Zürich 1975.

Liber Censuum, ed. P. Fabre and L. Duchesne, 3 vols., Paris 1889–1952.

Papal Registers: Innocent III, *PL*, 214–17, Paris 1889–91; Honorius III, ed. P. Pressutti, Rome 1888; Gregory IX, *Les Registres*, ed. L. Auvray, Paris 1890–1955; Innocent IV, *Les Registres*, ed. E. Berger, Paris 1881–1920; Alexander IV, *Les Registres*, ed. C. G. Bourel de la Roncière, Paris 1902–53; Urban IV, *Les Registres*, ed. L. Dorez, Paris 1892–1929; Clement IV, *Les Registres*, ed. E. Jordan, Paris 1893.

Regii Neapolitani Archivii Monumenta, 6 vols., Naples 1854–61.

Heinemann, L. von, *Normannischen Herzogs – und Königsurkunden aus Unteritalien und Sicilien*, Tübingen 1899.

Ménager, L. R., *Recueil des actes des ducs normands d'Italie 1046–1127*, I, *Les premiers ducs*, Bari 1981.

Codex Diplomaticus Regum Siciliae: Rogerii II Regis Diplomata Latina, ed. C. R. Brühl, Cologne 1987; *Tancredi et Willelmi III Regum Diplomata*, ed. H. Zielinksi, Cologne 1982; *Constantiae Imperatricis et Reginae Siciliae Diplomata (1195–1198)*, ed. T. Kölzer, Cologne 1983.

Die Urkunden der Kaiserin Konstanze, ed. T. Kölzer, *MGH*, Hanover 1990.

Huillard-Bréholles, J., *Historia Diplomatica Friderici Secundi*, 6 vols., Paris 1859–61.

Winkelmann, E., *Acta Imperii inedita saeculi XIII et XIV*, 2 vols., Innsbruck 1880–85.

Amelli, P., *Quaternus de excadenciis et revocatis Capitanate*, Monte Cassino 1903.

Conrad, H., T. von der Lieck Buyken and W. Wagner, *Die Constitutionen Friedrichs II von Hohenstaufen für sein Königreich Sizilien*, Cologne 1973.

Liber Augustalis, trans. J. M. Powell, Syracuse, N.Y. 1971.

Capasso, B., *Historia Diplomatica Regni Siciliae inde ab anno 1250 ad annum 1266*, Naples 1874.

Böhmer, J. F., *Regesta Imperii*, I, Innsbruck 1881; II, ed. J. Ficker and E. Winkelmann, Innsbruck 1892–1901.

Nachträge und Ergänzungen, ed. P. Zinsmaier, Cologne 1983.

Giudice, G. del, *Codice Diplomatico del Regno di Carlo I e II d'Angio*, Naples 1863.

Catalogus Baronum, ed. E. Jamison, *FSI*, 101, Rome 1972. *Commentario* by E. Cuozzo, *FSI*, 101*, Rome 1984.

Garufi, C., *I documenti inediti dell'epoca normanna in Sicilia. Documenti per servire alla storia di Sicilia*, series 1, diplomata 18, Palermo 1899.

Gattola, E., *Historia abbatiae Cassinensis*, Venice 1733.

Ad historiam abbatiae Cassinensis accessiones, Venice 1734.

Codex Diplomaticus Cajetanus, II (1053–1294), Monte Cassino 1891.

Leccisotti, T., *I Registri dell'Archivio di Monte Cassino*, 9 vols., 1964–74.

Morcaldi, M., *Codex Diplomaticus Cavensis*, 8 vols., 1873–93.

Tropeano, P. M., *Codice Diplomatico Verginiana*, I, Monte Vergine, 1977.

Mongelli, G., *Abbazia di Montevergine: Regesto delle Pergamene*, 3 vols., Rome 1956–7.

Filangieri di Candida, R., *Codice Diplomatico Amalfitano*, Naples 1917.

Mazzoleni, J., *Le Pergamene degli Archivi Vescovili di Amalfi e Ravello*, Naples 1972.

Le Pergamene di Capua, Naples 1957.

Salvati, C., *Le Pergamene dell'archivio vescovile di Ravello*, Naples 1974.

Carucci, C., *La provincia di Salerno dai tempi più remoti*, Salerno 1923.

Codice Diplomatico Salernitano del secolo XIII, Subiaco 1931.

Cassese, L., *Pergamene del monastero benedettino di San Giorgio*, Salerno 1950.

Caetani, G., *Regesto delle Pergamene dell'Archivio Caetani*, Perugia 1925.

Gallo, A., *Codice Diplomatico di Aversa*, Naples 1926.

Aversa Normanna, Naples 1938.

Bartolini, F., *Le più antiche carte dell'abbazia di San Modesto di Benevento*, Rome (Regesta Chartarum Italiae, 33), 1950.

Tescioni, G., *Caserta medievale e i suoi conti e signori*, Caserta 1965.

Codice Diplomatico Barese, 28 vols., published by various editors, Bari 1897–1985.

Prologo, A. di G., *Le carte che si conservano nell'archivio del capitolo metropolitano della città di Trani*, Barletta 1877.

Favaglia, N. F., *Codice Diplomatico Sulmonese*, Lanciano 1888.

Magliano, A., *Considerazioni storiche sulla città di Larino*, Campobasso 1895.

Crudo, G., *La SS Trinità di Venosa, memorie storiche diplomatiche archeologiche*, Trani 1899.

Camobreco, F., *Regesta di San Leonardo di Siponto*, Regesta Chartarum Italiae n. 10, Rome 1913.

Di Leo, A., *Codice Diplomatico Brindisino*, ed. G. M. Monti, I, Trani 1940.

Petrucci, A., *Codice Diplomatico del monastero benedettino di Santa Maria di Tremiti*, *FSI*, 98, Rome 1960.

Mastrobuono, E., *Castellaneta e i suoi documenti*, Bari 1969.

Tromby, B., *Storia critica-cronologica diplomatica del Patriarca san Brunone e dal suo Ordine Cartusiano*, II, Naples 1775.

Pometti, F., *Carte delle abbazie di Santa Maria di Corazzo e di San Giuliano di Rocca Fallucca in Calabria*, in *Accademia di Conferenze Storico-Giuridiche*, 22 (1901), 241–306.

Pratesi, A., *Carte Latine di Abbazie Calabresi proveniente dell'archivio Aldobrandini*, *ST*, 197, Vatican City 1958.

De Grossis, G. B., *Catania Sacra*, Catania 1654.

Lello, G. L., *Descrizione del Real Tempio e Monasterio di Santa Maria Nuova di Monreale*, Palermo 1702.

Garofalo, A., *Tabularium regiae et imperialis capellae collegiatae Divi Petri in regio Palermitano Palatio*, Palermo 1835.

Starrabba, R., *I Diplomi della cattedrale di Messina*, Palermo 1888.

Silvestri, G., *Tabulario di San Filippo di Fragalà e Santa Maria di Maniaci*, Palermo 1887.

Sciacca, G. G., *Patti e l'amministrazione del comune nel medio evo*, Palermo 1907.

Collura, P., *Le più antiche carte dell'archivio capitolare di Agrigento*, Palermo 1960.

Mirto, C., *Rollus Rubeus Privilegia ecclesiae Cephaleditane*, Palermo 1972.

Spata, G., *Le Pergamene Greche esistente nel grande archivio di Palermo*, Palermo 1862.

   Diplomi Greci inediti della Biblioteca Comunale di Palermo, Turin 1870.

Trinchera, F., *Syllabus Graecarum Membranarum*, Naples 1865.

Cusa, S., *Diplomi Greci ed Arabi di Sicilia*, Palermo 1868, 1882.

Introduction

Chalandon, F., *Histoire de la domination normande en Italie et en Sicile*, 2 vols., Paris 1907. Abridged English version in *Cambridge Medieval History*, V, *Contest of Empire and Papacy*, 1926, chapter 4, 'The Conquest of South Italy and Sicily by the Normans', pp. 167–83, and 'The Norman Kingdom of Sicily', pp. 184–207.

Guillou, A., F. Burgarella, V. von Falkenhausen, V. Rizzitano, V. Piacentini and S. Tramontana, *Il Mezzogiorno dai Bizantini a Federico II*, Turin 1983.

Amari, M., *Storia dei musulmani di Sicilia*, 2nd ed. C. A. Nallino, Catania 1933–9.

Jamison, E., *Studies on the History of Medieval Sicily and South Italy*, 3 vols., Aalen 1987–88.

Guillou, A., *Studies on Byzantine Italy* (Variorum Reprints), London 1970.

Abulafia, D., *Italy, Sicily and Mediterranean 1100–1400*, Aldershot 1987.

The Normans in Sicily and Southern Italy, Lincei lectures 1974. British Academy, London 1977.

Conference Proceedings: *Atti del Convegno Internazionale di Studi Ruggeriani*, 2 vols., Palermo 1955; *Atti delle Giornate Federiciane*, I (1968), II (1971), III (1974), IV (1977), V (1980), Bari; *Spoleto: Settimane di Studio XVI*, 1968, *I Normanni e la loro espansione in Europa nell alto medioevo*, Spoleto 1969; *Atti del Congresso Internazionale di Studi sulla Sicilia Normanna* (1972), Palermo 1973; *Roberto il Guiscardo e il suo tempo* (1973), Rome 1975; *Ruggero il Gran Conte e l'inizio dello stato normanno* (1975), Rome 1977; *Società, potere e popolo nell'età di Ruggero II* (1977), Bari 1979; *Potere, società e popolo nell'età dei due Guglielmi* (1979), Bari 1981; *Congresso Internazionale sulle fonti documenti e narrativi per la storia di Sicilia normanna*, Palermo 1981–2; *Potere, società età normanna ed età sveva (1189–1210)* (1981), Bari 1983; *Poetere, società e popolo nell'età sveva* (1983), Bari 1985; *Terra e uomini nel Mezzogiorno normanno-svevo* (1985), Bari 1987.

Gay, J., *L'Italie méridionale et l'empire byzantin 867–1071*, Paris 1904.

Giunta, F., *Bizantini e bizantinismo nella Sicilia normanna*, Palermo 1950.

Falkenhausen, V. von, *Untersuchungen über die byzantinische Herrschaft in Süditalien vom 9. bis ins 11. Jahrhundert*, Wiesbaden 1967.

Carabellese, F., *L'Apulia ed il suo comune nell'alto medioevo*, Bari 1905.

Hirsch, F. and M. Schipa, *La longobardia meridionale (570–1077)*, ed. N. Acocella, Rome 1968, for F. Hirsch, *Il ducato di Benevento* and M. Schipa, *Storia del principato longobardo di Salerno*.

Poupardin, R., *Etudes sur les institutions politiques et administratives des principautés lombardes de l'Italie méridionale*, Paris 1907.

Cilento, N., *Italia meridionale longobarda*, 2nd ed., Milan 1971.

Noble, T. F. X., *The Republic of St. Peter: the birth of the Papal state 680–825*, Philadelphia 1984.

Kehr, P., *Die Belehnungen der süditalienischen Normannenfürsten durch die Päpste 1059–1192*, Abhandlungen der Preussischen Akademie der Wissenschaften, Berlin 1934.

Deer, J., *Papsttum und Normannen*, Cologne 1972.

d'Alessandro, V., *Fidelitas Normannorum: Note sulla fondazione dello stato normanno e sui rapporti col papato*, Palermo 1969.

Trombetta, A., *La sovranità pontificia sull'Italia meridionale e sulla Sicilia*, Casamari 1981.

Decarreaux, J., *Normands papes et moines en Italie méridionale et en Sicile XIe–XIIe siècle*, Paris 1974.

Dormeier, H., *Montecassino und die Laien im 11 und 12 Jahrhundert*, M.G.H. Schriften, 27, Stuttgart 1979.

Bloch, H., *Monte Cassino in the Middle Ages*, Cambridge, Mass. 1986.

1 Southern Italy and the Normans before the creation of the monarchy

Angold, M., *The Byzantine Aristocracy IX to XIII Centuries*, BAR, International series 221, 1981.

Loud, G., 'Byzantine Italy and the Normans', in *Proceedings of XVIII Spring Symposium of Byzantine Studies*, Oxford 1984. ed. J. D. Howard-Johnston, *Byzantinische Forschungen*, 13 (1988), 215–33.

McQueen, W. B., 'Relations between the Normans and Byzantium 1071–1112', *Byzantion*, 56 (1986), 427–76.

Nicol, D., 'Byzantium and the Papacy in the Eleventh Century', *JEH*, 13 (1962), 1–20.

Tirelli, V., 'Osservazioni sui rapporti tra sede apostolica, Capua e Napoli durante i pontificati di Gregorio VII e di Urbano II', *Studi nel medioevo cristiano offerti a Raffaele Morghen*, II, Rome 1974, pp. 961–1010.

Blumenthal, V. R., *The Early Councils of Pope Paschal II*, Toronto 1978.

Rowe, J. G., 'Paschal II, Bohemund of Antioch and the Byzantine Empire', *BJRL*, 49 (1966–7), 165–202.

Cowdrey, H. E. J., *The Age of Abbot Desiderius*, Oxford 1983.

Loud, G., 'Abbot Desiderius of Montecassino and the Gregorian Papacy', *JEH*, 30 (1979), 305–26.

Joranson, E., 'Inception of the Career of the Normans in Italy', *Speculum*, 23 (1948), 353–96.

Hoffmann, H., 'Die Anfänge der Normannen in Süditalien', *QF*, 49 (1969), 95–144.

Clementi, D., 'Stepping Stones in the Making of the Regno', *BISIME*, 90 (1982–3), 227–93.

Loud, G., 'How Norman was the Norman Conquest of Southern Italy?', *Nottingham Medieval Studies*, 25 (1981), 13–34.

'The Gens Normannorum, Myth or Reality?' *ANS*, 4 (1981), 104–16.

Waley, D., 'Combined Operations in Sicily 1060–78', *BSR*, 22 (1954), 118–25.

Lopez, R., 'The Norman Conquest of Sicily', in K. M. Setton, *A History of the Crusades*, ed. M. W. Baldwin, 2nd ed., I, Madison 1969, pp. 54–67.

Kolias, G., 'Le motif et les raisons de l'invasion de Robert Guiscard en territoire byzantine', *Byzantion*, 36 (1966), 424–30.

Ménager, L. R., 'La byzantinisation religieuse de l'Italie méridionale et la politique monastique des Normands d'Italie', *Revue d'histoire ecclésiastique*, 53 (1958), 747–74; 54 (1959), 5–40.

'Les fondationes monastiques de Robert Guiscard', *QF*, 39 (1959), 1–116.

'Notes et documents sur quelques monastères de Calabre', *Byzantinisches Zeitschrift* 50 (1957), 7–30, 321–61.

Jordan, E., 'La politique ecclésiastique de Roger I de Sicile', *Le moyen âge*, 2nd series, 24 (1922), 237–73; 25 (1923), 32–65.

Starrabba, R., 'Contributo allo studio della diplomatica Siciliana dei tempi normanni. Diplomi di fondazione delle chiese episcopali di Sicilia, *ASS*, nuova serie, 18 (1893), 30–135.

Cowdrey, H. E. J., 'The Mahdia Campaign of 1087', *EHR*, 102 (1977), 1–29.
Cardini, F., 'La société italienne et les croisades', *CCM*, 28 (1985), 19–33.
Manselli, R., 'Normanni d'Italia alla prima crociata, Boemondo d'Altavilla', *Japigia*, 11 (1940), 45–79, 145–84.
Yewdale, R. B., *Bohemond I, prince of Antioch*, Princeton 1924.
Antonucci, C., 'Il Principato di Taranto', *Archivio Storico per la Calabria e la Lucania*, 8 (1938), 133–54.
Petrucci, A., 'Note di Diplomatica Normanna', *BISIME*, 71 (1959), 113–40; 72 (1960), 135–81.

2 The establishment of the kingdom

Caspar, E., *Roger II 1101–1154 und die Gründung der normannisch-sicilischen Monarchie*, Innsbruck 1904.
Curtis, E., *Roger of Sicily and the Normans in Lower Italy*, London 1912.
Bloch, H., 'The Schism of Anacletus II and the Glanfeuil Forgeries of Peter the Deacon of Monte Cassino', *Traditio*, 8 (1952), 159–264.
Gervasio, E., 'Falcone Beneventano e la sua cronaca', *BISIME*, 54 (1939), 1–128.
Zielinski, H., 'Zum königstitel Rogers II von Sizilien 1130–54', in H. Ludat and R. C. Schwingen, *Politik, Gesellschaft, Geschichtsschreibung*, Vienna 1982, pp. 165–82.
Rivera, C., 'L'annessione delle terre d'Abruzzo al regno di Sicilia', *Archivio Storico Italiano*, series 7 (6), 1926, 199–309.

3 The material resources of the kingdom

Bianchini, L., *Della Storia Economica Civile di Sicilia*, Naples 1841.
Lizier, A., *L'economia rurale dell'età pre-normanna nell'italia meridionale*, Palermo 1907.
Egidi, P., 'Ricerche sulla populazione dell'Italia meridionale nei secoli XIII e XIV', *Miscellanea di studi storici in onore di Giovanni Sforza*, Turin 1923, pp. 731–50.
Filangieri, A., *Territorio e popolazione nell'Italia meridionale*, Naples 1980.
Goitein, S. D., *A Mediterranean Society, The Jewish Communities of the Arab World, I, Economic Foundations*, Berkeley 1967.
Abulafia, D., *The Two Italies: Economic Relations between the Norman Kingdom of Sicily and the Northern Communes*, Cambridge 1977.
Citarella, A. O., 'The Relations of Amalfi with the Arab World before the Crusades', *Speculum*, 13 (1967), 299–312.
'Patterns in Medieval Trade: the Commerce of Amalfi before the Crusades', *Journal of Economic History*, 28 (1968), 531–55.
Galasso, G., 'Il commercio amalfitano nel periodo normanno', *Storia in onore di Riccardo Filangieri*, I, Naples 1959, pp. 81–103.
Krueger, H. C., 'The Italian Cities and the Arabs before 1095', in K. Setton, *History of the Crusades*, I, ed. M. W. Baldwin, 2nd ed., Madison 1969, pp. 40–53.

Battaglia di Nicolosi, G., *I Diplomi inediti relativi all'ordinamento della proprietà fondiaria in Sicilia sotto i Normanni e gli Svevi*, Palermo 1895.
Peri, I., *Città e campagna in Sicilia*, 2 vols., Palermo 1953–6.
Uomini, città e campagna in Sicilia dell'XI al XIV secolo, Bari 1978.
'La questione delle colonie "Lombarde" in Sicilia', *Bollettino Storico-Bibliografico Subalpino*, 57 (1959), 253–80.
Bresc, H., 'L'habitat médiéval en Sicile 1100–1450', *Atti del Colloquio Internazionale di Archeologia Medievale* (Palermo 1974), Palermo 1976, pp. 186–95.
'Féodalité coloniale en terre d'Islam: la Sicile 1070–1240', in *Structures féodales et féodalisme dans l'occident méditerranéen (Xe–XIIIe siècles)* (Ecole française de Rome), Rome 1980, pp. 631–47.
Un monde méditerranéen: économie et société en Sicile 1300–1450, Paris 1986.
Fumagalli, V. and G. Rossetti, *Medioevo Rurale: sulle tracce della civiltà contadina*, Bologna 1980, pp. 945–76.
Brassacchio, G., *Storia Economica della Calabria*, II, Chiaravalle 1977.
Guillou, A., 'Production and Profits in the Byzantine Province of Italy (Tenth to Eleventh Centuries): An Expanding Society', *DOP*, 28 (1974), 89–109.
Del Treppo, M., 'La vita economica e sociale in una grande abbazia del mezzogiorno – San Vincenzo al Volturno nell'alto medioevo', *ASPN*, 74 (1956), 31–110.
Tallarico, M. A., 'L'abbazia di Montevergine nell'età normanna. Formazione e sviluppo di una potenza economica e politica', *Samnium*, 45 (1972), 197–237.
Golella, G., *Toponomastica Pugliese*, Trani 1941.
Feller, L., 'Casaux et Castra dans les Abruzzes: San Salvatore a Maiella, San Clemente di Casauria, XIe–XIIIe siècles', *Mélanges*, 97 (1985), 145–82.
Toubert, P., 'Pour une histoire de l'environnement économique et social du Mont Cassin IXe–XIIe siècles', *Compte-rendue de l'Académie des Inscriptions et Belles-Lettres*, 1976, 689–702.
Sinatti d'Amico, F., 'Territorio, Città e Campagna in epoca Federiciana: exemplum Apuliae', *ASP*, 37 (1984), 3–42.
Giuffrida, A., 'Permanenza technologica ed espansione territoriale del mulino ad acqua siciliano', *ASSO*, 69 (1973), 193–215.
Iovio, R., 'Olive e olio in Terra di Bari in età normanna sveva', *Quaderni Medievali*, 20 (1985), 67–102.

4 The religious communities of the kingdom

Pellegrini, G. B., 'Terminologia Geografica Araba in Sicilia', in *Gli Arabismi nelle Lingue Neolatine*, Brescia 1972, pp. 237–332.
Abdul Wahab, H. H. and F. Dachraqui, 'Le régime foncier en Sicile au moyen âge, IX et X siècles, in *Etudes d'orientalisme dédiées à la mémoire de Lévi-Provençal*, II, Paris 1962, pp. 401–44.
Gabrieli, F., 'La politique arabe des Normands de Sicile', *Studia Islamica*, 9 (1958), 83–96.

Bercher, H., A. Courteaux and J. Mouton, 'Une abbaye latine dans la société musulmane: Monreale au XIIe siècle', *Annales*, 34 (1979), 525–47.

Johns, J., 'The Muslims of Norman Sicily *c*.1060–*c*.1194', D. Phil. thesis, University of Oxford, 1983 (unpublished).

Tamassia, N., 'Stranieri e ebrei nell'Italia meridionale dell'età romana alla sveva', *Atti del Reale Istituto Veneto di Scienze Lettere ed Arti*, 63 (2), 1903–4, 757–839.

Ferorelli, N., *Gli ebrei nell'Italia meridionale dall'età romana al secolo XVIII*, Turin 1915.

Straus, R., *Die Juden im Königreich Sizilien unter Normannen und Staufen*, Heidelberg 1910.

Ferrari, G., *I documenti greci medioevali di diritto privato dell'Italia meridionale*, Leipzig 1910.

Lake, K., 'The Greek Monasteries in South Italy', *Journal of Theological Studies*, 4 (1902–3), 345–68, 517–42; 5 (1904), 22–41, 189–202.

Robinson, G., 'Some Cave Chapels of Southern Italy', *Journal of Hellenic Studies*, 50 (1930), 186–209.

Scaduto, M., *Il monachesimo basiliano nella Sicilia medievale*, Rome 1947.

Guillou, A., *Les actes grecs de Santa Maria di Messina*, Istituto Siciliano di Studi Bizantini e Neoellenici Palermo, Testi, 8, 1963.
   'Grecs d'Italie du Sud et de Sicile au moyen âge: les moines', *Mélanges*, 75 (1963), 79–110.

Pertusi, A., 'Aspetti organizzativi e culturali dell'ambiente monacho greco dell'Italia meridionale', in *L'eremitismo in occidente nei secoli XI e XII*, *Miscellanea del Centro di Studi Medievali*, IV, Milan 1965, pp. 382–426.

Lavagnini, B., 'Aspetti e problemi del monachesimo greco nella Sicilia normanna', *Byzantino-Sicula, Quaderni: Istituto Siciliano di Studi Bizantini e Neoellenici*, 2 (1966), 51–65.

Patlagean, E., 'Recherches récentes et perspectives sur l'histoire du monachisme italo-grec', *Rivista di storia della chiesa italiana*, 22 (1968), 146–66.

Fonseca, C. D., 'L'organizzazione ecclesiastica dell'Italia normanna tra'l XI e il XII secolo', in *Le istituzione ecclesiastiche della Società Christiana dei secoli XI–XII*, *Miscellanea del Centro di Studi Medievali*, VIII, Milan 1977, pp. 327–52.

Ruggiero, B., *Principi, nobiltà e chiese nel mezzogiorno longobardo*, Naples 1973.
   'Per una storia della pieve rurale nel Mezzogiorno medievale', *Studi Medievali*, serie 3 (16), 1975, 583–626.

Federici, V., 'Ricerche per l'edizione del Chronicon Vulturnense del monaco Giovanni', *BISIME*, 23 (1939), 147–231.

Manaresi, C., 'Il liber instrumentorum seu Chronicorum Monasterii Casauriensis', *Rendiconti (Classe Lettere) Istituto Lombardo di Scienze e Lettere*, 80 (1947), 29–62.

Loud, G., *Church and Society in the Norman Principality of Capua 1058–1197*, Oxford 1985.
   'The Abbey of Cava, its Property and Benefactors in the Norman Era', *ANS*, 9 (1986), 143–77.

White, L. T., *Latin Monasticism in Norman Sicily*, Cambridge, Mass. 1938.

Jones, C. W., *St. Nicholas of Myra, Bari and Manhattan*, Chicago 1978.

Mongelli, G., 'Legenda de Vita et Obitu Sancti Guglielmi Confessoris et Heremite', *Samnium*, 33–5 (1960–2).

Russo, F., *Gioacchino da Fiore e le fondazioni fiorensi di Calabria*, Naples 1958.

La Piana, G., 'Joachim of Flora: a Critical Survey', *Speculum*, 7 (1932), 257–82.

Bloomfield, M. W., 'Joachim of Flora', *Traditio*, 13 (1957), 249–311.

5 Intellectual and artistic aspects of the kingdom

Bertaux, E., *L'art dans l'Italie méridionale*, Paris 1903; revised A. Prandi, Bari 1978.

Belting, H., 'Byzantine Art among Greeks and Latins in Southern Italy', *DOP*, 28 (1974), 3–29.

Cavallo, G., V. von Falkenhausen, *et al.*, *I Bizantini in Italia*, Milan 1982.

Lipinsky, A., 'Les arts somptuaires en Italie méridionale et en Sicile 900–1200', *CCM*, 18 (1975), 97–116, 239–56.

Jamison, E., 'The Sicilian Kingdom in the mind of Anglo-Norman contemporaries', *PBA*, 24 (1938), 237–85.

Pinder-Wilson, R. H. and C. N. L. Brooke, 'The Reliquary of St Petroc and the Ivories of Norman Sicily', *Archaeologia*, 104 (1973), 261–305.

Cotto, P. B., *Siculo-Arabic Ivories*, Princeton 1939.

de Stefano, A., *La cultura in Sicilia nel periodo normanno*, Palermo 1937, 2nd ed. 1954.

La cultura alla corte di Federico II imperatore, 2nd ed., Bologna 1950.

Shearer, C., *The Renaissance of Architecture in Southern Italy*, Cambridge 1935.

Bottari, S., *Chiese Basiliane della Sicilia e della Calabria*, Messina 1939.

di Stefano, G., *Monumenti della Sicilia normanna*, Palermo 1955, 2nd ed. W. Krönig, 1979.

Basile, F., *L'architettura della Sicilia normanna*, Catania 1975.

Schwarz, H. M., 'Die Baukunst Kalabriens und Siziliens in Zeitalter der Normannen', *Römisches Jahrbuch für Kunstgeschichte*, 6 (1942–4), 3–112.

Carbonara, G., *Iussu Desiderii: Monte Cassino e l'architettura campana-abruzzese nell'undecesimo secolo*, Rome 1979.

Bozzoni, C., *Calabria Normanna*, Rome 1974.

Occhiato, G., 'Rapporto culturale e rispondenze architettoniche tra Calabria e Francia in età romanica: l'abbaziale normanna di Sant'Eufemia', *Mélanges*, 93 (1981), 565–603.

Pace, V., 'Le componenti inglesi dell'architettura normanna in Sicilia nella storia della critica', *Studi Medievali*, serie 3 (16), 1975, 395–406.

Settis Frugoni, C., 'Per una lettura del mosaico pavimentale della cattedrale di Otranto', *BISIME*, 80 (1968), 213–56; 82 (1970), 243–70.

Monneret de Villard, V., *Le Pitture Musulmane al soffitto della Capella Palatina in Palermo*, Rome 1950.

'La tessitura palermitana sotto i Normanni e i suoi rapporti con l'arte bizantina', *Miscellanea Giovanni Mercati*, Studi III, 464–89; *ST*, Vatican City 1946.

Salvini, R., *Il chiostro di Monreale e la scultura romanica in Sicilia*, Palermo 1962.

Sheppard, C. D., 'Iconography of the Cloister of Monreale', *AB*, 31 (1949), 159–69.

'A Chronology of Romanesque sculpture in Campania', *AB*, 32 (1950), 319–26.

'A stylistic analysis of the cloister of Monreale', *AB*, 34 (1952), 35–41.

Leisinger, H., *Romanesque Bronzes*, London 1956.

Haskins, C. H., 'England and Sicily in the Twelfth Century', *EHR*, 26 (1911), 433–47, 641–65.

'Science at the Court of Frederick II', *AHR*, 27 (1922), 669–94.

Studies in the History of Medieval Science, 2nd ed., Cambridge, Mass. 1927.

Derenzini, G., 'All'origine della tradizione di opere scientifiche classiche: vicendi di testi e di codici tra Bisanzio e Palermo', *Physis*, 18 (1976), 87–103.

Burnett, C., ed., *Adelard of Bath: an English Scientist and Arabist of the Early Twelfth Century*, London 1987.

Lawn, B., *The Salernitan Questions*, Oxford 1963.

Thomson, R. M., '*Liber Marii de elementis* – the work of a hitherto unknown Salernitan Master', *Viator*, 3 (1972), 179–89.

Powell, J. M., 'Greco-Arabic Influences on the Public Health Legislation in the Constitutions of Melfi', *Atti delle Giornate Federiciane*, 4 (1977), 55–71.

Reeves, M., *The Influence of Prophecy in the Later Middle Ages*, Oxford 1969.

Jamison, E., *Admiral Eugenius of Sicily: his Life and Work and the Authorship of the Epistola ad Petrum and the Historia Hugonis Falcandi Siculi*, London 1957.

Lowe, E., *Beneventan Script*, Oxford 1914.

Newton, F., 'The Desiderian Scriptorium at Monte Cassino', *DOP*, 30 (1976), 37–54.

Canart, P., 'Le livre grec en Italie méridionale sous les règnes normands et souabes: aspects matériels et sociaux', *Scrittura e Civiltà*, 2 (1978), 103–63.

Magistrale, F., *Notariato e Documentazione in Terra di Bari*, Bari 1984.

Pratesi, A., 'La scrittura latina nell'Italia meridionale nell'età di Federico II', *Atti delle Giornate Federiciane*, 2, (1971), 133–50.

Langley, E. P., 'The Extant Repertory of the Early Sicilian Poets', *Publications of the Modern Language Association of America*, 28 (1913), 454–520.

Pavini, B., *La scuola poetica Siciliana*, Florence 1955, 1957, 1958.

van Waard, R., *Etudes sur l'origine et la formation de la Chanson d'Aspromonte*, Groningen 1937.

Becker, P. A., 'Aspremont', *Romanische Forschungen*, 60 (1947), 27–67; 61 (1948), 447–60.

Paris, G., 'La Sicile dans la littérature française du moyen âge', *Romania*, 5 (1876), 108–13.

Williams, H. F., 'La Sicile et l'Italie méridionale dans la littérature française au moyen âge', *BCSFLS*, 2 (1954), 85–92.

Reichenkron, G., 'Per la lingua dei normanni in Sicilia e dell'Italia meridionale', *BCSFLS*, 5 (1957), 97–103.

Rohlfs, G., 'Der sprachliche Einfluss der Normannen in Süditalien', *Mélanges Delbouille*, Gembloux 1964, pp. 565–72.

Ribezzo, F., 'L'elemento normanno nella letteratura e nella lingua della Sicilia e della Puglia', *BCSFLS*, 1 (1953), 107–14.

Varvaro, A., 'Notizie sul lessico della sicilia medievale: I francesimi', *BCSFLS*, 12 (1973), 72–104.

Avery, M., *The Exultet Rolls of South Italy*, Princeton 1936.

'The Miniatures of the Fables of Bidpai and of the Life of Aesop in the Pierpont Morgan Library', *AB*, 23 (1941), 103–16.

Cavallo, G., *Rotoli di 'Exultet' dell'Italia meridionale*, Bari 1973.

Daneu-Lattanzi, A., *Lineamenti di storia della miniatura in Sicilia*, Florence 1966–8.

Rotili, M., *La miniatura nella badia di Cava*, Cava dei Tirreni 1976.

Buchtal, H., 'The Beginnings of Manuscript Illumination in Norman Sicily', *BSR*, 24 (1956), 78–85.

'A School of Miniature Painting in Norman Sicily', *Late Classical and Medieval Studies in Honor of A. M. Friend Jr*, Princeton 1955, pp. 312–39.

Kauffmann, C. M., *The Baths of Pozzuoli: A Study of the Medieval Illuminations of Peter of Eboli's Poem*, Oxford 1959.

Grabar, A. and M. Manoussacas, *L'illustration du manuscrit de Skylitzes de Madrid*, Venice 1979.

Sevčenko, I., 'The Madrid Manuscript of the Chronicle of Skylitzes in the Light of its New Dating', *Osterreichischer Akademie der Wissenschaften Sitzungsberichte*, 432, Vienna 1984, pp. 117–30.

6 The ordering of society

Genuardi, L., *Il comune nel medioevo in Sicilia*, Palermo 1921.

Calasso, F., *La legislazione statutaria dell'Italia meridionale*, Rome 1929.

Cassandro, G. I., *Storia delle terre comuni e degli usi civici nell'Italia meridionale*, Bari 1943.

La Mantia, V., *Antiche Consuetudini delle città di Sicilia*, Palermo 1900.

Massa, T., *Le Consuetudini della città di Bari*, Bari 1903.

Giardini, L., 'I boni homines in Italia', *Rivista di storia del diritto italiano*, 5 (1932), 28–98, 313–94.

Orlando, D., *Il feudalismo in Sicilia*, Palermo 1847.

Palmarocchi, R., 'Sul Feudo Normanno', *Studi Storici*, 2 (1912), 349–76.

Padovan, C., *Delle origini economiche e finanzarie del feudalismo*, Padua 1935.

Cohen, C., *Le régime féodal de l'Italie normande*, Paris 1940.

Ebner, P., *Storia di un feudo del Mezzogiorno: la baronia di Novi*, Rome 1973.

Ménager, L. R., 'Inventaire des familles normandes et franques, émigrés en Italie méridionale et en Sicile XIe–XIIe siècles', *Guiscard Congress*, pp. 261–390.

Varvaro, A., 'Les normands en Sicile aux XIe et XIIe siècles', *CCM*, 23 (1980), 199–213.

Filangieri, A., 'La struttura degli insediamenti in Campania e in Puglia nei secoli XII–XIV', *ASPN*, 103 (1985), 61–86.

Cuozzo, E., 'Milites e testes nella contea normanna di Principato', *BISIME*, 88 (1979), 121–63.

Quei Maledetti Normanni, Cavalieri e organizzazione militare nel Mezzogiorno Normanno, Naples 1989.

Duby, G., 'Diffusion du titre chevalresque sur le versant méditerranéen', in P. Contamine, *La noblesse au moyen-âge – essais à la mémoire de Robert Boutruche*, Paris 1976, pp. 39–70.

Peri, I., *Il villanaggio in Sicilia*, Palermo 1965.

Aymard, M. and H. Bresc, 'Problemi di storia dell'insediamento nella Sicilia medievale e moderna 1100–1800', *Quaderni Storici*, 24 (1973), 945–76.

Girgensohn, D. and N. Kamp, 'Urkunden und Inquisitionen der Stauferzeit aus Patti', *QF*, 45 (1965), 1–240.

Tamassia, N., 'Ius Affidandi', *Atti del Reale Istituto Veneto di Scienze Lettere ed Arti*, 72(2), 1912–13, 343–90.

Fuiano, M., *Economia rurale e società in Puglia*, Naples 1978.

7 The kings in their kingdom

Ménager, L. R., 'L'institution monarchique dans les états normands d'Italie', *CCM*, 2 (1959), 303–31, 445–68.

Marongiu, 'A Model-State in the Middle Ages: the Norman and Swabian Kingdom of Sicily', *Comparative Studies in Society and History*, 6 (1964), 307–20.

Delogu, P., 'Idea sulla regalità: l'eredità normanna', in *Potere, società e popolo 1189–1210*, pp. 185–214.

Elze, R., 'Zum Königtum Rogers II von Sizilien', *Festschrift P. E. Schramm*, Wiesbaden 1964, pp. 102–16.

Wieruszowski, H., 'Roger II of Sicily, Rex-Tirannus in Twelfth-Century Political Thought', *Speculum*, 38 (1963), 46–78.

Siragusa, G. B., *Il regno di Guglielmo I in Sicilia*, Palermo, 2nd ed. 1929.

Fodale, S., *Comes et legatus Siciliae: sul privilegio di Urbano e la pretesa Apostolica legazione dei Normanni di Sicilia*, Palermo 1970.

Loud, G., 'Royal Control of the Church in the Twelfth-Century Kingdom of Sicily', *Studies in Church History*, 18 (1981), 147–59.

Niese, H., *Die Gesetzgebung der normannischen Dynastie*, Halle 1910.

Ménager, *Notes sur les codifications Byzantines et l'occident*, Paris 1957.
  'La législation sud-italienne sous la domination normande', in *Spoleto Congress*, pp. 439–96.

Zecchino, O., *Le Assise di Ruggiero II. Problemi di Storia delle Fonti e di Diritto Penale*, Naples 1980.

Zecchino, Ed., *Le Assise di Ruggiero II*, Naples 1984.

Ullmann, W., 'Public Law and Medieval Monarchy: Norman Rulership in Sicily', in Ullmann, *Jurisprudence in the Middle Ages*, London 1980, pp. 157–84.

Jamison, E., 'Judex Tarentinus', *PBA*, 53 (1967), 289–344.

Goldschmidt, A., 'Die Normannischen Königspaläste in Palermo', *Zeitschrift für Bauwesen*, 48, Berlin 1898, pp. 541–90.

Demus, O., *The Mosaics of Norman Sicily*, London 1949.

Kitzinger, E., 'The Mosaics of the Capella Palatina in Palermo', *AB*, 31 (1949), 269–92.

The Mosaics of Monreale, Palermo 1960.

'The First Mosaic Decoration of Salerno Cathedral', *Festschrift für Otto Demus. Jahrbuch der Osterreichische Byzantinistik*, 21, Vienna 1972, pp. 149–62.

Beck, I., 'The First Mosaics of the Capella Palatina in Palermo', *Byzantion*, 40 (1970), 119–64.

Thieme, T. and I. Beck, *La cattedrale normanna di Cefalù*, Odense 1977.

Deer, J., *The Dynastic Porphyry Tombs of the Norman Period in Sicily*, Cambridge Mass. 1959.

Valenziano, M. and C. Valenziano, 'La supplique des chanoines de la cathédrale de Cefalù pour la sépulture du roi Roger', *CCM*, 21 (1978), 3–30, 137–50.

Borsook, E., *Messages in Mosaic: the royal programmes of Norman Sicily 1130–87*, Oxford 1990.

8 Royal government and administration

Gregorio, R., *Considerazioni sopra la storia di Sicilia dai tempi normanni sino ai presenti*, Palermo 1805–16.

Caravale, M., *Il regno normanno di Sicilia*, Milan 1966.

Chalandon, F., 'La diplomatique des Normands de Sicile et de l'Italie méridionale', *Mélanges*, 20 (1900), 155–97.

Kehr, K. *Die urkunden der normannisch – sizilischen Könige*, Innsbruck 1902.

Enzensberger, H., *Beiträge zum Kanzlei-und Urkundenwesen der Normannischen Herrscher Unteritaliens und Siziliens*, Kallmünz 1971.

Brühl, C. R., *Urkunden und Kanzlei König Rogers II von Sizilien*, Cologne 1978.

Ménager, L. R., *Amiratus 'Amnpas. L'émirat et les origines de l'Amirauté*, Paris 1960.

Loewenthal, L. J. A., 'For the Biography of Walter Ophamil Archbishop of Palermo', *EHR*, 87 (1972), 75–82.

Takayama, H., 'The Financial and Administrative Organisation of the Norman Kingdom of Sicily', *Viator*, 16 (1985), 129–55.

'Familiares Regis and the Royal Inner Council in Twelfth-Century Sicily', *EHR*, 104 (1989), 357–72.

Jamison, E., 'The Norman Administration of Apulia and Capua', *BSR*, 6 (1913), 211–481.

'The Administration of the County of Molise in the Twelfth and Thirteenth Centuries', *EHR*, 44 (1929), 529–59; 45 (1930), 1–34.

Holtzmann, W., 'The Norman Royal Charters of San Bartolomeo di Carpineto', *BSR*, 24 (1956), 94–100.

Mazzarese-Fardella, E., *Aspetti dell'organizzazione amministrativa nello stato normanno e svevo*, Milan 1966.

Galasso, G., 'Mezzogiorno continentale e Sicilia nello stato normanno-svevo', *ASS*, serie 4 (2), 1976, 211–28.

Filangieri, C., 'Ipotesi sul sito e sul territorio di Demenna', *ASS*, serie 4 (4), 1978, 27–40.

Girgensohn, D. and N. Kemp, 'Urkunden und Inquisitionen der Stauferzeit aus Tarent', *QF*, 41 (1961), 137–234.

Abulafia, D., 'The Crown and the Economy under Roger II and his Successors', *DOP*, 37 (1983), 1–14.

Stern, S., 'Tari', *Studi Medievali*, serie 3 (11), 1970, 177–207.

Spahr, R., *Le Monete Siciliane dai Bizantini a Carlo I d'Angiò*, Zürich 1976.

Grierson, P., 'The Salernitan Coinage of Gisulf II (1052–77) and Robert Guiscard (1077–85)', *BSR*, 24 (1956), 37–59.

Lopez, R., 'Back to Gold', *Economic History Review*, 2nd series (9), 1956–7, 219–40.

9 The kingdom's defences and its enemies

Capasso, B., 'Sul Catalogo dei Feudi e dei Feudatari delle Provincie Napoletane', *Reale Accademia di Napoli*, 4 (1868), 293–371.

Cohn, W., *Die Geschichte der Normannischen-Sizilischen Flotte unter der Regierung Rogers I und Rogers II (1060–1154)*, Breslau 1910.

 Die Geschichte der sizilischen Flotte unter der Regierung Friedrichs II 1197–1250, Breslau 1926.

Loud, G., 'The Church, Warfare and Military Obligation in Norman Italy', *Studies in Church History*, 20 (1983), 31–45.

Sthamer, E., *Die Verwaltung der Kastelle im Königreich Sizilien unter Kaiser Freidrich II und Karl I von Anjou*, Leipzig 1914. *Ergänzungsband*, II, 2 vols., Leipzig 1912, 1926.

Santoro, R., 'Considerazioni generali sull'evoluzione della fortificazione siciliana dell'ultima amministrazione imperiali bizantina al consolidamento del regno di Sicilia', *ASS*, serie 4 (2), 1976, 27–52.

Bruschi, A. and G. M. Mariani, *Architettura sveva nell'Italia meridionale. Repertorio di Castelli*, Florence 1975.

Krönig, W., *Il castello di Caronia in Sicilia*, Rome 1977.

De Vita, R., ed., *Castelli, torri ed opere fortificate di Puglia*, Bari 1974.

Fuiano, M., 'Castelli in Puglia nei secoli X–XIII', *ASP*, 31 (1978), 25–45.

Maruotti, S., *Sant'Agata di Puglia nella storia medioevali*, Foggia 1981.

Lamma, P., *Comneni e Staufer: Ricerche sui rapporti fra Bisanzio e l'occidente nel secolo XII*, 2 vols., Rome 1955–7.

Clementi, D., 'The Relations between the Papacy, the Western Roman Empire, and the Emergent Kingdom of Sicily and South Italy 1050–1156', *BISIME*, 80 (1968), 191–212.

Parker, J. S. R., 'The Attempted Byzantine Alliance with the Norman Kingdom 1166–67', *BSR*, 24 (1956), 86–93.

Wieruszowski, H., 'The Norman Kingdom of Sicily and the Crusades', in K. M.

Setton, *A History of the Crusades*, II, *The Later Crusades 1189–1311*, ed. R. L. Wolff and H. W. Hazard, Madison 1969, pp. 3–42.

Abulafia, D., 'Ancona, Byzantium and the Adriatic 1155–73', *BSR*, 39 (1984), 195–216.

'The Norman Kingdom of Africa', *ANS*, 7 (1984), 26–49.

Johns, J., 'Malik Afriqiya. The Norman Kingdom of Africa and the Fatimids', *Libyan Studies*, 18 (1987), 89–101.

Day, G. W., 'Manuel Comnenus in Italy', *Journal of Economic History*, 37 (1977), 289–301.

Thomson, R., 'An English Eyewitness of the Peace of Venice', *Speculum*, 50 (1975), 21–32.

Jamison, E., 'Alliance of England and Sicily in the Second Half of the Twelfth Century', *Journal of the Warburg and Courtauld Institutes*, 6 (1943), 20–32.

Lavagnini, B., 'I Normanni di Sicilia a Cipro e a Patmo (1186)', *Byzantino-Sicula II. Miscellanea di Studi in memoria di Giuseppe Rossi Taibbi*, Palermo 1975, pp. 321–34.

Hunger, H., *Die Normannen in Thessalonike*, Graz 1955.

Saidi, O., ' The Unification of Maghrib under the Almohades', General History of Africa IV, ed. D. T. Niane, pp. 15–56. *Africa from the Twelfth to the Sixteenth Century*, UNESCO 1984.

10 The kingdom in disarray

Salvati, C., *Tancredi re di Sicilia e gli atti della sua cancelleria*, Naples 1973.

Clementi, D., 'The Circumstances of Count Tancred's Accession to the Kingdom of Sicily, Duchy of Apulia and the Principality of Capua', *Mélanges Antonio Marongiu*, Palermo 1967, pp. 57–80.

'An Administrative Document of 1190 from Apulia', *BSR*, 24 (1956), 101–6.

'Further Documents Concerning the Administration of Apulia and Terra di Lavoro during the Reign of Emperor Henry VI', *BSR*, 27 (1959), 170–82.

'Some Unnoticed Aspects of the Emperor Henry VI's Conquest of the Norman Kingdom of Sicily', *BJRL*, 36 (1954), 328–59.

'Calendar of the Diplomas of the Hohenstaufen Emperor Henry VI Concerning the Kingdom of Sicily', *QF*, 35 (1955), 86–225.

Baacken, G., 'Die Verhandlungen zwischen Kaiser Heinrich VI und Papst Coelestin III in den Jahren 1195–97', *DA*, 27 (1971), 457–513.

Zielinksi, H., 'Zu den Urkunden der beide letzen Normanner könige Sizilien Tankreds und Wilhelms III 1190–94', *DA*, 36 (1980), 453–86.

Fried, J., 'Eine unbekannte sizilische Königsurkunde Konstanzes von Aragon und Heinrichs (VII)', *DA*, 36 (1980), 567–74.

De Robertis, A. N., 'Il concordato del 1198 tra la Santa Sede e il regnum Siciliae e la sua validita formale', *Atti delle Giornate Federiciane*, 4 (1977), 249–58.

van Cleve, T. C., *Markward of Anweiler and the Sicilian Regency*, Princeton 1937.

Kennan, E., 'Innocent III and the First Political Crusade', *Traditio*, 27 (1971), 231–49.

Abulafia, D., 'Pisan Commercial Colonies and Consulates in Twelfth-Century Sicily', *EHR*, 93 (1978), 68–81.

Zinsmaier, P., 'Die Kanzleistare Friedrichs II in der deutscher Königszeit', *DA*, 38 (1982), 180–92.

Powell, J. M., *Anatomy of a Crusade 1213–1221*, Philadelphia 1986.

11 The kingdom revitalised

Kantorowicz, E., *Frederick the Second*, London 1931.

van Cleve, T. C., *The Emperor Frederick II of Hohenstaufen*, Oxford 1972.

Abulafia, D., *Frederick II*, London 1988.

'Kantorowicz and Frederick II', *History*, 62 (1977), 193–210.

Probleme um Friedrich II. Vorträge und Forschungen der Konstanzer Arbeitskreis XVI, Sigmaringen 1974.

Kamp, N., *Kirche und Monarchie in Staufischen Sizilien 1194–1266*, 4 vols., Münster 1973–82.

Dilcher, H., *Die sizilischen Gesetzgebungen Kaiser Friedrichs II*, Cologne 1975.

Frederick II, *De arte venandi cum avibus*, trans. C. A. Wood and F. M. Fyfe, Stanford 1943.

Haskins, C. H., 'The "De arte venandi cum avibus" of the Emperor Frederick II', *EHR*, 36 (1921), 334–55.

'Latin Literature under Frederick II', *Speculum*, 3 (1928), 129–51.

Maschke, E., 'Die Wirtschaftspolitik Kaiser Friedrichs II im Königreich Sizilien', *Vierteljahrschrift für Sozial-und Wirtschaftsgeschichte*, 53 (1966), 289–318.

Powell, J. M., 'Medieval Monarchy and Trade: the Economic Policy of Frederick II in the Kingdom of Sicily. A Survey', *Studi Medievali*, serie 3 (3), 1962, 426–521.

'Frederick II and the Church in the Kingdom of Sicily 1220–24', *Church History*, 30 (1961), 28–34.

Pybus, H. J., 'The Emperor Frederick II and the Sicilian Church', *Cambridge Historical Journal*, 3 (1930), 134–63.

d'Angelo, F., 'La monetazione di Muhammed ibn Abbad emiro rebelle a Federico II di Sicilia', *Studi Magrebini*, 7 (1975), 149–53.

Falco, G., 'I preliminari della pace di San Germano', *Archivio della Reale Società Romana di Storia Patria*, 23 (1910), 441–79.

Egidi, P., 'La colonia saracena di Lucera e la sua distruzione', *ASPN*, 36 (1911), 597–694; 37 (1912), 71–89, 664–96; 38 (1913), 115–44, 681–707; 39 (1914), 132–71, 697–766.

Heckel, R. von, 'Das päpstliche und Sizilische Registerwesen', *Archiv für Urkundenforschung*, 1 (1908), 371–510.

Sthamer, E., 'Studien über die sizilischen Register Friedrichs II', *Sitzungsberichte der Preussischen Akademie der Wissenschaften* (1920), 584–610; (1925), 168–78; (1930), 78–96.

Das Amtsbuch der Sizilischen Rechnungshofes, ed. W. E. Heupel, Text and research commissioned by the Preussischen Akademie der Wissenschaften, Burg 1942.

Heupel, W. E., *Der Sizilische Grosshof unter Kaiser Friedrich II, eine verwaltungsgeschichtliche studie*, *MGH*, Schriften, Leipzig 1940.

'Schriftuntersuchungen zur Registerführung in der Kanzlei Friedrichs II', *QF*, 46 (1966) 1–90.

Schaller, H. M., 'Die Kanzler Kaiser Friedrichs II ihr Personel und ihr Sprachstil', *Archiv für Diplomatik Schriftsgeschichte Siegel-und Wappen-Kunde*, 3 (1957), 207–86; 4 (1958), 264–327.

Zinsmaier, P., 'Beiträge zur Diplomatik der Urkunden Friedrichs II', *DA*, 41 (1985), 101–74.

Kölzer, T., 'Die sizilische Kanzlei von K. Constanze bis K. Manfred', *DA*, 40 (1984), 532–61.

Caruso, A., 'Il controllo dei conti nel regno di Sicilia durante il periodo svevo', *ASPN*, 64 (1939), 201–36.

Colliva, P., '"Magistri Camerarii" e "Camerarii" nel regno di Sicilia nell'età di Federico II', *Rivista di Storia del Diritto Italiano*, 36 (1963), 51–126.

12 The kingdom betrayed

Hampe, K., *Urban IV und Manfred (1261–64)*, Heidelberg 1905.

Bergmann, A., *König Manfred von Sizilien 1264–66*, Heidelberg 1909.

Arndt, H., *Studien zur inneren Regierungsgeschichte Manfreds*, Heidelberg 1911.

Merkel, C., 'L'opinione dei contemporanei sull' impresa italiana di Carlo I d'Angio', *Atti della Reale Accademia dei Lincei* (year 285), 1888. *Classe di scienze morali storiche e filologiche*, 4, 277–435.

Pontieri, E., *Richerche sulla crisi nella monarchia siciliana nel secolo XIII*, Naples 1942.

Morghen, R., *Il tramonto della potenza sveva in Italia*, Milan 1936.

Palumbo, P., *Contributi alla storia dell'età di Manfredi*, Rome 1959.

Colasanti, G., 'Il passo di Ceprano', *Archivio della Reale Società Romana di Storia Patria*, 35 (1912), 5–99.

Caffaro, P., 'Se i pugliesi furono bugiardi a Ceprano', *ASP*, 5 (1952), 243–50.

Sthamer, E., 'Bruchstücke mittelalterliche Enqueten aus Unteritalien: ein beitrag zur geschichte der Hohenstaufen', *Abhandlungen der Preussischen Akademie der Wissenschaften*, Berlin 1933.

Runciman, S., *The Sicilian Vespers*, Cambridge 1958.

Nicol, D., *Despotate of the Epirus*, Oxford 1957.

Strayer, J. F., 'The Political Crusades of the Thirteenth Century', in K. M. Setton, *A History of the Crusades*, II, *The Later Crusades 1189–1311*, ed. R. L. Wolff and H. W. Hazard, Madison 1969, pp. 343–75.

Housley, N., *The Italian Crusades*, Oxford 1982.

Waley, D., 'Papal Armies in the Thirteenth Century', *EHR*, 72 (1957), 1–30.

INDEX

399

Index

Cambridge Medieval Textbooks

Medieval Russia, 980–1584
JANET MARTIN

The Wars of the Roses: Politics and the Constitution
in England, *c.* 1437–*c.* 1509
CHRISTINE CARPENTER

Other titles are in preparation